SOCIAL AND ECONOMIC STUDIES OF POST-WAR FRANCE

Prepared under the auspices of the

COLUMBIA UNIVERSITY COUNCIL FOR RESEARCH IN THE SOCIAL SCIENCES

EDITED BY

CARLTON J. H. HAYES

PROFESSOR OF HISTORY IN COLUMBIA UNIVERSITY

VOLUME II

THE PROCESS OF INFLATION IN FRANCE 1914–1927

BY

JAMES HARVEY ROGERS

THE PROCESS OF INFLATION IN FRANCE

1914-1927

BY

JAMES HARVEY ROGERS

PROFESSOR OF ECONOMICS
UNIVERSITY OF MISSOURI

with the assistance of his students

AUGUST MAFFRY AND ROBERT E. LANDMAN

New York

COLUMBIA UNIVERSITY PRESS

1929

Published March, 1929.

PRINTED IN THE UNITED STATES OF AMERICA
BY THE PLIMPTON PRESS · NORWOOD · MASS.

To the power of
scrupulous honesty and unswerving patriotism
in a national crisis
a simple record of events again attests

PREFACE

Under the financial organization of society existing throughout the civilized world of to-day, currency and banking systems have taken on an importance little appreciated even by many historians. The Napoleonic era has been treated by many writers with hardly a mention of the extraordinary and far-reaching effects of the currency depreciation of that period. Even the accounts of the Civil War in the United States and of the more recent conflicts in the Balkan countries have been attempted by some without so much as a reference to the dominant rôles so often played by attendant financial disturbances.

But if currency and banking operations played an influential rôle in the earlier periods mentioned, what can be said of their importance in the decade just passed? Not only have our economic organizations become much more completely dominated by interlocking financial arrangements of many kinds, but the economic welfare of an ever increasing proportion of the total populations of all modern countries has been inextricably entwined in the complicated machinery of a money-and-credit age. During the war and post-war years this powerful and important but extremely delicately adjusted machinery has been subjected to severe strains and stresses both from within and from without. And while the machine as a whole has shown a capacity of adaptability beyond the expectations even of many of the more sanguine of its engineers, the processes of its adjustments have not failed in their turn to disturb greatly the still more intricate and more delicate — though perhaps less well understood — mechanisms of our social and political systems.

In a study of post-war France, therefore, it has been thought wise to devote one volume to an analysis of the process of inflation itself. While, in the existing state of statistical information (especially of that in France), such an analysis cannot possibly prove wholly satisfactory, it is hoped that something can be done to advance the understanding of some of the noteworthy financial happenings which, in the post-war period, have played such a vital and often tragic part in the lives of the French people.

It is further hoped that the study will throw light likewise upon the more general problems of monetary theory. In periods of great disturbance, happenings which might at other times pass unobserved are often greatly magnified and may even occupy temporarily the center of the stage. Moreover, it is frequently the abnormal rather than the usual functioning of a system which gives the greater insight into its inner workings.

The methods of investigation used in the study are principally the inductive and the statistical. While the shortcomings of both of these methods in the present state of our economic information are clearly recognized, the writer knows no other with greater promise of unbiased results. The processes used have been described carefully and can be duplicated by anyone who may care to undertake the laborious computations involved. The Pearsonian coefficient of correlation, which has been frequently used throughout the study, is acknowledged to be only an extremely crude measure of the degree of similarity of the time series under comparison, and evident technical errors involved in its use have been allowed for whenever possible. The reader will always be clearly informed, however, of such allowances, as well as of the reasons for making them.

The reader is asked to bear in mind that this study, made during a period of rapidly changing conditions, cannot but be out-of-date before it is published. Purely historical in character, it purports to do nothing more than to trace and interpret as nearly accurately as possible some of the happenings of an era filled alike with financial disaster and financial recovery, but above all else with financial experiment. Written in the late months of 1927, the final chapters attempt to depict conditions then existing.

For assistance in the prosecution of the study I am indebted to many.

Special acknowledgement is made to the following officials of the Finance Ministry of the French Government for the invaluable aid which they have given, not only in furnishing information elsewhere unavailable, but likewise in explaining many of the intricate details of the complicated operations of French government finance: Albert Adam, Albert Amet, Léon Araud, P. J. L. Goulin, Marcel Grémy, J. E. R. Jacquot, Albert Le Gal, J. J. Navaillès, Joseph Pisson,

Marcel Vaidie; to the following officials of various banking and other financial institutions in France: Charles Rist and Paul Ricard of the Bank of France, Pierre Meynial and M. Morize of Morgan et Cie., Louis Pommery of the Banque Nationale Française du Commerce Extérieur, Jean Vergeot of the Banque Ottomane, Théodore Laborde of the Caisse Nationale d'Épargne, Jean Laurent and Marcel Coué of the Caisses d'Épargne Ordinaires, Raoul Auberty of the Caisse des Dépôts et Consignations, Maurice Spire, G. H. Bousquet, and A. Bahuet of the Banque de l'Union Parisienne, Philip A. Rogers of the Equitable Trust Company (Paris Office), A. Despoisse and Léopold Ollier of the Caisse Nationale du Crédit Agricole, Georges Montérou of the Crédit National, Frédéric Fauvin of the Crédit Foncier; and to the following officials and publicists: L. Dugé de Bernonville of the Statistique Générale de la France, Urbain Durand of the Ministère du Travail—Contrôle des Assurances Privées, Georges Manchez of *Le Temps*, and Lewis A. Glynn of the *New York Herald* (Paris Edition).

To the Council for Research in the Social Sciences of Columbia University I am greatly indebted for the opportunity to undertake the investigation, and to the various members of its staff with whom I was associated in Paris I am further indebted for numerous suggestions and criticisms given in a spirit of complete coöperation almost daily during the course of the study. I am especially grateful to Professor Wesley C. Mitchell and to Professor Irving Fisher for their extremely helpful criticisms with regard to the "key" chapters of the work, and to Professors Robert M. Haig and James W. Angell for their kindness in reading and criticizing the manuscript as a whole.

Finally, my debt of gratitude to my two student assistants and to the other members of my little organization engaged in prosecuting the research is extremely great. In spite of the continual pressure of the work, no organization could have labored more loyally. August Maffry was with me from the beginning. Not only did he assist in every phase of the work, but in addition he took almost complete charge of the details of the statistical investigations. Robert E. Landman, on the other hand, did equally indispensable work in the gathering of much of the data on which the investigation rests.

Mlle. France M. A. Chalufour carefully compiled and checked most of the numerous tables and graphs which play such an important part in the study, and Miss Winifred Smeaton, although with the organization for only the last three months of the investigation, rendered excellent service in making statistical computations and in checking the final manuscript.

To all these, I wish to express my sincere thanks.

JAMES HARVEY ROGERS.

PARIS, FRANCE, January 4, 1928.

CONTENTS

CONTENTS

CHARTS

TABLES

CHAPTER I

INTRODUCTION

When the war broke out in 1914 there were many prophets ready to venture the opinion that it could not last more than a few months because of the impossibility of financing expensive operations on so gigantic a scale. They were wrong, as prophets usually are. The war lasted four years and a quarter, and as time went on was financed on an ever increasing scale. The importance of victory in the minds of the people and of their leaders brought forth the requisite funds. So instead of the difficulties of finance interrupting field operations, the finances were forced to adjust themselves to the exigencies of war. The resulting important and far-reaching effects on currency and on public and private finance which were felt successively in Russia, in Austria, in Poland, in Germany, and in many other of the belligerent countries of Eastern and Central Europe are generally familiar to all of us. Moreover, in spite of the widespread war propaganda to the contrary, it has become an open secret to students of the history of the period that these extraordinary economic phenomena had their genesis in excessive government spending and large treasury deficits. Hence this study of the process of inflation begins logically with a brief statement of government expenditures and deficits, which will be taken from the study of Professor Robert M. Haig entitled *The Public Finances of Post-War France.*

Referring to this study, government expenditures in France were found to have been double in 1914 what they were in 1913 and again in 1915 double what they were in 1914. Moreover, they continued to increase until the end of the war period, reaching for the year 1918 the gigantic total of 56½ milliards[1] of francs. Nor was

[1] Because the word *billion* has in England and in Germany a different significance from what it has in France and in the United States, the term *milliard* will be used throughout this study to denote a thousand millions.

there a substantial decrease in such expenditures until 1922, when for the first time after the war they fell below 50 milliards. Revenues, on the other hand, were less in 1914 than in 1913 and still less in 1915 than in 1914. For the remainder of the war period they increased slightly, but never by nearly enough to take care of more than a very small proportion of the simultaneous increase in expenditures. After the war they continued to increase notably but reached substantial equality with expenditures only in the now famous balanced budget of 1926.

Thus there arose large and increasing Treasury deficits, which continued to accumulate almost to the present time. These deficits were made up by borrowing the needed funds, partly abroad, but very largely at home. The home borrowings took on, by force of necessity, various forms. Long-term bond issues, subscribed to generally by investors throughout the country, were floated whenever possible. Funds which could not be secured on this basis, however, were raised in more dangerous ways. To meet the needs of individuals and institutions desiring short-term investments, two- to ten-year securities were provided; and, to tap the banking and money-market sources, obligations with maturities of one to twelve months, until recently, were issued in unlimited amounts. Besides, in order to attract all surplus cash in the hands of the banks and of the public, the Treasury invited the deposits of both, and, by allowing rates of interest ranging from 1½ to 3 per cent, acquired by the middle of 1927 a fund amounting to 18 milliards of francs. Finally, whatever of the needed resources could not be obtained in one of these ways was borrowed from the Bank of France.[2]

Thus France ended the war period with a total internal debt of approximately 144 milliards of paper francs and an external debt of but little less than 30 milliards of gold francs, whereas at the end of 1913 her total debt had amounted to but little more than 32½ milliards. The internal debt at the end of the war was composed of approximately 97 milliards of perpetual and long-term bonds, a half milliard of short-term obligations, and about 46½

[2] The French Government borrowed also from the Bank of Algeria. The total of such borrowings, however, bulked so small in comparison with those from the Bank of France that they may be neglected as insignificant.

milliards of francs in floating debt and advances from the Bank of France. By September, 1927, not only had this internal debt not diminished in amount, but it had reached a total of slightly more than double its amount at the end of 1918. Nor had the proportion of the floating to the total debt been materially reduced by that time. Likewise, the external debt, although on account of the negotiations with the British and American governments rendered somewhat uncertain in amount, had not been formally reduced.

In order to give the reader a clear picture of the debt situation from year to year, the following tables compiled from Professor Haig's study are presented.

TABLE 1

ANNUAL RECEIPTS, EXPENDITURES AND DEFICITS*

(In millions of francs)

Year	Receipts	Expenditures	Deficits	Deficits cumulated
1913	4,907	5,072	165	165
1914	4,196	10,371	6,175	6,340
1915	4,130	22,120	17,990	24,330
1916	4,932	36,848	31,916	56,246
1917	6,186	44,661	38,475	94,721
1918	6,791	56,649	49,858	144,579
1919	11,586	54,213	42,627	187,206
1920	20,100	58,100	38,000	225,206
1921	23,100	51,100	28,000	253,206
1922	24,200	48,900	24,700	277,906
1923	27,700	45,800	18,100	296,006
1924	31,100	40,200	9,100	305,106

* Sources: 1913–1918, *Projet de Budget pour l'exercice 1923, presenté par le Ministre des Finances*, p. 10 *et seq.;* 1920–1924, *Inventaire*, p. 21. The statistics of receipts and expenditures for this period are even today in a chaotic condition. The figures presented in Table 1 are only approximate.

In attempting to describe and explain the inflation process one soon discovers that it is inextricably connected with the operations of the banks and other financial institutions. This study will open, therefore, with a general analysis of the obvious and inevitable rôle of such institutions in every inflation process. Then, since it is French inflation which is to be examined, a general description

TABLE 2 — INTERNAL PUBLIC DEBT

(In millions of francs)

Date	Funded			Floating				Total
	Short-term bonds	Perpetual and long-term bonds	Total funded	Bank [a] borrowings	Treasury paper	Deposits with the Treasury and miscellaneous items	Total floating	
Dec. 31, 1913	.....	31,162	31,162	.....	410	1,022	1,432	32,594
Dec. 31, 1914	.....	31,966	31,966	3,925	1,735	1,802	7,462	39,428
Dec. 31, 1915	632	46,367	46,999	5,705	7,006	−269	12,442	59,441
Dec. 31, 1916	427	57,756	58,183	9,225	12,618	171	22,014	80,197
Dec. 31, 1917	516	69,904	70,420	15,805	19,552	1,339	36,696	107,116
Dec. 31, 1918	531	97,248	97,779	20,891	22,915	2,735	46,541	144,320
Dec. 31, 1919	914	101,722	102,636	29,490	48,052	5,449	82,991	185,627
Dec. 31, 1920	423	133,176	133,599	30,580	50,899	4,094	85,573	219,172
Dec. 31, 1921	10,309	138,392	148,701	28,742	60,362	3,621	92,725	241,426
Dec. 31, 1922	26,835	134,042	160,877	27,955	59,070	6,537	93,562	254,439
Dec. 31, 1923	39,975	143,775	183,750	27,883	57,720	5,938	91,541	275,291
Dec. 31, 1924	46,636	146,511	193,147	27,472	56,408	8,482	92,362	285,509
Dec. 31, 1925	39,461	153,232	192,693	41,163	48,128	9,609	98,900	281,593
Dec. 31, 1926	38,796	156,857	195,653	41,576	44,449	10,096	96,121	291,774
Sept. 30, 1927	27,739	180,687	208,426	30,206	44,379	14,330	88,915	297,341

[a] The advances from the Bank of Algeria and the Russian advances are included.

TABLE 3 — EXTERNAL PUBLIC DEBT

(In millions of gold francs)

Date	Total
December 31, 1913	......
December 31, 1914	510
December 31, 1915	1,971
December 31, 1916	7,453
December 31, 1917	20,038
December 31, 1918	29,282
December 31, 1919	33,566
December 31, 1920	35,959
December 31, 1921	35,655
December 31, 1922	35,444
December 31, 1923	35,725
December 31, 1924	36,479
December 31, 1925	36,439
December 31, 1926	36,744 [a]
September 30, 1927	36,664 [a]

[a] Issues of French railroad obligations floated abroad are included.

of French banks and other financial bodies will follow. This information provided, a study of the process itself may be undertaken. Statistical data of various sorts have been gathered with a view to discovering so far as possible and in a quantitative way what has actually happened in the affairs of the institutions through which the process has taken form. Comparisons of series thus found significant have been made with others of evident importance in picturing the character as well as the effects of the inflation process. To the explanation of the movements and relations discovered the rest of the study will be devoted.

CHAPTER II

THE INEVITABLE RÔLE OF THE BANKS IN EVERY INFLATION PROCESS

So frequently and so variously has inflation been defined that it would be naïve indeed to introduce this study with another attempt at acceptable definition. Yet it is the object of the research to describe the process of inflation. And, as this monograph is to constitute one of a series of studies devoted primarily to discovering, in a modern industrial and agricultural country, the outstanding effects of this same variously defined inflation, a definite use of the term becomes indispensable.

To some, inflation is nothing more or less than an increase in the circulating media — money and deposits. To others, there is no inflation unless the currency increase is accompanied by a general rise in prices. Some might even regard a general rise in prices unaccompanied by currency increase as a sort of unusual but equally true inflation. But, when prices move in one direction and currency supplies in the other, as is frequently the case, it is somewhat difficult to forecast whether most persons would regard the process as one of inflation or one of deflation. Still others would doubtless consider inflation as synonymous with monetary depreciation in the foreign exchange markets, in spite of the fact that such depreciation might or might not be accompanied by simultaneous increases in prices and in currency supplies.

It is evident, therefore, that to discuss the process of inflation in a way which will prove at all satisfactory to the general reader, the three phenomena — price levels, currency supplies, and exchanges rates — must alike be followed. Furthermore, in order to simplify exposition and to avoid embarrassing contradictions, the process will be defined in terms of one of the phenomena, prices, and the other two will be discussed in their relations to the first. Inflation will be defined, therefore, *for the purposes of this study*, as *an increase in the general level of prices growing out of an increase in expenditures while goods available for purchase are not correspondingly increased in amount.*

Increases in expenditures falling within this definition of inflation may occur in numerous ways. Increased buying on the part of governments without simultaneous reduction in the expenditures of others has frequently induced price increases continuing over long periods. In the spring of 1917, immediately after the entrance of the United States into the war, the large purchases made by the various departments of the national government led to a rapid and almost uninterrupted rise in prices for the next few years, a rise which in the early stages of the process was unaccompanied by comparable increases in the supplies of the circulating media. In most of the other belligerent countries similar price rises occurred and, without doubt, for a similar reason — enlarged purchasing without corresponding increase in the amounts of goods available for purchase. In France, to take another example, prices began to rise abruptly immediately after the war broke out and continued their upward trend with hardly a break until after the Armistice was signed.

Larger expenditures by business firms without corresponding increase in the supplies of goods offered are of frequent occurrence and, if long continued, lead to important rises in the general price level. This type of inflation seems to be characteristic of the prosperity period of almost every business cycle which has been analyzed. Also, in many cases, the inflation periods begun by increased governmental expenditures have been prolonged and at times even dominated by the ever increasing expenditures of business people lured to larger borrowing by the huge profits so characteristic of most periods of rapidly rising prices.

Finally, it is at least conceivable that larger expenditures by private individuals without a corresponding reduction in those of others and without a simultaneous increase in production might lead to inflated prices. Such a process of general impoverishment resulting from a sudden turn to spendthrift habits can hardly be anticipated in modern society. Yet it is interesting to note how closely, in one respect at least, it resembles the other two cases of inflation so familiar to all.

The rôle played by the banks in all such increases in expenditures is an important and inevitable one. In order to become large spenders, the governments, business firms, or private individuals alike must receive increased purchasing power. Ricardo, when appearing before a parliamentary investigating committee, was once asked in substance whether he regarded credit as a form of capital. "Credit, I think," he said, "is the means which is alternately transferred from one to another, to make use of capital actually existing; it does not create capital; it determines only by whom that capital should be employed."[1] In other words, whatever is borrowed by one is loaned by another, and the additional purchasing power received by the borrower is necessarily taken from the lender. Hence, the increased spending of the one is exactly and completely counterbalanced by the reduction in that of the other. The accuracy of his negative answer to the question propounded is hardly to be doubted. But, with respect to loans, his ultra-classical statement, far from tenable even in an economic society of the type in which Ricardo lived, becomes a ludicrous caricature of modern lending as it is done by our numerous powerful and immensely rich credit institutions. The great lenders of today, directly or indirectly, are our banks and other financial houses. It is important, therefore, to see how they provide the purchasing power for the additional spending which has been defined as the basis of the inflation process.

The act of lending, as understood in the financial world, *does* consist of the turning over of immediately available purchasing power by one person (or institution) to another. Contrary to Ricardo's statement, however, that received by the borrower is not at all necessarily taken from the lender. In fact, much of that borrowed from banking institutions — especially under our modern central banking systems — is, as effective purchasing power, something which would not exist at all except for the borrowing operation itself. Lest this statement be misunderstood, however,

[1] *Reports from Committees: The Bank of England, Resumption of Cash Payments* (Session 21 January — 13 July, 1819); Volume III, Second Report, p. 192.

it should be explained that to the extent that the borrowing operation leads to a general rise in prices — often appearing much later, if at all — the sum total of real purchasing power is reduced. But it should be added that on account of the usual lag in prices the reduction in purchasing power applies almost invariably to its future rather than to its present holders. Consequently, each loan can perhaps best be regarded as a net addition to purchasing power, the utilization of which often leads to a price rise, but a rise which, except in the cases of speculative and of other extremely sensitive markets, takes place too late to affect the purchasing power of the proceeds of the loan itself. Nor, for present purposes, are the security, the period, the terms, and certain other conditions of the loan of great importance. It is the celerity with which its proceeds are spent which matters most. A government borrows on good or poor security, at high rates or low rates, for short term or for long term; but, so far as the increases in the purchasing power of the government and in prices are concerned, the effect is the same *if the funds are speedily spent.* The same is true for loans made to business firms or to the public. Always the important question from the standpoint of prices is: How soon and for what are the borrowed funds spent?

In evaluating their influence in advancing inflation, however, there are other considerations of extreme importance for all loans. Are they so made as to reduce by their amounts the further lending power of the lenders? If so, Ricardo's statement, so far as the particular loans are concerned, holds. If not reduced by an equal amount, then to what extent is the lending ability of the lenders decreased? No lender has an infinite capacity for lending, and, in general, the making of one loan reduces his capacity for making others. By just how much is frequently an unsolved riddle, the exact amount often depending upon factors completely beyond the control of the lender and sometimes beyond his consciousness. Much will be said on this subject as the study proceeds.

Another consideration of equal importance is the effect of the loan in reducing the further spending power of the lender, as well as that of all others. A private individual lending to another person or institution funds which he would otherwise have used for consumption usually cuts his expenditures by the amount of the loan. Frequently during the war, however, in response to patriotic appeals, many persons loaned to their governments in much larger amounts than the economies which they were later willing to make in their expenditures. Hence, they in turn borrowed from the banks in order to retrieve some of the purchasing power which they had surrendered to their governments in too generous amounts. In a sense, "they had their cake and ate it too." On the other hand, as is well known to all, the advance of every inflation process through the excess spending of some brings forced economies to others. Individuals with fixed and semi-fixed incomes meet the rise in prices with reduced expenditures, for to them there is no other course open.

But the rôle of the banks in the inflation process is not exclusively that of lenders. In return for the notes and other paper of their borrowers, they issue, in most countries, deposits or current accounts. These accounts, being transferable by check, make up a large portion of the circulating media of the countries concerned. And the fact to be emphasized for present purposes is that a large proportion of this currency under certain circumstances may be manufactured out of whole cloth by the banking institutions themselves.

But, when a larger amount of deposits and current accounts comes into use, a need is gradually experienced for a somewhat correspondingly increased quantity of circulating notes or other form of money. This need arises much as that for additional small change whenever there is an increase in the quantity of money in circulation. In Anglo-Saxon countries, where deposit currency is in much more general use as a circulating medium than in other parts of the world, almost all business transactions (except retail trade and the payment of wages) are accomplished by the use of deposit currency. Retail trade, on the other hand, as often the payment of wages, is carried on very largely with cash. It happens further that the prices of most of the goods paid for with deposit currency are more sensitive than those paid for with cash. Consequently, at least in the United States, where their movements have been studied, they usually rise earlier, faster, and farther in periods of rising prices and fall earlier, faster, and farther in periods of falling prices. What is of chief interest here is that deposits subject to check do much the same thing in relation to the quantity of money in circulation. For these and other reasons it seems very clear that in the United States the quantity of money in circulation simply adjusts itself to the quantity of deposit currency in accordance with the demands of trade. Whether the adjustment takes place in a similar way in France, where deposit currency is relatively so little used, attempt will be made to discover in the course of the investigation which follows.

In this adjustment of the quantity of money in circulation to changes in the volume of trade handled with cash and in the prices at which such trade is carried on, the banks again play an extremely important rôle. Almost everyone in a country either directly or indirectly depends upon them to supply his needs for cash. A person with a banking account, seeing that his cash supply is becoming depleted because of a rise in the prices of articles which he purchases with cash or because of increased purchases of such goods, draws on his bank for a new supply. The paymaster, finding that his pay-roll has increased, likewise increases his drawings of cash. The banks must so regulate their affairs, therefore, as to be continually in a position to meet the new demands for cash which normally accompany a rising trend in prices and in the volume of trade. They do so by keeping in their tills a certain minimum of cash and in their portfolios various types of paper readily convertible into cash at short notice. Under most of our central banking systems they rely especially on their ability to rediscount or borrow at the central banks. When the Federal Reserve System was instituted in the United States perhaps more attention was given to securing the easy expansion and contraction of cash in response to the needs of the banks than to any other of its important provisions. Thus, by paying cash to depositors drawing on their accounts and to others in whose favor checks and drafts are drawn, the banks supply the currency needs of their customers, relying in turn upon their ability to provide for their own cash needs by borrowing from the central banks, by selling some of their marketable paper, or by demanding funds loaned on call.

Furthermore, besides providing the additional cash needs of their customers, the banks also serve as depositories for superfluous cash wherever and whenever it makes its appearance. The wholesaler, the retailer, "the butcher, the baker, the candlestick-maker," as well as most other persons in business or out of business, regularly deposit with their banks any incoming cash in excess of their immediate needs. This continued inflow is as a rule approximately balanced by a similar outflow. But, as at certain seasons of the year and during certain periods in longer intervals of time greater cash needs are experienced, so, in others, reduced needs are equally in evidence. The banks, on receiving the surplus cash use it to make new loans, to buy securities, to pay off indebtedness at the central banks, or in France, as will be seen later, to deposit in the Treasury. In the last two cases, it should be pointed out, a direct reduction in the available cash of the country follows.

In their rôles above enumerated — as lenders of credit, as providers of cash, and as receivers of surplus cash — the various types of banks play very different parts in advancing and in retarding the inflation process. The commercial banks, dealing largely in short-term loans, lend principally to business and to the public, although their loans to the government are at times far from negligible. They provide the purchasing power for the transaction of a large portion of the so-called commercial deals; within varying limits they expand deposit currency supplies irrespective of the source of its demand; and with the aid of the central banks they keep — however unconsciously — the cash supplies nicely adjusted to the volume of business and to price levels.

The investment banks, on the other hand, deal almost exclusively in long-term loans. And, while their loans in the form of the flotation of long-term securities are made more generally to business enterprises and to smaller governmental organizations, they are not infrequently floated for the national governments themselves, especially for foreign governments. The effects of such loans in advancing the inflation process are in some respects different from those resulting from the operations of the commercial banks. For while both classes of banks increase the purchasing power of the borrowers, they do not reduce alike the further lending power of the lenders; nor do investment loans provide directly for increases in the circulating media — money and deposits — as do the loans of commercial banks. The differences must, therefore, be carefully noted. In the first place, investment loans, although made directly by the bankers to the borrowers, are not held by them, as is generally the case with the commercial banks, but are sold to the investing public. Frequently, too, investment bankers have no recourse, as do the commercial banks, to the discount and lending facilities of the central banks. Their holdings of bonds and stocks naturally cannot be discounted, and, since the market for them is often unestablished, they may not in general serve as collateral for an advance from a central bank. Hence, the lending power of the investment banks is strictly limited by the capacity and willingness of the investing public and of financial institutions to absorb their securities.

With respect to the effect of investment operations on currency supplies, it should be noted that the purchasers of the securities floated by the investment banks usually pay for them with checks upon their accounts in the commercial banks, thus diminishing for certain of these banks the chief source of their lending powers. The deposits thus used in the purchase of securities, however, are simply transferred first by the purchaser to the investment banker and in turn by him to the borrower in whose interest the loan was floated. Obviously such transactions cause no net reduction in the total of deposit currency.

Moreover, while the floating of investment loans does not increase *directly* the deposit currency available, it does so *indirectly*. As observed above, the purchasers of securities transfer their deposits to the investment banker and he in turn to the borrowers. The borrowers thus find themselves in the possession of new purchasing power to the extent of their borrowings. The lenders, on the other hand, having invested only their normal savings, presumably continue their expenditures about as formerly. The net result is a greater purchase of goods or, in other words, a greater volume of trade. And an increase in trade, except to the extent (usually considered slight) that velocities of money and of deposits increase, requires an increase in the circulating media for its accomplishment. Hence, deposits and currency are borrowed in the normal way from the banks by those whose trade has become more active.

As a final consideration, it is mentioned that the funds loaned on long term by the investment bankers are in general spent almost as rapidly as those loaned by the commercial banks on short term. A business firm planning the construction of a new plant arranges with its banker to receive the necessary funds in amounts and on dates carefully estimated to meet its needs without loss of interest. Any idle funds arising from a faulty estimate are quickly loaned, and any shortage is made up by temporary borrowing from the commercial banks. Funds borrowed by municipalities, although generally handled less economically, are apt to be used to discharge current indebtedness created in anticipation of the receipt of the borrowed funds. Hence, as a rule, the rapidity with which funds received from investment loans are spent is presumably not less than in the case of commercial loans.

The savings banks have little to do either with advancing or retarding the inflation process. For present purposes, they may be regarded simply as gatherers and investors of savings. They receive the small deposits of their customers and pass them along to the investment and mortgage banks (or to the Government) in return for the securities they handle. To the extent that they deal directly with those borrowing on mortgage or other long-term security they may be regarded as performing the investment banking function and, consequently, as affecting the inflation process much as do the investment banks proper. Likewise the mortgage banks require no discussion. They, too, perform a kind of investment banking function and, consequently, fall under the foregoing discussion so far as their effects on inflation are concerned. The agricultural credit institutions are of such varied character that their treatment will be delayed to the chapter on the French banking system, where the *Crédit Agricole*, the French agricultural credit banking system, will be analyzed in some detail.

It remains to discuss the rôle of the central banks. Theirs

is in many ways the most potent influence in every inflation process. Often virtual controllers of the discount and interest policies of all the other banks, they are frequently in a position practically to determine the course of inflation. By raising their rates sufficiently to make unprofitable further borrowing by the commercial banks not only can they discourage credit expansion, but they can also encourage immediate contraction. Furthermore, most central banks make a practice of operating freely in certain classes of paper in the markets in which they are located. By selling securities when money is easy they frequently are able to tighten rates appreciably, and by buying when money is tight they can, reversely, often loosen rates to an extent frequently of great importance in determining the credit policies of the other banks. Finally, in making advances to a government a central bank increases directly the purchasing power of the state without at all reducing that of other spenders — until the subsequent rise in prices forces a painful economy upon persons with relatively fixed incomes. Unquestionably the most powerful influence in advancing the inflation process in France, as will be seen later, has been the large and long-continued advances of the Bank of France to the State.

All the banks of every sort, may, therefore, be regarded as dispensers of purchasing power and certain of them to a limited extent as its creators. Moreover, all the banks are dispensers of the circulating media, money and deposits, and certain of them, the commercial and central banks, to a large extent its creators. The question arises, therefore, as to whether or not, in a study of price phenomena, the additions to purchasing power and to the circulating media may not be regarded as identical or as two ways of looking at the same thing. In other words, does it make any difference (at least for purpose of analysis) whether it is decided to follow the changes in the amounts of purchasing power or the changes in the volume of the circulating media? Or, again, is not the total of purchasing power completely and exactly represented by the volume of the circulating media, money and deposits, outstanding? The distinction is a nice one. Aside from the consideration of velocities, were the commercial and other banks carrying deposits for their customers the only lenders (other than those lending cash and deposits directly), it might by some be considered an academic one only. There are, however, many other sorts of lenders, who, while influencing the amount of purchasing power, have no direct effect whatever on the quantity of the circulating media. In this class come all business firms lending on open account or otherwise to purchasers of their wares. Here are included a large proportion of the retailers, almost all of the wholesalers and jobbers, and, certainly in America, most of the manufacturing companies. By extending credit to their customers they increase the existing purchasing power without in any way influencing directly the amount of the circulating media. Again, certain of the banks themselves, especially in Europe, although their chief business is that of loan and deposit, maintain the policy of lending to many business customers through the allowing of overdrafts. To the extent that their lending takes this form there is no deposit or currency item corresponding to the increase in purchasing power resulting from the opening or enlarging of a line of credit. Hence, here also is to be found a change in available purchasing power unconnected with a change in the amount of the circulating media. Furthermore, it will be found that, while changes in expenditures growing out of changes in purchasing power evidently in general precede price movements, currency movements usually follow prices at a considerable interval.

Viewed in another way, velocities of circulation of money and deposits are continually changing (1) because of the lending operations of the non-banking bodies and (2) because of the lending of banks by overdrafts. It is clear, therefore, that the existing purchasing power and the supplies of circulating media are far from identical and that one may change without in any way affecting directly the other. And, since it is purchasing power which is of primary importance for present purposes, the quantities of circulating media must be discarded as an inaccurate measure.

CHAPTER III

THE FRENCH BANKING SYSTEM

In France, as in England and in Germany, the banking system is essentially centralized in form. At the apex is the Bank of France, exclusive bank of issue, bank of discount for other banks, banker for the Government, and clearing house for the great mass of the country's banking transactions. Constituting perhaps less important but nevertheless vital elements of the French banking structure are the commercial banks, headed by the *grandes sociétés de crédit;* the investment banks, *la haute banque* and *les banques d'affaires;* the savings banks, *la Caisse Nationale d'Épargne* and *les caisses d'épargne ordinaires;* the mortgage banks, *le Crédit Foncier;* the agricultural banks, *le Crédit Agricole;* and a number of other financial institutions combining banking with other functions. In addition, there are in Paris and in certain other commercial centres numerous branches of foreign banks, usually with functions similar to those of their head-offices abroad, but likewise with many of those peculiar to the French banks with which they must of necessity coöperate.

In order to comprehend the course of the French inflation, which, as in all other countries, has been largely determined by the operations of the banks, a brief study of the nature and functions of each of these institutions will be needed.

The Bank of France

Until the beginning of the nineteenth century banking in France was very largely in the hands of a few private houses, many of them banks of issue and all operating with extremely limited means as separate and independent institutions. Napoleon is reported to have remarked as late as 1806: "France lacks men who know what a bank is; it is a race of men to be created."[1] The banking history of France may be said to have begun in 1800 with the establishment of the Bank of France.

On February 20, 1800, this new institution opened its doors. Formed originally as a consolidation of the *Caisse des Comptes Courants*, an association of bankers established four years earlier for the purpose of issuing notes and discounting commercial paper, of the *Caisse d'Escompte du Commerce*, an association of merchants created three years earlier, likewise for the purpose of issuing notes and discharging primary banking functions, and of several other organizations of a similar character, it soon became and has since remained the outstanding financial institution of France. To the new Bank was assigned no less important a duty than that of serving the needs of commerce. It discounted sixty-day bills, accepted deposits, and issued notes in such amounts "that, with the cash reserves held by the Bank and with the commercial paper in its portfolio, it should at no time be in danger of deferring the payment of its obligations."[2] After its creation a hundred and twenty-eight years ago its functions gradually expanded, its resources increased, and its organization developed until toward the middle of the last century, when accorded the exclusive privilege of issue, it assumed its present dominant position in the French banking system.

The Bank of France is a private corporation, its shares being sold freely on the Paris bourse. In its earliest years its control was likewise completely in the hands of its stockholders or, more exactly, in those of the two hundred largest holders of its stock, who formed the General Assembly of the Bank (*l'Assemblée Générale*). This group in turn chose the fifteen regents (*Conseil d'Escompte*) and the three censors (*Censeurs*) in whom was vested the general administration of the Bank. Since 1806, however, the general direction has been delegated to a governor and two deputy

[1] "La France manque d'hommes qui sachent ce que c'est que la Banque; c'est une race d'hommes à créer."—E. Kaufmann, *La Banque en France considérée principalement au point de vue des trois grandes Banques de Dépôts* (Paris, Giard et Brière, 1914), p. 6.

[2] ". . . telles qu'au moyen du numéraire réservé dans les caisses de la Banque et des échéances du papier de son portefeuille, elle ne peut dans aucun temps être exposée à différer le paiement de ses engagements." — *Statuts Primitifs du 24 Pluviôse An VIII.*

governors, at first appointed by the Emperor and now selected by the *Chef de l'État*. The regents and censors were thus deprived of many of their powers, but they still discharge extremely important duties, particularly that of determining the discount policy of the Bank. Nevertheless, it can scarcely be disputed that, despite its private ownership and despite the measure of control exercised by some of its stockholders, the Bank of France has become more than a *semi-public* institution. In many respects, as will be seen later, it has recently taken on the appearance even of a government bureau.

In the functions of the Bank is found an explanation of its extraordinary position in the French banking system as a whole. In fact, it holds its place by virtue of the peculiar and indispensable services which it renders to the other banks and to the State.

As holder of the exclusive right of issuing circulating notes, legal tender in the payment of all debts, the Bank of France has gradually become guardian of the currency supply of the country. While in pre-war days there were gold and silver coins in considerable quantities in circulation, early in the war period they largely disappeared, going partly into the stockings of the peasants, partly, no doubt, though illegally, abroad, but for the greatest part into the vaults of the Bank of France. With their disappearance the notes of the Bank of France became the only circulating medium of the country, exception being made, of course, for the moneys of small denominations issued to meet the need for small change. Naturally there have continued in circulation the nickel and copper minor coins. One still finds, too, in some of the departments "chamber of commerce" notes, remnants of issues put out, on the security of equal amounts of Bank of France notes of larger denomination, to provide the pressing need for small change which arose as the inflation progressed. And since 1919 the metallic *jetons* coined by the French Government to replace the "chamber of commerce" notes (now practically all withdrawn) have been in general circulation. Nevertheless, since all of these small change moneys together bulk small in comparison with total circulation and since it may be assumed with some degree of certainty that such small change remains a nearly constant proportion of the total, recent fluctuations in the amount of Bank of France notes in circulation have probably corresponded almost exactly to changes in the quantity of money in circulation in the country.[3]

The Bank of France is holder of the real money reserves for the other banks and for the country as a whole. To it even the gold of the private hoards has been gradually released — during the war, in response to patriotic appeals and, more recently, by direct sale to the Government or to the Bank. As a result, its present (December 1927) holdings amount to the huge sum of 5.5 milliards of gold francs,[4] certainly a very large proportion indeed of the gold money supply of France. This gold reserve, once serving as a pledge of security for the notes issued by the Bank and for the deposits entrusted to its keeping, exists now as an important potential source of control over the position of the franc in the international exchange markets.

As banker to the French banks the central institution affords a service of fundamental importance and wields thereby much influence in promoting or checking the inflation process. It stands ready at all times to discount acceptable paper submitted by persons entitled as holders of properly qualifying accounts to make use of the service. To such persons it will also grant loans on collateral. To avail themselves of these and other services, practically all of the banks maintain accounts[5] and are thus enabled at all times to replenish their cash supplies by discounting paper from their portfolios at the nearest office of the Bank of France. Since the branches of the Bank are very widely distributed through

[3] Various estimates place the proportion of metallic to paper money in circulation in France in 1913 at approximately 50 per cent. In 1925 and 1926 *jetons* constituted only 1.8 per cent of the outstanding Bank of France notes.

[4] Of this amount 1.5 milliards are deposited abroad as security for loans from foreign governments.

[5] These accounts are reported to be small. Since, in the reports of the commercial banks, deposits at the Bank of France and at the Treasury are combined with the item "cash" and since the Bank of France in its statement does not separate deposits of banks from other private deposits, it is impossible to state the exact amount. It is an open secret, however, that they are not large, probably never amounting to more than 600,000,000 francs and usually perhaps to considerably less.

the country, it follows that at least one is within easy reach of every other banking office. It is by virtue of this wide geographical extension of the Bank's services that the amounts of idle cash in the tills of other banks have been reduced to a surprisingly low minimum.[6]

The clearing and transfer services of the Bank of France are valued in high degree not only by other banks but almost equally so by the railroad companies and by big business firms maintaining branches in various parts of the country and experiencing, therefore, the necessity of daily transfers of funds. Sums deposited at any office of the Bank are promptly credited at any other office to anyone designated. Or, if there is no office located in the vicinity of the transferee, the credit will, upon request, be placed at the local Post Office. Reversely, the Bank undertakes to collect checks, drafts, and matured notes payable in various parts of the country. No charge is made for these services to those maintaining sufficient balances to take care of the transactions involved. To other banks this transfer accommodation not only affords a means of transferring funds from one of their branches to another but also enables them to meet the demands of customers desiring either to make payments to various parts of the country or to collect out-of-town checks.

Besides its dealings with other banks and with large business firms, the Bank of France, especially at its branches located in country districts, does a small but important business with farmers and local merchants. For them, as for all other customers, it discounts commercial paper, transfers funds, and collects items payable in distant parts of the country. Such accounts, being very small, are naturally far from lucrative to the Bank, and the extension of its branches to communities offering business of such an unprofitable character has been brought about as a kind of price demanded by the Government in consideration of the successive renewals of the Bank's charter. This policy of geographical expansion into parts of the country which would otherwise have remained devoid of banking facilities has, however, doubtless had

[6] It seems likely that the proportion of till money held at the banks to their sight deposits is about 3 per cent. See Chap. XI, p. 284 and accompanying footnote.

much to do with winning for the Bank the position of prestige and of esteem which even the Government itself has sometimes been unable to command.

Finally, and for the purposes of this study most important of all its functions, the Bank provides invaluable services for the State itself. Besides acting in the capacity of fiscal agent of the Government in financial transactions not assigned to government bureaus or to specially created bodies such as the *Caisse Autonome d'Amortissement* or the *Crédit National*, it has since the beginning of the war regularly accorded to the State in large or small amounts and for various purposes funds for which a need was expressed. So large indeed have been these advances in recent years that they have almost completely dominated the affairs of the Bank. Ranging in amount as high as six times the portfolio of the Bank, including all non-governmental advances, and *in paper francs* as high as nine times its cash reserve, they have necessarily determined in large measure the amount of the liabilities of the Bank, viz. its notes in circulation and its deposits. During the early months of 1925, as at various times previously, the Bank even made *indirect* advances to the State in excess of the maximum set for direct ones and, in unduly increasing these advances, created the situation which led in 1925 to the infringement of the law fixing the maximum of notes in circulation. This it did in spite of the fact that it receives only an insignificant net interest for such advances.[7] Whatever may be said, therefore — and it is much — in defense of the policy of the Bank in thus lending financial aid to the Government in violation of the spirit of the law and in concealing in its published statements the resulting increased note circulation, the fact remains that during recent years it has functioned much more as a bureau of the Finance Ministry than as a privately owned and controlled central bank chiefly interested in fostering the needs of commerce and industry.

[7] Since April 7, 1925 the Bank of France has received in consideration of its advances to the State a nominal interest of 3 per cent. But, after deduction is made for that part of the interest going to the amortization funds for the debt of the State, the net interest accruing to the Bank is trifling: up to 21 milliards .50 per cent, from 21 to 22 milliards .375 per cent, from 22 to 26 milliards no interest whatsoever, and above 26 milliards .20 per cent.

The Commercial Banks (Les Grandes Sociétés de Crédit)

Approximately one-half of the commercial banking business in France is transacted by only four large banks, generally known in France as *les grandes sociétés de crédit.* In order of size they are: the *Crédit Lyonnais*, the *Société Générale pour favoriser le Développement du Commerce et de l'Industrie en France*, the *Comptoir National d'Escompte de Paris*, and the *Société Générale du Crédit Industriel et Commercial.* While created under varying circumstances and for somewhat different purposes, these four banks are, nevertheless, much alike in their organization and government and have come to exercise essentially similar functions. All are private corporations, their stock being quoted regularly on the Bourse. All except the *Crédit Industriel et Commercial*[8] maintain numerous branches throughout France, the central offices being in each instance at Paris. To councils of administration (*conseils d'administration*) elected by the stockholders are assigned all of the powers of control and many of the duties of administration. These councils, in turn, choose the officers, certain of whom, with designated members of the administrative councils, form the executive committees. The form of organization is democratic and would seem to insure a considerable measure of control by the stockholders; but here, as in the case of so many governmental bodies, the democracy is more apparent than real. Actually, the administrative councils are little more than self-perpetuating oligarchies. Not only do they nominate their successors, but their nominees are invariably accepted by the assembly of stockholders. The approval has, in fact, come to be regarded as a sort of vote of confidence, and a refusal to approve leads ultimately, unless reversed, to the resignation of the entire council. The effects of such a forced resignation of its admistrative council on the affairs of a bank are not hard to imagine. Naturally it does not occur, for the simple reason that the stockholders do not dare force it. Furthermore, small stockholders are effectively eliminated from control by the

[8] The *Crédit Industriel et Commercial* maintains, however, close relations with many provincial banks, especially with those having no Paris office.

stipulation, uniformly present in the charters of the banks, that members of the administrative councils must be holders of sizable amounts of stock.

There are, to be sure, a certain number of *commissaires des comptes* required by French corporation law to act as a board of control for every corporation. They too, however, although elected by the assembly of stockholders, are in practice chosen by the councils of administration and, being in line for promotion to lucrative executive positions or even to places on the council itself, from which in either case the nomination proceeds, regularly acquiesce in the programs and policies of the administrators.

Operating under such a completely autocratic control and without any effective supervision, these "Big Four" banks have come to occupy a position of power and of unaccountability to the public almost without parallel in other industrial countries. Never having been seriously interfered with, they have grown to resent public regulation or private investigation. Never having felt the necessity of publishing comprehensive information as to their operations, they see no reason why the public should be entitled to any, and content themselves with meagre and almost meaningless monthly statements but slightly amplified in their annual or semi-annual reports. Meanwhile the great majority of the stockholders, as well as the public, remain in ignorance of the nature and extent of their important operations.[9]

With respect to functions, the *grandes sociétés de crédit* are primarily institutions of discount and deposit and provide, in general, all the services offered by American commercial banks. But, unlike English and most American banks, these establishments combine extensive investment operations with their commercial banking functions. They not only participate frequently in the sale of securities floated by other syndicates but also not infrequently undertake individually the flotation of an entire issue, confining themselves in these undertakings, however, to the issues of governments, municipalities, and well established business firms, leaving to the *banques d'affaires* and to the private banks the more

[9] *Cf.* E. Kaufmann, *La Banque en France considérée principalement au point de vue des trois grandes Banques de Dépôt* (Paris, Giard et Brière, 1914), pp. 333–341.

speculative issues. The *Crédit Industriel et Commercial*, for example, although doing an extensive commercial banking business, is often classified, and perhaps properly so, with the *banques d'affaires*, the investment banks.

In addition to their regular investment banking operations, the French commercial banks, and many private banks as well, trade largely on the Bourse in both securities and foreign exchange.

The Investment Banks (La Haute Banque et les Banques d'Affaires)

Investment banking in France is managed by two groups of institutions so different in character as to require separate description.[10] The first and older group is known as *la haute banque*, the name given to the group of Paris bankers operating under the Restoration. Formerly the most powerful banking interests in the country and, in the case of Rothschild's, likewise on the entire Continent, the banks of this classification have in time come to occupy positions of secondary importance only. There have persisted in France only seven or eight, all private banks and some of them dating from long before the establishment of the Bank of France and even from before the beginnings of modern banking on the Continent. Besides administering the fortunes of the families to which they belong, these houses now act as bankers to various foreign governments, particularly in the capacity of paying interest on outstanding bonds and of floating small new loans. In the case of important issues of foreign governments, however, they usually become mere intermediaries between the government in question and one of the *banques d'affaires*. They serve, too, as administrators of estates and retain a certain measure of control in the banks and industrial companies in the establishment of which they have aided.

The *banques d'affaires*, which constitute the second group of French investment banks, play a much more important rôle in the present financial system of France. Headed in size and in im-

[10] The importance of the large commercial banks in investment operations has already been referred to (pp. 24–25).

portance by the *Banque de Paris et des Pays-Bas*,[11] they undertake the sale of the great bulk of securities intended for the French market. Unlike the more strictly commercial banks, which are serious competitors only for the seasoned issues, the *banques d'affaires* will undertake the financing of promising but still unestablished industries. The *Banque de Paris et des Pays-Bas* began its existence as little more than an association of big capitalists[12] organized for the purpose of forming and managing syndicates. It was not long, however, before its competition became a serious menace to the operations of the *haute banque*, which, with the exception of Rothschild's, was fast being reduced to a rank of complete dependence. In an attempt to maintain their fast waning position, some of these private bankers organized the *Banque de l'Union Parisienne*, which entered into active competition with their new and dangerous rival. Hence this bank, second in size of the *banques d'affaires*, is in a sense the permanent head of a syndicate composed of a number of the *haute banque* as members. The present (1928) governing council of administrators is made up almost entirely of important figures among the private bankers.

As the chief agencies through which long-term financing, other than that of the French Government and of its smaller political divisions, is accomplished, these banks inevitably exerted a large part of whatever influence investment banking as a whole had in the process of inflation. As will be seen later, however, the emission of such securities was much reduced during most of the inflation period, and consequently the influence of the banking institutions responsible for their issue was correspondingly diminished.

On the other hand, one of the important banking developments during the inflation period was the great extension of the commercial banking operations of these larger investment banks. Prior to the war the *Banque de Paris et des Pays-Bas*, for example, maintained deposit accounts for its investment-banking customers only. Since 1920, however, the service has been opened to everyone, and by December 1926 its total deposits were several

[11] The other most important *banques d'affaires* are: *la Banque de l'Union Parisienne*, *la Banque Française pour le Commerce et l'Industrie*, and *le Crédit Mobilier Français*.

[12] *Cf.* E. Kaufmann, *op. cit.*, p. 124.

times as large as those of the *Crédit Industriel et Commercial*, the smallest of the "Big Four," and almost half as large as those of the *Comptoir National d'Escompte*. A similar change occurred in the affairs of the *Banque de l'Union Parisienne*. Presumably the influence of these banks in the later inflation was much more important as commercial than as investment banks. Like the "Big Four" banks, however, they have never informed the public or even their stockholders of their really significant operations. By the device of combining several items under a single caption in their statements, they have succeeded in making their published reports almost meaningless.

The Paris Money Market

A money market in the Anglo-Saxon sense of the term has never existed in Paris. To be sure, bankers' acceptances and other types of high-grade commercial paper are bought and sold regularly outside the banks, and at times — especially prior to 1914 — the volume of transactions in such *beau papier*, as the Parisians call it, has been very considerable. Nevertheless, even for prime commercial paper there is no continuous market with standard quoted rates, nor a market of sufficient breadth to be depended upon either by banks desiring to adjust their portfolios or by those wishing to invest idle funds for short periods of time.

The explanation of the failure of the Paris money market to develop seems to lie firstly in the policies and organizations of the leading commercial banks, which almost completely determine banking sentiment in France, and secondly in the extraordinary borrowing methods practiced by the French Treasury.

The large banks are buyers of high-grade commercial paper, but rarely sellers. To them it is a sign of weakness to take paper from their portfolios and to offer it for sale. This view seems to be much the same as that which a decade and a half ago was held by many of the American banks with respect to interbank loans. In the case of the large French banks, however, which, as has been pointed out, do a large portion of the commercial banking business of the country, this feeling is exceptionally strong and is generally shared by the smaller banks. Moreover, the bankers reason, and rightly, that a purchasing competitor might easily use the paper they would sell to discover and wean away some of their most profitable customers.

Equally efficacious in retarding the development of the Paris money market is the fact that the big banks with their numerous branches operating throughout a country of such varied industries have usually found it possible, in their holdings of customers' paper, to secure suitable maturities as well as sufficient diversity of industry and locality and, consequently, have not felt a pressing need for the services of an active money market.

But, of more importance still, the French Treasury began early in the war period (*décret du 13 septembre 1914*) to issue in any desired amounts National Defense Bonds (*Bons de la Défense Nationale*) of three, six, and twelve months' maturity. Since 1824 and even earlier it had been accustomed to issue other treasury bonds of short maturity, termed, in the earlier days, *bons royaux* and, in the later days, *Bons du Trésor*. In 1918 (*arrêté du 16 avril*) the issue of National Defense Bonds[13] was extended to include Treasury paper of one month maturity. By purchasing these obligations the banks were enabled to place surplus cash, to adjust maturities according to need, and to replenish their cash supplies without danger of loss of customers. Thus these short-term government securities have in great measure provided a substitute for the commercial paper so plentiful in other money markets. More recently, as will be seen later, the banks have had recourse to the deposit facilities offered by the Treasury, from which they have received a rate of interest varying from $1\frac{1}{2}$ to 3 per cent.

Two types of loans have necessarily become of importance despite the slight development of the money market as a whole. These more common types are *l'escompte hors banque* and *prêts au jour le jour* ("discount outside the banks" and "loans from day to day"). The market for the former has failed to develop normally for reasons already given. Nevertheless there are certain kinds of paper which

[13] The term "bond" in referring to short-term issues such as *Bons de la Défense Nationale* and *Bons du Trésor* will be replaced hereafter in this volume by "Treasury paper" to avoid confusion with long-term issues.

are frequently sold in important quantities outside the banks. Drafts arising from the import of standard raw materials, bills of big commission houses, and many of the best bankers' acceptances having an origin essentially commercial are often discounted on the Paris money market at rates ranging sensibly lower than those charged at the same time by the banks. Maturities of paper thus discounted are usually of forty-five to ninety days, although in the period of rapid currency depreciation there was a tendency for the period to shorten. The chief dealers are the large banks, principally buyers and rarely sellers; the foreign banks, equally buyers and sellers; the private banking houses, regularly purchasers and sometimes sellers; the railroad companies; the *Crédit Foncier;* and certain large business firms having bills for discount or disposable funds to invest.

The market for the second type of loan, the *prêts au jour le jour*, has developed only under serious difficulties. The stringency of French law in respect to the pledging of securities as collateral for loans (*gage*) renders impossible, for the present, a broad market like that existing for call loans in New York. In this situation the French banks have ordinarily resorted to one of two devices in the making of this type of loan: either the borrowing bank gives the lending bank a check (*mandat*) on the Bank of France dated the following day, or the loan is arranged by the simultaneous purchase and sale of certain bonds of short maturities held by the borrowing bank.

The French Savings Banks

Savings in France are handled not only by most of the commercial and investment banks in the form of time deposits of various sorts but also by two sets of specialized institutions devoted to their accumulation and investment. The older of these two organizations, that comprising the private and municipal savings banks (*les caisses d'épargne ordinaires*), made its appearance early in the nineteenth century in the form of a small savings bank in Paris. Similar institutions entirely independent of one another arose subsequently in various other parts of the country. In 1883, however, they united into a general conference which might be regarded as a sort of extremely loose administrative union. This association has persisted until the present time. At the end of 1926 there were in the organization approximately 550 banks and 1800 branches, exclusive of those located in Alsace-Lorraine. These latter savings banks, numbering about 140 banks with some 700 branches, belong to the association, but, having grown up under the regulations of German law, they have not yet become completely identified with the others. As a consultative and advisory body for the entire association a superior commission of 26 members, 13 of whom are presidents or members of the administrative councils of the commercial banks, is maintained; local councils, each composed of 15 citizens, determine budgetary questions and administer the private resources of the several banks. The *caisses d'épargne ordinaires* are owned by their depositors, no profits being distributed except as interest payments on deposits.

The national savings bank (*la Caisse Nationale d'Épargne*) was established in 1881 and began operations the following year. It is owned by the Government and is managed as a subdivision of the Ministry of Commerce and Industry, under the control of which its services have been extended over a field wider yet than that of the private and municipal savings banks — every post office is an auxiliary office and every rural mail carrier an agent.[14]

Both institutions have as their primary purpose the stimulation of savings among the peasants, workers, and poorer classes, large depositors being practically forbidden participation by the stipulation of a low maximum deposit.[15]

The funds of the banks of both classes are administered by a government institution, the *Caisse des Dépôts et Consignations*, a body performing banking functions, chiefly those of investment and administration of funds, for many governmental and non-governmental institutions. Because of legal requirements and because of

[14] At the end of 1925, 13,000 offices were being maintained.

[15] In 1926 (August 20) the maximum deposit was fixed at 12,000 francs for private individuals and at 40,000 francs for philanthropic and other non-business societies. (Before that time the maximum was considerably lower.) The nature of the clientèle of the savings banks is clearly shown by the fact that in the private banks 71 per cent, and in the national banks 75 per cent of the accounts were for amounts less than 500 francs.

the policy of the government-appointed executives of this organization, practically all of the deposits of the savings banks are placed in government securities.[16] The surplus and reserves of the banks are likewise largely invested in government bonds. Furthermore, the banks of both savings organizations assist in the placement of government issues and at the request of depositors arrange gratuitously for the purchase of state securities. Surplus deposits (deposits beyond the maximum allowed) are automatically placed at the disposal of the Government through investment in state obligations. In short, the French Government has turned the small savings[17] of the country to its own use and has thereby tapped a source of credit not usually available. Its policy has also bound up the savings of some millions of workers, housewives, and peasants with the ups-and-downs of state finances.

For the purposes of this report and in the process of the French inflation, the operations of the savings banks are of minor importance only. In the same measure that the State receives new purchasing power from its absorption of savings deposits, purchasing power has been relinquished by private individuals. Or, reversely, the withdrawal by holders of savings accounts of a portion or all of their deposits merely reduces by an equal amount the disposable purchasing power of the Government and may, on occasion, force it to increase its advances from the Bank of France. Following the movements of savings deposits may reveal something of the relation (if any) between inflation and the saving dispositions of small gentry, but thereby is missed the great bulk of the savings of the country — those of corporations and of the wealthy classes. That problem is treated elsewhere.[18]

Le Crédit Foncier de France

Founded in 1852 as an agricultural relief measure, the *Crédit Foncier* had as its chief function the granting of mortgage loans to

[16] All of the deposits of the *Caisse Nationale d'Épargne* and 95 per cent of the deposits of the *caisses d'épargne ordinaires* were thus placed December 31, 1926.

[17] At the end of 1926 the total deposits of the two savings banks exceeded 15 milliards of francs.

[18] See Chap. X, pp 269–277.

farmers. In fact, until 1876 it held a legal monopoly of such business. But, in spite of its original purpose, the urban loans of the *Crédit Foncier* have more recently become much larger and hence more important than its rural ones. Moreover, since 1860 it has loaned extensively to communes, to municipalities, and to a less extent to certain of the departments. Hence it can no longer be regarded as a purely mortgage-banking institution.

The loans of this bank to city real-estate holders and to governmental divisions, like its mortgage loans to farmers, are long-term, ranging from ten to seventy-five years. All are amortized gradually by the payment at each interest date of a sum which when put at interest and combined with all similar sums will take care of the payment of the principal at the date of maturity.

To secure the funds required for its long-term lending operations the *Crédit Foncier* issues its own bonds on the security of its holdings of mortgages or of communal loans. These bonds are sold to the investing public, which in buying provides the bank with its loanable resources.

Besides its regular long-term loan operations, the *Crédit Foncier* lends on mortgage security for a period of time up to nine years, giving in return current accounts to the borrowers. It transacts, too, a small commercial banking business, extending credit in particular to holders of its obligations who pledge them as security for advances. The total of its current accounts, however, must not exceed the par value of its capital stock, and, consequently, these accounts form but an insignificant portion of its total business.

Despite the importance of the *Crédit Foncier* in the economic life of the French people, the institution seems to have played a relatively unimportant part in the inflation process. True, at the end of 1926, the total of outstanding loans amounted to more than 9 milliards of francs, and in 1921 alone more than $1\frac{1}{3}$ milliards of new loans were granted. Also, in 1923 and in 1924 new loans aggregated in each year almost a milliard. Such loans, however, derived as they are from the proceeds of sales of securities to the investing public, lead to few increases in expenditures not balanced by economies elsewhere.

In its organization the French mortgage bank is very similar to the Bank of France. A council of administration elected by the stockholders holds the nominal governing power, but the chief authority seems to rest with the governor and two deputy-governors, all appointed by the State.

Le Crédit Agricole

Agricultural credit in France is provided by a group of coöperative banks generally known as the *Crédit Agricole*. Until 1920 they were organized under the direct control of the Ministry of Agriculture; but on August 5 of that year the management was transferred to a central organization, the *Caisse Nationale de Crédit Agricole*, which is directed by a council of administration named and controlled by a plenary commission of thirty members, which, in turn, is presided over by the Minister of Agriculture.

At the head of the French agricultural credit organization is the *Caisse Nationale*. In dependence upon it are the regional banks (*les caisses régionales*), numbering about one hundred,[19] one or more of which are located in each department. And, as subsidiary institutions to the regional banks, there exist numerous local banks (*les caisses locales*). Of these last-named there were in all about 5300 at the end of 1926.

The resources of the *Caisse Nationale* accrue in large part from the annual rentals paid by the Bank of France for the privilege of note issue. Other resources consist of a sum of forty million francs exacted in 1897 by the Government from the Bank as a price demanded for the renewal of its charter and gifts and legacies of various sorts. The central office administers these funds, but their division into amounts to be made available respectively for short-term, medium-term, and long-term advances is determined by a joint decree of the Ministers of Agriculture and of Finance.

The resources of the regional banks, aside from those represented by their capital and reserves, are derived principally from advances granted by the national office. Such funds are distributed to the various regional offices several times a year according to their needs, the relative amounts allowed each being largely de-

[19] As of December 1926.

termined on the basis of its capitalization. In addition, the regional offices are permitted to receive deposits, from which certain amounts of funds available for short-term advances may be drawn. The regional banks also borrow directly from the Bank of France by discounting short-term paper or by securing advances on pledge of collateral. The local banks similarly derive most of their resources from advances granted them by the regional banks. They likewise receive deposits and in this way obtain funds for short-term lending.

As mentioned above, each local organization is a form of coöperative bank. Only farmers and local agricultural coöperative societies can become members, and only members have the privilege of borrowing. The nominal membership fee paid for admission takes the form of a subscription to the stock of the local bank, which is, therefore, both owned and controlled by the stockholder-members.

The farmer or local coöperative society desiring a loan makes application to the manager of the local bank. When approved by the manager and his loan committee, the advance — if a short-term one — is made usually from funds derived from discounting the original instrument at the regional office, which may in turn provide itself with any funds required for this or further advances by rediscounting it at the Bank of France.

Medium- or long-term loans to farmers are made directly by the regional offices, but only after the approval of one of the local banks. The long-term loans to agricultural societies are made only by the central organization. In either case the requisite funds are derived from those received by the national bank from the Government and allotted among the various uses by joint decree of the Ministers of Agriculture and Finance.

All of the loans of the *Crédit Agricole* are thus of types which might affect the inflation process. Those for short maturities increase the purchasing power in the hands of ready spenders often by expanding the discounts of the Bank of France and hence carry no counterpart of saving elsewhere in the system, while those for medium and long maturities place in the hands of equally quick spenders funds which otherwise might not be used. In fact, however, the inflationary effects of such loans have probably been negligible because of their relatively small size. The total outstanding loans of the system at the end of 1926 were but 863 millions of francs. The additions to lending during that year were 156 millions of intermediate and long-term and 361 millions of short-term loans. And only 83 millions of discounts were made by the regional offices at the Bank of France. In earlier years these amounts were generally even smaller.

Le Crédit National

In 1919 the French Government created the *Crédit National* as a special organization to take care of the indemnification of the inhabitants of the zone of conflict who had suffered property loss during the war. Although established as a joint-stock company with shares held by the general public,[20] in its functions it is little more than a department of the Treasury. All of the funds necessary for its operations (except for insignificant amounts to be mentioned later) come either from government appropriations or from the flotation of long-term securities with government guarantee. Interest, as well as principal reimbursement at maturity, are naturally direct charges upon the annual budget of the Treasury.

The general direction of the *Crédit National* is vested in a council of administration composed of a director-general, two directors, and from twenty to twenty-four other members elected by the general assembly of stockholders. The executive heads — the director-general and the two directors — are named by the President of the Republic after presentation of the names of the nominees to the council of administration for approval.

In order to provide for a satisfactory dividend payment to the stockholders, several minor sources of income are available. The capital funds are invested in government or government-guaranteed securities. The various reserve funds and unclaimed interest are also invested in similar securities. Furthermore, the State turns over fifteen days in advance of due dates the funds required for meeting interest payments on the obligations of the company. These funds are invested in the interim. Finally, there is a profit derived from loans made on a limited scale for industrial and commercial exploitations.

[20] They are not, however, quoted on the Bourse.

In all, eight loans were floated by the company between 1919 and 1924.[21] After the failure of the eighth loan in 1924, however, the *Crédit National* was obliged to make its payments in the settlement of indemnity claims partly in cash and partly in government securities.[22]

Thus, in its effective control and in its functions, the *Crédit National* is essentially an organ of the State. Its work merely relieves the Treasury of the administration and adjustment of war claims. All obligations issued by the society are guaranteed as to interest and principal by the Government and are to be considered as accretions to the debt of the State.

[21] The loans aggregated in nominal value 27 milliards of francs.

[22] For this purpose government bonds of from 4- to 30-year maturities were used. 15- to 30-year government annuities were also used.

CHAPTER IV

TEMPORARY CHANGES IN THE FRENCH BANKING SYSTEM

SINCE the beginning of the inflation, banking in France has undergone many changes. In January 1921[1] demand deposits began to be received by the Treasury both from banks and from the public. Interest was offered on such deposits, and all banks, as well as business firms and private individuals, were invited to leave their idle funds.

Thus a new practice in central banking is being[2] tested. It is a time-honored tradition, sanctioned by long usage, that a central bank must not pay interest on any of its deposits. Such payments are held by many to be incompatible with the function of note issue. It is also evident that to allow a return on deposits would tend in certain banking systems to defeat other important purposes of the central banking institution, such as those of loan and discount at the official bank rate and the purchase and sale of securities and of paper on the open market at any rate even approximating the official one. On the other hand, it has long been recognized that the elasticity provisions of most of our banking systems are to a certain extent inadequate to bring about a speedy contraction of money and of deposits as soon as the need for them has passed. Hence, the French innovation assumes a peculiar interest.

The French banking system is now essentially a system with two central banks, one paying interest on deposits and the other not. Viewed purely from the standpoint of central banking policy, the device is, to say the least, an ingenious one. The old difficulties with respect to the paying of interest on deposits by a central bank have

[1] By terms of the *arrêté* of December 17, 1920.

[2] The reader is asked to bear in mind that this chapter as well as those which follow were written in the latter months of 1927. The present tense is accordingly used throughout to describe conditions then existing.

been completely avoided, and all the advantages of the practice have been gained. Most of the banks are now depositors both at the Treasury and at the Bank of France. They continue to deposit at the Bank of France as formerly in order to avail themselves of its discount and transfer privileges. But such deposits need not be large. Hence, all the otherwise idle cash of the banks — recently much increased in volume by the prohibition against the export of capital and by the large purchases of foreign exchange by the Bank of France — instead of being sent to the Bank of France or being held in their own vaults, is now sent to the Treasury in order to draw the rate of interest there offered. Immediately after the Treasury has received such funds, however, they are turned over to the Bank of France in payment of some of its advances to the State. And, since the advances of the Bank to the State bear a net rate of interest varying from zero to .50 per cent, the operation, *from one point of view*, amounts to the State's paying 1 per cent to 3 per cent in order to secure for the Bank of France the speedy return of all surplus cash falling into the hands of the banks or of the public.[3]

In times of easy money it is to be expected that the deposits of the banks and of the large business firms with the Treasury will be considerably augmented and that, consequently, advances by the Bank of France to the State will be correspondingly reduced. There is no doubt, as will be seen later, that just this order of events has been produced by the economic depression beginning with August 1926 and continuing until the present (December 1927) and that the flow of funds released from business use accounts for a considerable part of the repayments to the Bank of France by the State. In periods of increasing trade activity and rising prices just the reverse situation is certain to appear. Private depositors will naturally procure from their banks the increased amount of funds needed for business purposes; and the banks, increasing their loans and deposits, will meet their additional reserve and till-money requirements by drawing on their accounts at the Treasury. Because of interest considerations they will thus exhaust their accounts at the Treasury before beginning to rediscount at the Bank of France.

[3] That is, the rate offered by the Treasury has ranged from 1.5 per cent to 3 per cent.

Hence, the deposits at the Treasury will be reduced, and the Treasury, in order to meet the demands of its depositors, will be forced to increase its borrowings at the Bank of France.

The effects of the banking operations of the Treasury on the volume of note circulation of the Bank of France are in the long run probably not great. True, in periods of depression idle funds are doubtless retired earlier than they otherwise would be, and the average volume of notes in circulation is consequently reduced. The reduction probably does not, however, bulk large. But, except to the extent that the new operations thus enhance contraction elasticity, they have little effect upon currency supplies. The interest payments are hardly sufficient to attract funds other than those completely idle. Hence, the deposits in the Treasury cannot be expected to be large except in periods of business inactivity or at times when, as recently in its purchase of foreign exchange, the Bank of France persists in issuing funds in considerable amounts. So, while, in general, currency supplies (notes and deposits) will be reduced by an amount substantially equivalent to the deposits made at the Treasury, the reduction will occur only when excess funds have already been put out by the Bank of France and will last only so long as additional currency supplies are not needed by commerce and industry. Immediately upon finding it to their advantage to expand their loans, the banks will withdraw such deposits to meet their cash and reserve needs. Then the Treasury will of necessity proceed once more to borrow from the Bank, which will, in turn, issue notes to the extent demanded.[4]

The effects of its banking operations on the Treasury itself are also easy to see. First and most important, the Government liquidates its current indebtedness to the Bank of France by borrowing on demand from the French banks and, to a limited extent, from the French public. Moreover, since the advances of the Bank to the State are virtually free of interest charge,[5] the operation amounts to the replacing of a substantially non-interest-bearing

[4] Attention is called to the searching analysis of certain of the features of the new French banking system made by Robert Wolff in his recent monograph, *Note sur le Système monétaire français* (Paris, Gauthier-Villars et Cie., 1927).

[5] See above, Chap. III, footnote 7.

obligation payable entirely at the option of the Government by one carrying a net charge of 1.5 to 3 per cent and payable on demand. When the deposits at the Treasury are called for and have to be returned, however, the necessary funds may again be received by the negotiation of new advances from the Bank of France. Thus the Government, in order to reduce that part of its current indebtedness which has received the widest publicity and the most severe public condemnation, has done so by creating another form of current indebtedness which is payable on demand and which, except for the fact that it is reconvertible at any time into the original type of indebtedness, would consequently be more dangerous as well as more expensive. But the new type of loan (that of deposits at the Treasury) has the great advantage of having so far escaped the attention, and, consequently, the adverse criticism, of the rank and file of the French public.

It should perhaps be added, in fairness to the French Government, that the advantages gained from its banking operations are important and not to be underestimated. In the first place, the Treasury gets most of the surplus funds in the French money markets without delay and at small cost. The alternative policy of floating new bond issues more frequently than has been done would probably have cost the State in interest charges three or four times as much as those paid on deposits. In the second place, the funds received, whether in the form of deposits or of notes, are turned over immediately to the Bank of France and immediately cancelled. Thus the ordinary, as opposed to forced, contraction elasticity of the French banking system has been greatly enhanced. As a result, whatever influence the idle cash in the French money markets might otherwise have had in supplying an unhealthy stimulus to trade and to prices and in increasing the incentives of banks and of others to place idle funds in foreign markets has been diminished. What is more, by providing a ready investment for the otherwise idle funds of the banks the Government has at least made tolerable the discontinuance of its practice of issuing *at all times and in any amounts demanded* its short-term Treasury paper. Without some such provision the stringent regulations against the export of capital would probably early have broken down under the resistance of the banks. Finally, and perhaps most important of all, the confidence of the French public in their Government and in the Bank of France has been greatly increased at a time when confidence above all things else was a prime necessity.

But how far and for how long are these benefits assured? The dangers of investment abroad or of the export of capital have received so much public attention that little further exposition of them is necessary. Suffice it to say that, to the extent that the commercial and other banks throughout the country supply the necessary foreign exchange, deposits are transferred from the buyers' banks to the selling banks, which in turn buy the exchange from business or speculating sellers. Thus the funds which were originally in the hands of the buyers of foreign securities come finally to those of the sellers of the necessary foreign exchange, so that thus far no apparent shrinkage or enlargement of deposits has been occasioned. It is only when the Bank of France comes into the picture to save the franc from depreciation that the situation changes materially. To the extent that it supplies the necessary exchange, as it would be obliged to do should the flight of capital again become large, it receives in payment funds that were formerly deposited in the banks or perhaps at the Treasury. The banks, losing cash thereby, draw on their accounts at the Treasury for like amounts — or the Treasury may be drawn upon directly by other buyers — and the State is obliged to apply to the Bank of France for new advances to the amount of its deposit losses. Hence, while the Bank of France would have increased its cash (or reduced its notes and private deposits) to the extent of its sales of foreign exchange, the much dreaded advances of the Bank to the State could not but be increased by a somewhat like amount. Also, to the extent (if any) that these operations affect prices and the volume of trade, the need for new currency supplies would be likewise affected. Should the volume of the operations be so great as to depress considerably the value of the franc or should the Bank of France for any reason not interfere to prevent its depreciation, the resultant increases in the volume of trade and in prices would soon bring in their train a notable increase in the volume of currency and of bank credit. Under the pre-war system the Bank of France would have lost gold by export, and money rates in Paris would have tightened in consequence; under the present (December 1927) system the Bank will close part of its foreign exchange holdings and will suffer an augmentation of its advances to the State.

Against the danger of the export of capital the French Government attempted to provide by two stringent and very painful measures. Not only was there a practically complete prohibition against the export of capital, but, in addition, a tax of 25 per cent was imposed on most interest and dividend payments from abroad.[6] The force of these restrictions is, to say the least, doubtful. There is at present (December 1927) much foreign capital in France, and against its withdrawal there can naturally be no effective prohibition. Coming into France, as much of it did, during the recent stock-market boom, it had the effect of weakening the markets of foreign exchange. At the same time, on account of the resulting large purchases of exchange by the Bank of France, it loosened considerably the money-market rates in Paris and increased the deposits of the banks at the Treasury. Should this capital be suddenly withdrawn, the reverse effects may be anticipated. In order to maintain the franc at its present level the Bank of France would be obliged to sell some of its holdings of sterling and of dollars, while the Treasury, according to the above analysis, would lose deposits and, as a consequence, be obliged to increase its borrowings from the Bank of France.

There remains continually in the background the extraordinary but sentimentally important danger of business prosperity. Strange as it may seem at first thought, any substantial increase in the

[6] These restrictions began with the Decree of July 3, 1915 prohibiting the exportation of gold. By the Decree of April 12, 1916 the restriction was extended to silver and by that of April 3, 1918 to almost all sorts of capital and securities. Recent regulations have not affected the applicability of these measures. An executive order of July 23, 1927 permitted the sale of foreign currency and credits to French tourists and to French citizens residing abroad. The *arrêté* of August 16, 1927 provided that the proceeds of the sale of foreign securities might be used again for the purchase of an equivalent value of foreign securities, thus permitting to banking houses operating for their own accounts the reëxportation of capital to the extent of its repatriation. For further recent and drastic revisions with regard to the temporary export of capital, see Chap. XIII, p. 333. For a full treatment of the entire subject the reader is referred to an excellent treatise entitled *Changes et Monnaies* by Louis Pommery (Paris, Marcel Giard, 1926).

volume of trade or in prices must lead eventually to an increase in the advances of the Bank of France to the State. A revival of trade or a rising price level is invariably accompanied by larger borrowing from the banks on the part of the business public. In order to meet this new demand for credit, as well as for cash, the banks will draw upon their resources at the Treasury, and the Treasury must in turn secure new credit from the Bank. As a result, the feared expansion of the Bank's advances to the State again will make its appearance. Against this danger the Government has interposed no safeguard.[7] And, while business depression continues, none will be needed.

The advantages of the new banking arrangement to the Government are not to be underestimated nor the attendant dangers given too much weight. It has recently been learned that, at least in France, political confidence may be of greater importance, even in its effects on financial and currency stability, than financial solvency itself. It may be better, therefore, to let the French public believe that the steady reduction in the advances of the Bank of France to the State represents a real amelioration of the financial status of the Treasury. The trust inspired by the belief is perhaps a prerequisite to the successful carrying through of the reforms which will bring a permanent betterment of the situation.

Changes in the Paris Money Market

The changed relations between the Treasury and the banks have produced important changes also in the Paris money market. As explained above, the French banks for a long period relied upon short-term Treasury paper (*Bons de la Défense Nationale* and *Bons du Trésor*) as the chief source of investment for their surplus funds. The former being issued in unlimited amounts with maturities from one to twelve months[8] and both being salable at any time as well

[7] The deposit of the *Caisse d'Amortissement* at the Bank of France amounts to approximately 7 milliards of francs (December 1927). There is no legal restriction against this fund being deposited in the Treasury. Should this be done, no increase in advances would be necessary.

[8] The actual maturities were for one, three, six, and twelve months. The one-month Treasury paper could be kept at the option of the holders for one, two, or three months.

as readily discountable at the Bank of France, alike they served admirably as a substitute for high-grade commercial paper and provided a good form of secondary reserve for the French banks.

How important an element the short-term Treasury paper had become in the Paris money market may be judged by the indignation among the banks when in March 1924 the Bank of France recommenced its interference in the exchange market. In an attempt to prevent the use of Treasury obligations as a means of securing funds for accomplishing the sale of francs, the Bank at that time refused to grant credit on National Defense Bonds. Thus, at a moment when the aid of all the banks was being sought in an attempt to block the disastrous manipulation of French exchange from abroad, much confusion was aroused at home. With their secondary reserves very largely invested in National Defense Bonds, the banks suddenly found an important part of their assets almost completely frozen. Such pressure on the part of the Bank of France was especially resented by the foreign banks, which began immediately to find other employments for their funds.

Again in the critical days of April 1925, when the political situation had once more become tense, and almost at the moment when it was announced on the floor of the Senate that the Bank of France had for a number of months been resorting to misrepresentations in its statements, another money market crisis loomed on the banking horizon. There had been talk from time to time of various projects for the consolidation of the floating debt, but none of these projects had previously received much serious political attention. Beginning in April 1925, however, certain formulae for forced consolidation appeared to be meeting with favorable consideration. Again the affairs of the banks were thrown into confusion by the threatened compulsory conversion of their most liquid assets into entirely unliquid ones. By November of that year the fear of consolidation had provoked a veritable panic among the bankers, who, in the absence of an organized money market, could not be assured of the normal functioning of their organizations.[9]

Finally, in the late summer of 1926, just after the exchange

[9] *Cf. La France économique en 1926*, published by *La Revue d'Économie Politique*, 1927, p. 354, "Le Marché monétaire et les Changes."

crisis which brought the franc to the lowest point on record, came the legal limitation of the total amount of the floating debt. And, while this maximum was made flexible within narrow limits, the departure from the former practice of unlimited issue of National Defense Bonds caused considerable anxiety among the banks. The restriction was especially annoying because of the critical situation prevailing at the time. With the return of political stability and of public confidence in the Poincaré Government, the repatriation of capital coupled with large purchases of securities by foreigners at steadily rising prices was adding continually to the abundance of funds in the Paris market. Furthermore, the continued business depression, keeping down the demand for such funds from business sources, aggravated in increasing measure the position of the banks. With plentiful funds in but slight demand for business purposes and with the supply of short-term government securities (the former resort in such periods) narrowly limited, they were left the choice of depositing the excess of their funds with the Treasury at 1.5 per cent interest or of buying securities with the attractive yields which many of them still offered. Indications are that they did both on a large scale, although, if their operations[10] on the security market were as extensive as the rise in security prices might lead one to believe, their monthly reports are as successful in disguising them as they are reputed to be in concealing most of their other interesting operations. Statistical evidence is extremely strong, however, that a very large proportion of the surplus cash coming into the hands of the banks through deposit as well as through the retirement of Treasury paper was deposited with the Treasury and by it used either for the purchase of foreign exchange or for repayment of advances from the Bank of France.[11] Thus, the acceptance of interest-bearing demand deposits by the Treasury has provided a form of short-term investment for the banks to replace the withdrawn National Defense Bonds and has again made possible com-

[10] No inconsiderable portion of the recent rise in the security markets has been attributed (though probably erroneously) to their operations. *Cf. La France économique en 1926*, p. 355.

[11] *Cf.* statistical analysis of the operations of the large commercial banks, Chap. IX, pp. 216 and 220.

plete liquidity in those of their assets represented by government borrowings.

La Caisse Autonome d'Amortissement

The *Caisse d'Amortissement*,[12] although a continuation of a series of older institutions of similiar nature and functions, in its relations to the Treasury and to the Bank of France properly constitutes an element of the "new French banking system". And, since frequent reference will be made later to its activities, a clear conception of its character and functions becomes desirable. Strictly speaking, the creation of the present *Caisse d'Amortissement* has introduced no new feature into the relations between the Bank of France and the Treasury. In its administration of outstanding short-term government securities and in the disposition of its funds it operates much as the Treasury itself would were the *Caisse* not in existence. Its revenues, derived from the earnings of the tobacco monopoly and from the proceeds of the real-estate transfer and inheritance taxes, come from sources formerly exploited by the Treasury. In paying the interest on, redeeming, and renewing *Bons de la Défense Nationale* it obviously performs Treasury functions. Moreover, its issue of long-term obligations on the security of tobacco receipts is nothing more or less than a funding operation undertaken for the Treasury, and the obligations issued are no less debts of the State than Treasury bonds themselves. In discounting government bonds received as subscriptions to new issues, the *Caisse* turns over to the Treasury only funds which are really the Treasury's. Finally, in depositing its funds at the Bank of France it places at the disposition of the central bank amounts which would ordinarily have been placed there by the Treasury itself in the repayment of advances and which constitute as much a fund for the reduction of the debt of the State at the Bank as if they were in the Treasury account proper.

There is, however, the point to be noted that the resources of the *Caisse d'Amortissement* at the Bank of France serve as a "cushion" to the disparities between current disbursements and current

[12] The present *Caisse d'Amortissement*, created by the law of August 7, 1926, began operations on October 1 of the same year.

receipts of the Treasury from the redemption or issue of National Defense Bonds. That is, when reimbursements exceed the proceeds of new loans, the extra funds needed are secured, not as formerly from the Bank of France as an increase in advances to the State, but from the resources of the *Caisse*. Likewise when the proceeds of new loans exceed reimbursements, the additional funds go, not to the Bank of France as a reduction in advances to the State, but to the *Caisse* in augmentation of its account at the Bank. Thus, the establishment of the *Caisse d'Amortissement* has secured for the Treasury the advantage that the changing relations between repayments and receipts are not reflected as continual and undesirable fluctuations in the advances of the Bank of France to the State.

CHAPTER V

PUBLIC DEBTS AND INFLATION

In attempting an inductive study of the inflation process it will be necessary first to gain a general view of certain evidently related phenomena. Accordingly, in this chapter several outstanding series from various parts of the economic field will be presented, and their more general relationships with one another and with important political and economic happenings will be discussed. The more detailed statistical analyses of the operations of particular institutions must be reserved for the chapters which follow.

In view of the important rôle in the process of inflation usually assigned to government deficits and to government borrowing, this statistical chronicle will begin with a further reference to the Treasury deficits accumulated during the war and post-war years. The resulting internal borrowings of the State, the part of these borrowings constituted by the floating debt, and, finally, the part of the floating debt represented by the advances from the Bank of France to the State will be compared with these deficits and, in turn, with the various measures of the extent of the inflation.

From Table 4 and the accompanying graph (Chart I) it is seen, as would naturally be expected, that total government borrowings at home and deficits correspond closely. The excess of deficits (barring errors of computation) was made up by borrowing abroad. On the other hand, the floating debt makes up, of course, only a portion of the total borrowings of the Government and the advances of the Bank of France to the State only a portion of the floating debt. The relative proportions are apparent in the graph.

With respect to annual data for wholesale prices, dollar exchange and note circulation of the Bank of France — the three measures of the extent of the inflation — there are to be noted certain remote, other close, and still other striking similarities in the movements of all three series as compared with those of the series just discussed.

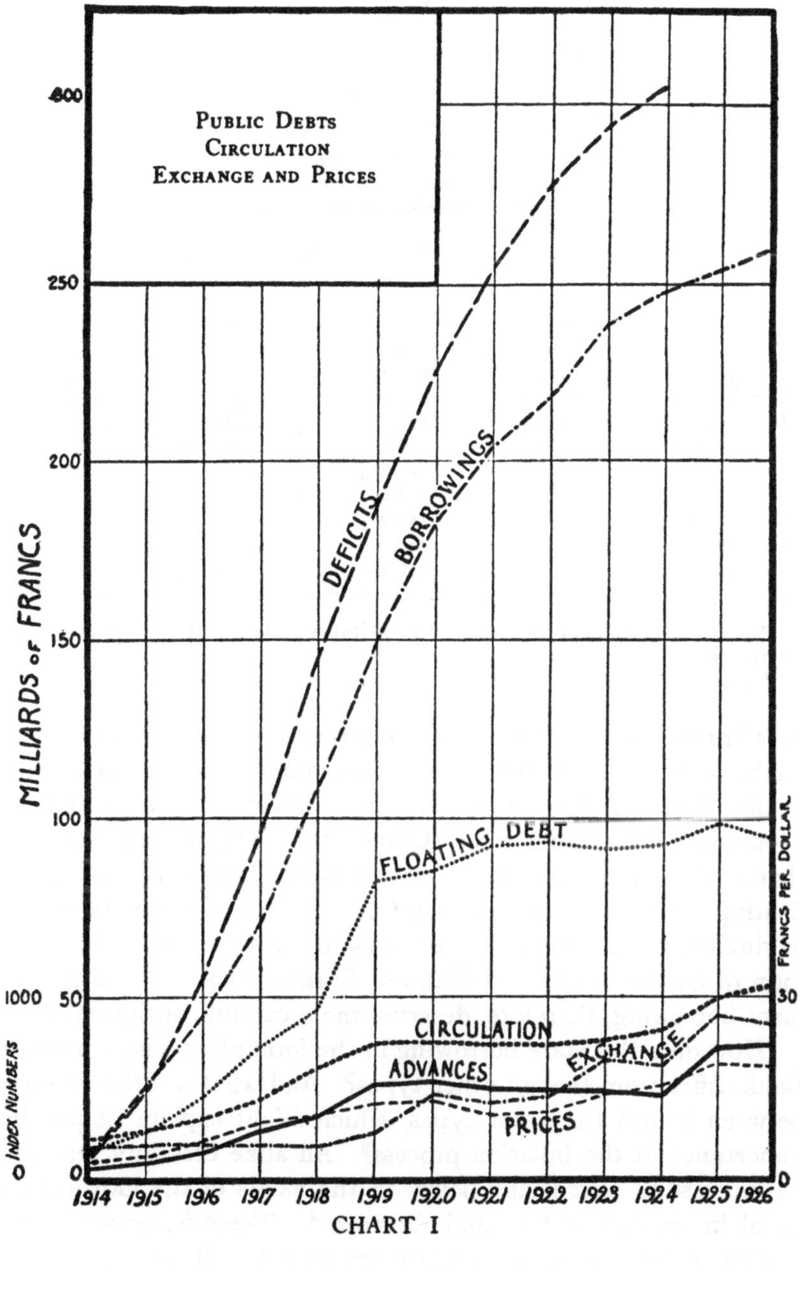
PUBLIC DEBTS
CIRCULATION
EXCHANGE AND PRICES
MILLIARDS OF FRANCS
INDEX NUMBERS
FRANCS PER DOLLAR
DEFICITS
BORROWINGS
FLOATING DEBT
CIRCULATION
ADVANCES
EXCHANGE
PRICES
300
250
200
150
100
1000
50
30
0
0
0
1914 1915 1916 1917 1918 1919 1920 1921 1922 1923 1924 1925 1926

CHART I

TABLE 4

DEFICITS AND GOVERNMENT BORROWINGS

(In millions of francs)

Date	Deficits cumulated	Total internal borrowings of Government	Total[a] floating debt	Advances of Bank of France to the State cumulated
Dec. 31, 1914	6,175[b]	6,834	6,030	3,900
Dec. 31, 1915	24,165	26,847	11,010	5,000
Dec. 31, 1916	56,081	47,603	20,582	7,400
Dec. 31, 1917	94,556	74,522	35,264	12,500
Dec. 31, 1918	144,414	117,726	45,109	17,150
Dec. 31, 1919	187,041	153,033	81,559	25,500
Dec. 31, 1920	225,041	186,578	84,141	26,600
Dec. 31, 1921	253,041	208,832	91,293	24,600
Dec. 31, 1922	277,741	221,845	92,130	23,600
Dec. 31, 1923	295,841	242,697	90,109	23,300
Dec. 31, 1924	304,941	252,915	91,930	22,600
Dec. 31, 1925		248,999	97,468	35,950
Dec. 31, 1926		259,180	94,689	36,000

[a] These totals do not include 1,432 million francs floating debt outstanding December 31, 1913.
[b] Deficit for 1914.

It is immediately seen that all six series have at least remote resemblances one to another. On closer examination, however, it may be observed that the curve of advances is very strikingly like that of circulation and much more like both those of prices and exchange than is that of deficits, that of total internal borrowings, or that of floating debt. It appears, therefore, that the type of borrowing having the most obvious connection with the inflation is that in the form of advances from the Bank of France. This type of government borrowing, therefore, deserves more careful consideration.

How does the State borrowing in the form of advances from the Bank differ from that of other types? And what are the relations between it and the other types, which might explain its peculiar importance in the inflation process? All alike certainly represent an increase in purchasing power in the hands of the Government equal in amount to the funds borrowed. There is, however, this obvious difference between advances from the Bank and govern-

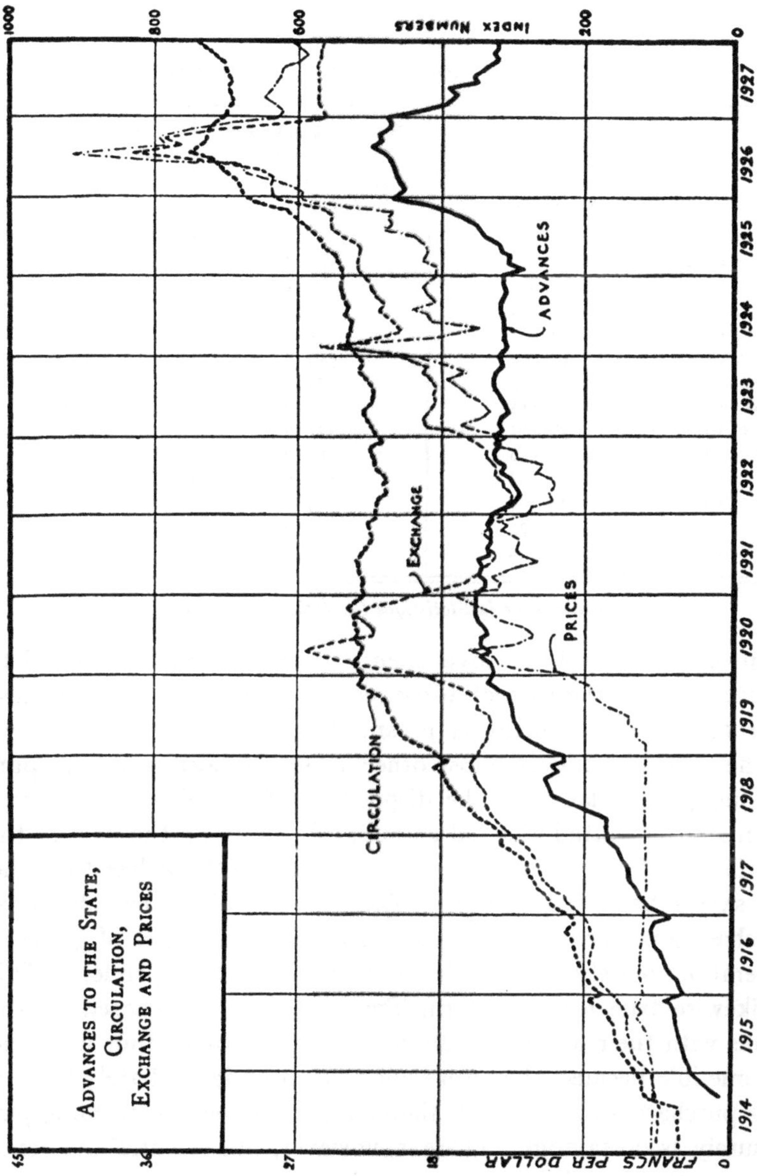
ADVANCES TO THE STATE,
CIRCULATION,
EXCHANGE AND PRICES
ADVANCES
EXCHANGE
PRICES
CIRCULATION
INDEX NUMBERS
FRANCS PER DOLLAR
MILLIARDS OF FRANCS
1914
1915
1916
1917
1918
1919
1920
1921
1922
1923
1924
1925
1926
1927

CHART II

TABLE 5

CIRCULATION, PRICES, AND EXCHANGE

Date	Circulation (end-of-month data in millions of francs)	Wholesale prices (end-of-month index numbers of B.S.G.F.[a])	Exchange (end-of-month averages; francs per dollar)
Dec. 1914	10,043	110.5	5.17
Dec. 1915	13,201	163.2	5.85
Dec. 1916	16,679	203.5	5.84
Dec. 1917	23,337	304.3	5.70
Dec. 1918	30,250	352.8	5.45
Dec. 1919	37,275	422.7	10.52
Dec. 1920	37,444	434.8	17.04
Dec. 1921	36,487	325.7	12.40
Dec. 1922	36,359	361.9	13.74
Dec. 1923	37,905	458.6	19.59
Dec. 1924	40,604	507.2	18.56
Dec. 1925	49,993	632.4	26.90
Dec. 1926	52,234	626.5	25.25

[a] *Bulletin de la Statistique Générale de la France.*

ment obligations sold as investments to private individuals and to institutions: in the case of advances the purchasing power turned over to the Government is balanced by no reduction elsewhere in the system, while in most other types of borrowing the purchasing power placed at the disposition of the Government represents a substantially[1] equal amount of savings on the part of the purchasers of the securities. Hence, what the State has to spend the savers have economized. There is, therefore, no additional purchasing power pitted against the available supplies of goods in general but merely a change in the personnel of the spenders. This is likewise true for short-term Treasury paper purchased by the banks with their otherwise idle funds, for the funds thus used had become idle because they were not to be used immediately for further purchase and represent, therefore, reductions in spending just as surely as do savings. There is, however, this essential difference between the flotations of short- and of long-term government se-

[1] In France, as in other countries, some of the purchases of long-term obligations of the Government were undoubtedly financed with bank credit; but the practice of borrowing to make such purchases was certainly less general than in the United States.

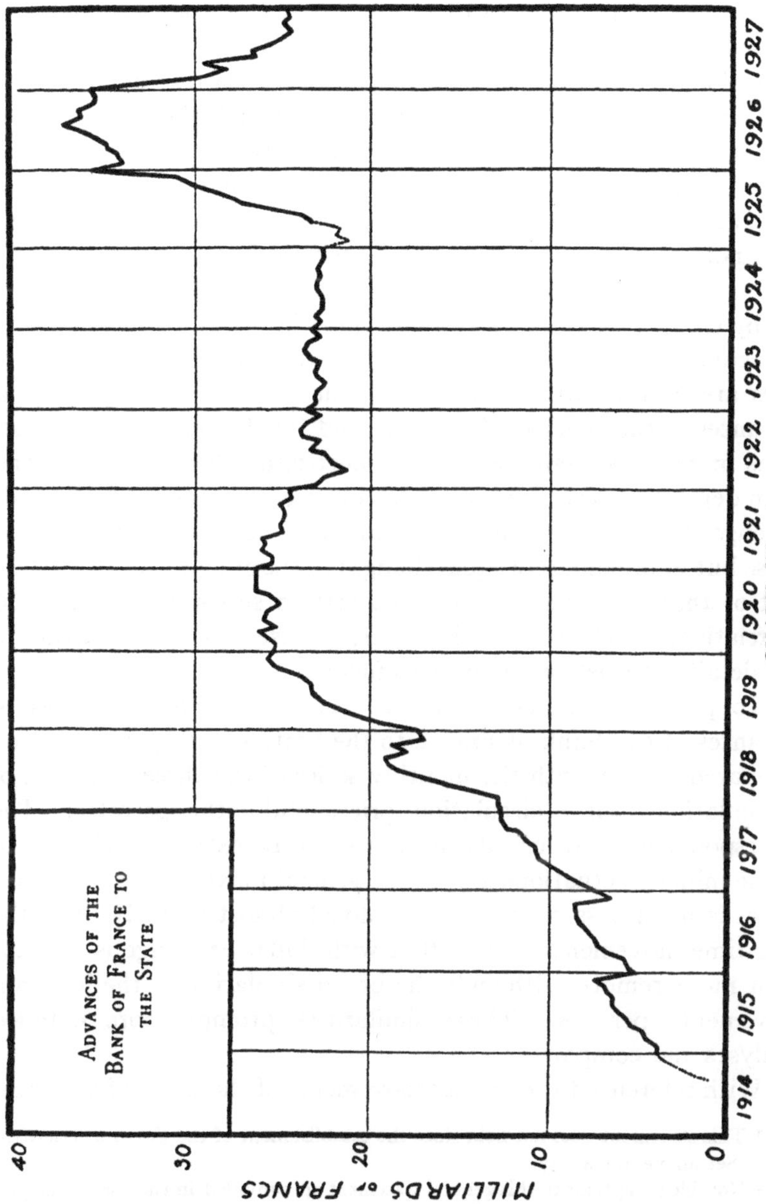
ADVANCES OF THE
BANK OF FRANCE TO
THE STATE
1914
1915
1916
1917
1918
1919
1920
1921
1922
1923
1924
1925
1926
1927
0
10
20
30
40
MILLIARDS of FRANCS

CHART III

curities in their relations to advances. When the proceeds of the purchase of short-term paper by banks (or others) reach the Treasury, they almost invariably appear immediately in corresponding reductions in the advances of the Bank to the State,[2] whereas the funds subscribed by the public to long-term obligations are generally used either to refund maturing issues or to fund outstanding floating debt and are, consequently, reflected only slightly in advances.[3] The points of greatest importance, therefore, as explained in detail later in this chapter, are (1) that, except as compensated for by changes in expenditures elsewhere in the system, excesses or reductions in government spending above or below the customary ones are almost invariably accompanied by like changes in the advances of the Bank to the State; and (2) that excesses or reductions in receipts from the sale of short-term Treasury paper and from deposits in the Treasury — as opposed to those from the sale of longer-term issues — in general appear almost immediately in reverse but approximately equal changes in the amounts of advances.[4] Out of these relationships between certain series grow important correlations — which must, however, be reserved for discussion in the detailed statistical analysis to follow.

To proceed with the inductive study, the monthly series of advances of the Bank of France to the State will be presented and compared in turn with the monthly series of the three measures of the inflation itself — circulation, prices, and exchange rates. The correspondence with circulation is seen to be extremely close both in the minor fluctuations and in the general movements; that with prices is much less close and is confined almost exclusively to the long-time movements; while that with dollar exchange is perhaps even more remote, although the broad similarity in the long-run movements persists. These similarities prompt more detailed analyses and comparisons.

With reference to the broad movements of the series of advances

[2] This statement does not hold since the establishment of the *Caisse d'Amortissement*. See above, pp. 46–47.

[3] Notable exceptions to this general statement are provided in the use of the proceeds of the 6 per cent *obligations amortissables en 50 ans* of 1927 and of several wartime issues.

[4] See footnote 2.

TABLE 6

ADVANCES OF THE BANK OF FRANCE TO THE STATE*

(Total outstanding at end of month in millions of francs)

	1914	1915	1916	1917	1918	1919	1920
Jan.		3900	5400	8100	12800	19550	25300
Feb.		4400	5700	8800	12950	20500	25800
Mar.		4700	6700	9500	14000	21600	26300
Apr.		5200	7200	9900	15650	22400	25300
May		5500	7500	10500	16800	22900	26050
June		6000	7900	10600	18450	23250	26000
July		6300	8300	10700	18900	23300	25550
Aug.		6300	8400	11200	19150	23600	25800
Sept.	2100 [a]	6700	8500	11650	18000	24150	26600
Oct.		6900	8600	12150	18800	25450	26600
Nov.		7400	6500	12550	17000	25850	26600
Dec.	3900 [b]	5000	7400	12500	17150	25500	26600

	1921	1922	1923	1924	1925	1926	1927
Jan.	25600	23000	23100	22800	21200	34200	32550
Feb.	25600	22500	23200	23100	21900	34500	29600
Mar.	26200	21500	23100	22700	21800	35000	28150
Apr.	26000	22100	22500	22700	23250	35150	29300
May	26200	22450	23000	22700	23850	35900	26600
June	25000	23300	23100	23000	25650	36600	26850
July	25100	23000	23000	23000	27250	37450	25650
Aug.	24900	23900	23400	22800	27750	36450	25050
Sept.	24900	24000	23700	23000	28900	36650	24400
Oct.	25100	23600	23400	22700	29950	35750	24850
Nov.	24500	22900	22800	22600	31950	35700	24450
Dec.	24600	23600	23300	22600	35950	36000	24550

[a] October 1.

[b] December 24.

* Sources: 1915–1919, *Journal Officiel;* 1920–1925, 1927, *L'Économiste Français;* 1926, *Bulletin de Statistique et de Législation Comparée.* The data for advances of the Bank of France to the State are taken from the last weekly report of each month issued by the Bank. The first advances were accorded by the Bank in August 1914 in pursuance of the law of August 5. Except for isolated dates, however, the amounts for that year were not published.

of the Bank of France to the State, it is observed (Chart III) that for the period under consideration (August 1914 to July 1926) they passed through four distinct phases. The first, from August 1914 — when the earliest advances of the war period were made — to the end of 1919, was a period of general and continuous rise with an average annual increase of appromixately 44 per cent. Such an increase in government indebtedness in general was, no doubt, to be expected during the war years.

The second phase comprises the two years 1920 and 1921. This short period may be regarded as one of financial readjustment to peace conditions after the extremely expensive war years. But it was likewise a period of the culmination of business prosperity and of the beginnings of depression, as well as one of fantastic, politically inspired dreams of the golden flood which would begin soon to flow from recently conquered enemies. The advances of the Bank to the State maintained during those two years the high level reached at the end of 1919; but — let it be said to the credit of the French finance ministry — in spite of the generally held hope of extravagant yields from German reparations, at least this form of public indebtedness was kept from further substantial increase. Indeed, by the end of 1921 a slight reduction had been effected. This reduction can probably be explained, however, by the purchase by the banks of short-term Treasury paper with the rapidly accumulating funds set free by the advancing business depression.

In the next phase, comprising the three years 1922–1924, a level was likewise maintained, but one somewhat below that of the preceding two years. No pronounced tendency either upward or downward developed during the entire five years of the second and third phases.

The fourth phase immediately following, however, is clearly characterized by the waning confidence of the public in German reparations and with it the declining credit of the Government. The most abrupt rise of the entire period in the advances of the Bank to the State began in April 1925 and continued at an increasing rate until the end of the year. Unable to meet the payment of its rapidly maturing floating obligations in addition to the heavy demands upon it for current expenses, the Treasury was forced to

TABLE 7

WHOLESALE PRICE INDEX OF THE *STATISTIQUE GÉNÉRALE DE LA FRANCE**

(Index numbers based on end-of-month data. Base 100 in 1913)

	1914	1915	1916	1917	1918	1919	1920
Jan.	99.0	119.5	172.7	215.6	312.8	347.6	486.8
Feb.	99.9	124.5	177.9	225.6	319.4	340.4	521.9
Mar.	99.5	129.5	185.9	228.9	327.1	335.7	554.5
Apr.	98.7	133.0	190.9	248.0	333.4	332.2	587.5
May	99.6	135.2	190.4	256.0	335.5	325.1	550.1
June	99.3	137.4	188.4	266.2	328.7	328.7	492.7
July	97.9	139.8	184.5	268.0	337.3	348.6	495.6
Aug.	102.2	140.7	186.0	270.0	350.0	347.5	501.3
Sept.	102.9	144.5	188.7	279.9	355.1	360.0	525.7
Oct.	103.8	151.3	192.9	283.6	359.9	381.8	501.7
Nov.	106.7	158.9	197.4	293.2	357.9	405.0	460.7
Dec.	110.5	163.2	203.5	304.3	352.8	422.7	434.8

	1921	1922	1923	1924	1925	1926	1927
Jan.	406.6	313.8	386.9	494.0	514.4	633.5	621.8
Feb.	377.4	306.4	421.8	543.7	515.0	635.6	631.6
Mar.	359.9	307.4	424.0	499.3	513.5	631.8	641.4
Apr.	347.1	313.7	414.7	450.0	512.8	650.1	636.3
May	329.4	316.8	406.5	458.5	519.8	687.9	628.3
June	325.0	325.0	408.6	465.3	542.6	738.4	622.6
July	330.1	325.1	406.7	481.0	556.8	836.2	619.9
Aug.	331.3	331.2	413.1	476.6	557.2	769.5	617.9
Sept.	344.0	329.3	423.6	485.6	555.7	786.9	600.3
Oct.	331.3	337.4	420.5	497.1	572.3	751.5	587.5
Nov.	331.8	352.1	442.9	503.5	605.5	683.8	594.4
Dec.	325.7	361.9	458.6	507.2	632.4	626.5	604.2

* Sources: 1914–1918, calculated from the index numbers on the base 1901–1910 published in the *Bulletin de la Statistique Générale de la France;* 1919–1927, *League of Nations Bulletin of Statistics.*

The monthly index numbers of wholesale prices prepared and published by the *Statistique Générale de la France* are based upon the prices of 45 commodities, taken during the last week of each month. The price of each article is referred to its average price during the period 1901–1910, and the general index number is then obtained by computing the simple arithmetic mean of the 45 individual relative prices. For the period 1914–1918, the conversion of the index to the base 1913 = 100 was accomplished by dividing each of the monthly indices on the base 1901–1910 = 100 by the index number for 1913 on the same base, the result being multiplied by 100. For the period 1919–1927, the index numbers on the base 1913 = 100 taken from the *League* borrow in ever increasing amounts from the central bank. After the end of 1925 the most rapid part of the rise was over, and in January 1926, for the first time in five years, the Treasury actually lived up to its agreement with the Bank of France to repay at the end of each year two milliards of francs. But with February the rise began once more and continued, though at a slower rate than in the preceding year, until with the desperate crisis of July 1926 it reached the huge total of more than 37 milliards of francs.

After July 1926 began a period of decline of advances, developing slowly at first and then becoming extremely rapid with the beginning of 1927. This decline is attributable very largely, if not entirely, as will be explained later, to the private deposits received by the Treasury, mainly from the banks but partly, too, from individuals and from business firms. Hence, representing, as it does, from the standpoint of the Treasury, an exchange of an obligation with indefinite maturity and bearing not more than one-half of one per cent interest for one payable on demand and bearing from 1½ per cent to 3 per cent, the reduction of advances from the Bank hardly represents in itself a real betterment of the position of the Treasury or a change of permanent significance.

---

of Nations Bulletin of Statistics were converted from the original base in exactly the same manner. The obvious error involved in the calculations is certainly slight and may be neglected.

The 45 commodities which enter into the composition of the general index are principally agricultural products, raw materials, or semi-finished products. The list of products follows:

I. Agricultural products and foodstuffs (20 commodities).
   A. Vegetable products: wheat, wheat flour, rye, barley, oats, maize, potatoes, rice.
   B. Animal products: beef (first quality), beef (second quality), mutton (first quality), mutton (second quality), pork, salted meat, butter, cheese.
   C. Colonial products: raw sugar, refined sugar, coffee, cocoa.

II. Industrial products (25 commodities).
   A. Minerals: coal, pig iron, cast iron, copper, tin, lead, zinc.
   B. Textiles: cotton, wool, silk, hemp, flax, jute.
   C. Sundries: leather (salted), hides, tallow, rapeseed oil, linseed oil, alcohol, petroleum, carbonate of soda, nitrate of soda, benzol, lumber, rubber.

All of the prices going into the calculation of the index represent end-of-month prices. Most of them are secured on the last Friday of each month from various private and published sources. For those of foodstuffs (potatoes, meat, butter, and cheese) an average price is struck for each commodity from the total quantity of that commodity sold during the last seven days of the month in the *Halles Centrales* and the total sum of money paid.

TABLE 8

DOLLAR EXCHANGE IN PARIS *

(End-of-month daily rates, 1914–1918, and averages of daily rates for final weeks of each month, 1919–1927; francs per dollar)

	1914	1915	1916	1917	1918	1919	1920
Jan.	5.18[a]	5.18	5.87	5.84	5.70	5.45	13.07
Feb.	5.18	5.28	5.87	5.84	5.70	5.45	14.25
Mar.	5.18	5.31	5.97	5.84	5.70	5.92	14.50
Apr.	5.15	5.33	5.94	5.70	5.70	6.05	16.77
May	5.15	5.42	5.93	5.70	5.70	6.43	13.15
June	5.15	5.50	5.91	5.70	5.70	6.45	12.06
July	5.15	5.68	5.91	5.70	5.70	7.12	12.95
Aug.	5.12[b]	5.95	5.89	5.70	5.50	8.03	14.37
Sept.	....	5.75	5.85	5.70	5.47	8.52	14.68
Oct.	5.18	5.97	5.84	5.70	5.47	8.67	15.67
Nov.	5.10[c]	5.91	5.84	5.70	5.47	9.68	16.40
Dec.	5.17	5.85	5.84	5.70	5.45	10.52	17.04

	1921	1922	1923	1924	1925	1926	1927
Jan.	14.04	12.31	15.57	21.74	18.49	26.77	25.32
Feb.	13.92	11.00	16.45	25.57	19.38	27.49	25.55
Mar.	14.30	11.12	15.23	18.32	19.06	28.65	25.54
Apr.	13.22	10.82	14.84	15.45	19.20	30.15	25.53
May	11.79	11.07	15.15	18.80	19.83	30.60	25.53
June	12.40	11.99	16.32	18.88	21.56	34.93	25.54
July	12.98	11.96	16.84	19.86	21.11	41.15	25.56
Aug.	12.96	13.02	17.65	18.48	21.30	35.12	25.51
Sept.	14.00	13.15	16.15	18.96	21.12	35.66	25.48
Oct.	13.74	14.19	17.19	19.13	23.92	32.52	25.47
Nov.	14.23	14.38	18.51	18.82	26.09	28.11	25.43
Dec.	12.40	13.74	19.59	18.56	26.90	25.25	25.40

[a] January 22.
[b] August 8.
[c] November 18.
* Sources: 1914–1918, *L'Économiste Français;* 1919, *Journal Officiel;* 1920–1926, calculated from material furnished by the *Statistique Générale de la France;* 1927, *Cote des Agents de Change.*

The rates given in the table are, for the years 1914–1918 inclusive, daily average rates for the last Thursday of each month as given by *L'Économiste Français;* and for the years 1919–1927 inclusive, arithmetic averages of daily rates for the last week of each month during which there were at least four quotation days. For 1919 the average rates were computed from the daily rates published in the *Journal Officiel;* for the years 1920–1926 from material furnished by the *Statistique Générale de la*

Generally speaking, therefore, it may be said that during the war period and for one year thereafter the advances of the Bank of France to the State, like all other forms of government indebtedness, increased continually and by larger amounts each year. During the subsequent two years (1920 and 1921) an increase in advances was successfully prevented, although borrowing in other forms continued on a large scale. Then, at the beginning of 1922 there was effected an actual reduction in their amount, and substantial increases were avoided during the succeeding three years. During the turbulent period of 1925 and the first half of 1926, however, advances again showed a rapid rise which ended only with the coming of the now justly famous Poincaré Government. There followed a period of slow decline during the remaining five months of 1926 and one of precipitate decline during the first half of 1927. But, as has been observed, since probably more than enough funds to liquidate the advances from the Bank actually repaid during this decline were derived from the deposit of funds on demand, there is good reason to question whether there was any real reduction at all in the advances of the Bank to the State.

With regard to the movements of the note circulation of the Bank of France, it is seen (Charts IV and V) that in the large, as well as in detail, they were almost exactly similar to those of the advances of the Bank to the State. Furthermore, the almost complete correspondence of movements holds for the entire twelve-year period 1915–1926 — the Pearsonian coefficient of correlation being +.98 (145). In 1927, however, the similarity disappeared altogether. The significance of the disparity of movement in this year is probably as far-reaching as that of the similarity in all the other years. Accordingly, both similarities and divergences will be carefully analyzed below.

France and compiled by it; for the period 1920–February 1924, from the daily rates given by the *Journal Officiel;* for the period February 1924–1927, from those published in the *Cote des Agents de Change.* The daily rates given in the table and those used in computing the average rates represent averages of highest and lowest quotations during official exchange hours, except those taken from the *Journal Officiel,* which are single prevailing daily rates.

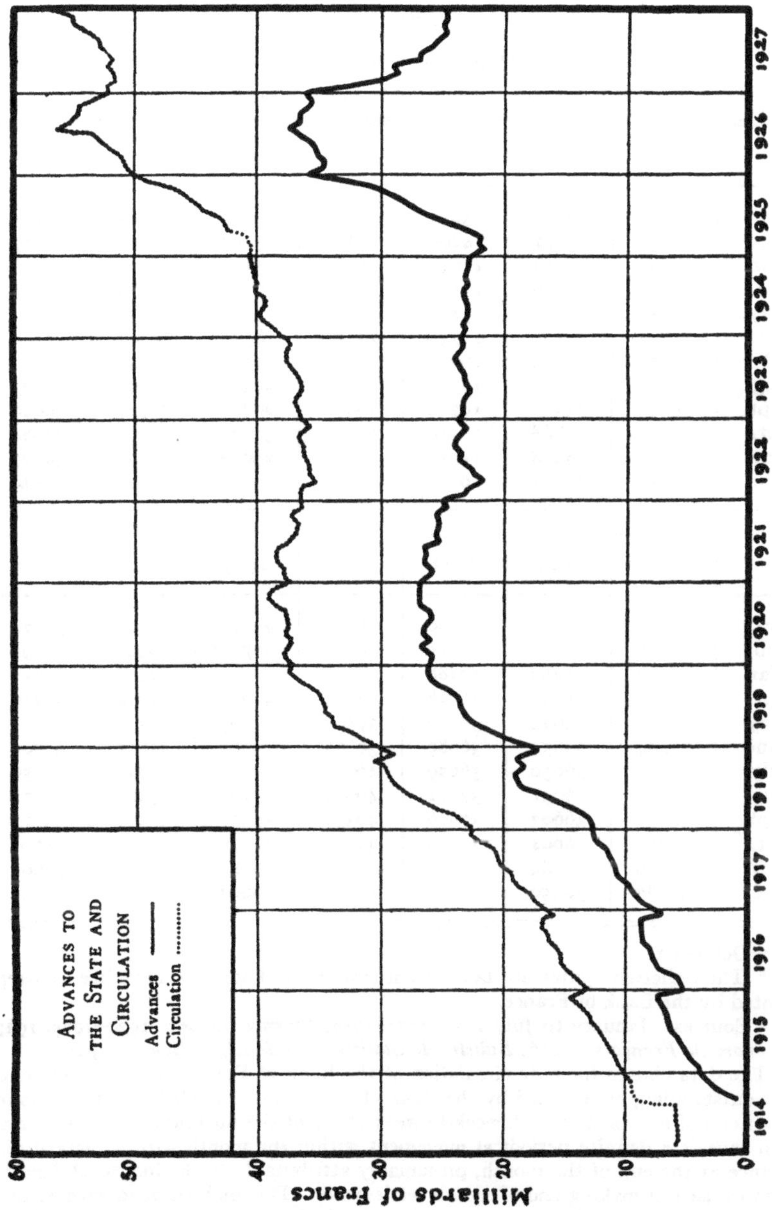
Advances to
the State and
Circulation
Advances
Circulation
1914
1915
1916
1917
1918
1919
1920
1921
1922
1923
1924
1925
1926
1927
0
10
20
30
40
50
60
Milliards of Francs

CHART IV

TABLE 9

NOTE CIRCULATION OF THE BANK OF FRANCE *

(Selected end-of-month data in millions of francs)

	1914	1915	1916	1917	1918	1919	1920
Jan.	5894	10474	13858	17328	23163	31794	37583
Feb.	5763	10962	14295	17889	23986	32492	37889
Mar.	5743	11177	14847	18460	25179	33772	37569
Apr.	5805	11540	15278	19010	26395	33978	37327
May	5812	11828	15435	19395	27073	34134	37915
June	5852	12105	15735	19823	28550	34442	37544
July	5912	12593	16091	20202	29148	34932	37696
Aug.	....	12950	16376	20469	29434	35090	37905
Sept.	9299[a]	13310	16714	20995	29922	35787	38690
Oct.	....	13868	16589	21705	30721	36769	39084
Nov.	....	14278	15952	22414	29072	37424	38807
Dec.	10043	13201	16679	22337	30250	37275	37444

	1921	1922	1923	1924	1925	1926	1927
Jan.	37913	36433	36780	38329	*40516*[b]	50618	52172
Feb.	37808	36151	37055	38895	*40792*[b]	50991	51697
Mar.	38133	35282	37188	39950	*40892*[b]	51492	51912
Apr.	38211	35787	36548	39824	42662	52014	52210
May	38233	35674	36386	39403	42703	52735	51800
June	37494	35852	36689	39665	43000	53073	52107
July	36941	36050	36929	40082	44221	56022	52756
Aug.	36783	36051	37111	40034	44702	55147	52672
Sept.	36921	36603	37626	40339	45557	54507	53773
Oct.	37154	36694	37670	40460	46679	54578	54700
Nov.	36336	35789	37159	40447	48085	53263	54962
Dec.	36487	36359	37905	40604	49993	52234	56551

[a] October 1.

[b] The italicized figures are taken from statements known to have been misrepresented by the Bank of France.

* Sources: January to July 1914, 1915–1919, *Journal Officiel;* 1920–1925, 1927, *L'Économiste Français;* 1926, *Bulletin de Statistique et de Législation Comparée.*

The data chosen for note circulation of the Bank of France are the amounts of notes outstanding, as reported by the Bank of France in its published statements on *selected* end-of-month dates. A week-to-week study of the fluctuations of note circulation reveals a definite periodical movement within the month with a marked disturbance at the end of the month, presumably attributable to the increased demand for notes used in making end-of-month settlements. This high point in each month, however, on account of the varying dates on which the month-end reports of the Bank of France appear, falls sometimes on the last reporting date of the month and sometimes (when the last reporting date comes relatively early) on the first reporting

In magnitude the note circulation was always considerably greater than the advances of the Bank to the State. By years the proportions of advances to circulation were as follows:[5]

1915	.46	1921	.68
1916	.47	1922	.64
1917	.53	1923	.62
1918	.60	1924	.57
1919	.67	1925	.60
1920	.74	1926	.78

It will be noted that during the period 1915–1919, in which both advances and circulation were increasing, and for a year beyond, there was a steady increase in the proportion of advances. Then, during the period of relative stability of both series, there was a gradual reduction in the proportion. This decline was followed by a rapid rise in the period of increase of 1925 and of the first half of 1926. The significance of such variations in the proportion is not altogether clear, especially in view of the close correspondence between the movements of the two curves. They seem to indicate that while there was an immediate and almost exactly similar movement in circulation caused by every increase in advances, there may also have been a long-time effect on circulation which took some time to reach culmination. More specifically, the purchases of the Government (normally made considerably before the advances providing for their payment) caused a similar rise in circulation simultaneous with the granting of the advances. As time went on,

[5] The figures are obtained by dividing, for each year, the sum of the month-end data for advances by the sum of those for circulation.

date of the following month, occurring necessarily early in that month. Hence end-of-month circulation figures taken without regard to the date to which they refer would sometimes include the month-end rise, and at other times not, with the result that such data would fail to meet the requisite of complete uniformity and would show fluctuations of an obviously distorting character. In order to fix exactly the date limits within which the month-end disturbance fell, it was established that the last report of the month showed the disturbance only when it was made on one of the last two days of the month. (Bank of France weekly reports are prepared on Wednesday of each week and are published on Thursday. The discussion refers to publishing dates.) Otherwise the rise was shown in the first weekly report of the following month. To free the circulation data from this disturbance, the figures chosen are those for the last reporting date of each month, *except when that report falls on one of the last two days of the month*, in which case they are for the next to last reporting date.

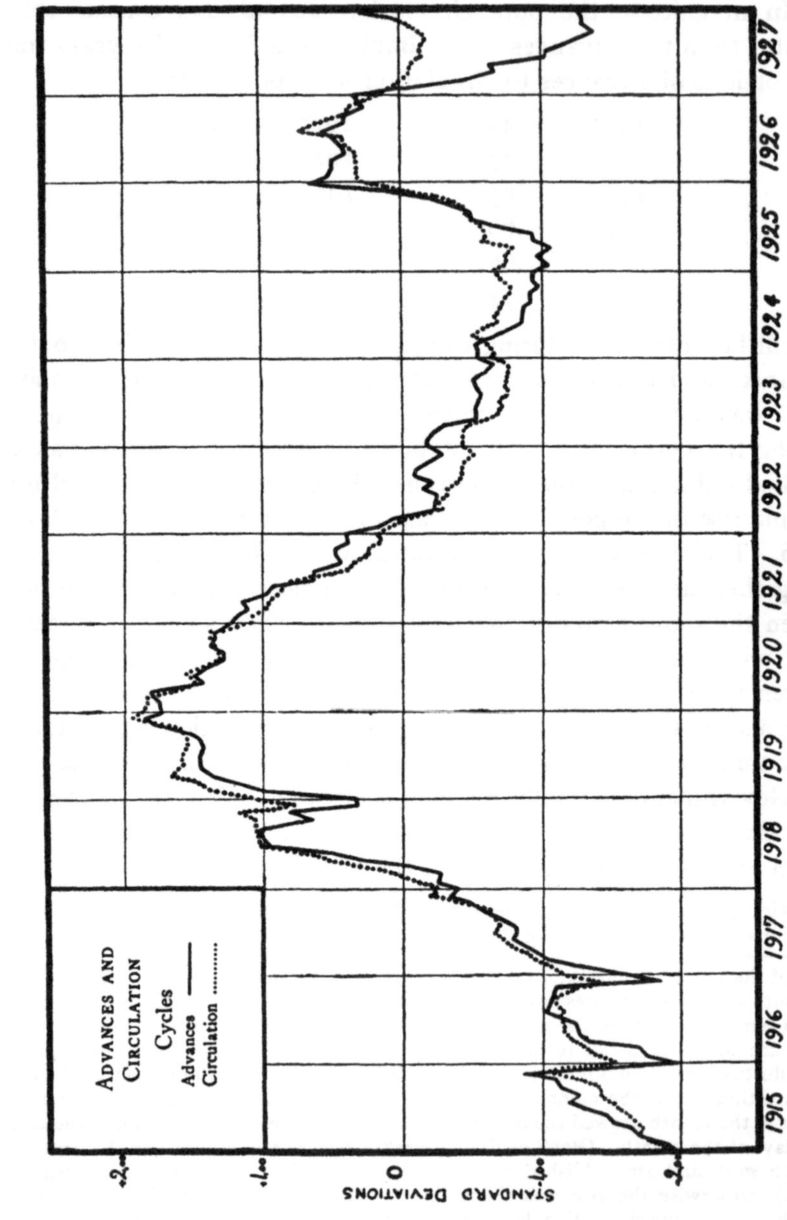

Advances and Circulation Cycles
Advances
Circulation
1915
1916
1917
1918
1919
1920
1921
1922
1923
1924
1925
1926
1927
+2.00
+1.00
0
-1.00
-2.00
Standard Deviations

CHART V

however, the effects of the original payments on both prices and the volume of trade spread not only forward and backward but also sidewise and, in spreading, grew. Forward, the new purchases affected the prices of all goods into the manufacture of which the articles purchased entered; and backward, by stimulating the demand for these articles, they encouraged trade in and boosted the prices of all articles entering into the various phases of their production. Here should be included even wages, which are generally raised in one industry after another as the effects of rising prices and of increasing business activity spread. Moreover, the sidewise effects of increased government purchasing on goods serving as substitutes for or as adjuncts to those originally demanded, cannot be neglected. But the important point is that the spreading, of whatever sort it may be, requires time. Hence, it is not surprising that the full quota of circulation required for financing a gradually increasing volume of sales at perhaps even more gradually increasing prices should have been slow in making its appearance.

TABLE 10

ADVANCES OF THE BANK OF FRANCE TO THE STATE *

(Percentage deviations from secular trend expressed as percentages of standard deviation, allowance made for seasonal variations)

	1914	1915	1916	1917	1918	1919	1920
Jan.		− 1.90	− 1.75	− 1.21	− 0.23	+ 1.03	+ 1.75
Feb.		− 1.69	− 1.68	− 1.02	− 0.25	+ 1.20	+ 1.79
Mar.		− 1.62	− 1.33	− 0.86	− 0.03	+ 1.39	+ 1.81
Apr.		− 1.50	− 1.26	− 0.86	+ 0.32	+ 1.44	+ 1.44
May		− 1.46	− 1.24	− 0.76	+ 0.54	+ 1.45	+ 1.50
June		− 1.29	− 1.15	− 0.80	+ 0.94	+ 1.46	+ 1.41
July		− 1.19	− 1.03	− 0.80	+ 1.02	+ 1.43	+ 1.27
Aug.	− 3.83	− 1.26	− 1.05	− 0.69	+ 1.02	+ 1.44	+ 1.27
Sept.	− 3.21	− 1.13	− 1.07	− 0.60	+ 0.63	+ 1.51	+ 1.39
Oct.	− 2.67	− 1.09	− 1.08	− 0.48	+ 0.80	+ 1.77	+ 1.35
Nov.	− 2.29	− 0.86	− 1.85	− 0.34	+ 0.32	+ 1.87	+ 1.36
Dec.	− 1.96	− 1.99	− 1.53	− 0.38	+ 0.33	+ 1.75	+ 1.33

* For the calculation, a straight-line secular trend was fitted to monthly data for a period of 145 months from December 1914 to December 1926. The equation, with origin (0,0) so chosen that December 1914 represents the zero point of the abscissas, and a zero volume of advances that of the ordinates, was found to be

TABLE 10 (Continued)

	1921	1922	1923	1924	1925	1926	1927
Jan.	+1.19	+0.18	−0.18	−0.55	−1.05	+0.51	−0.01
Feb.	+1.12	+0.04	−0.21	−0.54	−0.98	+0.50	−0.42
Mar.	+1.16	−0.22	−0.29	−0.67	−1.06	+0.50	−0.66
Apr.	+0.98	−0.23	−0.51	−0.78	−0.96	+0.41	−0.63
May	+0.93	−0.25	−0.51	−0.85	−0.94	+0.43	−1.03
June	+0.63	−0.15	−0.54	−0.85	−0.73	+0.47	−1.04
July	+0.62	−0.21	−0.56	−0.86	−0.51	+0.58	−1.19
Aug.	+0.53	−0.09	−0.53	−0.91	−0.47	+0.41	−1.28
Sept.	+0.49	−0.11	−0.51	−0.91	−0.33	+0.41	−1.38
Oct.	+0.49	−0.20	−0.58	−0.97	−0.20	+0.27	−1.33
Nov.	+0.40	−0.29	−0.64	−0.94	+0.11	+0.30	−1.33
Dec.	+0.41	−0.18	−0.55	−0.94	+0.66	+0.34	−1.31

$y = +182.4x + 7266$, m being + 182.4 and b 7266 millions of francs. The data for 1914 and 1927 were added to the calculation by extending the same line of secular trend to those years. The seasonal variations were calculated by the method of link relatives.

TABLE 11

NOTE CIRCULATION OF THE BANK OF FRANCE*

(Percentage deviations from secular trend expressed as percentages of standard deviation, allowance made for seasonal variations)

	1914	1915	1916	1917	1918	1919	1920
Jan.	−3.26	−1.82	−1.38	−1.05	−0.10	+1.36	+1.84
Feb.	−3.44	−1.69	−1.31	−0.95	+0.05	+1.45	+1.83
Mar.	−3.56	−1.72	−1.21	−0.87	+0.29	+1.66	+1.64
Apr.	−3.63	−1.66	−1.15	−0.78	+0.54	+1.61	+1.49
May	−3.68	−1.61	−1.16	−0.72	+0.66	+1.58	+1.57
June	−3.72	−1.56	−1.11	−0.64	+1.01	+1.59	+1.42
July	−3.83	−1.51	−1.14	−0.68	+1.02	+1.56	+1.31
Aug.	−2.34	−1.42	−1.09	−0.64	+1.04	+1.54	+1.32
Sept.	−2.09	−1.41	−1.10	−0.61	+1.04	+1.58	+1.36
Oct.	−2.18	−1.26	−1.22	−0.46	+1.18	+1.74	+1.39
Nov.	−2.05	−1.04	−1.39	−0.18	+0.79	+1.96	+1.39
Dec.	−1.91	−1.53	−1.16	−0.24	+1.07	+1.88	+1.08

* For the calculation, a straight-line secular trend was fitted to monthly data for a period of 145 months from December 1914 to December 1926. The equation of this line, with origin (0,0) so chosen that December 1914 represents the zero point of the abscissas and a zero circulation that of the ordinates, was found to be $y = +261.5\,x + 14020$, m being 261.5 and b 14020 millions of francs. The data for 1914 and 1927 were added to the calculation by extending the same line of secular trend to those years. The seasonal variation was calculated by the method of link relatives.

	1921	1922	1923	1924	1925	1926	1927
Jan.	+ 1.08	+ 0.09	− 0.41	− 0.64	− 0.74	+ 0.32	+ 0.09
Feb.	+ 0.98	− 0.03	− 0.42	− 0.60	− 0.75	+ 0.32	− 0.03
Mar.	+ 0.95	− 0.28	− 0.47	− 0.50	− 0.80	+ 0.32	− 0.07
Apr.	+ 0.88	− 0.25	− 0.65	− 0.58	− 0.59	+ 0.33	− 0.08
May	+ 0.84	− 0.31	− 0.70	− 0.67	− 0.60	+ 0.41	− 0.16
June	+ 0.64	− 0.31	− 0.68	− 0.66	− 0.58	+ 0.43	− 0.14
July	+ 0.40	− 0.39	− 0.76	− 0.70	− 0.51	+ 0.73	− 0.16
Aug.	+ 0.34	− 0.41	− 0.74	− 0.72	− 0.45	+ 0.59	− 0.18
Sept.	+ 0.25	− 0.41	− 0.75	− 0.77	− 0.42	+ 0.41	− 0.13
Oct.	+ 0.25	− 0.43	− 0.77	− 0.78	− 0.28	+ 0.39	− 0.03
Nov.	+ 0.17	− 0.51	− 0.76	− 0.68	+ 0.02	+ 0.30	+ 0.10
Dec.	+ 0.19	− 0.41	− 0.63	− 0.65	+ 0.30	+ 0.17	+ 0.31

Moreover, the striking similarity in the two curves, in spite of the changes in their absolute proportions, may be more completely accounted for. With increases in the advances of the Bank to the State, government disbursements in payments for purchases already made increased in like amount. And, what is of especial importance in the case of funds thus secured, the new spending of the Government was not balanced by a corresponding amount of saving on the part of others. Hence, its full effect must have appeared on the pecuniary volume of trade — perhaps partially (and ultimately almost entirely) in prices, but immediately most largely in the volume of goods sold. It follows that a like volume of currency (money and deposits) required for accomplishing the payments for sales was naturally added to that already in use for other purposes. Moreover, not only all salary payments to government employees but likewise most Treasury payments (of less than 3000 francs) for supplies are made in notes of the Bank of France. Consequently, the immediate expansion in circulation arising from the extra expenditures represented by the new advances of the Bank were, in general at least, similar in amount to that of such advances — as, indeed, is found to have been the case.

Some critic will immediately object, however, and, superficially, with good reason, that the advances of the Bank, making up, as they do, only a small proportion of the funds spent by the Government, cannot possibly have such a dominating influence over note circulation. "The whole approach, therefore, from the standpoint of the volume of expenditures instead of from that of the amount of currency in circulation," he will say, "thus becomes ridiculous." Is this contention true?

In France, as in most other countries, the normal revenues of the Government, such as taxes and incomes from government monopolies and other industrial undertakings, come in, some continuously, others periodically at short intervals, and still others quite irregularly or only at long intervals of time. And, what is of primary importance for present purposes, they represent savings or, at least, deductions from funds which would otherwise have been spent by their holders. Expenditures, likewise, are met, some continuously, others periodically at short intervals, and still others irregularly and only occasionally. Naturally, when big obligations have to be met, special effort is made to raise funds in correspondingly big amounts, and, when current obligations are too large in comparison with current revenues, some will be funded into obligations with long maturities whenever such an operation seems practicable.

But, when all is said and done, and this is the point to be especially noted, if extra expenditures above those taken care of by normal revenues (including subscriptions to *Bons Ordinaires du Trésor* and *Bons de la Défense Nationale*)[6] were necessary, they were met by increasing the advances from the Bank of France. Correspondingly, reduced expenditures led to a cancellation of a portion of such advances. In other words, *the advances of the Bank of France to the State constituted the elastic and the emergency element in the revenue system of the Government.*[7] And, since, in addition, increases or decreases in this source of revenue gave rise to additional or

[6] Since the reëstablishment of the *Caisse d'Amortissement* subscriptions to National Defense Bonds do not add to general government revenues.

[7] To this generalization one apparent exception appears. When increases in advances came as the result of unexpected reimbursements of short-term Treasury paper, the Government was thereby provided with no additional purchasing power. The funds thus withdrawn from the Treasury, however, even in France, but rarely went into private hoards. Those taken by the banks were withdrawn for lending to business or for investing otherwise; those received by private individuals were secured for some sort of expenditures — even though at times for the purchase of foreign securities; and all represented immediately effective purchasing power for their new holders. Hence, although all new advances might not have provided the Government with additional

reduced purchasing power, usually immediately effective and against which there was temporarily[8] no counterbalancing change in expenditures elsewhere, is there any wonder that, so far as the effects of government spending were concerned, the immediate changes in note circulation should have corresponded as closely as they did to such advances?

This is, however, only part of the story. As was pointed out in an earlier part of this chapter, the proportion of advances to circulation changed in such a way as to indicate a long-time as well as a short-time effect of government spending on the volume of currency in general use. It should be further noted here that it is the general movements of the two curves from year to year rather than the month-to-month fluctuations which show the more striking similarity. The linear secular trends are somewhat different: $y = +182.4x + 7266$ for advances, as opposed to $y = +261.5x + 14020$ for circulation;[9] and the month-to-month movements are only generally similar. Yet there is a correlation between the movements of the two curves of +.98(145). Nor is this correlation in any sense accidental because of the close correspondence between a few points with large ordinates or for any other mechanical reason. The curves are actually strikingly similar in their broad general year-to-year movements. What is the explanation?

It would seem that throughout much of the period, until late 1926, expansion and contraction of circulation were dominated by changes in advances of the Bank to the State. Government spending, as has been seen above, led to immediate issues of notes in quantities somewhat similar to the amount of the new advances. Only the fact that some of the payments to big industrial or other firms were made, not with notes, but with Treasury *mandats* or by *virements* kept the correspondence between increases in circulation

purchasing power nor have signified an increase in government expenditures, to the extent that they did not, they provided others with additional purchasing power and for them signified increased spending.

[8] After prices have changed, forced economies or enlarged purchasing capacities of those with relatively fixed incomes lead naturally to corresponding changes in the amounts of goods purchased.

[9] Straight-line trends fitted by method of least squares to monthly data for the two series.

and advances from showing any greater similarity than they did. Moreover, the spending on the part of the Government led, as has also been observed above, to spending in somewhat similar amounts on the part of receivers of the payments. This was true whether the payments were made in notes, by *mandats*, or otherwise. As the spending spread through the economic system, the amounts of notes and of deposits used in making the attendant payments gradually approximated their normal proportion, which in France is about 1 to .7. But, to the extent that the funds originally released by government expenditures were not kept in use for this continued spending, they drifted naturally to the banks. Surplus funds thus received by any of the banks, on account of the centralized form of the French banking system, soon reached their head offices, for the most part located in Paris. And funds thus accumulating in the Paris banks, as has been noted in Chapters III and IV above, were usually immediately invested very largely in short-term Treasury obligations[10] — until recently issued in any amounts demanded. Thus, such funds were again turned over to the Government,[11] which, in turn, used them to pay off its advances from the Bank. Hence, to the extent that the funds put out by government spending did not continue to circulate, they came back in the form of subscriptions to Treasury paper and led, therefore, to a like reduction in the advances of the Bank to the State. Needless to add, certain of the funds becoming idle would be invested directly in government obligations by their holders without passing through the hands of the banks. The result is obviously the same. Consequently, an extremely high degree of similarity between the series of advances and note circulation was certainly to be anticipated for the years 1915–1926, for which, in fact, the correlation of +.98 (145) was found.

For the last four months of 1926 and for the year 1927, however, as has been previously observed, the similarity between the curves almost completely disappeared. It was no longer the ad-

[10] Instead of buying Treasury paper the banks might deposit directly with the Treasury. The result is obviously the same.

[11] The reader is again cautioned that the period under discussion extends only to the middle of 1926.

vances of the Bank to the State which were even apparently dominating the changes in circulation, but rather the purchases of foreign exchange by the Bank which dominated the output of new funds into circulation and, as a result, the movement of advances. The process was presumably as follows. With the return of confidence in the position of the franc after the formation of the Poincaré National Union Cabinet, funds from abroad in the form both of capital being repatriated and of foreigners' holdings seeking investment began to come into the country in large quantities. The resulting sales of large amounts of foreign drafts on the Paris market brought a notable recovery of the franc during the fall of 1926. Except for the interference of the Government through the Bank of France, the franc would probably have risen to a value sufficient to cripple seriously French exports as well as a large part of the country's internal industry. The Bank of France, however, acting for the Government, began to purchase foreign exchange on a large scale and thus accumulated by the middle of 1927 foreign balances of a value of not less than 20 milliards of francs.

The funds thus paid out for foreign exchange were used very largely in the purchase of securities and of investments of various sorts, and consequently did not stimulate business as much as would have done the purchase of commodities and the payment of wages to a similar amount by the Government or by anyone else. To the extent that they were not required for commercial purposes, the funds thus put into circulation by the Bank of France, whether in the shape of notes or of deposits, drifted speedily, therefore, to the banks, which invested them, partly in Treasury paper as formerly, but more largely as deposits with the Treasury, for the amounts of Treasury paper of short maturity which could be issued had by that time been narrowly limited.[12] The funds

[12] The *arrêté* of December 16, 1926 suppressed the issue of *Bons de la Défense Nationale* of one month maturity; that of December 22, 1926, those of three months maturity; that of January 29, 1927, those of six months; and that of June 2, 1927, those of one year. Since this last date only two-year bonds may be issued. Treasury paper of short maturity (*Bons Ordinaires du Trésor*) is still issued in limited quantities, the maximum being fixed annually at the time that the budget for the year is formulated by the Chamber of Deputies.

thus accruing to the Treasury were used to pay off advances from the Bank of France. Consequently, during this period, while advances were regularly reduced by the return flow of the notes and other funds put out, the note circulation was kept up by a continuance of the output and by the demands of business and of the public for appropriate supplies of cash purchasing power with which to meet their needs. Doubtless, too, a part (however small) of the monetary output remained in circulation to bear the additional burden imposed upon the currency by the transfers connected with the purchase of exchange and of securities.

So much for the relation between advances of the Bank to the State and circulation. But what of private borrowings from the banks? Did they have no effect at all on the volume of circulation? In order to answer the question, a comparison will be made between the lendings of the commercial banks and the outstanding note circulation of the Bank of France. The best available source of data for this purpose seems to be the monthly statements of the "Big Four" banks — the *Crédit Lyonnais*, the *Société Générale*, the *Comptoir National d'Escompte*, and the *Crédit Industriel et*

TABLE 12

PORTFOLIO OF THE "BIG FOUR" COMMERCIAL BANKS *

(Data from end-of-month reports in millions of francs)

	1914	1915	1916	1917	1918	1919	1920
Jan.	6702	....	*4000*	4676	5338	7323	*12820*
Feb.	6870	....	*4021*	4623	5706	7421	13663
Mar.	6834	....	4054	4741	5872	7635	13122
Apr.	6948	3832	4107	5005	5711	7768	13623
May	6937	....	4115	5161	6003	8266	13994
June	6572	3837	4201	5276	6028	8847	13849
July	....	....	4309	5357	6152	9578	13786
Aug.	....	....	4317	5669	6496	10042	13668
Sept.	....	3884	4464	5496	6819	10643	14062
Oct.	....	....	*4383*	*5722*	7557	11102	14268
Nov.	....	....	4377	5863	*6656*	11835	14057
Dec.	3834	3982	4508	5985	7120	12372	13451

* Source: The data for all the years were taken from the records of the Bank of France. Italicized figures indicate estimated amounts for months in which the balance sheet of one of the four banks failed to appear. The amounts given are those

	1921	1922	1923	1924	1925	1926	1927
Jan.	13650	13660	14092	15416	15252	19901	21445
Feb.	13449	13357	13878	15523	15306	19969	21455
Mar.	13338	13165	13933	15667	15368	19727	20851
Apr.	13893	13751	13906	15448	15361	19838	20154
May	13660	13672	14339	15286	16150	20595	19145
June	12973	14253	14525	15409	16472	21306	17218
July	13312	13765	14400	15743	17248	21945	18495
Aug.	13185	13608	14557	16172	17386	21554	19265
Sept.	13410	13905	15354	15672	18119	21009	19307
Oct.	13988	14088	14541	15567	18547	21960	21895
Nov.	13605	13781	14420	15967	17979	21153	21988
Dec.	13587	14029	14931	14894	19003	21299	22642

for three of the banks with allowance made for the fourth by adding the portfolio holdings of that bank for the preceding month.

The above series is a compilation of items in the balance sheets of the "Big Four" commercial banks under various captions but all representing a type of loan. Three main categories may be established: *Portefeuille Commercial*, *Avances et Reports*, and *Comptes Courants Débiteurs*. The *Portefeuille Commercial* includes holdings of commercial paper and of National Defense Bonds, both, with some exceptions, of a maximum maturity of three months. *Avances et Reports* represent, for the first, short-term loans guaranteed by the deposit of securities, mortgages, goods, etc. and, for the second, loans on the collateral of Bourse securities to operators on the Bourse. *Comptes Courants Débiteurs* comprise overdrafts, bank acceptances, and bills left for collection. Until July 1922 the *Société Générale* included correspondent balances at home and abroad and miscellaneous assets in this last account, but from that date these items were excluded.

Commercial. Unfortunately, however, there is no way of separating in their statements the commercial portfolio from holdings of *Bons de la Défense Nationale* and short-term Treasury paper. Consequently, a series made up of the sum of these two items plus two others — *Avances et Reports* (loans on security and stock exchange loans) and *Comptes Courants Débiteurs* (overdrafts) — has been compiled.

By reference to the accompanying graphs (Charts VI and VII), it is immediately seen that after 1920 their movements were very much alike. In 1918 and 1919 and again in 1927, however, they were very dissimilar indeed. For the sake of simplicity in presentation the period of great similarity (1921–1926) will be considered first and then the exceptional years of dissimilarity (1918–1920 and 1927) will be taken up in turn.

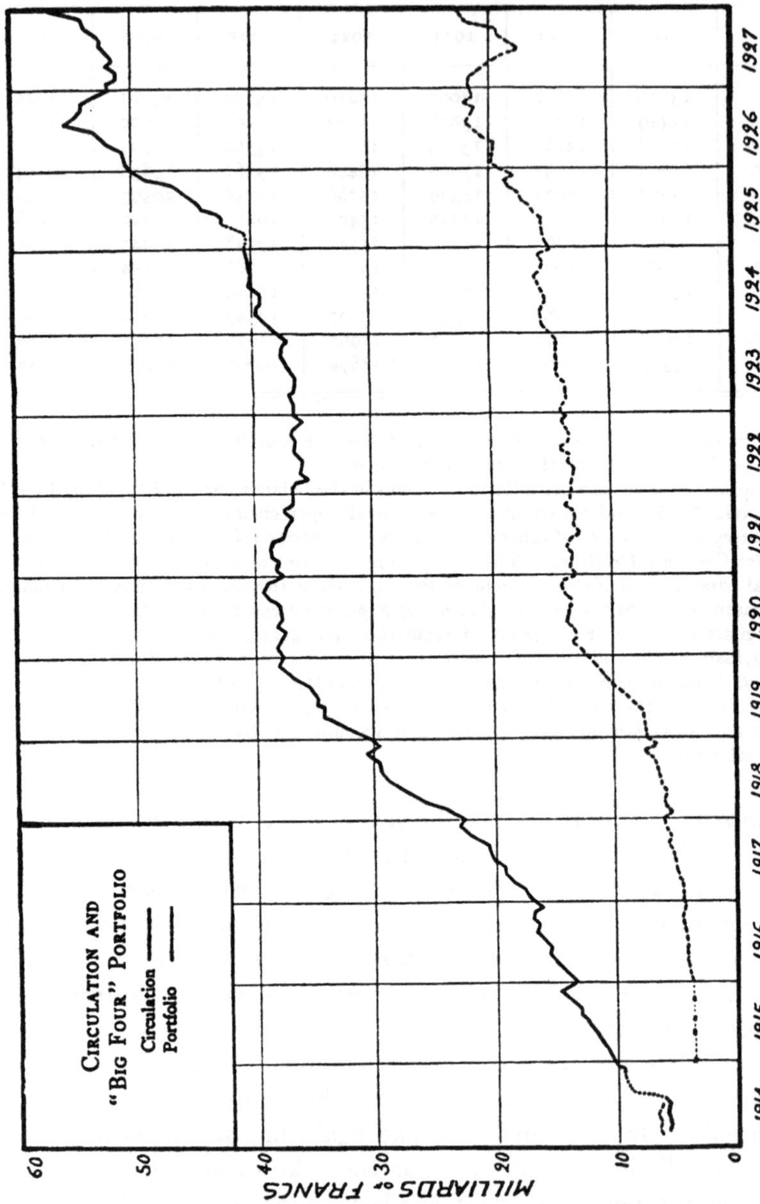
CIRCULATION AND
"BIG FOUR" PORTFOLIO
Circulation
Portfolio
60
50
40
30
20
10
0
MILLIARDS of FRANCS
1914
1915
1916
1917
1918
1919
1920
1921
1922
1923
1924
1925
1926
1927

CHART VI

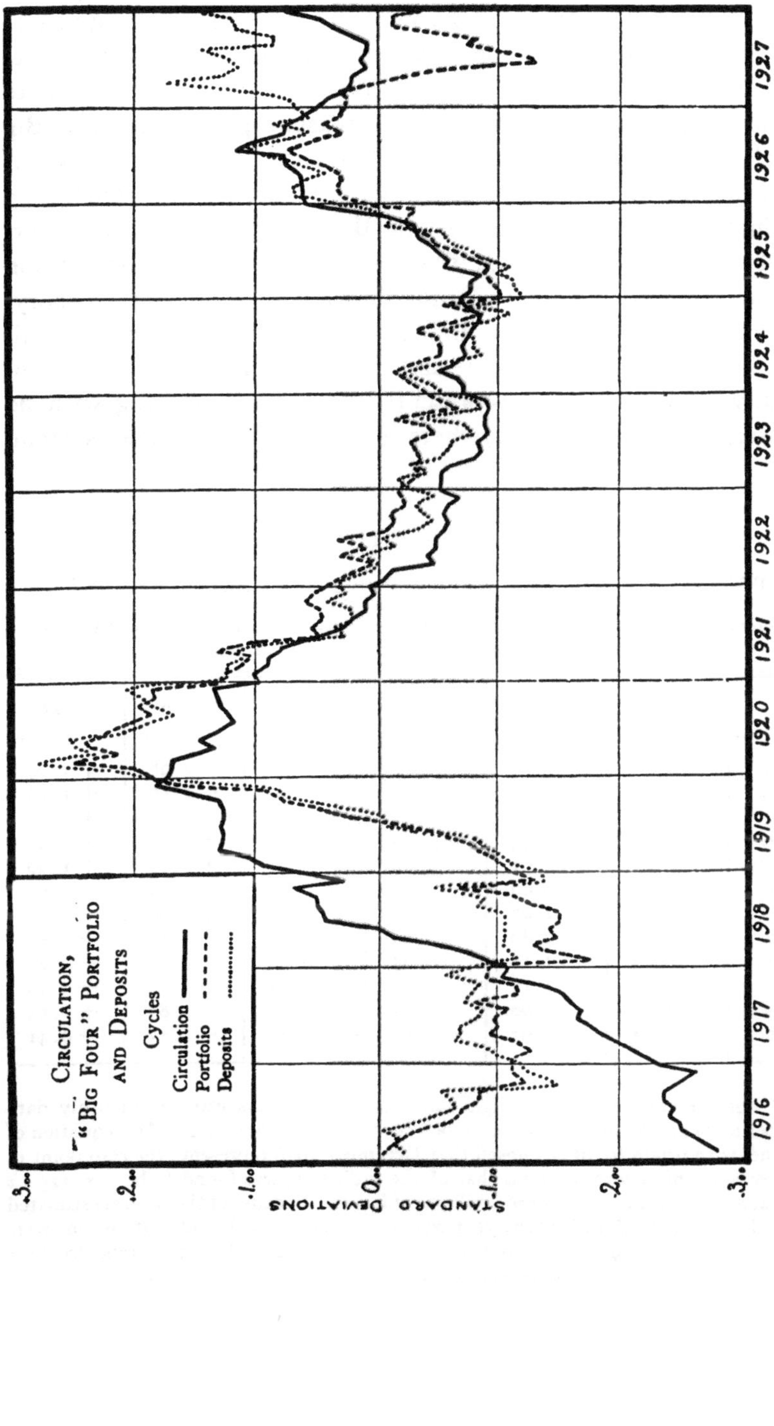
Circulation,
"Big Four" Portfolio
and Deposits
Cycles
Circulation
Portfolio
Deposits
Standard Deviations
3.00
2.00
1.00
0.
1.00
2.00
3.00
1916
1917
1918
1919
1920
1921
1922
1923
1924
1925
1926
1927

CHART VII

With respect to the period 1921–1926 the question arises as to how circulation could possibly have corresponded so closely in movement both to advances of the Bank of France to the State and to "loans plus holdings of short-term Treasury paper" of the "Big Four" banks. The answer, while certainly not obvious, seems to be attainable. Assume first that circulation was completely dominated by the advances of the Bank to the State, as superficially seems to have been the case. (The reverse assumption will be discussed in turn.) Funds thus advanced to the Treasury, as was explained earlier in this chapter, not only were spent almost immediately, but also — and this point should be borne continually in mind — they represented a type of spending with no counterpart of saving anywhere else in the economic system.

TABLE 13

PORTFOLIO OF THE "BIG FOUR" COMMERCIAL BANKS *

(Percentage deviations from secular trend expressed as percentages of standard deviation, allowance made for seasonal variations)

	1916	1917	1918	1919	1920	1921
Jan.	− 0.03	− 1.13	− 1.78	− 1.06	+ 1.98	+ 1.29
Feb.	− 0.13	− 1.25	− 1.41	− 0.99	+ 2.56	+ 1.16
Mar.	− 0.21	− 1.16	− 1.28	− 0.82	+ 2.12	+ 1.07
Apr.	− 0.30	− 0.94	− 1.51	− 0.78	+ 2.38	+ 1.35
May	− 0.59	− 1.00	− 1.44	− 0.59	+ 2.41	+ 1.00
June	− 0.64	− 0.99	− 1.51	− 0.22	+ 2.20	+ 0.51
July	− 0.70	− 1.07	− 1.54	+ 0.21	+ 1.99	+ 0.57
Aug.	− 0.81	− 0.80	− 1.27	+ 0.51	+ 1.86	+ 0.46
Sept.	− 0.83	− 1.18	− 1.13	+ 0.80	+ 1.94	+ 0.45
Oct.	− 1.23	− 1.17	− 0.70	+ 0.92	+ 1.85	+ 0.59
Nov.	− 1.14	− 0.90	− 1.35	+ 1.59	+ 1.85	+ 0.53
Dec.	− 1.14	− 0.91	− 1.07	+ 1.85	+ 1.33	+ 0.41

* For the calculation, a straight-line secular trend was fitted to monthly data for a period of 121 months from December 1916 to December 1926. The equation of this line, with origin (0, 0) so chosen that December 1916 represents the zero point of the abscissas and a zero portfolio that of the ordinates, was found to be $y = 125.5x + 5364$, m being + 125.5 and b 5364 millions of francs. Because of the several estimated figures for 1916, the data for that year were not included in the calculation, but were added, as were the 1927 data, by extending the same line of secular trend to those years. The seasonal variations were computed by the method of link relatives.

	1922	1923	1924	1925	1926	1927
Jan.	+ 0.30	− 0.28	− 0.33	− 1.00	+ 0.27	+ 0.26
Feb.	+ 0.15	− 0.36	− 0.25	− 0.94	+ 0.33	+ 0.30
Mar.	+ 0.04	− 0.31	− 0.17	− 0.88	+ 0.27	+ 0.12
Apr.	+ 0.32	− 0.36	− 0.30	− 0.91	+ 0.28	− 0.15
May	+ 0.09	− 0.33	− 0.54	− 0.75	+ 0.40	− 0.65
June	+ 0.33	− 0.29	− 0.54	− 0.67	+ 0.61	− 1.35
July	− 0.04	− 0.46	− 0.49	− 0.46	+ 0.75	− 1.00
Aug.	− 0.15	− 0.40	− 0.32	− 0.41	+ 0.59	− 0.73
Sept.	− 0.12	− 0.15	− 0.65	− 0.23	+ 0.28	− 0.82
Oct.	− 0.22	− 0.70	− 0.86	− 0.23	+ 0.46	− 0.12
Nov.	− 0.20	− 0.57	− 0.50	− 0.26	+ 0.36	+ 0.12
Dec.	− 0.17	− 0.42	− 1.03	+ 0.06	+ 0.33	+ 0.36

TABLE 14

SIGHT DEPOSITS OF THE "BIG FOUR" COMMERCIAL BANKS*

(Data from end-of-month reports in millions of francs)

	1914	1915	1916	1917	1918	1919	1920
Jan.	5417	....	*3637*	4457	5656	7045	*12475*
Feb.	5530	....	*3727*	4631	5825	7208	13372
Mar.	5583	....	3808	4812	5848	7368	12788
Apr.	5708	3664	3936	5032	6109	7724	13332
May	5833	....	3971	5238	6340	8232	13769
June	5455	3717	4030	5258	6494	8931	13387
July	....	....	4111	5421	6678	9214	13433
Aug.	....	....	4219	5603	6976	9623	13193
Sept.	....	3815	4364	5673	7000	10308	13591
Oct.	....	....	*3940*	*5769*	7515	10643	13984
Nov.	....	....	4108	5981	*6612*	11423	14063
Dec.	3709	3596	4256	5940	6729	11948	13231

* Source: The data for all years were taken from the records of the Bank of France. Italicized figures indicate estimated amounts for months in which the balance sheet of one of the four banks failed to appear. The amounts given are those for three of the banks with allowance made for the fourth by adding the deposit item of that bank for the preceding month.

The deposit item of the "Big Four" commercial banks includes both current accounts and sight deposits. The checking accounts included are maintained as credit balances, but the current accounts carry the privilege of overdraft. Both items represent the deposits of corporations, private individuals, and the balances of correspondents. Until July 1922, the *Société Générale* included its miscellaneous liabilities with current accounts, but from that date these items were eliminated. The comparison between the "Big Four" portfolio and deposit series is not materially disturbed by the inclusion, until July 1922, of correspondent credits at home and

TABLE 14 (Continued)

	1921	1922	1923	1924	1925	1926	1927
Jan.	13132	13368	14116	15152	15008	20732	22760
Feb.	13248	13137	13864	15583	15120	20910	23658
Mar.	12954	12864	13913	15505	15312	20476	25160
Apr.	13440	13505	13872	15219	15396	20516	24637
May	13552	13390	14102	15018	16422	21636	24753
June	12628	13822	14258	15375	16879	22419	25091
July	13025	13546	14132	15659	17604	23335	26171
Aug.	12856	13340	14342	16128	17732	22692	24467
Sept.	12975	13601	15158	15442	18901	22123	24553
Oct.	13514	13946	14418	15328	18996	23120	25717
Nov.	13122	13488	14243	15860	19321	22101	25515
Dec.	13320	13973	14948	14857	19943	22469	26404

abroad and of miscellaneous assets in the portfolio item of the *Société Générale* and of miscellaneous liabilities in the same bank's current accounts, for the two groups of heterogeneous assets and liabilities roughly balance each other. In the balance sheet for December 31, 1922, the total of the former was 218 million francs and that of the latter 201 million francs.

TABLE 15

SIGHT DEPOSITS OF THE "BIG FOUR" COMMERCIAL BANKS *

(Percentage deviations from secular trend expressed as percentages of standard deviations, allowance made for seasonal variation)

	1916	1917	1918	1919	1920	1921
Jan.	− 0.22	− 1.00	− 1.19	− 1.13	+ 2.18	+ 1.26
Feb.	− 0.14	− 0.89	− 1.10	− 1.06	+ 2.78	+ 1.25
Mar.	− 0.19	− 0.63	− 1.05	− 0.86	+ 2.34	+ 1.10
Apr.	− 0.01	− 0.66	− 1.06	− 0.81	+ 2.46	+ 1.16
May	− 0.30	− 0.66	− 1.05	− 0.58	+ 2.54	+ 1.01
June	− 0.47	− 0.85	− 1.05	− 0.11	+ 2.08	+ 0.26
July	− 0.64	− 0.87	− 1.06	− 0.06	+ 1.90	+ 0.34
Aug.	− 0.61	− 0.73	− 0.81	+ 0.24	+ 1.66	+ 0.20
Sept.	− 0.54	− 0.77	− 0.89	+ 0.73	+ 1.86	+ 0.22
Oct.	− 1.53	− 0.86	− 0.54	+ 0.82	+ 1.97	+ 0.41
Nov.	− 1.26	− 0.58	− 1.40	+ 1.52	+ 2.07	+ 0.24
Dec.	− 1.18	− 0.76	− 1.38	+ 1.84	+ 1.38	+ 0.30

* For the calculation, a straight-line secular trend was fitted to monthly data for a period of 121 months, from December 1916 to December 1926. The equation of the line, with origin (0, 0) so chosen that December 1916 represents the zero point of the abscissas and a zero deposit item that of the ordinates, was found to be $y = 131.3x + 5026$, m being 131.3 and b 5026 millions of francs. Because of the several esti-

	1922	1923	1924	1925	1926	1927
Jan.	+ 0.29	− 0.18	− 0.42	− 1.15	+ 0.66	+ 0.79
Feb.	+ 0.09	− 0.38	− 0.26	− 1.14	+ 0.70	+ 1.10
Mar.	0.00	− 0.26	− 0.19	− 0.94	+ 0.62	+ 1.77
Apr.	+ 0.14	− 0.52	− 0.57	− 1.13	+ 0.41	+ 1.34
May	− 0.14	− 0.58	− 0.85	− 0.86	+ 0.67	+ 1.19
June	− 0.01	− 0.61	− 0.78	− 0.75	+ 0.89	+ 1.23
July	− 0.33	− 0.82	− 0.79	− 0.58	+ 1.10	+ 1.49
Aug.	− 0.46	− 0.72	− 0.56	− 0.51	+ 0.86	+ 0.87
Sept.	− 0.36	− 0.34	− 0.91	− 0.04	+ 0.60	+ 0.87
Oct.	− 0.30	− 0.84	− 1.09	− 0.12	+ 0.87	+ 1.18
Nov.	− 0.46	− 0.82	− 0.73	+ 0.13	+ 0.58	+ 1.22
Dec.	− 0.24	− 0.51	− 1.22	+ 0.34	+ 0.69	+ 1.50

mated figures for 1916, the data for that year were not included in the calculation, but were added, as were the 1927 data, by extending the same line of secular trend to those years. The seasonal variation was computed by the method of link relatives.

TABLE 16

NOTE CIRCULATION OF THE BANK OF FRANCE*

(Percentage deviations from secular trend expressed as percentages of standard deviation, allowance made for seasonal variations)

	1916	1917	1918	1919	1920	1921
Jan.	− 2.82	− 2.20	− 0.92	+ 0.95	+ 1.72	+ 1.01
Feb.	− 2.72	− 2.07	− 0.74	+ 1.06	+ 1.72	+ 0.91
Mar.	− 2.60	− 1.97	− 0.47	+ 1.33	+ 1.52	+ 0.88
Apr.	− 2.52	− 1.86	− 0 16	+ 1.28	+ 1.35	+ 0.81
May	− 2.50	− 1.77	0.00	+ 1.28	+ 1.47	+ 0.78
June	− 2.42	− 1.66	+ 0.41	+ 1.30	+ 1.31	+ 0.55
July	− 2.45	− 1.69	+ 0.43	+ 1.28	+ 1.19	+ 0.27
Aug.	− 2.36	− 1.63	+ 0.48	+ 1.27	+ 1.22	+ 0.21
Sept.	− 2.36	− 1.58	+ 0.49	+ 1.34	+ 1.28	+ 0.11
Oct.	− 2.47	− 1.39	+ 0.67	+ 1.55	+ 1.33	+ 0.12
Nov.	− 2.60	− 1.05	+ 0.26	+ 1.82	+ 1.35	+ 0.04
Dec.	− 2.34	− 1.10	+ 0.60	+ 1.76	+ 0.99	+ 0.08

* The results of this calculation being specifically intended for comparison with the series of portfolio and of sight deposits of the "Big Four" commercial banks, a straight-line secular trend was fitted to monthly circulation data (Table 9) for the period corresponding to that chosen for the above-mentioned series: one of 121 months from December 1916 to December 1926. The equation of this line, with origin (0, 0) so chosen that December 1916 represents the zero point of the abscissas and a zero circulation that of the ordinates, was found to be $y = +222.4x + 23295$, m being $+222.4$ and b 23295 millions of francs. The data for 1916 and 1927 were

TABLE 16 (Continued)

	1922	1923	1924	1925	1926	1927
Jan.	−0.03	−0.53	−0.72	−0.77	+0.63	+0.41
Feb.	−0.16	−0.53	−0.66	−0.77	+0.64	+0.27
Mar.	−0.46	−0.60	−0.53	−0.84	+0.64	+0.22
Apr.	−0.41	−0.80	−0.63	−0.56	+0.66	+0.21
May	−0.47	−0.86	−0.74	−0.58	+0.77	+0.12
June	−0.47	−0.82	−0.71	−0.54	+0.80	+0.15
July	−0.56	−0.91	−0.76	−0.45	+1.18	+0.12
Aug.	−0.58	−0.88	−0.78	−0.36	+1.02	+0.10
Sept.	−0.56	−0.88	−0.83	−0.31	+0.79	+0.18
Oct.	−0.59	−0.91	−0.84	−0.14	+0.78	+0.31
Nov.	−0.66	−0.89	−0.72	+0.24	+0.66	+0.47
Dec.	−0.53	−0.72	−0.67	+0.60	+0.50	+0.75

added by extending the same line of secular trend to those years. Correction for seasonal movements was made by employing the indices of seasonal variation calculated for the first circulation series (Table 11).

The spending of these funds by the Government led to an immediate increase in the pecuniary volume of trade, an increase which spread backwards, forwards, and sidewise in the manner above described. In the process of this spreading, most of the funds originally put out as new advances from the Bank to the State passed successively in and out of the banks in making their numerous revolutions against the goods and services which they purchased: *in*, in the shape of deposits of shops, of business firms and of private individuals; *out*, in the form of advances or of loans to industry and commerce. Thus the funds once spent tended to continue their endless movements through the complicated mechanism of a modern economic system. But, as is well known, many things may happen to arrest or diminish this normal and continuous flow. Immediately the funds begin to accumulate in the banks. And herein lies the secret of the close correspondence with circulation of two series so apparently unrelated as those of the advances of the Bank to the State and of "loans plus holdings of short-term Treasury paper" of the banks. When funds for which there were no commercial or industrial demands accumulated in the banks, they were almost at once employed to purchase short-term Treasury paper. To the extent that they continued to circulate against goods and services, the funds originally put out continued likewise to maintain the loans and deposits of the banks. To the extent that they ceased to circulate, they augmented the purchase of short-term Treasury paper [13] — and thereby reduced the advances of the Bank of France to the State. Hence, while in periods of credit contraction the new purchases of Treasury paper by the banks naturally reduced the shrinkage of portfolio items at the same time that they effected reductions in the advances of the Bank to the State, the more gradual downward adjustments of circulation kept the general movements of that series in reasonably close correspondence with those of both the others. And, since most of the period under discussion was one of general credit expansion, a close correlation between the series of circulation and of portfolios was certainly to have been expected.

To take up the reverse assumption, suppose next that it was the business borrowing, instead of the advances of the Bank to the State, which dominated the amounts of the currency (money and deposits) in circulation. In this case, as in the preceding, any new spending by the Government with funds derived from advances from the Bank or from the sale to the banks or to others of short-term Treasury paper naturally added its influence to that already exerted by the business and other spending. But, to the extent that business spending increased and loans and deposits of the banks expanded, the withdrawals of funds from the banks would naturally multiply and the subscriptions to short-term Treasury paper would decrease. Hence the State would be obliged to increase correspondingly its borrowings from the Bank of France. But, should business spending become less, as it would sooner or later, funds would accumulate in the banks and would, except to the extent of the unpaid borrowings of the banks from the central bank or elsewhere, be used to purchase short-term Treasury paper,[14] thus providing the Treasury with money either to pay off its advances from the Bank of France or to reduce their increase. Thus, there is no doubt

[13] After the middle of 1925 the volume of deposits made by the banks at the Treasury assumed proportions sufficient to modify this relationship.

[14] See footnote 10, p. 70.

that the ups and downs of business may dominate circulation and advances of the Bank to the State as completely as advances may dominate circulation and business.

With these analyses all the apparent mystery aroused by the great similarity of series so diverse as those under consideration seems to be dispelled. It remains, however, to explain the divergences in the movements of note circulation and of the two "Big Four" bank series — loans, etc. and deposits — in the period 1918–1920 and again in 1927.

In the dark days of 1918, when government borrowings in general and the advances of the Bank of France to the State in particular were expanding rapidly, French industry, on account of the many uncertainties of the economic situation, not to mention the loss of territory to the Germans, was apparently not expanding its borrowings. Funds put into circulation by the Bank of France as advances to the State had, accordingly, a tendency to stagnate after serving their first function of making purchases for the Government. Under normal conditions they would have drifted naturally to the banks in the form of deposits by those into whose hands they had come. The banks, in turn, would have invested such funds in short-term Treasury obligations. In 1918, however, with the victorious enemy pressing ever closer to Paris, there were continuous and urgent appeals to the public to subscribe to the long-term obligations of the Government. Hence, the idle funds, instead of flowing to the banks in amounts normal for such circumstances, were in large part invested directly by their holders in government securities. As a result, many of them never appeared as bank deposits at all, and, of those that did so appear, a large part was evidently quickly transferred by their depositors to the Treasury in payment for the securities purchased. Thus, the funds were returned to the Treasury for use again without at all, or only for short periods, appearing as deposits and, consequently, without swelling the holdings by the banks of short-term Treasury obligations. Hence, during 1918, items of the series both of deposits and of "loans plus holdings of short-term Treasury paper" might have been expected to fall far short of correspondence with those of the circulation series —

as they actually did.[15] This explanation finds ample confirmation in the data of flotations of long-term government obligations (Table 2 above). In 1918 such flotations amounted to 27.4 milliards as compared with 12.2 milliards in 1917 and 4.8 milliards in 1919.

With the return of business prosperity in 1919 and with the great reduction in the flotation of long-term government obligations, the curves of deposits and of "loans plus holdings of Treasury paper" of the "Big Four" banks rapidly approached again the curve of circulation, as was to be expected. Then, at the height of industrial activity in 1920 both of the "big four" series went considerably above that of circulation. This movement seems to violate what has just been said above with regard to the necessary correspondence of the curves. The violation, however, is perhaps only an apparent one. In a period of rapidly rising prices like that of the latter half of 1919 and of the first four months of 1920, deposits and loans of commercial banks usually increase more rapidly than does circulation. In other words, in such periods a given amount of circulation will support a considerably larger expansion of bank loans and of deposits. It seems that, on account of the fact that the prices of raw materials, of manufacturers' goods, and of goods at wholesale in general, many of which, even in France, are paid for by check or draft, rise much more rapidly and much farther than do wages or retail prices, which, on the other hand, are very largely paid in cash, a given volume of circulation will support a considerably larger expansion of bank loans and deposits. Therefore, since the normal proportion between deposit currency and note circulation was temporarily distorted in favor of deposits, it was certainly to be expected that the curves of the two factors would have separated as they did in 1920.

It remains to discuss the separation of the series in 1927 (Chart VIII). Even by the middle of 1925 an extremely important influence causing the series of loans and of deposits to diverge had made its appearance. After January 1, 1921 the Treasury was authorized to accept deposits not only from the banks but

[15] The series used for the comparison are percentage deviations from secular trend expressed in terms of the respective standard deviations.

likewise from business firms and from private individuals. Partly on account of the large initial deposits required the totals of such deposits did not become important in magnitude until about the middle of 1925. Thereafter, however, they grew gradually until in June 1927 their total amounted to the substantial sum of 17.8 milliards of francs. The effect of the growth of such deposits — in so far as they were made by the "Big Four" banks — on the separation of the series of loans and of deposits under consideration, is at once obvious. Since such deposits, unlike investments in short-term Treasury paper, are not included with portfolio and other loan items but with cash and since the funds deposited in the Treasury by the banks were largely those previously received on deposit by them, it is evident that to the extent of their deposits in the Treasury those held for their customers would tend to exceed the amounts of portfolio plus other loans.

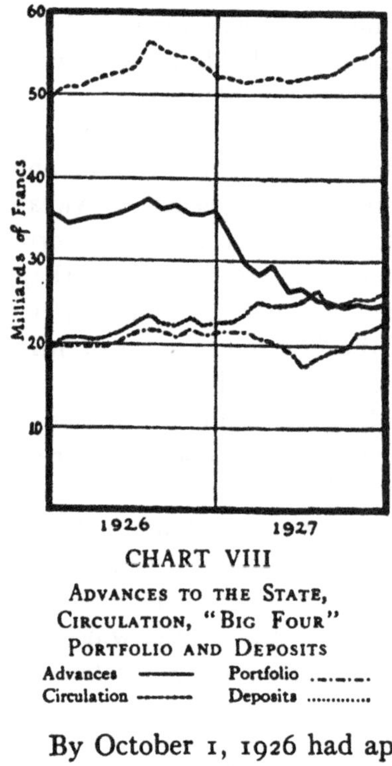

CHART VIII

ADVANCES TO THE STATE, CIRCULATION, "BIG FOUR" PORTFOLIO AND DEPOSITS

Advances ——— Portfolio ._._._.
Circulation ------- Deposits ....

By October 1, 1926 had appeared another important influence destined to disturb greatly not only the relationship between subscriptions and reimbursements of *Bons de la Défense Nationale* and advances of the Bank of France to the State, but also that between such advances and the note circulation of the Bank of France. At that time the newly organized *Caisse Autonome d'Amortissement* began its important operations. Thereafter all subscriptions to *Bons de la Défense Nationale*, which during the entire period until somewhat after the beginning of 1927 made up practically the entire volume of short-term Treasury obligations, were paid into the *Caisse*, and all reimbursements were made from its resources. Moreover, all but a small portion of the funds thus received were kept on deposit at the Bank of France, only a fixed required minimum of 1.2 milliards of francs being maintained at the Treasury. Consequently, purchases and reimbursements of such obligations no longer had their earlier effects of reducing or increasing advances of the Bank to the State but, on the contrary, simply enlarged or diminished the account of the *Caisse* at the Bank of France. And this influence — sufficient in itself to disturb greatly the above-described relationship between advances and the changes in purchasing, whether of the Government or of business, when combined with the increasing use by the banks of Treasury deposits instead of short-term Treasury obligations as investments for otherwise idle funds, destroyed completely the former correspondence between note circulation and the advances of the Bank to the State.

The wide separation during 1927 between the loans and deposits of the "Big Four" is, therefore, to be accounted for largely by the shifting of the investment of the surplus funds of the banks from short-term Treasury paper to deposits in the Treasury. The failure of the note circulation to move like either of these two series, or like that of advances of the Bank to the State, may be ascribed to the failure of any of the three series longer to represent even remotely the volume of spending (and hoarding), while the note circulation continued to adjust itself to such influences. That the note circulation would not increase proportionately as much as deposits is clear from the fact that, when large deposits of idle funds are transferred to the Treasury and by it to the Bank of France, a considerable cancellation of notes necessarily followed. That it would not fall by so much as loans, might have been anticipated from the fact that the reduction in this item below deposits represented the entire shift from investments in short-term paper to deposits in the Treasury, while a portion of the funds deposited in the Treasury, although being used to reduce advances from the Bank, during much of the period were being again issued by the Bank of France to accomplish its large purchases of foreign exchange. Advances, on the other hand, fell more rapidly and more drastically than any of the others, not only because other funds than those of the banks were being deposited in the

Treasury but because, too, while such advances were being reduced by practically the total of funds thus deposited, the Bank was in turn putting out new funds with which to pay for its large purchases of foreign exchange. These new funds, being paid largely to capital repatriators and to foreign purchasers of French securities, flowed quickly to the banks, which, as a result, found their deposits and to a certain extent their loans increased; and the return of these new funds to the Treasury led to a corresponding further reduction in advances. In a word, deposits were increased and advances reduced at each circuit of the funds,[16] whereas loans fluctuated only with subscriptions to and reimbursements of short-term Treasury paper (by that time relatively unimportant in amount) and with movements in the volume of loans to customers and of other business credits.

An important illustration of the intricate and but little understood relationships just discussed is furnished by the effects of the government loan of July 10, 1927.[17] When the loan was announced it was confidently expected by many in France not only that sight deposits in the Treasury would be reduced, another slice of short-term Treasury paper would be disposed of, and a large payment of advances of the Bank to the State would be accomplished *but also that a considerable volume of the notes of the Bank of France would be retired.* All of the first three anticipated effects were amply realized. Since *Bons de la Défense Nationale* were accepted from subscribers to the issue in lieu of cash, it came about that something over a milliard and a quarter of such government obligations were retired.

Moreover, Treasury deposits were likewise immediately reduced. No doubt some of the direct business or private depositors in the Treasury withdrew funds in order to make payment for their subscriptions; but much more important in their total effects were the actions of subscribers from the rank and file of the population. By drawing funds from the banks and paying for their new bonds in cash — as most of them doubtless did — or by simply writing checks on their deposit balances in their banks, they produced

[16] For a full description, see pp. 293-295.

[17] *Rentes françaises 6% amortissables 1927.*

the same effect on the total of deposits in the Treasury as did their fellow-subscribers who drew directly therefrom. For, to meet the cash demands of their customers or to procure the funds with which to cash the checks presented either by the Treasury or by the Bank of France as its agent, the banks were in turn forced to draw upon their deposits at the Treasury. Consequently, the net result of most of the payments other than those made in the form of *Bons de la Défense Nationale* was an almost equivalent reduction of the deposits at the Treasury. The Treasury, having put out and received substantially the same amount of funds, found its position, except to the extent that it had been paid with hoarded funds or with checks on the Bank of France, otherwise unaffected by the operations connected with the loan.

To the extent that *Bons de la Défense Nationale* were received in payment for subscriptions, however, the Treasury, by the terms of a previous authorization, discounted these obligations at the *Caisse d'Amortissement* and with the proceeds was enabled to reduce its advances from the Bank of France. Hence the net effect was a turning over of the bonds to the *Caisse* for cancellation at maturity, a corresponding reduction of the deposit account of the *Caisse* at the Bank of France, and, to the extent that the funds thus realized by the Treasury were actually used for that purpose, a like reduction in the advances of the Bank of France to the State.

The total nominal subscriptions amounted to 4,642 millions of francs, of which 3,250 millions were in cash and 1,392 millions in *Bons de la Défense Nationale.* But, since the subscriptions were made at the rate of 460 francs for each 500-franc bond, the net yields were in cash 2,990 millions and in *Bons de la Défense Nationale* 1,281 millions. In the period from June 30 to September 1, during which the effects of the loan should have been largely realized, the reduction in the private deposits of the Bank of France was about 1.75 milliards. However, since this reduction covers not only the withdrawals of the *Caisse d'Armortissement* but also those of other depositors at the Bank of France paying for subscriptions with checks on their accounts in that institution (as well as all the other unrelated private operations affecting the total of private deposits at the Bank), the correspondence with the amount of subscriptions paid in *Bons de la Défense Nationale* is reasonably close. The reduction of deposits at the Treasury, on the other hand, amounted to slightly over 4 milliards as against cash subscriptions of a little less than 3 milliards. Evidently, therefore, although there were other influences likewise reducing them, their movement was in the direction anticipated. Finally, the reduction of advances of the Bank to the State amounted to a little more than 2 milliards as opposed to bond paid subscriptions of 1.3 milliards.[18] Hence, here, too, the influences set in motion by the flotation of the new bond issue were apparently being assisted by others producing similar effects. In the note circulation during the same period, however, not only was there no reduction but an actual increase of approximately half a milliard of francs. What is the explanation?

In the above description of the effects of cash subscriptions it was seen that the cash or deposit credit transferred by the subscribers to the Treasury was counterbalanced by the cancellation of an almost exactly equivalent amount of deposits at the Treasury, which were withdrawn to provide the wherewithal to make payments. Since the Treasury received in cash, however, almost exactly the same amounts that it paid out in cash, the operations involved — except possibly very temporarily — neither expansion nor contraction of the note circulation of the Bank of France. Moreover, in the case of subscriptions paid for with short-term Treasury obligations, the bonds received were discounted, as has been observed, at the *Caisse d'Amortissement*, which paid the proceeds by transferring to the Treasury a portion of its deposit account at the Bank of France. Hence, these operations likewise involved no issue of new notes nor a cancellation of old ones. Consequently, note circulation was practically unaffected by the operations as a whole. The half milliard increase doubtless came from unrelated influences having to do primarily with business and private currency needs and, for short periods at a time, with the Bank's activities in the foreign exchange market.

[18] Of the 1.3 milliards of subscriptions in the form of *Bons de la Défense Nationale* only approximately 1 milliard was discountable at the *Caisse d'Amortissement*. Some 500 millions of francs additional from the Bank's amortization account for the advances to the State were used in the reduction of advances.

CHAPTER VI

EXCHANGE, PRICES, CIRCULATION, AND BANK DEPOSITS

THE preceding chapter was devoted to a discussion of the relations between government borrowing on the one hand and the various measures of inflation — exchange, prices, and circulation — on the other. The task of this chapter is to study the interrelations among the several measures themselves; and, on its completion, at least the outstanding features of the French inflation process should be apparent.

The changed relationships between exchange and prices since the departure from the gold standard are of signal importance. Under the former system of uniform metallic standards prevailing throughout most of the commercial world, certain interconnections were obvious and almost automatic. For example, should similar articles in two countries on the gold standard command widely different prices, commerce between the countries could be depended upon in the long run (barring trade barriers or prohibitive shipping costs) to reduce to reasonable proportions the inequalities in prices. The demand would be stimulated in the cheaper market and the supply correspondingly increased in the dearer, both influences leading toward a price equalization. Moreover, the international payments, being made in gold, would tend probably — depending upon the banking and currency organizations and policies of the two countries — to bring about similar price adjustments. Such a correspondence in prices could be anticipated at least for all commodities entering into international commerce, and indices based largely on the prices of such commodities could likewise be expected to correspond at least roughly. Furthermore, since in all of our modern economic systems prices of widely differing commodities are often closely connected in many ways, the general price indices in the various commercial and industrial countries could be expected to maintain at least a remote similarity. Indeed, all these expectations were realized in the civilized world as it existed at the time of the outbreak of the Great War. Moreover, in countries on the same metallic standard, exchange rates, on account of provisions maintaining the standard, combined with those guaranteeing free traffic in the money metals, were kept nearly constant. And, being kept relatively fixed, they in turn kept the price levels of gold standard countries in a comparatively constant proportion one to the other.

Altogether different are the relations between exchange rates and prices under our modern systems of paper standards and of controlled commerce in the money metals. Or perhaps it would be more accurate to say that relations once kept from appearing on account of the restrictions of the metallic systems now stand out in bold relief under the prevailing paper standards. Should the prices of similar articles be very different in two countries, at least one of which is on a paper standard, naturally (in the absence of prohibitive trade or transportation restrictions) there would be, as before, a tendency for them to adjust themselves — the cheaper upward, and the dearer downward. But an important difference becomes at once apparent. The relative cheapness or dearness of the article in one country or the other depends directly on the rate of exchange between the moneys used in its purchase. And the important point is that, unlike rates between two gold standard (or any other metallic standard) countries, these rates themselves have no necessary fixity. In fact, the very process by which the adjustment in prices is arrived at tends to bring about a change in the exchange rates which causes the price differences to be reduced. On the other hand, if the rates of exchange between the currencies of the countries move for any other reason, as very frequently happens, the changes establish price differences which often lead to trade movements otherwise unprofitable. But, just as in the case of exchange rates adjusting themselves to prices the process of adjustment causes the rates of exchange to move in such a way as to make the adjustment less necessary, so in the reverse case of prices moving to an equilibrium with exchange rates the process of their moving so reacts on exchange rates as to make their change ever less imperative.

Thus it is clear that, in the absence of artificial restrictions, exchange rates and prices will tend to adjust themselves naturally to each other and that each in so doing will tend to make less necessary the adjustment of the other. It may, therefore, often be difficult — if not impossible — to determine which way the adjustment will take place.

Of the relations between exchange and circulation there are several varieties. In the first place, it is evident that purchases of foreign exchange, representing, as they do, an increase in the pecuniary volume of trade, require some form of currency (usually deposits) for their accomplishment. But more important for the purposes of this study is the unusual but, at the present time in France, the extremely instructive case in which the central bank participates in the purchase of exchange. These purchases involve a release of funds by the central bank equivalent to the value of the exchange purchased, and, since usually the new funds are placed in the hands of those actively engaged in commerce and industry, they are apt to continue in use and to spread their influence to remote parts of the economic system. Such has not been the experience in France, however, as will be explained in detail below.

The relations between prices and circulation have been the subject of so many volumes on monetary theory that it would be indeed preposterous to attempt in a paragraph anything more than the briefest sketch of the positions of various schools. All the controversy about the quantity theory is involved. And, since it is especially desired to avoid in this study fruitless wranglings about any theory, it is only with hesitation that the classical position of its advocates is even suggested. Suffice it to say that in general the quantity theorists, not content with the qualified proportionality statistically evident between prices and circulation, have usually urged with equal vigor the causal relationship from circulation to prices. Most of the anti-quantity theorists — especially the bullionists — have generally urged, on the other hand, the reverse causal relationship from prices to circulation. As this study proceeds it will become increasingly evident that the adjustments occur both ways and in response, presumably, to changes in the kinds and amounts of expenditures and to the lags in time between purchases and payments.

Finally, the obvious relationship between circulation and deposits presents itself. In most Anglo-Saxon countries cash seems usually to adjust its quantity to that of deposits rather than the reverse, as is frequently assumed. This adjustment, as explained in Chapter II above, is not very different from that which takes place between the total monetary circulation and the amount of small change in use. It is a matter of common knowledge that the minor coins are minted as required and are issued to the banks in whatever quantities they are demanded by the spending public. The obvious explanation is that, since the great mass of cash purchases are made with notes and with coins of higher denominations and since there is a mutual adjustment between prices and the quantities of such circulation, the small change required naturally adjusts itself to the prices already established in the existing equilibrium between money and prices. In much the same manner, in countries like England and the United States, where the great bulk of purchases are paid for with check or draft, the equilibrium is established between prices and deposit circulation, with the monetary circulation — playing, as it does, a secondary rôle — simply adjusting itself accordingly.[1] Viewed in a purely mechanical way, the adjustment takes place through the pursuance by most people of the practice of depositing all surplus cash in their banks and of withdrawing therefrom all needed cash supplies. The amounts of both types of currency are thus kept adjusted to the convenience of the public in meeting their cash payments. The amounts of the cash payments are in turn determined by the quantities of things thus paid for and by the prices at which they are bought. And, since the prices have in large part been

[1] Lest this statement be misunderstood, attention is called to the fact that, on account of the much greater draughts on the lawful money resources of the central banks usually occasioned by the issue of additional supplies of money as opposed to those of deposits, the potential issues of the latter are very strictly limited by the amount of the issue of the former. For a quantitative treatment of the subject under the Federal Reserve System of the United States, the reader is referred to a forthcoming publication entitled *A Third Approximation in Monetary Theory*, by the author of this work.

already established in mutual adjustments with deposit currency, the quantity of money in circulation can do little more than adjust itself accordingly — much as the number of nickels in New York City becomes adjusted to the heavy demands placed upon that coin so utterly indispensable to the riding and talking public.

On the other hand, the potential amounts of deposit currency are closely related to the amounts of cash released from circulation. In spite of the ample borrowing facilities provided for the banks in most central banking systems and in spite of the easy issue by the central banks of additional circulating notes, it still remains true that increases in cash received by the banks lead in general to expansions of loans and deposits and, similarly, decreases, to contractions; and it is also true that in issuing circulating notes central banks which maintain definite reserve policies reduce their capacity for further lending of deposit credit always by as much as the amount of the additional note issues and sometimes by even more. Hence the mutual relationships here, as in the case of circulation and prices, must be kept continually in mind.

An example of extraordinary relationship between cash and deposits is found in France during the summer and fall of 1927. The amounts of funds issued by the Bank of France in its purchases of foreign exchange continued large throughout the spring and the first two summer months. This exchange arose in large part from the repatriation of capital by French investors and from purchases by foreigners of French securities, and, since in both cases the derived funds were mainly used for the purchase of securities already outstanding, the resulting expenditures in France did not have their normal effect of stimulating trade and prices. Industry continued in the depressed condition which had existed since the middle of 1926. Hence there was little use for the additional funds in commerce and industry. Under such circumstances they flowed naturally to the banks as increases in deposits. But instead of expanding their loans, the banks purchased Treasury paper or increased their deposits at the Treasury, which used them to pay off advances from the Bank of France. Thus during the summer there was a continual flow of funds from the Bank back to the Bank, a flow which left in its wake an ever increasing item of deposits in the banks and, presumably,[2] one of corresponding dimensions[3] in the Treasury, without, however, occasioning any substantial expansion of bank loans or of circulating notes.

In discussing the movements of French exchange during the war and post-war years, it must be borne in mind that during much of the period the rates were artificially maintained. Definite control was exercised during the war years from the middle of 1916 to March 1919, again during the recovery from the exchange crisis of the spring of 1924, for at least a year and a half after July 1926,[4] and doubtless for very short intervals at various other times during the period considered. Since, however, it was with March 1919 that the war-time control was relinquished, the series for the detailed study of French exchange will start with the beginning of that year. With the few exceptions mentioned, the movements of exchange rates after that time were usually of significance.

During the war years the prices of many articles were likewise controlled, as some of them have continued to be until the present time. There seems, however, no available means of making proper allowance for such regulation, and consequently, for the purposes of this study, the price indices of the *Statistique Générale de la France* will be used without modification.[5] The detailed comparison of the two series, prices and exchange, will cover the period 1919–1926.

In passing, then, to a consideration of the series of dollar exchange rates and of prices,[6] observation will first be made of their

[2] It will be remembered that the issue of *Bons de la Défense Nationale* of maturities of less than two years had by that time been discontinued (see Chap. V, footnote 12, p. 71).

[3] In spite of this flow of funds, there was during August 1927 a reduction in the deposits of the Treasury of 3.5 milliards attributable without doubt to the withdrawal of funds at the time of the 6 per cent, 50-year bond issue of the Government. Again, toward the middle of 1927 a slight revision of the restrictions against the export of capital was instituted in order to make possible the temporary export by the banks of certain of their disposable funds (see Chap. XIII, p. 333.) To this revision is doubtless attributable a further reduction in the deposits at the Treasury.

[4] The control was evidently still in force at the end of 1927.

[5] The data used are the index numbers of wholesale prices of the *Statistique Générale de la France* on the base 100 in 1913 as published in the *League of Nations Bulletin of Statistics*.

[6] For the description of these series see Chap. V, Tables 7 and 8.

long-time movements. While the linear secular trends computed for the period 1919–1926 are very different [$y = 3.1x + 312.7$; $(1 + \frac{nm}{b} = 1.95)$[7] for prices as opposed to $y = +.224x + 6.19$; $(1 + \frac{nm}{b} = 4.47)$ for dollar exchange], the proportional changes over pre-war rates and prices are much more nearly alike. Some confusion arises from the fact that exchange rates were kept down throughout the war years by artificial control, whereas during the same period prices, in spite of all the efforts of the Government to keep them from increasing, rose to three times their pre-war level. The peak of exchange in July 1926, however, is proportionately considerably higher than that of prices.

TABLE 17

DOLLAR EXCHANGE IN PARIS *

(Percentage deviations from secular trend expressed as percentages of standard deviation)

	1918	1919	1920	1921	1922
Jan.		− 0.70	+ 2.01	+ 0.88	− 0.69
Feb.		− 0.83	+ 2.44	+ 0.73	− 1.17
Mar.		− 0.64	+ 2.40	+ 0.78	− 1.18
Apr.		− 0.68	+ 3.31	+ 0.28	− 1.32
May		− 0.56	+ 1.46	− 0.33	− 1.30
June		− 0.67	+ 0.83	− 0.19	− 1.07
July		− 0.38	+ 1.11	− 0.06	− 1.13
Aug.		+ 0.02	+ 1.61	− 0.14	− 0.88
Sept.		+ 0.18	+ 1.61	+ 0.14	− 0.89
Oct.		+ 0.13	+ 1.89	− 0.02	− 0.65
Nov.		+ 0.55	+ 2.06	+ 0.07	− 0.65
Dec.	− 0.56	+ 0.86	+ 2.19	− 0.60	− 0.88

* For the calculation, a straight-line secular trend was fitted to monthly data for a period of 97 months from December 1918 to December 1926. The equation of this line, with origin (0, 0) so chosen that December 1918 represents the zero point of the abscissas and a zero exchange rate that of the ordinates, was found to be $y = +.224x + 6.19$, m and b being measured in francs per dollar. The data for 1914–1918 were not added to the calculation, since during those years the exchange value of the franc was artificially controlled. The data for 1927 were added to the calculations by extending the same line of secular trend to that year. The seasonal movements being but poorly defined, no allowance was made for seasonal variations.

[7] In order to make a direct comparison of linear secular trends when the items of the two series are in entirely different units, the following device is introduced for the

TABLE 17 (Continued)

	1923	1924	1925	1926	1927
Jan.	− 0.43	+ 0.44	− 0.83	+ 0.28	− 0.43
Feb.	− 0.25	+ 1.26	− 0.69	+ 0.37	− 0.43
Mar.	− 0.63	− 0.45	− 0.79	+ 0.54	− 0.46
Apr.	− 0.78	− 1.14	− 0.80	+ 0.76	− 0.50
May	− 0.75	− 0.44	− 0.71	+ 0.79	− 0.53
June	− 0.50	− 0.46	− 0.41	+ 1.51	− 0.56
July	− 0.42	− 0.29	− 0.54	+ 2.54	− 0.59
Aug.	− 0.27	− 0.64	− 0.54	+ 1.44	− 0.63
Sept.	− 0.69	− 0.57	− 0.61	+ 1.48	− 0.66
Oct.	− 0.48	− 0.58	− 0.12	+ 0.89	− 0.69
Nov.	− 0.21	− 0.69	+ 0.24	+ 0.11	− 0.73
Dec.	− 0.01	− 0.78	+ 0.35	− 0.41	− 0.76

TABLE 18

WHOLESALE PRICE INDEX OF THE *STATISTQUE GÉNÉRALE DE LA FRANCE* *

(Percentage deviations from secular trend expressed as percentages of standard deviation)

	1918	1919	1920	1921	1922
Jan.	....	+ 0.49	+ 1.84	+ 0.21	− 1.29
Feb.	....	+ 0.33	+ 2.26	− 0.19	− 1.40
Mar.	....	+ 0.20	+ 2.64	− 0.45	− 1.41
Apr.	....	+ 0.11	+ 3.02	− 0.64	− 1.36
May	....	− 0.04	+ 2.46	− 0.88	− 1.35
June	....	− 0.04	+ 1.64	− 0.96	− 1.29
July	....	+ 0.20	+ 1.62	− 0.93	− 1.31
Aug.	....	+ 0.15	+ 1.65	− 0.95	− 1.27
Sept.	....	+ 0.28	+ 1.90	− 0.83	− 1.32
Oct.	....	+ 0.54	+ 1.54	− 1.01	− 1.25
Nov.	....	+ 0.82	+ 0.97	− 1.03	− 1.21
Dec.	+ 0.62	+ 1.01	+ 0.60	− 1.13	− 1.04

* For the calculation, a straight-line secular trend was fitted to monthly data for a period of 97 months from December 1918 to December 1926. The equation of this line, with origin (0, 0) so chosen that December 1918 represents the zero point

convenience of the reader. What seems most desirable is a statement of the multiple the final ordinate of secular trend is of the original one.

Let y_o = original ordinate at the point $x = 0$.

Let y_n = final ordinate at the point $x = n$.

$$n + 1 = \text{number of items.}$$

Then $\dfrac{y_n}{y_o} = \dfrac{nm + b}{b} = 1 + \dfrac{nm}{b}.$

	1923	1924	1925	1926	1927
Jan.	− 0.81	− 0.07	− 0.21	+ 0.49	+ 0.08
Feb.	− 0.47	+ 0.38	− 0.24	+ 0.48	+ 0.13
Mar.	− 0.48	− 0.08	− 0.28	+ 0.42	+ 0.18
Apr.	− 0.60	− 0.58	− 0.31	+ 0.54	+ 0.12
May	− 0.71	− 0.52	− 0.27	+ 0.83	+ 0.03
June	− 0.72	− 0.48	− 0.10	+ 1.21	− 0.04
July	− 0.76	− 0.36	0.00	+ 1.98	− 0.08
Aug.	− 0.73	− 0.43	− 0.02	+ 1.40	− 0.12
Sept.	− 0.65	− 0.37	− 0.06	+ 1.51	− 0.28
Oct.	− 0.70	− 0.29	+ 0.05	+ 1.19	− 0.40
Nov.	− 0.51	− 0.26	+ 0.31	+ 0.62	− 0.37
Dec.	− 0.38	− 0.25	+ 0.51	+ 0.14	− 0.32

of the abscissas and a zero price level that of the ordinates, was found to be $y = + 3.1x + 312.7$. The data for 1927 were added to the calculation by extending the same line of secular trend to that year. The seasonal movements being but poorly defined, no allowance was made for seasonal variations.

By considering the two monthly series in detail, it is seen (Charts IX and X) that in general their movements show a high degree of similarity. Most of the important as well as many of the minor peaks and troughs of one of the series appear, usually simultaneously, with similar ones in the other. Naturally the movements of exchange (even as weekly averages) were much sharper and of greater range than those of prices. A simultaneous correlation of the two series gave a coefficient of + .845(97). With prices moved one month to the left, the coefficient was + .809(96); and one month to the right, + .812(96). For the period as a whole, therefore, there is no discoverable lag of prices behind exchange or of exchange behind prices.

Since the wholesale price index used in the above comparison is a composite one, being made up partly of the prices of domestic goods and partly of those of imported commodities, it seems desirable to make likewise the comparison of the separate indices with exchange rates. For imported goods' prices and exchange, as for prices in general and exchange, the similarity of the curves is very noticeable (Charts XI and XII). The general movements are, in fact, strikingly alike. Here, as above, there is no discoverable lag in the movements of one series as compared with those of the other. The simultaneous correlation of the two series yielded a

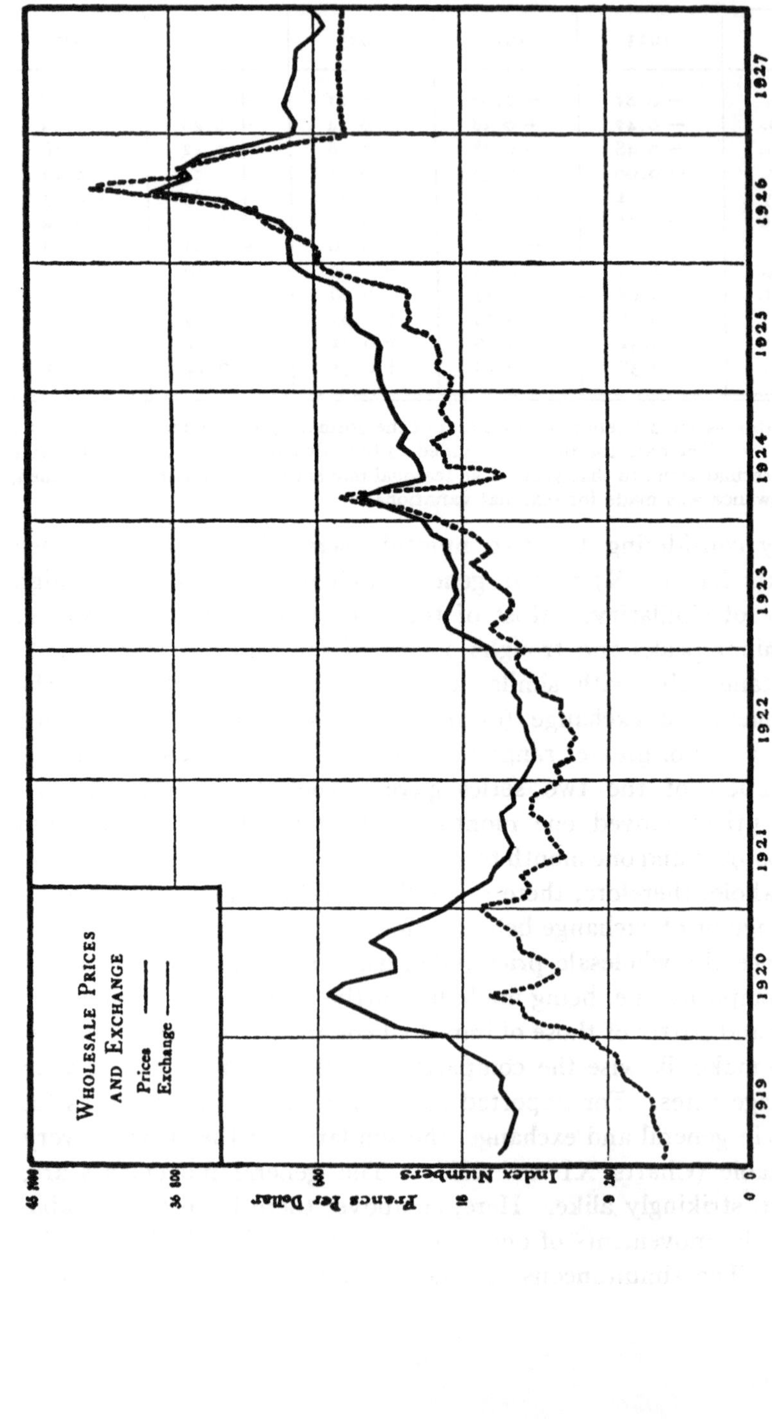
Wholesale Prices and Exchange
Prices
Exchange
1919
1920
1921
1922
1923
1924
1925
1926
1927
Index Numbers
Francs Per Dollar

CHART IX

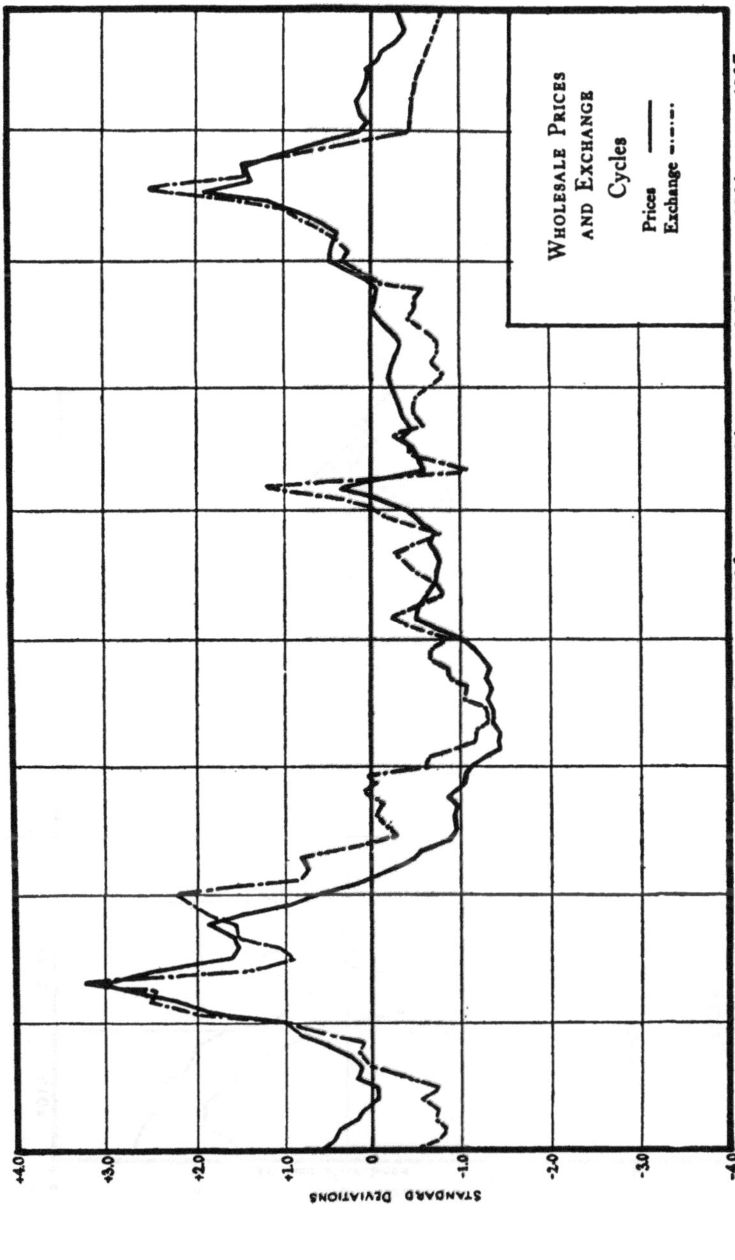
Wholesale Prices
and Exchange
Cycles
Prices
Exchange
1919
1920
1921
1922
1923
1924
1925
1926
1927
+4.0
+3.0
+2.0
+1.0
0
-1.0
-2.0
-3.0
-4.0
Standard Deviations

CHART X

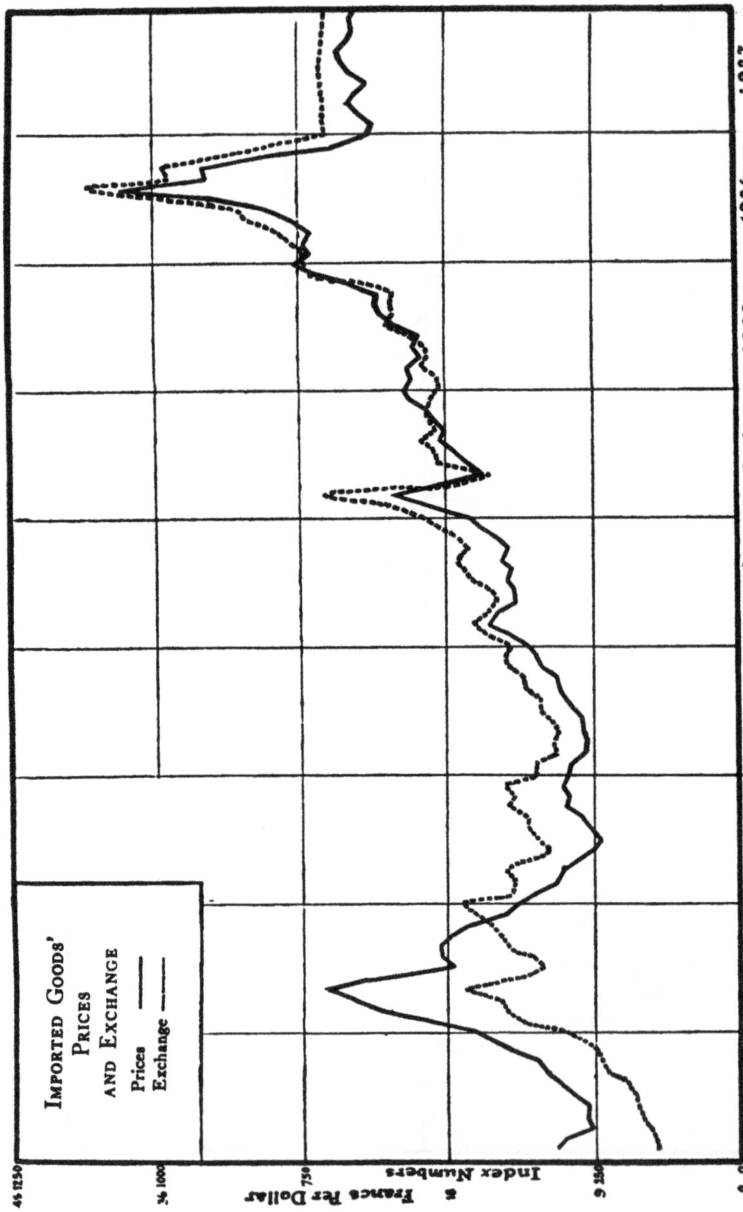
Imported Goods' Prices and Exchange
Prices
Exchange
1919
1920
1921
1922
1923
1924
1925
1926
1927
Index Numbers
Francs Per Dollar

CHART XI

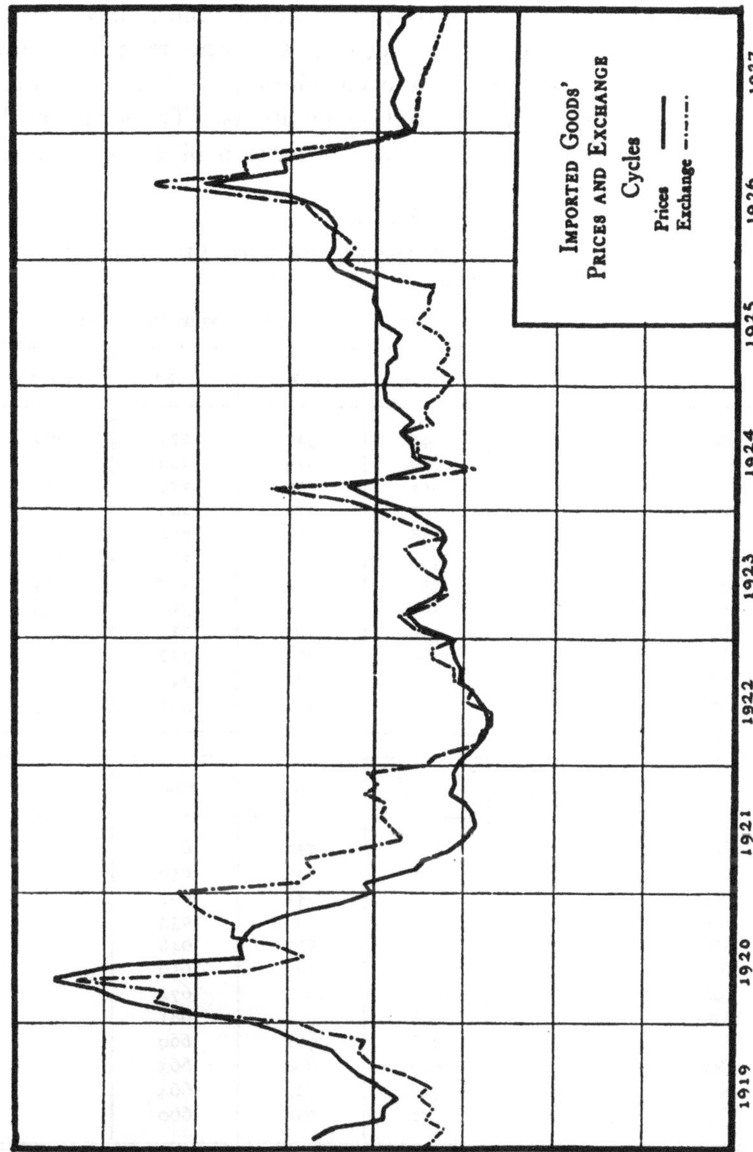
IMPORTED GOODS'
PRICES AND EXCHANGE
Cycles
Prices
Exchange
1919
1920
1921
1922
1923
1924
1925
1926
1927
+4.0
+3.0
+2.0
+1.0
0
-1.0
-2.0
-3.0
-4.0
STANDARD DEVIATIONS

CHART XII

coefficient of + .818(96). With prices moved one month to the left, the coefficient became + .739(97); and one month to the right, + .799(95). The maximum correlation, as before, is that found in the comparison of simultaneous items. The same result was obtained by making a minute comparison of the two series reduced to cycles.

TABLE 19

IMPORTED GOODS' PRICE INDEX OF THE *STATISTIQUE GÉNÉRALE DE LA FRANCE**

(Index numbers based on end-of-month data; base 100 in July 1914)

	1919	1920	1921	1922	1923
Jan.	317	547	349	277	396
Feb.	300	606	314	262	421
Mar.	252	651	306	259	402
Apr.	257	706	279	260	377
May	257	638	255	264	378
June	276	498	247	276	387
July	305	510	256	292	383
Aug.	322	509	266	310	403
Sept.	341	499	295	312	395
Oct.	383	468	292	337	405
Nov.	417	404	297	343	444
Dec.	452	370	288	351	467

	1924	1925	1926	1927	
Jan.	531	558	741	624	
Feb.	598	559	743	650	
Mar.	506	547	741	667	
Apr.	434	553	766	653	
May	463	550	817	646	
June	475	591	883	659	
July	509	609	1074	674	
Aug.	502	618	902	681	
Sept.	520	616	912	669	
Oct.	539	667	808	663	
Nov.	556	726	700	664	
Dec.	561	752	628	660	

* Source: *Bulletin de la Statistique Générale de la France*, April 1926 and following numbers.

The description of the wholesale price index of the *Statistique Générale de la France* (Chap. V, Table 7) applies likewise to the index for imported goods' prices as far as the method of computation and the collection of price data are concerned.

TABLE 20

IMPORTED GOODS' PRICE INDEX OF THE *STATISTIQUE GÉNÉRALE DE LA FRANCE* *

(Percentage deviations from secular trend expressed as percentages of standard deviation)

	1919	1920	1921	1922	1923
Jan.	+ 0.69	+ 2.30	+ 0.15	− 1.05	− 0.51
Feb.	+ 0.43	+ 2.81	− 0.47	− 1.18	− 0.37
Mar.	− 0.18	+ 3.14	− 0.57	− 1.22	− 0.52
Apr.	− 0.17	+ 3.59	− 0.82	− 1.23	− 0.70
May	− 0.22	+ 2.85	− 1.04	− 1.22	− 0.71
June	− 0.06	+ 1.50	− 1.12	− 1.16	− 0.68
July	+ 0.20	+ 1.54	− 1.08	− 1.07	− 0.73
Aug.	+ 0.34	+ 1.48	− 1.02	− 0.97	− 0.63
Sept.	+ 0.48	+ 1.32	− 0.82	− 0.97	− 0.69
Oct.	+ 0.86	+ 1.00	− 0.87	− 0.83	− 0.66
Nov.	+ 1.14	+ 0.39	− 0.86	− 0.81	− 0.45
Dec.	+ 1.44	+ 0.07	− 0.95	− 0.78	− 0.34

	1924	1925	1926	1927	
Jan.	+ 0.02	− 0.13	+ 0.51	− 0.30	
Feb.	+ 0.38	− 0.14	+ 0.50	− 0.19	
Mar.	− 0.18	− 0.23	+ 0.46	− 0.14	
Apr.	− 0.61	− 0.22	+ 0.55	− 0.22	
May	− 0.47	− 0.26	+ 0.77	− 0.27	
June	− 0.42	− 0.07	+ 1.05	− 0.23	
July	− 0.26	0.00	+ 1.91	− 0.18	
Aug.	− 0.32	+ 0.02	+ 1.08	− 0.17	
Sept.	− 0.24	− 0.01	+ 1.10	− 0.24	
Oct.	− 0.16	+ 0.22	+ 0.60	− 0.28	
Nov.	− 0.09	+ 0.49	+ 0.09	− 0.29	
Dec.	− 0.09	+ 0.59	− 0.26	− 0.33	

* For the calculation, a straight-line secular trend was fitted to monthly data for a period of 97 months from January 1919 to January 1927. The equation of this line, with origin (0, 0) so chosen that January 1919 represents the zero point of the abscissas and a zero price level that of the ordinates, was found to be: $y = + 4.5x + 259$. The data for 1927 were added to the calculation by extending the same line of secular trend to that year. The seasonal movements being but poorly defined, no allowance was made for seasonal variations.

The original base (July 1914 = 100) was kept, there being no data available for making the conversion to a 1913 base. Of the 45 articles going to make up the general index, the following 15 enter into the composition of the index of imported goods' prices: maize or Indian corn, rice, coffee, cocoa, copper, tin, lead, zinc, cotton, flax, jute, wool, oxen hides, benzol, nitrate of soda, rubber.

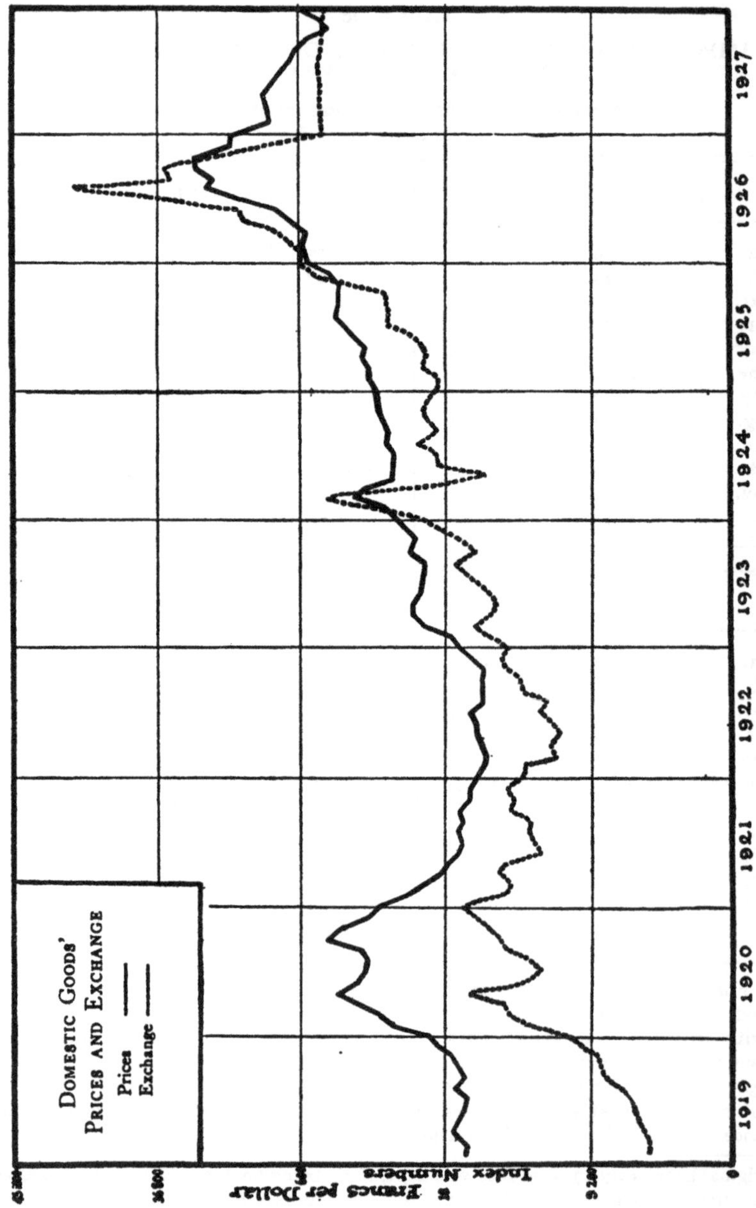
Domestic Goods'
Prices and Exchange
Prices
Exchange
1919
1920
1921
1922
1923
1924
1925
1926
1927
Index Numbers
Francs per Dollar

CHART XIII

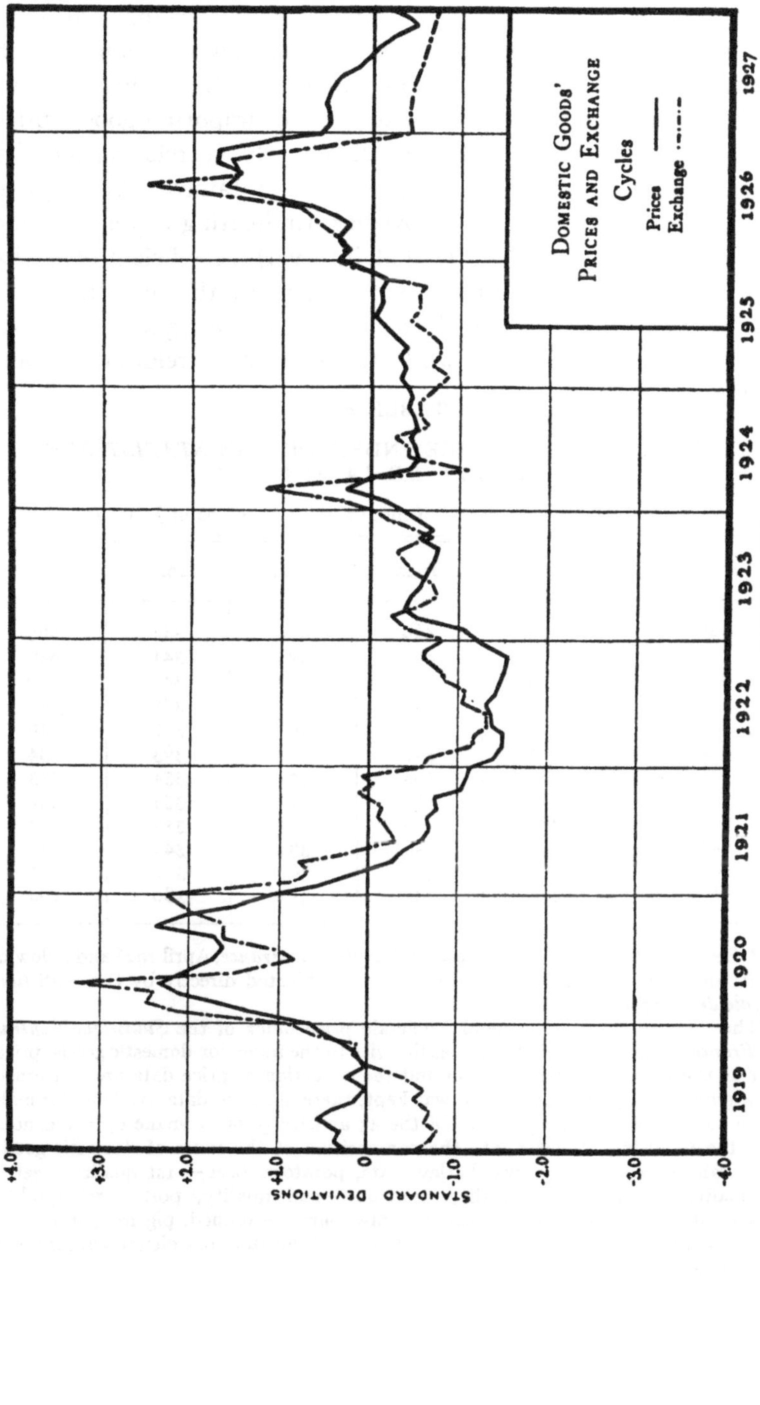
DOMESTIC GOODS'
PRICES AND EXCHANGE
Cycles
Prices
Exchange
1919
1920
1921
1922
1923
1924
1925
1926
1927
+4.0
+3.0
+2.0
+1.0
0
-1.0
-2.0
-3.0
-4.0
STANDARD DEVIATIONS

CHART XIV

In turning, finally, to the comparison of exchange rates and domestic goods' prices, strange as it may seem, it was found that the correspondence of movement was closer than that between either wholesale prices in general and exchange or imported goods' prices and exchange (Charts XIII and XIV). By correlating simultaneously, a coefficient of + .843(96) was obtained. With prices moved one month to the left, however, (indicating a precedence of exchange rates over prices by that interval) a coefficient of + .820 (97) resulted. Shifting prices two months to the left, the coefficient became +.772(96); and one month to the right, + .802(95). It is clear, therefore, that while the highest correlation between

TABLE 21

DOMESTIC GOODS' PRICE INDEX OF THE *STATISTIQUE GÉNÉRALE DE LA FRANCE**

(Index numbers based on end-of-month data; base 100 in July 1914)

	1919	1920	1921	1922	1923
Jan.	375	469	452	344	395
Feb.	374	492	425	341	436
Mar.	393	520	402	344	450
Apr.	385	541	397	353	449
May	374	520	382	357	436
June	368	507	379	363	434
July	384	504	382	354	433
Aug.	374	514	379	354	432
Sept.	382	558	383	350	453
Oct.	393	538	364	349	443
Nov.	412	507	361	368	457
Dec.	421	485	357	380	469

* Sources: *Bulletin de la Statistique Générale de la France*, April 1926 and following issues; for 1922, corrected index numbers communicated directly by the *Statistique Générale de la France*.

The description of the general wholesale price index of the *Statistique Générale de la France* (Chap. V, Table 7) applies likewise to the index for domestic goods' prices as far as the method of computation and the collection of price data are concerned. The original base (July 1914 = 100) was kept, there being no data available for making the conversion to a 1913 base. Of the 45 articles going to make up the general index, the following 26 enter into the composition of the index of domestic goods' prices: wheat, wheat flour, rye, barley, oats, potatoes, beef — 1st quality, beef — 2nd quality, mutton — 1st quality, mutton — 2nd quality, pork — 1st quality, salted meat, butter, dry cheeses, sugar — raw, sugar — refined, pig iron, iron, coal, hemp, silk, leather, tallow, rapeseed oil, linseed oil, alcohol, petroleum, carbonate of soda, lumber.

	1924	1925	1926	1927	
Jan.	490	507	594	640	
Feb.	531	507	597	643	
Mar.	512	512	593	647	
Apr.	475	507	607	648	
May	471	521	639	639	
June	475	533	682	623	
July	481	545	733	611	
Aug.	478	541	722	603	
Sept.	483	540	743	582	
Oct.	490	538	745	564	
Nov.	491	559	698	575	
Dec.	494	587	647	593	

the two series is found by correlating simultaneous items, the coefficient was but little reduced by comparing exchange rates of one month with prices of the following. Accordingly, the result was

TABLE 22

DOMESTIC GOODS' PRICE INDEX OF THE *STATISTIQUE GÉNÉRALE DE LA FRANCE* *

(Percentage deviations from secular trend expressed as percentages of standard deviation)

	1919	1920	1921	1922	1923
Jan.	+ 0.35	+ 1.39	+ 0.58	− 1.42	− 1.04
Feb.	+ 0.30	+ 1.70	+ 0.12	− 1.48	− 0.53
Mar.	+ 0.58	+ 2.12	− 0.26	− 1.47	− 0.37
Apr.	+ 0.40	+ 2.39	− 0.36	− 1.36	− 0.42
May	+ 0.16	+ 2.01	− 0.62	− 1.35	− 0.61
June	+ 0.02	+ 1.74	− 0.69	− 1.28	− 0.67
July	+ 0.24	+ 1.65	− 0.69	− 1.43	− 0.71
Aug.	+ 0.03	+ 1.75	− 0.76	− 1.46	− 0.75
Sept.	+ 0.12	+ 2.40	− 0.74	− 1.53	− 0.51
Oct.	+ 0.26	+ 2.03	− 1.04	− 1.58	− 0.66
Nov.	+ 0.53	+ 1.51	− 1.12	− 1.35	− 0.52
Dec.	+ 0.64	+ 1.11	− 1.19	− 1.21	− 0.39

* For the calculation, a straight line secular trend was fitted to monthly data for a period of 97 months from January 1919 to January 1927. The equation of this line, with origin (0, 0) so chosen that January 1919 represents the zero point of the abscissas and a zero price level that of the ordinates, was found to be: $y = + 2.5 x + 355$. The data for 1927 were added to the calculation by extending the same line of secular trend to that year. The seasonal movements being but poorly defined, no allowance was made for seasonal variations.

TABLE 22 (Continued)

	1924	1925	1926	1927	
Jan.	−0.16	−0.30	+0.36	+0.51	
Feb.	+0.32	−0.33	+0.37	+0.52	
Mar.	+0.05	−0.30	+0.29	+0.53	
Apr.	−0.43	−0.38	+0.42	+0.52	
May	−0.52	−0.25	+0.74	+0.40	
June	−0.49	−0.14	+1.18	+0.19	
July	−0.45	−0.03	+1.70	+0.05	
Aug.	−0.51	−0.10	+1.55	−0.06	
Sept.	−0.48	−0.14	+1.74	−0.30	
Oct.	−0.42	−0.19	+1.74	−0.51	
Nov.	−0.44	+0.03	+1.19	−0.42	
Dec.	−0.43	+0.30	+0.62	−0.26	

tested by a careful point-to-point comparison of the two series reduced to cycles. Such a procedure yielded twenty-three points of comparison which were hardly mistakable. Of these, twelve matched simultaneously, eight indicated a lag of prices behind exchange of one month, and three a similar lag of two months. It would seem, therefore, that there was a lag in price movements, but one averaging somewhat less than a month.

A study for individual periods was next made in order to determine whether any variations in the length of the lag could be discovered. Accordingly, the entire period was broken into two sub-periods, 1919–1922 and 1923–1926. New trends were not fitted for the sub-periods, but the products entering into the computation of the correlation coefficient for the entire period were summed separately for each sub-period, first with items compared simultaneously, then with lags allowed both ways. And, in order to make proper allowance for the varying number of items, each sum thus obtained was divided by the number of products entering into that sum.[8] By proceeding in this way it was discovered that for the first sub-period a comparison of simultaneous items yielded almost exactly the same index as when prices were displaced one month to the right (indicating their precedence of dollar exchange

[8] The exact method of making these computations is discussed on p. 119 and accompanying footnote 15.

by that interval). On the other hand, by pushing prices one month to the left (indicating a precedence of exchange rates by the same interval), a considerable reduction appeared.[9] It seems clear, therefore, either that during most of this period dollar exchange and domestic goods' prices were moving nearly together or else that prices were in general preceding exchange by approximately one month.

Similar indices were next made for the last four years of the original period, 1923–1926. In that case the maximum was obtained by the comparison of items with prices pushed one month to the left. Pushing them two months to the left, however, did not materially reduce the index, which remained above that for the simultaneous comparison. Displacing prices one month to the right, on the other hand, very greatly lowered the index.[10] Hence, it appears that for that period the lag of prices behind dollar exchange rates averaged more than one month but not as much as two.

In the comparison of wholesale prices in general and circulation for the period 1915–1926,[11] the correspondence in their long-time movements was found to be reasonably close. The linear secular trend, fitted by the method of least squares to monthly circulation data in millions of francs and with origin at December 1914, is $y = 261.5\,x + 14020$ $\left(1 + \frac{nm}{b} = 3.69\right)$, while that for prices measured in percentages of the 1913 level and with the same

[9] These sums, when divided by the number of items involved, were:
For the comparison of

Simultaneous items	+ 1.244
Items with prices moved one month to right	+ 1.248
Items with prices moved two months to right	+ 1.220
Items with prices moved three months to right	+ 1.162
Items with prices moved one month to left	+ 1.174

[10] The indices obtained are as follows:
For the comparison of

Simultaneous items	+ .443
Items with prices pushed one month to left	+ .459
Items with prices pushed two months to left	+ .444
Items with prices pushed one month to right	+ .365

[11] The tables of figures and the descriptions of the data used may be found in Chap. V, those of wholesale prices, Table 7, and those of note circulation, Table 9.

origin is $y = 3.27\,x + 148.3$ $(1 + \frac{nm}{b} = 4.18)$. It is apparent, therefore, that the increase in the ordinates of secular trend of prices during the period was by a greater percentage of itself than was that of circulation.[12] More will be said with regard to the relative increases in the two quantities in the theoretical chapter to follow (Chapter XI).

With respect to the month-to-month movements, however, two important differences are obvious. It is immediately noted (Charts XV and XVI) that the fluctuations of prices were much wider and sharper than those of circulation. On close observa-

TABLE 23

WHOLESALE PRICE INDEX OF THE *STATISTIQUE GÉNÉRALE DE LA FRANCE* *

(Percentage deviations from secular trend expressed as percentages of standard deviation)

	1914	1915	1916	1917	1918	1919	1920
Jan.	− 0.62	− 1.11	− 0.50	− 0.33	+ 0.85	+ 0.67	+ 2.09
Feb.	− 0.72	− 1.03	− 0.44	− 0.17	+ 0.90	+ 0.48	+ 2.55
Mar.	− 0.85	− 0.95	− 0.30	− 0.17	+ 0.97	+ 0.35	+ 2.96
Apr.	− 1.01	− 0.92	− 0.25	+ 0.18	+ 1.02	+ 0.23	+ 3.37
May	− 1.08	− 0.94	− 0.35	+ 0.28	+ 0.98	+ 0.06	+ 2.75
June	− 1.19	− 0.95	− 0.48	+ 0.42	+ 0.79	+ 0.06	+ 1.85
July	− 1.35	− 0.96	− 0.64	+ 0.39	+ 0.88	+ 0.33	+ 1.83
Aug.	− 1.28	− 1.02	− 0.68	+ 0.36	+ 1.04	+ 0.26	+ 1.85
Sept.	− 1.35	− 0.98	− 0.68	+ 0.49	+ 1.06	+ 0.40	+ 2.13
Oct.	− 1.40	− 0.86	− 0.65	+ 0.49	+ 1.07	+ 0.68	+ 1.73
Nov.	− 1.39	− 0.72	− 0.61	+ 0.61	+ 0.97	+ 0.98	+ 1.11
Dec.	− 1.34	− 0.68	− 0.54	+ 0.75	+ 0.82	+ 1.19	+ 0.70

* For the calculation, a straight-line secular trend was fitted to monthly data for a period of 145 months from December 1914 to December 1926. The equation of this line, with origin (0, 0) so chosen that December 1914 represents the zero point of the abscissas and a zero price level that of the ordinates, was found to be $y = 3.27\,x + 148.3$. The data for 1914 and 1927 were added to the calculation by extending the same line of secular trend to those years. The seasonal movements being but poorly defined, no allowance was made for seasonal variations.

[12] It is recognized that such a comparison is not altogether satisfactory and would not be necessary had the circulation data been reduced to 1913 relatives. Estimates of 1913 circulation are so undependable, however, that their use was avoided.

	1921	1922	1923	1924	1925	1926	1927
Jan.	+0.27	−1.38	−0.88	−0.11	−0.28	+0.46	−0.01
Feb.	−0.17	−1.50	−0.52	+0.37	−0.31	+0.44	+0.05
Mar.	−0.45	−1.51	−0.53	−0.12	−0.35	+0.38	+0.10
Apr.	−0.65	−1.47	−0.67	−0.65	−0.39	+0.51	+0.04
May	−0.93	−1.46	−0.79	−0.60	−0.35	+0.81	−0.05
June	−1.02	−1.39	−0.80	−0.56	−0.16	+1.22	−0.13
July	−0.98	−1.42	−0.84	−0.43	−0.06	+2.03	
Aug.	−1.01	−1.37	−0.81	−0.50	−0.09	+1.41	
Sept.	−0.87	−1.42	−0.72	−0.45	−0.13	+1.53	
Oct.	−1.07	−1.36	−0.79	−0.36	−0.01	+1.19	
Nov.	−1.09	−1.22	−0.58	−0.33	+0.26	+0.58	
Dec.	−1.20	−1.14	−0.45	−0.33	+0.48	+0.06	

tion it is further seen that there was a consistent lag in the movements of circulation behind those of prices. Moreover, it appears that the length of the lag was not constant but varied considerably from time to time.

A comparison of synchronous items of the two series for the entire period December 1914 to December 1926 yielded a coefficient of correlation of +.670(145). With circulation pushed one month to the right, the coefficient was reduced to +.643(144). Pushing it one month to the left, on the other hand, raised the coefficient to +.682(144); pushing it two months to the left gave +.687(143); three months to the left, +.691(142); and four months, +.693(141). Displacing circulation by more than four months to the left lowered the coefficient.

In order to determine whether or not the coefficient might be raised by varying the lags within the period, each series was broken into four sub-periods: (1) December 1914 to April 1920; (2) May 1920 to March 1922; (3) April 1922 to June 1925; and (4) July 1925 to December 1926.[13] The sums of the products involved in the correlation process *for the entire period* were then

[13] The division into sub-periods was made after a painstaking point-to-point comparison of the movements of the two series and secured, in general, periods in which the lags in the movements of circulation behind those of prices seemed to show a fair degree of constancy. Moreover, it will be noted that the sub-periods chosen break both curves into intervals of time in which the general movements are the same. Thus the first is a period of steady rise, the second a period of decline, the third one of gradual rise, and the fourth one of sharp rise and subsequent abrupt fall.

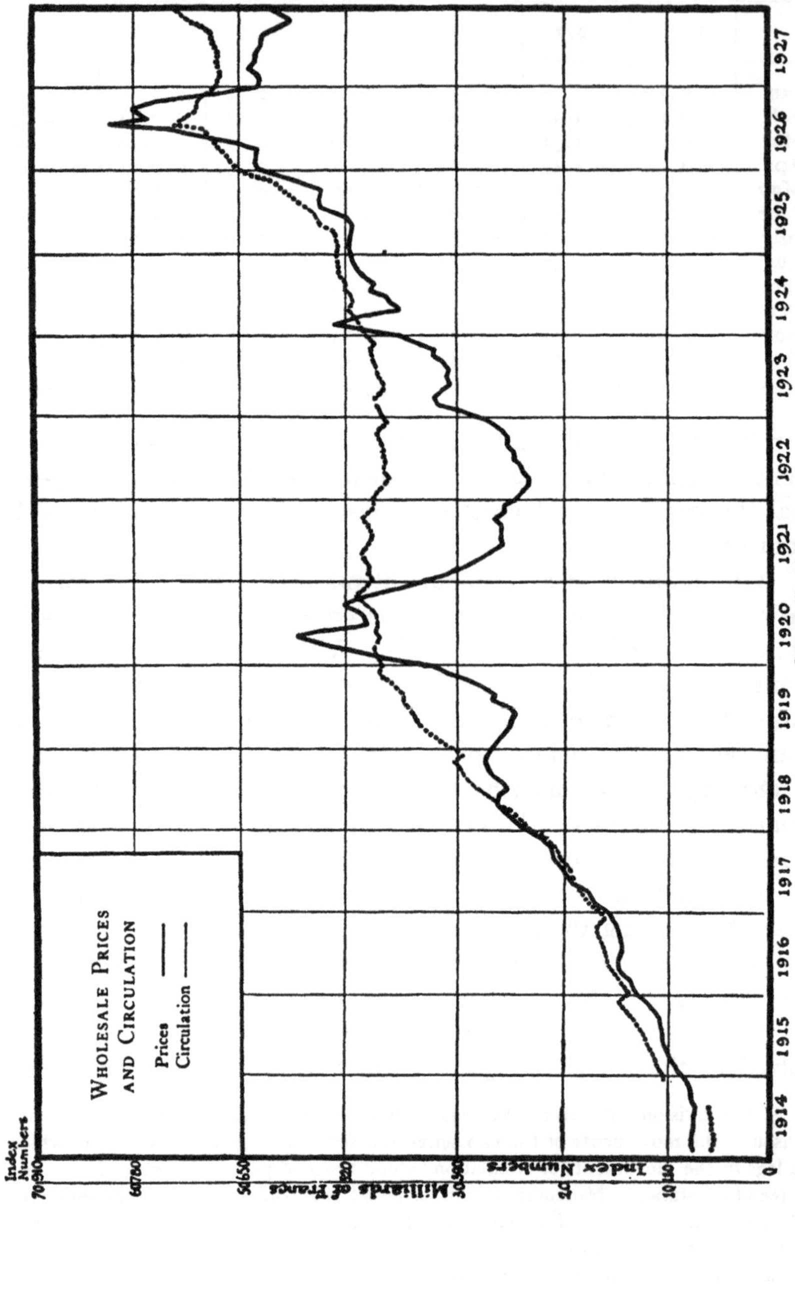

Wholesale Prices
and Circulation
Prices
Circulation
Index Numbers
Milliards of Francs
1914
1915
1916
1917
1918
1919
1920
1921
1922
1923
1924
1925
1926
1927

CHART XV

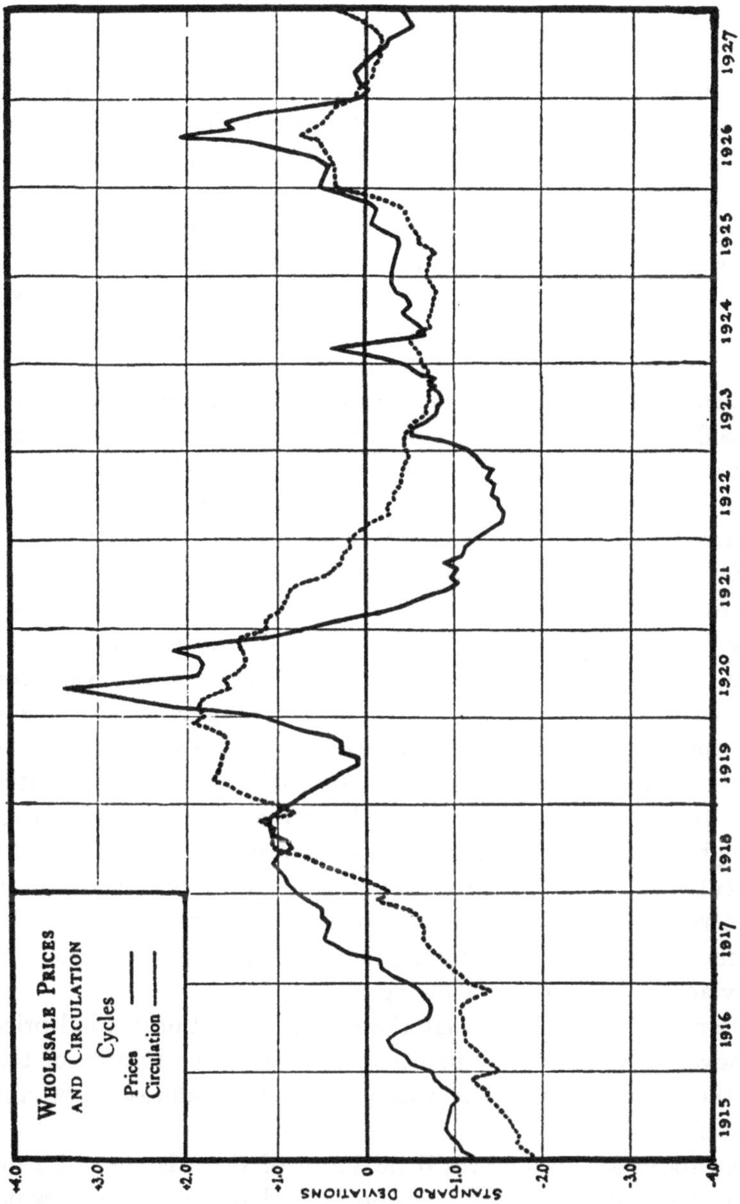
Wholesale Prices
and Circulation
Cycles
Prices
Circulation
Standard Deviations
+4.0
+3.0
+2.0
+1.0
0
-1.0
-2.0
-3.0
-4.0
1915
1916
1917
1918
1919
1920
1921
1922
1923
1924
1925
1926
1927

CHART XVI

made for each sub-period with lags allowed varying from zero to seven months in each. In this way it was discovered that the maximum coefficient for the entire period could be obtained by pushing prices four months to the left for the period December 1914 to June 1925 and by comparing the items simultaneously thereafter. The resulting coefficient was + .711(141).

From these two sets of correlations it seems, therefore, that there was a consistent lag in circulation throughout most of the period. It appears also that this lag either disappeared completely or else became considerably less than one month during the last year and one-half of the period for which the data were analyzed. In view of the fact, however, that the variations in the coefficients of correlation obtained were relatively slight and because, too, it is clearly recognized that, even when the number of items compared are as numerous as they were in the above comparisons, the correlation process provides at best but a crude measure of similarity of widely fluctuating time series, a minute point-to-point comparison of the two original series was considered indispensable. This study indicated clearly that for the war period, December 1914 to December 1918, there was a very considerable, but variable, lag in circulation ranging from three to seven months. During the transition year 1919 the two series moved so radically differently that no satisfactory determination of lags proved possible. Again in the period 1920–1921, however, although the price series moved much more widely than did that of circulation, a fairly clearly defined lag of six or seven months is discernible. By 1922 the lag appears to have been somewhat shortened, and the shortening process seems to have been distinctly accelerated in the following two years.

After the beginning of 1925 the lag of circulation behind prices was never more than two months; and after the middle of that year the movements of the two series appear almost invariably synchronous.

The above analysis leaves little doubt of the existence of a distinct but variable lag of circulation behind prices, but one which by the latter part of 1922 had become very greatly shortened and by the middle of 1925 practically eliminated so far as monthly data can indicate. To establish these results more conclusively, however, another set of correlations was run for each of three selected sub-periods. These periods, which, for the purposes of the calculations, necessarily differ from those chosen above, were: (1) December 1914 to December 1918; (2) December 1919 to December 1924; and (3) December 1924 to December 1926. The year 1919 was omitted, as explained above, because of the radically different movements of the two series during that year. Individual linear secular trends were fitted by the method of least squares to the data for each period, and separate correlations made of the percentage deviations from secular trends resulting from each pair of calculations. An exception was made with respect to correlation for the middle period where, as was observed above, the lags are evidently of greatly varying lengths. In this case, the secular trends, as for the other sub-periods, were fitted for the entire period, but in computing the correlation coefficient the lags in the sub-periods 1920–1921 and 1922–1924 were each

TABLE 24

WHOLESALE PRICE INDEX OF THE *STATISTIQUE GÉNÉRALE* DE LA FRANCE*

(Percentage deviations from secular trend expressed as percentages of standard deviation)

	1914	1915	1916	1917	1918
Jan.	......	+ 2.34	+ 0.29	− 1.28	+ 0.60
Feb.	......	+ 2.17	+ 0.26	− 0.97	+ 0.65
Mar.	......	+ 2.00	+ 0.46	− 1.08	+ 0.75
Apr.	......	+ 1.65	+ 0.42	− 0.22	+ 0.78
May	......	+ 1.17	− 0.08	− 0.06	+ 0.60
June	......	+ 0.74	− 0.66	+ 0.22	+ 0.02
July	......	+ 0.37	− 1.35	0.00	+ 0.15
Aug.	......	− 0.14	− 1.62	− 0.20	+ 0.49
Sept.	......	− 0.31	− 1.77	+ 0.05	+ 0.46
Oct.	......	− 0.17	− 1.82	− 0.05	+ 0.42
Nov.	......	+ 0.05	− 1.85	+ 0.17	+ 0.09
Dec.	+ 1.92	− 0.06	− 1.75	+ 0.46	− 0.37

* For the calculation, a straight-line secular trend was fitted to monthly data for a period of 49 months from December 1914 to December 1918. The equation of this line, with origin (0, 0) so chosen that December 1914 represents the zero point of the abscissas and a zero price level that of the ordinates, was found to be $y = + 5.48\,x + 98.2$. No allowance was made for seasonal variations.

chosen so as to make the sums of the products entering into the correlation computation in each case a maximum. Again, on account of the estimated big lag in circulation during the first period (December 1914 to December 1918), the secular trend for circulation during that period was fitted to a series beginning just five months (the estimated lag) later than that for prices. During the last period, when the movements of the two series were evidently almost synchronous, no such refinement of method was needed.

TABLE 25

NOTE CIRCULATION OF THE BANK OF FRANCE *

(Percentage deviations from secular trend expressed as percentages of standard deviation)

	1915	1916	1917	1918	1919
Jan.	......	+ 0.39	− 1.00	− 0.66	+ 0.59
Feb.	......	+ 0.33	− 0.94	− 0.51	+ 0.64
Mar.	......	+ 0.33	− 0.92	− 0.24	+ 0.86
Apr.	......	+ 0.25	− 0.87	+ 0.06	+ 0.73
May	+ 2.43	+ 0.03	− 0.89	+ 0.16	+ 0.63
June	+ 2.14	− 0.07	− 0.88	+ 0.60	......
July	+ 1.93	− 0.27	− 1.02	+ 0.52	......
Aug.	+ 2.80	− 0.34	− 1.06	+ 0.48	......
Sept.	+ 1.50	− 0.51	− 1.10	+ 0.39	......
Oct.	+ 1.53	− 0.88	− 0.95	+ 0.52	......
Nov.	+ 1.63	− 1.33	− 0.61	− 0.09	......
Dec.	+ 0.30	− 1.07	− 0.78	+ 0.25	......

* For the calculation, a straight-line secular trend was fitted to monthly data for a period of 49 months from May 1915 to May 1919. The equation of this line, with origin (0, 0) so chosen that May 1915 represents the zero point of the abscissas and a zero volume of note circulation that of the ordinates, was found to be $y = + 471.0x + 9739$, m being + 471.0 and b, 9739 millions of francs. The correction for seasonal movements was made by using the indices of seasonal variation calculated for the period 1915–1926.

In the first period, December 1914 to December 1918, the coefficient of correlation, with circulation pushed five months to the left, was + .837(49). With a lag of six months allowed, the coefficient became + .793(48); and with one of four months, + .790 (48). It is very clear, therefore, that during this period the movements of circulation lagged in general [14] approximately five months behind those of prices.

[14] There is no accurate terminology in use to describe the type of average lag thus indicated by the correlation process.

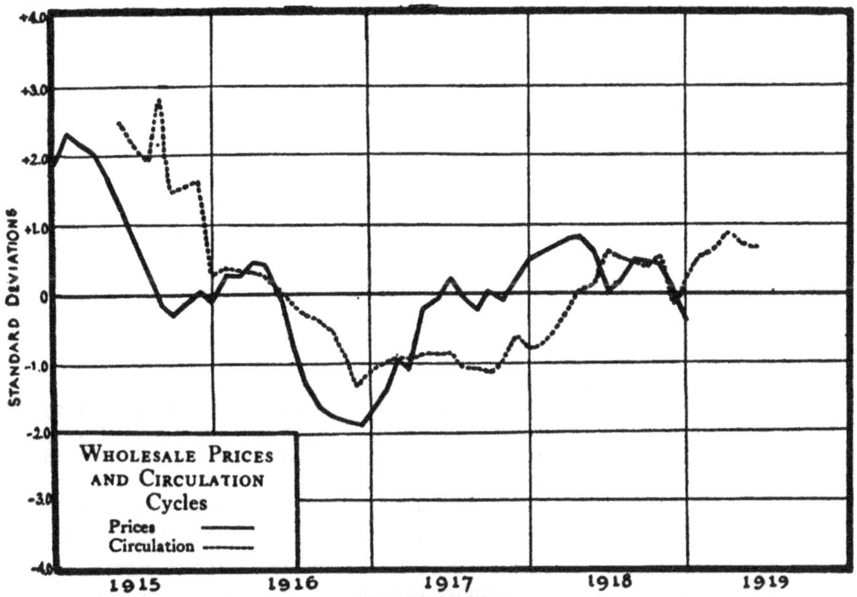

CHART XVII

TABLE 26

WHOLESALE PRICE INDEX OF THE *STATISTIQUE GÉNÉRALE DE LA FRANCE* *

(Percentage deviations from secular trend expressed as percentages of standard deviation)

	1919	1920	1921	1922	1923	1924
Jan.	......	+ 0.98	− 0.10	− 1.34	− 0.42	+ 0.92
Feb.	......	+ 1.44	− 0.49	− 1.43	+ 0.03	+ 1.56
Mar.	......	+ 1.86	− 0.71	− 1.42	+ 0.05	+ 0.99
Apr.	......	+ 2.30	− 0.88	− 1.34	− 0.07	+ 0.36
May	......	+ 1.80	− 1.11	− 1.30	− 0.17	+ 0.46
June	......	+ 1.05	− 1.17	− 1.20	− 0.15	+ 0.55
July	......	+ 1.08	− 1.11	− 1.20	− 0.18	+ 0.74
Aug.	......	+ 1.15	− 1.10	− 1.12	− 0.10	+ 0.68
Sept.	......	+ 1.46	− 0.94	− 1.15	+ 0.03	+ 0.79
Oct.	......	+ 1.15	− 1.10	− 1.05	− 0.01	+ 0.94
Nov.	......	+ 0.61	− 1.10	− 0.86	+ 0.28	+ 1.02
Dec.	+ 0.15	+ 0.27	− 1.18	− 0.74	+ 0.48	+ 1.06

* For the calculation, a straight-line secular trend was fitted to monthly data for a period of 61 months from December 1919 to December 1924, the equation of this line, with origin (0, 0) so chosen that December 1919 represents the zero point of the abscissas and a zero price level that of the ordinates, was found to be $y = + .21 x + 411.6$. No allowance was made for seasonal variations.

TABLE 27

NOTE CIRCULATION OF THE BANK OF FRANCE *

(Percentage deviations from secular trend expressed as percentages of standard deviation)

	1919	1920	1921	1922	1923	1924
Jan.	......	+0.85	+0.82	−0.62	−0.59	+0.32
Feb.	......	+1.00	+0.65	−0.91	−0.47	+0.68
Mar.	......	+0.59	+0.74	−1.76	−0.53	+1.32
Apr.	......	+0.26	+0.71	−1.47	−1.15	+1.12
May	......	+0.76	+0.76	−1.53	−1.24	+0.82
June	......	+0.53	+0.21	−1.35	−0.97	+1.06
July	......	+0.29	−0.59	−1.53	−1.12	+1.06
Aug.	......	+0.56	−0.62	−1.44	−0.88	+1.09
Sept.	......	+0.91	−0.76	−1.26	−0.74	+1.09
Oct.	......	+1.24	−0.56	−1.18	−0.71	+1.18
Nov.	......	+1.56	−0.68	−1.35	−0.56	+1.71
Dec.	+0.76	+0.56	−0.41	−0.76	+0.18	+1.97

* For the calculation, a straight-line secular trend was fitted to monthly data for a period of 61 months from December 1919 to December 1924. The equation of this line, with origin (0, 0) so chosen that December 1919 represents the zero point of the abscissas and a zero volume of note circulation that of the ordinates, was found to be $y = + 28.7\,x + 36793$, m being + 28.7 and b, 36793 millions of francs. The correction for seasonal movements was made by using the indices of seasonal variation calculated for the period 1915–1926.

For the second sub-period, December 1919 to December 1924, a comparison of synchronous items yields a coefficient of correlation of + .694(61). A study of the movements of the two series, as explained above, seems to indicate, however, a distinct lag of circulation behind prices and a lag much longer for the first two years than for the latter three. The problem, therefore, resolved itself into a separate determination of the lag for each of the two intervals. The natural procedure would have been to break the sub-period under discussion into two additional sub-periods, to fit secular trends to each of the series for each of these new sub-periods, and to compute separate correlation coefficients. Such an attack proved infeasible, however, because of the extraordinarily wide movement of prices as compared with those of circulation, movements which distorted completely the two- and three-year linear trends which would have had to be used. Consequently, another device was employed. The secular trends, as

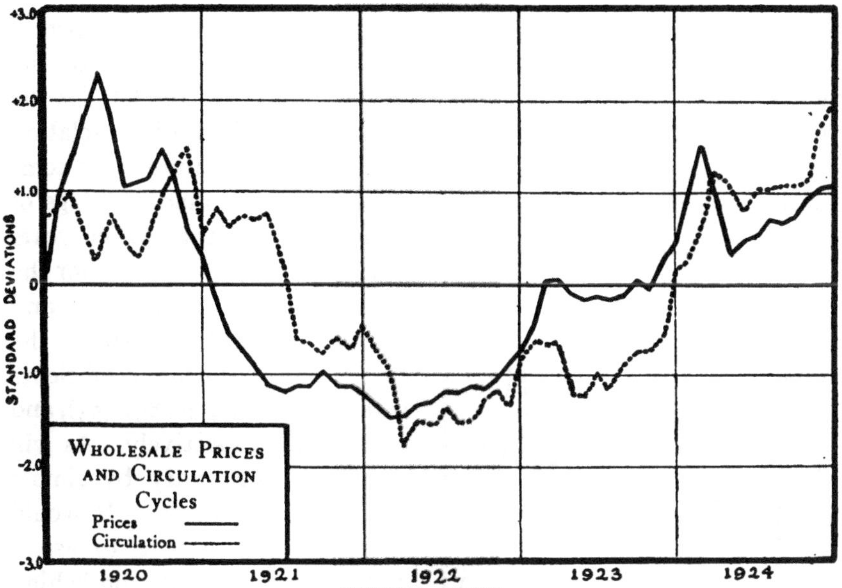

CHART XVIII

noted above, were fitted to each of the two series for the entire sub-period December 1919 to December 1924. Then, dividing the sub-period into two further sub-periods (1920–1921 and 1922–1924) and proceeding to note separately for each of these new sub-periods the sums of the products entering into the correlation computation for the entire period, different lags were allowed with a view to determining what displacement of circulation for each sub-period would yield the maximum coefficient of correlation for the entire five-year period 1920–1924.[15] In this manner it was

[15] The actual computation consisted of making for each sub-period first simultaneously, and then with various lags, the sums of the products entering into the correlation calculation for the entire period 1920–1924, these sums being then divided by the number of item-comparisons made in each case. The results (*which are not correlation coefficients*) were as follows:

For the period 1920–1921

For the comparison of

Simultaneous items	+ .483
Items with circulation pushed six months to the left	+ .827
Items with circulation pushed seven months to the left	+ .833
Items with circulation pushed eight months to the left	+ .750

established that the maximum coefficient for the entire sub-period could be obtained by pushing circulation seven months to the left for the years 1920 and 1921 and one month to the left for the remaining three years. The resulting coefficient of correlation was + .862(53), as compared with that for the simultaneous comparison of + .694(61). Computations were also made for lags of six months for the earlier years and one for the later; six for the earlier and two for the later; and seven for the earlier and two for the later. The resulting coefficients were + .859(54), + .851 (53), and + .853(52) respectively. As will be noted, they vary by almost negligible differences. It would certainly not be safe to assert that the lag of circulation behind prices was in general seven months for 1920 and 1921 and one month for 1922, 1923, and 1924, as opposed to six and one, six and two, or even seven and two. Undoubtedly it would be more nearly correct to say that the lag in circulation was between six and seven months on the average[16] for the earlier two years and between one and two for the later three. Furthermore, it should be remarked that the lag probably does not change abruptly from six or seven months to one or two. In fact, 1922, which appears to be the transition year, seems to show lags of from five

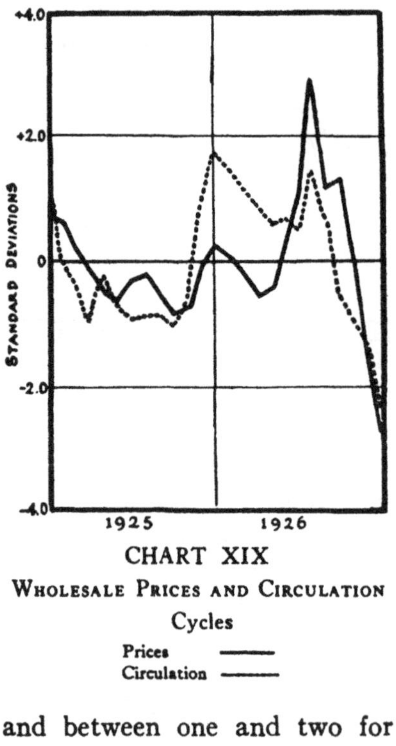

CHART XIX

WHOLESALE PRICES AND CIRCULATION Cycles

Prices ———
Circulation ---------

For the period 1922–1924

For the comparison of

Simultaneous items	+ .841
Items with circulation pushed one month to the left	+ .877
Items with circulation pushed two months to the left	+ .864

[16] *Cf.* footnote 14.

to two months. In the process of allowing for the different lags during the two periods, however, half of that year was dropped necessarily from the computations.

Finally, with respect to the period December 1924 to December 1926, the maximum coefficient resulted from a comparison of simultaneous items. In magnitude it is + .646(25). With circulation moved one month to the left, however, it became + .236 (24); and one month to the right, + .505(24). It seems entirely certain, therefore, that during this last sub-period any lag of circulation behind prices or of prices behind circulation was one of less than a month.

In summary of the results thus obtained with regard to the order of movement of exchange rates, prices, and circulation, the following inductive conclusions may be set forth.

1. With respect to the movements of dollar exchange rates as compared with those of wholesale prices:

TABLE 28

WHOLESALE PRICE INDEX OF THE *STATISTIQUE GÉNÉRALE DE LA FRANCE**

(Percentage deviations from secular trend expressed as percentages of standard deviation)

	1924	1925	1926
Jan.	......	+0.61	+0.02
Feb.	......	+0.26	−0.21
Mar.	......	−0.12	−0.56
Apr.	......	−0.47	−0.39
May	......	−0.59	+0.20
June	......	−0.27	+1.05
July	......	−0.20	+2.89
Aug.	......	−0.48	+1.18
Sept.	......	−0.80	+1.29
Oct.	......	−0.67	+0.30
Nov.	......	−0.11	−1.30
Dec.	+0.74	+0.27	−2.67

* For the calculation, a straight-line secular trend was fitted to monthly data for a period of 25 months from December 1924 to December 1926. The equation of this line, with origin (0, 0) so chosen that December 1924 represents the zero point of the abscissas and a zero price level that of the ordinates, was found to be $y = +11.51x + 483.3$. No allowance was made for seasonal variations.

TABLE 29

NOTE CIRCULATION OF THE BANK OF FRANCE *

(Percentage deviations from secular trend expressed as percentages of standard deviation)

	1924	1925	1926
Jan.	......	+0.11	+1.50
Feb.	......	−0.32	+1.18
Mar.	......	−0.96	+0.86
Apr.	......	−0.18	+0.61
May	......	−0.64	+0.71
June	......	−0.86	+0.54
July	......	−0.82	+1.64
Aug.	......	−0.82	+0.71
Sept.	......	−0.96	−0.43
Oct.	......	−0.61	−0.82
Nov.	......	+0.61	−1.39
Dec.	+0.96	+1.71	−2.25

* For the calculation, a straight-line secular trend was fitted to monthly data for a period of 25 months from December 1924 to December 1926. The equation of this line, with origin (0,0) so chosen that December 1924 represents the zero point of the abscissas and a zero volume of note circulation that of the ordinates, was found to be $y = +688.2x + 40025$, m being $+688.2$ and b, 40025 millions of francs. The correction for seasonal movements was made by using the indices of seasonal variation calculated for the period 1915–1926.

(*a*) For the period 1919–1922 it appears either that dollar exchange and domestic goods' prices were moving nearly together or else that prices were in general preceding exchange by approximately one month.

(*b*) For the period 1923–1926 a clear lag of the prices of domestic goods behind dollar exchange rates was discovered by the use of the correlation process, the lag averaging approximately one month. A point-to-point comparison, however, showed the lag to be sometimes one month, sometimes two months, and frequently zero or less than one month.

(*c*) The correlation process indicated no lag either way between the movements of the series of dollar exchange rates and that of imported goods' prices. A point-to-point analysis showed a few lags of one or two months of prices behind exchange, but in general the lag was either zero or less than one month.

(*d*) No lag either way was indicated by correlation coefficients between the general index of wholesale prices and dollar exchange rates. A point-to-point comparison seemed to indicate, nevertheless, a lag of prices behind dollar exchange rates of somewhat less than a month.

2. With respect to the movements of wholesale prices as compared with those of the note circulation of the Bank of France:

(*a*) There was apparent a distinct lag of circulation behind prices for the entire period December 1914 to December 1926 considered as a whole. Both correlation coefficients and point-to-point comparisons indicated considerable lags.

(*b*) For the period December 1924 to December 1926 no consistent lag either way was indicated by correlation coefficients. A point-to-point comparison, however, showed a few cases of one- or two-month lags of circulation behind prices. It would seem safe to conclude that there was a lag averaging somewhat less than one month.[17]

(*c*) The lag of circulation behind prices for the period December 1914 to December 1918, while somewhat variable, clearly averaged approximately five months.

(*d*) For the period 1920–1921 the lag of circulation behind prices was apparently between six and seven months.

(*e*) For the period 1922–1924 the lag of circulation behind prices, clearly evidenced by both correlation coefficients and point-to-point comparisons, averaged between one and two months.[18]

It remains to explain the hardly disputable facts revealed by the foregoing statistical analysis.

First, with regard to the movements of exchange rates and prices, although there was no discoverable lag one way or the other

[17] Circulation data for the early months of 1925 are disturbed by reason of the misrepresentations in the balance sheets of the Bank of France at that time.

[18] Attention is called to the investigation of M. Albert Aftalion, Professor in the Faculty of Law, University of Paris, in his book, *Monnaie, Prix, et Change* (Paris, Recueil Sirey, 1927). With respect to exchange and prices, the author concludes that prices in France have in general followed the movements in the external purchasing power of the franc; and, as regards prices and circulation, his results indicate that circulation has lagged on the average five months behind prices for the years 1920–1921 and two months during the years 1922–1924.

between dollar exchange rates and either imported goods' prices or wholesale prices in general, there was a clear lag of at least one month of domestic goods' prices behind exchange rates during the four-year period 1923–1926 and perhaps a very slight precedence of less than one month during the earlier period 1919–1922. Certainly it was to be expected that any lag of prices behind exchange rates or of exchange rates behind prices would appear more clearly in the movements of domestic goods' prices. As was pointed out in the early part of this chapter, any considerable differences between prices in two countries, one of which, like France, is on a paper standard, tend to be eliminated by the adjustment between the two countries of prices, of exchange rates, or of both. And, since, in any case, in the absence of credit adjustments, it is the flow of internationally sold products which largely operates to bring the two into correspondence, the prices of such products would usually be affected first when the adjustment began to take place. The general wholesale price index, including, as it does in the case of the one used in this study, price data of both imported and domestic goods, is naturally simultaneously though less affected. Hence, since the series used in the statistical analyses above is made up of monthly data only, it is not surprising that lags of such short lengths as those discovered should appear only in the comparisons involving the prices of domestic goods alone.

But why should a lag in prices appear in the last four years of the period, while in the first four, if there was any lag at all, it was one in dollar exchange rates? What seems to have been happening was this: When the artificial control of exchange rates was relinquished in March 1919, these rates naturally adjusted themselves gradually to prices. Having been kept depressed by artificial means, they recovered gradually as soon as the control was lifted. And, since the chief force operating to bring about the recovery was the purchase of foreign goods made unnaturally cheaper than domestic ones by the artificially low rates on foreign exchange, it was altogether normal that the movements of exchange rates during that period of adjustment should follow those of prices. If domestic prices increased, foreign goods serving the same needs would be purchased in larger quantities. Foreign exchange rates would in turn rise as soon as the new demands for means of payment began to be felt. If domestic goods fell in price, the demand for foreign goods would be correspondingly cut off, and foreign exchange rates might be expected to fall in consequence, but only after the reduced demand for means of foreign payment (or perhaps an increased supply of bills drawn on foreign buyers to pay for purchases in France) made itself felt.

Such a statement is, however, far from complete. 1920 was a year of important economic happenings in other parts of the world. In the middle of 1920, for example, prices began falling rapidly in both England and the United States, as well as in certain other countries. In France, domestic goods' prices, imported goods' prices, and dollar exchange rates all likewise fell rapidly and greatly. How much of the fall was a result of the internal situation and how much the effect of the external it is impossible to say, but certainly drastically reduced prices in the United States of staple articles of import, as of cotton, for example, could not but affect the demand in France for exchange with which to pay for them. The statistics of imports into France showed a great increase during 1919 and 1920 of both weights and values. Their value was also far in excess of that of exports. Since this situation was not at all maintained in 1921 and the succeeding years, the data lend support to the contention that 1919 and 1920 were years of adjustments of exchange rates to prices. In 1921 and 1922 there seems to be no apparent reason why either exchange rates or prices should lead or follow, and a study of the series indicates that their movements during that period were probably synchronous.

The second sub-period, on the other hand, covering the years 1923–1926, in which a well-defined lag of prices behind dollar exchange rates was discovered, was one of frequent if not continuous speculation in French exchange. The mark completely collapsed during the first year of that period, and it was continually rumored in Berlin that the "flock of vultures which for three years had been hovering over the German corpse had taken their flight to Paris."

Speculation for a fall in exchange is accomplished through the sale of what has come to be known as "forward exchange." When in the judgment of a New York[19] speculator, for example, the franc was destined soon to lose in value with respect to other currencies, he would proceed as follows. Applying to a foreign exchange banker either directly or through his broker, he would ask for a contract whereby the banker agreed to buy from him thirty, sixty, or ninety[20] days hence a specified amount of French exchange at a price which, for reasons to be explained presently, was very close to that prevailing for immediate or "spot" purchases. This arrangement the banker could make, frequently requiring, however, a minimum deposit by the speculator as a form of protection. Payment would be made when the francs were delivered. If, during the period covered by the contract, the franc depreciated as was expected, the speculator would buy the cheaper francs, deliver them to his banker according to the terms of his contract, and pocket the profits.

But what is of interest in connection with this study of the precedence of exchange rates over prices is the effect of the forward deals on the movements of "spot" rates of exchange. This effect will be apparent if the illustrative example above is followed a little further. The banker, having bought the forward exchange from the speculator, finds himself, in the absence of counterbalancing contracts, in the awkward position of speculating for a rise in French exchange. To escape from this position he sells simultaneously an equal amount of francs for delivery either immediately or else during the life of the original contract. When there is a great volume of speculation for a fall, most of such speculation will necessarily result in corresponding sales of "spot" francs — as there would not be, presumably, a sufficient demand for forward francs. Hence, the "spot" market would be depressed to approximately the same extent as the forward. As a matter of fact, the discount or premium on forward as opposed to "spot" francs tends to correspond exactly to the difference in money market rates in the two centres involved —

[19] Very little of such speculation originated in New York. Most of it came from continental centres.

[20] These were the usual periods, though others could be arranged.

provided that sufficient credit for the purpose is available in the centre against which the speculation is directed. The reason is obvious. In buying the forward contract the New York banker protected himself by selling "spot" francs. To do so he either drew on his balance with a Paris correspondent or else, in the absence of such a balance, was forced to borrow the requisite funds on the Paris market, paying therefor the rate prevailing in that market. On the other hand, the sale of the franc draft in New York yielded him the dollar proceeds of the sale. His added costs (or profits) for handling the particular deal under discussion are therefore represented by the difference in having money in New York rather than in Paris or, in other words, the difference in interest on the given sum in the two markets. If the discount (or premium) should fail to correspond substantially with this difference in interest, an arbitrage profit would appear. Foreign exchange houses, seeking to take advantage of such profit, would soon engage in transactions leading quickly to an adjustment of such discount or premium to the normal above described.

Speculation for a rise in the franc, on the other hand, often takes the form of purchases of "spot" francs. In that event its effects on the movements of exchange rates are direct and obvious. Instead of buying "spot" francs, however, the speculator may, in order to avoid an interest charge, buy francs for forward delivery. In such a case the bank is placed in the position of selling forward. Consequently, in order to avoid itself speculating for a fall, it must in turn purchase "spot" (or perhaps forward) francs to an amount equivalent to its sales of forward francs. Thus, the effect on the movements of exchange rates is the same as though the speculator had bought "spot" francs directly.

The speculation in francs in foreign centres (as well as in Paris) led during this period to abrupt and wide movements in French exchange rates. And each time one of these movements appeared, prices in France became, to most[21] foreign purchasers, correspondingly cheap or dear according to the direction of the swing. As

[21] In certain countries, like Germany, during the first year of the period under discussion, the more rapid inflation often more than counteracted the influence of the increasing depreciation of the franc.

a result, the values abroad of articles importable into France were increased or diminished, and purchases abroad by French merchants were accordingly reduced or enlarged, all these influences leading to an adjustment of prices to the ever fluctuating movements of exchange rates. Such adjustments were evidently and naturally speedy for the prices of imported goods but necessarily required time for those of domestic goods. For, in spite of the fact that late in the inflation period many prices — as in the last stages of the German inflation — were changed almost automatically with any considerable movement of exchange rates, the great bulk of them evidently were not. The adjustments of prices apparently averaged, for those prices included in the domestic goods' price index used, at least a month or perhaps longer, but certainly less than two months.

The large and varying lags revealed between the movements of prices and those of circulation remain to be explained. For the period December 1914 to December 1918 it will be remembered that there appeared a consistent lag in circulation of approximately five months. This period almost coincides with that of the war and was one of rapidly and continually rising prices. Large quantities of goods were being daily contracted for by the Government, and in turn the sellers to the Government were contracting for almost equally large quantities of raw materials and machinery, while the producers of raw materials and machinery were, in their turn, contracting for the articles necessary for increasing and speeding up their production. Most of the goods in this unending series being ordered or purchased — as they frequently are — long in advance of the date of delivery and payment, or even of production, began to show early increases in price. Only months later did many of the funds needed in paying for them — through *mandats* on the Treasury, through *virements* on the Bank of France, through checks and drafts on any of the banks, or through additional note issues — even come into existence. In fact, it was only as dates of payment approached that there was any need for funds with which to pay. For making payments on business purchases the funds usually appeared first as deposit balances derived from advances received from banks or sometimes merely as increased lines of credit on which overdraft privileges were allowed. For discharging those of the Government they probably made their appearance first as an increase in the current account of the Government at the Bank or more often, without ever appearing as a deposit account at all, as increased advances of the Bank to the State. At times, too, when used for the payment by the government of salaries, wages, and minor expenditures, the requisite funds made their appearance as notes of the Bank of France held in the Treasury or withdrawn from the Bank for the specific purpose of making such payments.

In all cases increases in note circulation almost inevitably resulted. For, whatever the form of the original payments, the initial purchases usually started a chain of further purchases, some of which (and in France a considerable portion of which) necessarily had to be paid in cash. Hence, the various other types of funds were changed at the banks for notes of the Bank of France. Sometimes there would be no delay at all in this new demand for notes. Indeed, if, before the original payments were made, the price rise should spread to the retail market or to wages or to any other significant group of prices usually paid in cash, it is conceivable that the increase in note circulation might even precede the time of the payments for the original purchases which were making the increases necessary. In general, however, the expansion of notes would normally follow the initiating payments, which for the period under consideration, as has been seen, were made some time after the purchases being paid for had occurred. That in a period of rapidly rising prices and of insistent government and private borrowing there should be a considerable lag between the movements of prices and those of note circulation seems, therefore, to require no further explanation. But why it should be five rather than some other interval is, in the existing state of statistical information, probably impossible to explain. Perhaps one influence in particular (described in detail in connection with the discussion of the next period) tended to lengthen the interval of lag. Retail prices and wages, almost invariably paid in cash, lag much behind wholesale prices, paid often, even in France, with some form of bank credit. Consequently, cash needs do not expand immediately when wholesale prices increase.

The second period, covering the years 1920 and 1921, was, except for the first few months of 1920, one of rapidly and almost continually falling prices. For it the lag of circulation behind prices seemed to be between six and seven months. It should further be noted that during those two years the magnitude of the price decline was altogether out of proportion to that of note circulation, which, following prices at a long interval, continued to rise steadily until October 1920. The explanation of the very long lag is perhaps not quite so clear as that for the shorter one during the first period discussed. Nevertheless a satisfactory one seems to be at hand. A considerable lag in the movements of circulation behind those of prices is always to be anticipated in a period of falling prices. There are many instances of a similar phenomenon in American statistics. In the case of the United States the reason is not far to seek. What seems to happen is this: When prices fall, it is usually those of raw materials, those of producers' goods in general, and almost invariably those set by manufacturers, by jobbers, and by wholesalers which fall first. Moreover, it so happens, under our present day economic organization, that these prices, even in France, are rarely paid for in cash but rather almost invariably with some form of check or draft. On the other hand, sales at retail, wages, and, in France, salaries are usually paid in cash. These last-named prices lag far behind those mentioned above, and especially so during a price decline.[22] Hence, so far as variations in prices change the cash needs of the country, reduction in circulating notes should naturally follow by

[22] The *Statistique Générale de la France* prepares an index number which is called a retail price index (*indices des prix de détail*). For present purposes, however, it is completely useless. It contains the prices of but thirteen articles, all but three of which are foodstuffs. Furthermore, of these foodstuffs, the prices of two, bread and milk, have during a considerable part of the period been fixed by municipal decree. The rest (except sugar and meat) are all local farm products. The two non-food products, coal oil and alcohol, as well as sugar and meat, clearly have their prices determined in the international markets and, consequently, even when sold at retail, could hardly be expected to carry lagging prices. The list of the articles entering into the index is as follows: bread, meat, lard, butter, eggs, milk, cheese, potatoes, beans, sugar, salad oil, coal oil, wood alcohol.

a considerable interval those of wholesale prices in general — indices of which incidentally, almost without exception, include many raw materials and generally exclude completely wages and most other of the laggards in the movement. But it will be immediately objected that there are two other influences quantitatively per-

TABLE 30

CLEARING OPERATIONS OF THE PARIS *CHAMBRE DE COMPENSATION* *

(Monthly totals in millions of francs)

	1917	1918	1919	1920	1921	1922
Jan.	....	2,903	3,863	10,914	16,426	12,229
Feb.	....	2,983	3,611	11,685	14,187	11,746
Mar.	....	3,499	4,136	14,126	14,447	12,286
Apr.	....	2,983	4,734	14,705	15,599	9,860
May	....	4,289	5,265	14,084	15,976	11,805
June	....	3,151	5,470	13,783	15,144	11,856
July	717	2,856	5,856	13,920	10,946	13,487
Aug.	1,927	2,993	5,738	13,913	12,135	12,789
Sept.	1,833	3,360	7,507	13,521	14,383	12,586
Oct.	2,370	3,271	7,927	14,147	11,583	14,451
Nov.	2,177	3,071	8,296	16,105	12,621	18,794
Dec.	2,285	3,186	10,536	16,220	13,711	15,756

	1923	1924	1925	1926	1927
Jan.	18,864	36,847	23,913	37,293	30,288
Feb.	19,005	37,252	24,650	37,770	28,500
Mar.	20,376	46,651	29,170	47,473	26,503
Apr.	18,252	34,643	27,889	44,589	26,264
May	16,995	33,705	25,390	48,661	26,352
June	19,063	31,058	33,895	49,582	24,131
July	19,122	25,229	29,454	55,843	23,704
Aug.	19,855	25,017	24,283	46,228	23,859
Sept.	19,020	24,019	24,716	42,172	20,593
Oct.	23,674	24,532	39,812	45,138	24,604
Nov.	22,980	21,979	42,105	49,800	26,363
Dec.	21,515	27,126	46,379	43,302	26,544

* Sources: July 1917 — December 1926, Reports of the *Chambre de Compensation des Banquiers de Paris;* 1927, *Bulletin de la Statistique Générale de la France.*

The figures represent the total for each month of checks, drafts, etc. presented at the Paris Clearing House for clearance.

haps just as important as prices in determining the cash needs of a country. These are the volume of transfers made against cash and, relatedly, the volume of cash carried regularly in the tills of merchants and of other business and non-business organizations and in the pockets and stockings of the people.

While the volume of production in France — *exclusive of building operations in the devastated regions, which were very large* — undoubtedly decreased during those two years (Chart XXXI), it is interesting to note that, in spite of the drastic decline in prices, the pecuniary volume of business transferred by means of checks, drafts, and similar instruments, as indicated by bank clearings (Chart XX), maintained a high though fluctuating level until the middle of 1921. Hence, any considerable decline in the pecuniary volume of business *done with cash* could hardly have been anticipated.

It remains to investigate the amount of notes held in the tills of business and other organizations and in the pockets and private hoards of the people, as opposed to that held as till-money and reserves by the banks. It is the sum of these two amounts that makes up practically the entire note circulation of the Bank of France. For the details of the division of total money supplies into these two uses, the reader is referred to Chapter XII. It seems to be a well established fact that in most countries in periods of rapidly falling prices most people keep in cash as well as in deposits actually considerably larger amounts of purchasing power than is their usual practice.[23] The reason seems to be that the amounts of cash and of deposits held have become much a matter of custom, and one not quickly changed in periods of rapid price movements. Especially is this true with regard to cash holdings; for the lagging retail prices, as well as those partly or completely fixed by custom, by law, or by agreement, are just the ones which are paid out of cash supplies. In such periods deposits, too, decrease much more slowly than do prices and for the

[23] *Cf.* J. M. Keynes, *Monetary Reform* (New York, Harcourt, Brace and Company, 1924) for the English experiences and Irving Fisher, *Purchasing Power of Money* (New York, The Macmillan Company, 1925) for a theoretical discussion of the subject.

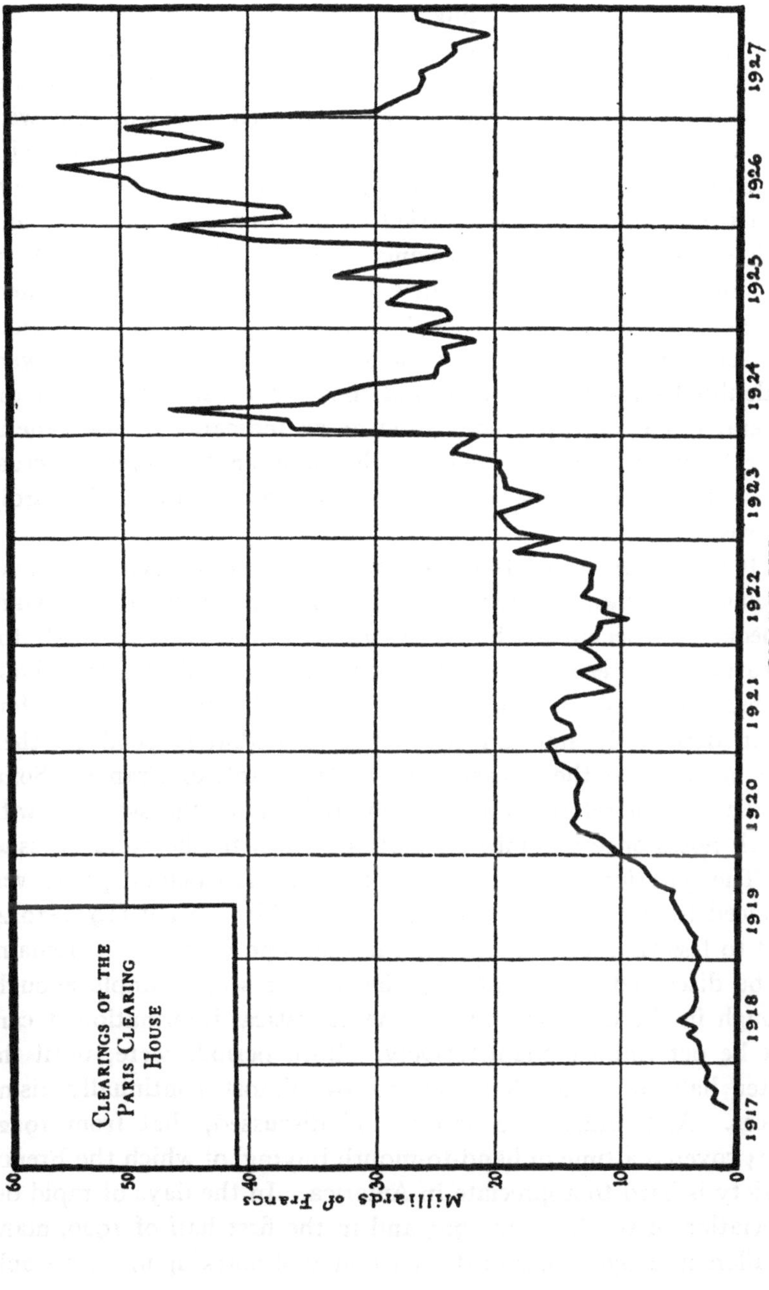
CLEARINGS OF THE PARIS CLEARING HOUSE
Milliards of Francs
0
10
20
30
40
50
60
1917
1918
1919
1920
1921
1922
1923
1924
1925
1926
1927

CHART XX

reason of inertia in changing one's habits. Consequently, supporting till-money reserves cannot be reduced. Or, explained in another way, velocities of circulation of money and deposits decrease greatly in such periods. Hence, it seems evident that with cash transactions not declining substantially in total value, with velocities of circulation decreasing greatly or (what is equivalent) with the amounts of cash carried or hoarded by the people and their organizations not decreasing, and with the requirements of till-money held in the banks not being substantially reduced, there was no possibility of any considerable decline in total circulation. And, since the prices of goods and services paid for with cash were undoubtedly lagging much behind most of those included in the general wholesale price index used as an indicator of the general price level, the lag of seven months between the minor fluctuations of circulation as compared with those of prices is hardly surprising.

It should be added that the contraction elasticity, even under so elastic a banking system as that of France, is far from instantaneous. Especially before the practice of depositing with the Treasury had become general, idle funds accumulating in private or business tills often lay there for considerable periods before being deposited; nor did the banks immediately send on their idle balances to the Treasury or to the Bank of France. Some of the lag, therefore, can be accounted for by the slowness with which notes once put into circulation return to the bank of issue.

The question of why the lag of circulation behind prices was reduced to less than two months for the third period (1922–1924) and to less than one month for the final one (1925–1926) remains to be discussed. Qualitatively the answer seems simple enough, though in the existing state of the statistical information it cannot be determined quantitatively. Both periods were, until the latter half of 1926, characterized by almost continually rising prices. And, unlike the first period discussed, that from 1922–1924 covered a time of hand-to-mouth buying, of which the French variety is hard to appreciate in America. In the days of rapid depreciation of the franc in 1925 and in the first half of 1926, many retailers no longer continued their policy of marking up prices only on the receipt, at higher cost, of new stocks from the wholesalers, but often, like those higher up, took an advance of dollar or sterling exchange as a sufficient excuse for an increase in selling prices. Thus, the normal lag between wholesale and retail prices either vanished or was shortened. Moreover, if general comment can be trusted, there is little doubt that as the position of the franc became more and more threatened the intervals of time between purchases and payments were much shortened in almost all phases of French economic life. In many lines of business open credits were practically abandoned, and in others they were reduced to a minimum both in extent and in time. Also, since, as in all periods of rising prices, business activity was generally high, the note circulation under the elastic French banking system expanded easily and quickly in response to generally increased spending at continually higher prices. In the last six months of 1926, when prices were falling rapidly, several influences were operating to prevent a substantial lengthening of the lag. Unlike in the decline of 1920–1921, the pecuniary volume of business, as indicated by bank clearings, fell off sharply. Cash in the hands of the public (see Table 85) not only did not increase as it did after the break in prices in 1920, but actually declined throughout all the remaining months of the year. Apparently otherwise idle cash was being quickly utilized either to deposit in the banks or else to purchase the ever available *Bons de la Défense Nationale*. Under the influence of these forces combined with renewed hand-to-mouth buying the lag of circulation behind prices increased but slightly.

A further question arises with regard to the varying gains from exchange accruing to holders of foreign currencies. Since it is the failure of prices to adjust themselves rapidly and completely to the movements of exchange rates which gives rise to much of this gain, it might be anticipated that the extent of the gain would depend very largely on the rapidity of the rise or fall in exchange rates. Accordingly, in order to discover any such relationship which may have existed during the period under discussion, a comparison will next be made between a monthly series of the first derivatives of dollar exchange rates $\frac{d\,e}{d\,t}$ and a similar series of the monthly percentage gains and losses from exchange.

TABLE 31

DOLLAR EXCHANGE IN PARIS

(First derivatives of a six-month moving average)

	1919	1920	1921	1922	1923
Jan.	.....	+0.99	+0.18	−0.12	+0.60
Feb.	.....	+1.04	−0.08	−0.32	+0.57
Mar.	.....	+0.99	−0.06	−0.48	+0.35
Apr.	.....	+1.35	−0.41	−0.49	+0.11
May	.....	+0.58	−0.77	−0.53	+0.12
June	.....	+0.26	−0.77	−0.06	+0.43
July	+0.28	−0.02	−0.18	−0.06	+0.22
Aug.	+0.43	+0.02	−0.16	+0.33	+0.20
Sept.	+0.43	+0.03	−0.05	+0.34	+0.15
Oct.	+0.44	−0.19	+0.09	+0.56	+0.39
Nov.	+0.54	+0.55	+0.41	+0.56	+0.56
Dec.	+0.68	+0.83	.00	+0.29	+0.55

	1924	1925	1926	1927	
Jan.	+0.81	−0.23	+0.94	−2.64	
Feb.	+1.32	+0.15	+1.03	−1.59	
Mar.	+0.36	+0.02	+1.26	−1.69	
Apr.	−0.29	+0.01	+1.04	−1.17	
May	+0.05	+0.17	+0.75	−0.43	
June	−0.12	+0.50	+1.34	+0.05	
July	−0.31	+0.43	+2.39	+0.04	
Aug.	−1.18	+0.32	−1.27	0.00	
Sept.	+0.11	+0.35	+1.17	−0.01	
Oct.	+0.61	+0.78	+0.40	−0.01	
Nov.	0.00	+1.05	−0.42	−0.02	
Dec.	−0.05	+0.89	−1.61	−0.02	

This latter series was constructed in the following way. Monthly purchasing power parities were computed by the use of the wholesale price index of the *Statistique Générale de la France* and that of the United States Bureau of Labor Statistics, both on a

TABLE 32

PERCENTAGES OF GAIN OR LOSS OF PURCHASING POWER OF DOLLARS AS COMPARED WITH FRANCS IN FRANCE

	1919	1920	1921	1922	1923
Jan.	......	+ .207	+ .132	+ .044	+ .212
Feb.	......	+ .222	+ .138	− .023	+ .182
Mar.	......	+ .181	+ .189	− .009	+ .102
Apr.	......	+ .349	+ .088	− .048	+ .098
May	......	+ .140	+ .002	− .002	+ .121
June	......	+ .147	+ .046	+ .068	+ .179
July	− .164	+ .215	+ .070	+ .100	+ .206
Aug.	− .037	+ .277	+ .072	+ .175	+ .237
Sept.	− .041	+ .218	+ .107	+ .179	+ .133
Oct.	− .076	+ .272	+ .136	+ .249	+ .207
Nov.	+ .001	+ .346	+ .167	+ .229	+ .226
Dec.	+ .071	+ .353	+ .029	+ .143	+ .245

	1924	1925	1926	1927	
Jan.	+ .282	+ .110	+ .272	+ .154	
Feb.	+ .379	+ .169	+ .294	+ .143	
Mar.	+ .062	+ .153	+ .326	+ .116	
Apr.	− .020	+ .127	+ .351	+ .116	
May	+ .163	+ .141	+ .302	+ .130	
June	+ .135	+ .204	+ .390	+ .137	
July	+ .171	+ .170	+ .431	+ .150	
Aug.	+ .122	+ .180	+ .314	+ .165	
Sept.	+ .123	+ .173	+ .316	+ .214	
Oct.	+ .129	+ .274	+ .250	+ .247	
Nov.	+ .103	+ .314	+ .175	+ .227	
Dec.	+ .109	+ .280	+ .145	+ .207	

1913 base. These purchasing power parities were regarded as the normal exchange rates which anyone should expect to receive. Consequently, the variations of the actual rate away from this normal were regarded as gains or losses. By reducing these variations to percentages of the normal, a monthly series of percentage gains and losses from exchange was obtained. The first derivative of a six-month moving average of exchange rates (with the average given as of the final month in each case) was used instead of a direct derivative. The two curves to be compared are represented in Chart XXI.

A glance at the chart shows a very high degree of similarity indeed between the two curves. It will be seen, too, that in 1919 and for a few months in 1922, as well as for the single month of April 1924, there were actual losses in exchange to holders of dollars. In all other parts of the period, however, the gains were considerable. Since the derivatives are of six-month moving averages entered at the end of the period in each case, it is evident, too, that there was in general a slight lag of the gains or losses in exchange behind the derivative of the original rates.

The greatest gains appeared in April and in December of 1920, in February 1924,[24] and in July 1926 — the maxima occurring in each case coincidently with the maxima of the derivatives. Likewise, most of the minima in the percentage gains appear simultaneously with minima in the derivatives. The few exceptions are easily explainable. In 1919, for example, the loss occurred because of the failure of exchange rates to recover from their but recently abandoned "pegged" position. The minimum in the derivative for August 1924, on the other hand, is one which arises most largely from the fact that the "lows" of March and April were still included in the six-month average. Consequently this minimum should be disregarded.

It may be concluded, therefore, that in general the gains or losses from exchange coincided closely with the rapidity of the movements of exchange rates themselves. In general, when exchange rates were moving rapidly upward, the gains were large and the more rapid the upward movements the larger were the gains. Reversely, when exchange rates were moving rapidly downward, the gains decreased or even losses appeared, and the more rapid the downward movements the smaller were the gains or the greater were the losses. Moreover, in general, when the rate of movement upward decreased, the percentage gains likewise decreased, and, when the rate of movement downward diminished, the percentage losses decreased or the percentage gains increased.

[24] The actual maximum undoubtedly occurred in March, but the gain at the end of February was greater than that at the end of March, to which dates the computations apply.

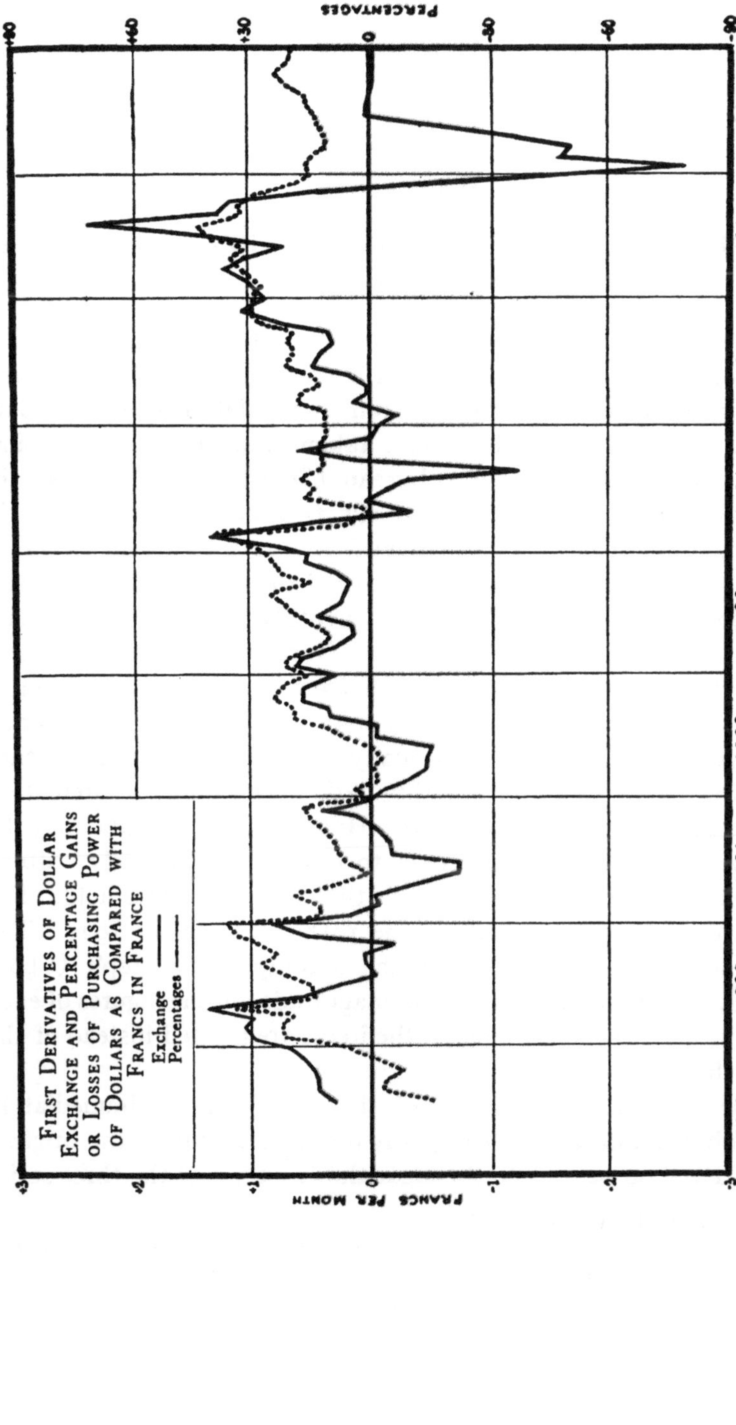
First Derivatives of Dollar Exchange and Percentage Gains or Losses of Purchasing Power of Dollars as Compared with Francs in France
Exchange
Percentages
Percentages
Francs per Month
1919
1920
1921
1922
1923
1924
1925
1926
1927

CHART XXI

CHAPTER VII

EXCHANGE, PRICES, AND CIRCULATION IN GERMANY 1918–1923

IN order to establish more conclusively the sequence of movement of exchange rates, prices, and circulation, series for the three phenomena have been compiled from the inflation régime in Germany. The statistical data were taken from a special compilation of the official statistical bureau (*Statistisches Reichsamt*) in *Wirtschaft und Statistik* (*Zahlen zur Geldentwertung in Deutschland 1914 bis 1923*).[1] For exchange, the data represent averages for each month of daily exchange rates of the dollar in Berlin. The data for prices represent likewise monthly averages, the official index used being based on monthly averages of wholesale prices. The data for circulation, on the other hand, apply to month ends. Thus, while the data for exchange and prices approximate coincidence in time, it must be continually borne in mind that the data for prices are averages for monthly periods and those of circulation for the ends of the same periods. Hence, the price data may be said in general to be applicable to dates approximately[2] fifteen days in advance of those for which the circulation data hold. The period considered is that from June 1918 to December 1923. The three series are represented in the accompanying graph (Chart XXII). Because of the extreme magnitude of the figures of each series in 1923, the logarithms of the items are plotted instead of the items themselves.

The steep concave ascents of the series indicate immediately the probable difficulty of fitting any ordinary trends to the original data. Even on passing to the logarithmic curves of the three series

[1] Berlin, Verlag von Reimar Hobbing, 1925.

[2] In periods of very rapid inflation the higher figures applicable to the latter portion of the month would cause the effective interval to be much shorter.

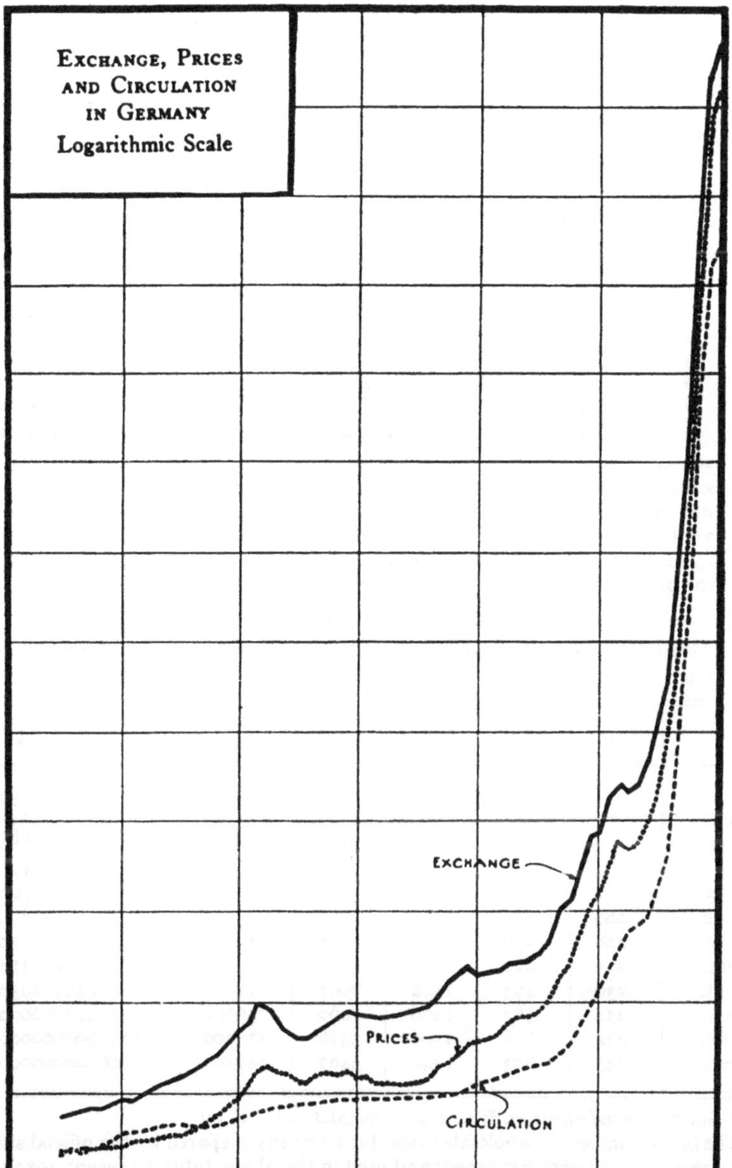
Exchange, Prices
and Circulation
in Germany
Logarithmic Scale
Exchange
Prices
Circulation
1918
1919
1920
1921
1922
1923

CHART XXII

TABLE 33

DOLLAR EXCHANGE IN BERLIN *

(Averages of daily rates for each month; marks per dollar)

	1918	1919	1920	1921	1922	1923
Jan.	....	8.20	64.80	64.91	191.81	17972.00
Feb.	....	9.13	99.11	61.31	207.82	27918.00
Mar.	....	10.39	83.89	62.45	284.19	21190.00
Apr.	....	12.61	59.64	63.53	291.00	24457.00
May	....	12.85	46.48	62.30	290.11	47670.00
June	5.36	14.01	39.13	69.36	317.44	109996.00
July	5.79	15.08	39.48	76.67	493.22	353412.00
Aug.	6.10	18.83	47.74	84.31	1134.56	4620455.00
Sept.	6.59	24.05	57.98	104.91	1465.87	98860000.00
Oct.	6.61	26.83	68.17	150.20	3180.96	25260000000.00
Nov.	7.43	38.31	77.24	292.96	7183.10	2193600000000.00
Dec.	8.28	46.77	73.00	191.93	7589.27	4200000000000.00

* Source: *Sonderhefte zu Wirtschaft und Statistik, Sonderheft 1*, "Zahlen zur Geldentwertung in Deutschland 1914 bis 1923," (Berlin, Verlag von Reimar Hobbing, 1925).

The data represent averages of daily exchange rates of the dollar in Berlin for each month. The daily rates used in computing the monthly averages are in turn the averages of the highest and the lowest quotations for each day.

TABLE 34

OFFICIAL WHOLESALE PRICE INDEX FOR GERMANY *

(Index numbers based on average monthly price data. Base 100 in 1913)

	1918	1919	1920	1921	1922	1923
Jan.	...	262	1256	1439	3665	278500
Feb.	...	270	1685	1376	4103	558500
Mar.	...	274	1709	1338	5433	488800
Apr.	...	286	1567	1326	6355	521200
May	...	297	1508	1308	6458	817000
June	209	308	1382	1366	7030	1938500
July	208	339	1367	1428	10059	7478700
Aug.	235	422	1450	1917	19200	94404100
Sept.	230	493	1498	2067	28700	2394889300
Oct.	234	562	1466	2460	56600	709480000000
Nov.	234	678	1509	3416	115400	72570000000000
Dec.	245	803	1440	3487	147500	126160000000000

* Source: *Sonderhefte zu Wirtschaft und Statistik, loc. cit.*

The index numbers of wholesale prices for Germany prepared by the official statistical bureau (*Statistisches Reichsamt*) and used in the above table represent 1913 relatives of weighted arithmetic averages of 800 price quotations for 38 commodities. The weights are taken as the relative importance of the articles in national consumption during the period 1908–1913. Though the index has recently been enlarged in scope, for the years considered (1918–1923) the prices of raw materials and of semi-finished products only are taken into account.

TABLE 35

TOTAL CIRCULATION IN GERMANY *

(End-of-month data in millions of marks)

	1918	1919	1920	1921	1922	1923
Jan.	.....	34536	51079	78764	124426	2014587
Feb.	.....	35254	54456	79995	129017	3552399
Mar.	.....	37237	59607	80412	140494	5558050
Apr.	.....	38518	62424	81220	150752	6616978
May	.....	39917	64296	81735	162546	8653821
June	20668	42701	68310	84902	180767	17400458
July	21010	41905	69824	86664	203246	43890025
Aug.	22473	40881	72404	88833	252858	692028000
Sept.	24673	42299	75831	94941	332563	28653353400
Oct.	26704	43405	77379	99812	484685	5186219738700
Nov.	29283	45417	77429	109261	769500	1487800000000000
Dec.	33106	50173	81628	122963	1295228	2273600000000000

* Source: *Sonderhefte zu Wirtschaft und Statistik, loc. cit.*

The data represent for the years 1918–1922 sums of the following components for end-of-month dates: (1) *Reichsbanknoten* (outstanding notes of the *Reichsbank*); (2) *Privatbanknoten* (outstanding notes of the private banks of issue); (3) *Darlehnskassenscheine* (notes of the mutual loan societies); (4) *Reichskassenscheine* (Treasury notes); and (5) *Münzen* (net coinage of subsidiary coins, deduction made for those no longer usable for the making of payments. The amounts are estimated.) The compilations are those of the German official statistical bureau (*Statistisches Reichsamt*) published in a special issue of *Wirtschaft und Statistik* ("Zahlen zur Geldentwertung in Deutschland 1913 bis 1923").

For 1923 the totals were computed from material contained in the same report. They include for all months: (1) *Reichsbanknoten*, (2) *Privatbanknoten*, (3) *Darlehnskassenscheine*, (4) *Reichskassenscheine*, and (5) *Notgeld* (emergency currency issued by municipalities and corporations); for the months September–December in addition: (6) *Reichsbahnnotgeld* (emergency currency of the state railways); and for the months October–December, converted into paper marks, the following types of stabilized currency: (7) *Rentenmark* (notes of the *Rentenbank*), (8) *Goldanleihenoten* (notes of the *Goldanleihebank*); (9) *Reichsbahnnotgeld* (stabilized form); and (10) *Goldanleihenotgeld* (emergency currency of the *Goldanleihebank*). The latter four sorts of stabilized currency were prepared for addition to the paper currencies by multiplication by the value of a gold mark in terms of paper marks

$$\frac{\text{exchange rate of the dollar in Berlin}}{\text{par of dollar exchange (4.20)}}$$

on the last day of each month.

The value of the metal coins in circulation is lacking for the months October-December 1922, January-March 1923, and September-December 1923. On account of the great magnitude of total circulation in these months, however, the accuracy of the data is in no way impaired.

it was found that the concavity was so great that compound interest curves could furnish but the remotest approximations to satisfactory trends for the period as a whole. Accordingly, the process was carried even further, and straight-line secular trends were fitted[3] to third logarithms in each case. In this way apparently satisfactory trends were secured.[4] These trends were then converted to corresponding trends for the first logarithmic curves and were found to fit extremely well. The stellar magnitudes of the original data for the last year of the period, however, caused the deviations from such trends even of the first logarithms to be extremely large for that year. Consequently, in reducing the series to final form for correlation,[5] the standard deviation for each series was found to be so magnified as to conceal almost completely the movements in the earlier years.

Accordingly, each series was divided into two sub-periods and separate compound-interest secular trends fitted in each case to the second logarithms of the original items. And, since the sequence of movements only was sought, deviations of the items of the second logarithmic series were taken in each case from the curve of secular trend fitted to that series and those deviations divided by the standard deviation from the trend.

For the comparison of dollar-exchange rates and prices the periods used were June 1918 to June 1922, and June 1922 to December 1923. On account of a peculiar movement of circulation appearing in late 1918 and early 1919, however, the first period chosen for the comparison of *prices and circulation* was June 1919 to June 1922. The second period was the same as that chosen for the comparison of exchange and prices.

The comparison of dollar-exchange rates and prices will first be made. The second logarithmic curves of each of the two series

[3] The method of least squares was used throughout.

[4] It is clearly recognized that the logarithms of the items of each series, and, consequently, the resulting secular trends for the logarithmic series, depend directly on the selection of the position of the decimal point in the items of the original series. It was placed, therefore, for each series so that the range of the resulting logarithmic series would be substantially the same. Care was also taken to avoid the necessity of including in any of the series the logarithm of an extremely small decimal.

[5] Each item was expressed in terms of its percentage deviation from secular trend divided by the standard deviation.

for the period June 1918–June 1922 reduced to percentage deviations from their compound-interest secular trends divided by their respective standard deviations are represented in the accompanying graph (Chart XXIII).

By observing the resulting movements of the two series it will be seen that a reasonably clear similarity exists. And, while there is evidence of a lag of prices behind exchange, it is entirely clear that many of the important movements were synchronous. To

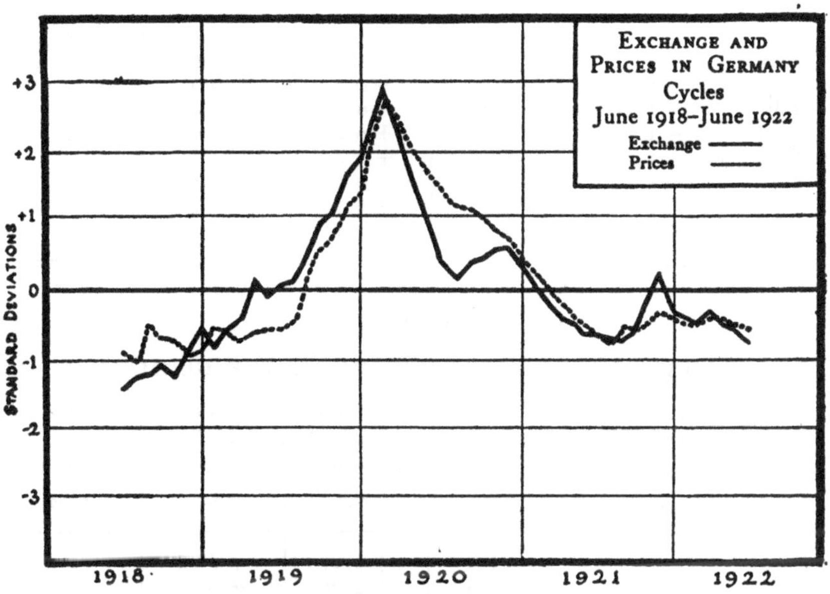

CHART XXIII

determine more definitely the prevailing sequence of movements resort was again made to the correlation process.[6]

A comparison of synchronous items yielded a coefficient of + .912(49). With prices pushed one month to the right, indicating a lag of exchange behind prices by that interval, the coefficient was reduced to + .830(48). With prices pushed one month to the left, however, indicating a precedence by that interval of the movements of dollar exchange, the coefficient was raised to + .941(48). Push-

[6] To compute coefficients, the items of the two series expressed in percentage deviations from their compound-interest trends and divided by their respective standard

TABLE 36

DOLLAR EXCHANGE IN BERLIN

(Percentage deviations of second logarithms of original data from compound-interest secular trend expressed in terms of standard deviation)

	1918	1919	1920	1921	1922
Jan.	......	− 0.85	+ 2.36	+ 0.05	− 0.49
Feb.	......	− 0.64	+ 2.97	− 0.21	− 0.56
Mar.	......	− 0.37	+ 2.44	− 0.35	− 0.38
Apr.	......	+ 0.07	+ 1.58	− 0.49	− 0.53
May	......	− 0.04	+ 0.91	− 0.68	− 0.69
June	− 1.43	+ 0.03	+ 0.38	− 0.68	− 0.77
July	− 1.25	+ 0.08	+ 0.22	− 0.70	......
Aug.	− 1.19	+ 0.51	+ 0.41	− 0.73	......
Sept.	− 1.03	+ 0.96	+ 0.45	− 0.58	......
Oct.	− 1.18	+ 1.03	+ 0.68	− 0.29	......
Nov.	− 0.89	+ 1.67	+ 0.70	+ 0.22	......
Dec.	− 0.65	+ 1.90	+ 0.43	− 0.32	......

TABLE 37

OFFICIAL WHOLESALE PRICE INDEX FOR GERMANY

(Percentage deviations of second logarithms of original data from compound-interest secular trend expressed in terms of standard deviation)

	1918	1919	1920	1921	1922
Jan.	......	− 0.62	+ 2.27	+ 0.19	− 0.53
Feb.	......	− 0.64	+ 2.70	− 0.05	− 0.57
Mar.	......	− 0.72	+ 2.49	− 0.25	− 0.46
Apr.	......	− 0.67	+ 2.08	− 0.42	− 0.48
May	......	− 0.66	+ 1.79	− 0.59	− 0.62
June	− 0.84	− 0.66	+ 1.41	− 0.68	− 0.69
July	− 1.01	− 0.44	+ 1.19	− 0.76	......
Aug.	− 0.44	+ 0.19	+ 1.11	− 0.52	......
Sept.	− 0.71	+ 0.53	+ 0.98	− 0.57	......
Oct.	− 0.76	+ 0.76	+ 0.73	− 0.51	......
Nov.	− 0.90	+ 1.12	+ 0.62	− 0.30	......
Dec.	− 0.81	+ 1.38	+ 0.36	− 0.43	......

deviations were multiplied together in pairs and the sum of the products in turn divided by the number of items paired. The resulting coefficients are evidently not identical with correlation ratios but are seemingly equally dependable measures of similarity and better adapted to the character of the data.

ing prices two months to the left reduced the coefficient to + .923 (47), a figure, nevertheless, slightly above that yielded by the comparison of simultaneous items. It is fairly clear, therefore, that in general during this period there was a lag of prices behind exchange rates of at least a month and perhaps somewhat more, though of less than two months.

In an attempt to discover further whether there was a consistent variation in the lag of prices behind exchange rates within the sub-period under consideration, the period was divided into two still shorter sub-periods: June 1918 to July 1920 and August 1920 to June 1922. These new sub-periods were found too short for the fitting of satisfactory trends. Hence, the products entering into the computation of the correlation coefficient for the entire original sub-period were summed separately for each of the new sub-periods, and the resulting sums were divided by the number of item-comparisons involved in each.[7] In this way, indices, *which are in no sense correlation coefficients*, were computed for each of the new sub-periods. By thus proceeding it was found that for the period June 1918 to July 1920 prices lagged in general behind dollar exchange by at least one month but by less than two.[8]

By making similar computations for the second sub-period, August 1920 to June 1922, it was found that the movements of the two series were in general simultaneous, with perhaps a tendency of dollar-exchange rates to lag slightly behind prices but by less than one month.[9]

[7] For a full description of the process see Chap. VI, p. 119, and accompanying note.

[8] The indices obtained are as follows:

For the period June 1918–July 1920

For the comparison of	
Simultaneous items	+ 1.466
Items with prices pushed one month to the right	+ 1.333
Items with prices pushed one month to the left	+ 1.518
Items with prices pushed two months to the left	+ 1.490

[9] The indices obtained are as follows:

For the period August 1920–June 1922

For the comparison of	
Simultaneous items	+ .286
Items with prices pushed one month to the right	+ .282
Items with prices pushed one month to the left	+ .260

With the above results in view a *correlation coefficient* was finally computed for the entire sub-period, June 1918 to June 1922, with prices pushed one month to the left for the period June 1918 to June 1920 and with simultaneous items compared thereafter. In this way the coefficient of correlation was raised from + .941(48), discovered above when a lag in prices of one month was allowed for the entire sub-period, to + .954(48).

In summary, for the sub-period June 1918 to June 1922 it appears evident that, while there was in general a tendency for prices to lag behind dollar-exchange rates by a month or a little more, the lag seems to have been confined to the earlier part of that sub-period and that in the latter part the movements of the two series were in general approximately simultaneous, but with a tendency for prices to precede dollar-exchange rates by less than a month.

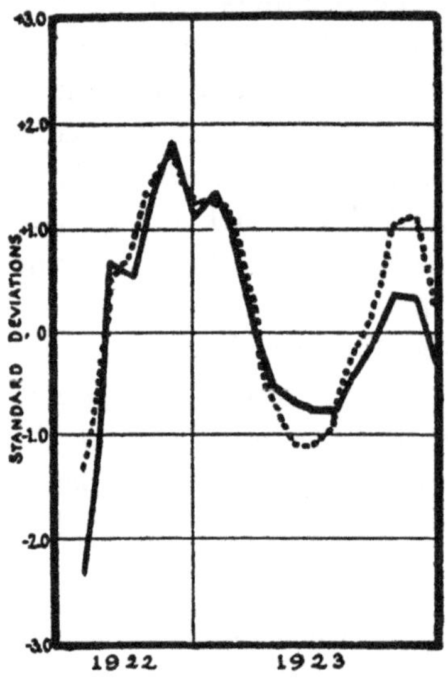

CHART XXIV

Exchange and Prices in Germany

Cycles

Exchange ———
Prices ---------

For the comparison of dollar-exchange rates and prices for the second original sub-period, June 1922 to December 1923, the second logarithms of the items of each series were used, as in the other comparison, instead of the items themselves, and the series were reduced, as before, to percentage deviations of these second logarithms from their compound-interest secular trends, the resulting percentage deviations being then divided by the standard deviations of the respective series. Such a procedure, as explained above, is permissible since only the sequence of movements is sought. The series thus transformed are pictured in the accompanying graph (Chart XXIV). There is at once apparent a very high degree of similarity indeed in the directions as well as in the times of their movements. Computations of correlation coefficients yielded the following results:

TABLE 38

DOLLAR EXCHANGE IN BERLIN

(Percentage deviations of second logarithms of original data from compound-interest secular trend expressed in terms of standard deviation)

	1922	1923
Jan.	......	+1.34
Feb.	......	+0.99
Mar.	......	+0.01
Apr.	......	−0.55
May	......	−0.68
June	−2.34	−0.78
July	−1.20	−0.79
Aug.	+0.63	−0.40
Sept.	+0.51	−0.15
Oct.	+1.32	+0.34
Nov.	+1.83	+0.31
Dec.	+1.09	−0.30

TABLE 39

OFFICIAL WHOLESALE PRICE INDEX FOR GERMANY

(Percentage deviations of second logarithms of original data from compound-interest secular trend expressed in terms of standard deviation)

	1919	1920	1921	1922
Jan.	......	+1.87	−0.02	−0.15
Feb.	......	+2.57	−0.30	−0.13
Mar.	......	+2.40	−0.54	+0.15
Apr.	......	+1.93	−0.73	+0.20
May	......	+1.61	−0.92	+0.06
June	−2.66	+1.16	−0.97	0.00
July	−2.31	+0.93	−1.03	......
Aug.	−1.41	+0.91	−0.54	......
Sept.	−0.87	+0.81	−0.55	......
Oct.	−0.49	+0.53	−0.37	......
Nov.	+0.09	+0.46	+0.08	......
Dec.	+0.54	+0.16	−0.06	......

For the comparison of

Simultaneous items	+ .921(19)
Items with prices pushed one month to the right	+ .680(18)
Items with prices pushed one month to the left	+ .699(18)

It is entirely clear, therefore, that during this period of extremely rapid inflation any lag in either direction in the movements of the two series was so extremely short as to be completely undiscoverable

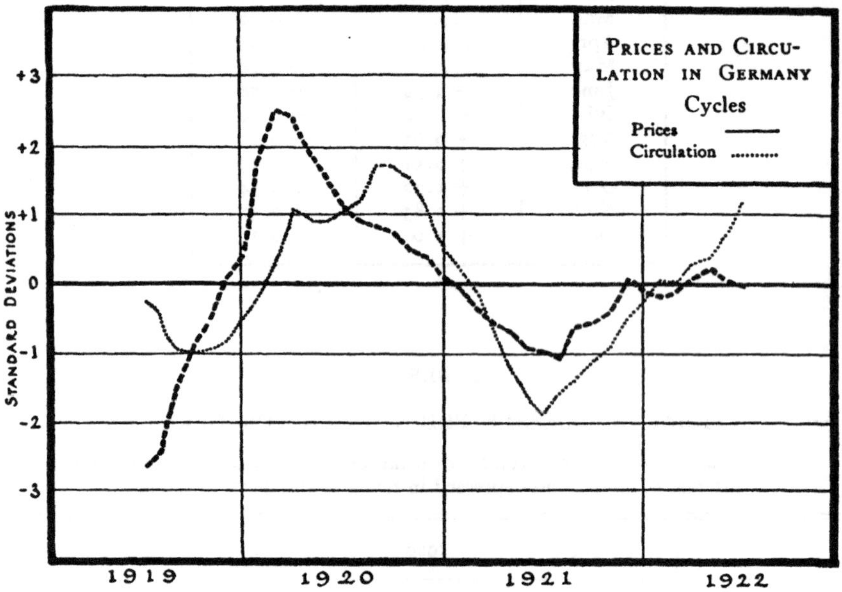

CHART XXV

by applying the correlation process to monthly series. It might be added that this result corresponds completely with personal observations made in Berlin in the summer of 1923. In many of the shops no prices would be quoted at all until the Bourse rate on dollars or other stable exchange was learned by telephone.

A study of the movements of circulation as compared with those of prices was next made. For careful comparisons of the sequence of movements of the two series each — as in the comparisons already made — was reduced to second logarithms, and compound-interest trends were fitted to the resulting items. The percentage deviations from the secular trend for each of the series thus transformed were then divided by the respective standard deviations. The resulting series for the period June 1919 to June 1922 are represented in the graph (Chart XXV).

While the similarity of the two curves is not nearly so marked as was the case in the comparisons just made of exchange rates and prices, a very distinct lag of circulation behind prices is immediately evident, a lag, however, which during the middle months of 1921 seems to have been greatly reduced, only to appear again lengthened a few months later.

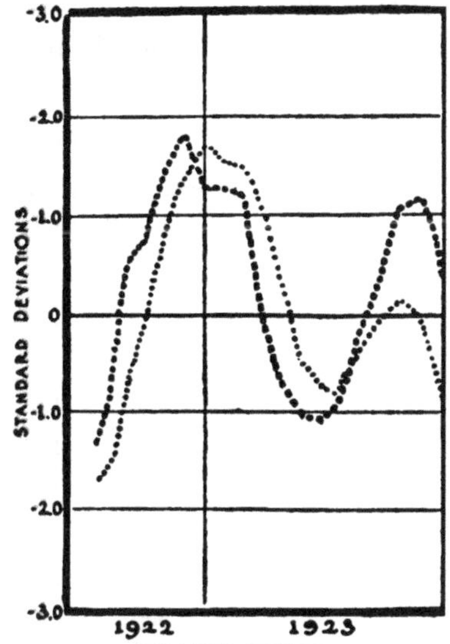

CHART XXVI

PRICES AND CIRCULATION IN GERMANY

Cycles

Prices ———
Circulation ....

Computations of coefficient of correlation yielded the following results:

For the comparison of

Simultaneous items	+ .682(37)
Items with circulation pushed one month to the right	+ .520(36)
Items with circulation pushed one month to the left	+ .839(36)
Items with circulation pushed two months to the left	+ .917(35)
Items with circulation pushed three months to the left	+ .897(34)

The highest coefficient is obtained, therefore, by comparing prices of one month and circulation of two months later. In other words, the movements of prices have in general during the period under consideration preceded those of circulation by approximately two months — a result entirely comparable with that discovered in the more recent period in France.

In the last nineteen months of the inflation period in Germany the precedence of prices over circulation was greatly reduced. The graphs of the two series for this period, transformed as in the other cases to percentage deviations from compound interest secular trends fitted

TABLE 40

OFFICIAL WHOLESALE PRICE INDEX FOR GERMANY

(Percentage deviations of second logarithms of original data from compound-interest secular trend expressed in terms of standard deviation)

	1922	1923
Jan.	......	+1.23
Feb.	......	+1.18
Mar.	......	+0.10
Apr.	......	−0.69
May	......	−1.05
June	−1.39	−1.10
July	−0.78	−0.94
Aug.	+0.50	−0.34
Sept.	+0.70	+0.19
Oct.	+1.36	+1.04
Nov.	+1.79	+1.15
Dec.	+1.23	+0.34

TABLE 41

TOTAL CIRCULATION IN GERMANY

(Percentage deviations of second logarithms of original data from compound-interest secular trend expressed in terms of standard deviation, allowance made for seasonal variation)

	1919	1920	1921	1922
Jan.	......	−0.09	+0.21	+0.07
Feb.	......	+0.41	−0.03	+0.05
Mar.	......	+1.02	−0.68	+0.30
Apr.	......	+0.95	−1.27	+0.36
May	......	+0.97	−1.57	+0.79
June	−0.10	+1.07	−1.83	+1.19
July	−0.44	+1.33	−1.60	......
Aug.	−0.91	+1.76	−1.36	......
Sept.	−0.99	+1.74	−1.15	......
Oct.	−0.96	+1.63	−0.92	......
Nov.	−0.82	+1.06	−0.39	......
Dec.	−0.45	+0.60	−0.15	......

to the second logarithms of the items of the original series and with the percentage deviations divided by the respective standard deviations, are reproduced graphically (Chart XXVI).

The lag, while reduced below that of the earlier period, is clearly apparent and seems to persist until about the end of the summer of 1923, after which the monthly movements evidently become approximately synchronous.

Computations of correlation coefficients for the entire sub-period yielded the following results:

For the comparison of

Simultaneous items	+ .754(19)
Items with circulation pushed one month to the right	+ .429(18)
Items with circulation pushed one month to the left	+ .806(18)
Items with circulation pushed two months to the left	+ .698(17)

For the period considered as a whole, therefore, it can be said that in general the circulation series lagged behind that of prices by approximately one month. To discover the lags within the period, however, further resort was made to summing separately for the two sub-periods June 1922 to June 1923 and July 1923 to December 1923 the products entering into the computation of the coefficients for the entire period.[10] The results were as expected. For the first period, June 1922 to June 1923, there was indicated a clearly defined lag of one month. For the remainder of the sub-period there was evidenced a tendency for the circulation series to

[10] These products divided by the number of item-comparisons involved in each case gave the following indices:

For the period June 1922–June 1923

For the comparison of

Simultaneous items	+ 1.037
Items with circulation pushed one month to the right	+ .561
Items with circulation pushed one month to the left	+ 1.161
Items with circulation pushed two months to the left	+ .982

For the period July 1923–December 1923

For the comparison of

Simultaneous items	+ .138
Items with circulation pushed one month to the right	+ .166
Items with circulation pushed two months to the right	+ .008
Items with circulation pushed one month to the left	− .118

precede, also by one month. The explanation of this latter precedence is entirely clear, however, when it is recalled that average prices for each month were compared with circulation for the ends of the months. On account of the differences in the dates to which the factual material entering the two series applies, it is obvious that there should appear an automatic precedence of approximately fifteen days of circulation over prices. Hence, in spite of the fact that the rapidity of the inflation in the final stages of the process

TABLE 42

TOTAL CIRCULATION IN GERMANY

(Percentage deviations of second logarithms of original data from compound-interest secular trend expressed in terms of standard deviation)

	1922	1923
Jan.	......	+1.59
Feb.	......	+1.50
Mar.	......	+1.05
Apr.	......	+0.23
May	......	−0.44
June	−1.63	−0.71
July	−1.41	−0.92
Aug.	−0.70	−0.39
Sept.	−0.02	−0.06
Oct.	+0.74	+0.13
Nov.	+1.37	0.00
Dec.	+1.73	−0.87

would certainly reduce this precedence to much less than fifteen days, it is clear that even though the movements of the two series became substantially synchronous, a lag of prices behind circulation might nevertheless appear. It cannot be stated definitely, however, that circulation did not precede prices during several of the final months of 1923.

Following the computation of the *indices* for the two separate sub-periods, the indicated lags (one month for circulation in the first and one month for prices in the second) were allowed, and the correlation coefficient again computed. In this way the maximum correlation for the entire sub-period June 1922 to December 1923 was raised from + .806(18), previously found when a lag of one month was allowed for the entire period, to + .884(17).

In summary, therefore, it can be stated with much assurance:

1. With respect to exchange rates and prices:

(*a*) That during the inflation régime in Germany, as during that in France, the movements of dollar exchange rates seem *in general* to have preceded those of prices.

(*b*) That in the German inflation as in the French, however, there was a period when prices seemed to precede exchange rates, but always by less than one month.

(*c*) Hence, to the extent that conclusions may be drawn from the limited number of cases observed, that when the movements of prices preceded those of exchange (if at all) the adjustments between the two factors were extremely rapid, while when movements of exchange preceded those of prices (as was usually the case) the adjustments were much more slowly effected.

(*d*) That in the final stages of rapid inflation in both countries the lags either way seemed to disappear very largely or else completely.

2. With respect to prices and circulation:

(*a*) That during the inflation régime in Germany, as during that in France, the movements of prices in general preceded definitely and by a considerable interval those of circulation.

(*b*) That, while in the French inflation there appeared no period during which it was evident that the movements of circulation were preceding those of prices, in the final months of the German inflation it is not certain that circulation did not precede prices, yet there is no conclusive evidence that they did.

(*c*) Hence, when movements of circulation preceded those of prices (if at all), that the adjustments between the two phenomena were extremely rapid indeed, while when movements of prices preceded those of circulation the adjustments were in general extremely slow.

(*d*) That in the final stages of rapid inflation in Germany, as in France, the lags either way became either completely or largely eliminated.

CHAPTER VIII

THE OPERATIONS OF THE BANK OF FRANCE

The detailed analysis of the operations of various financial institutions playing important rôles in the inflation process may well be introduced with a consideration of certain series taken from the statements of the Bank of France. The obvious importance of the operations of this institution in the process of inflation has been discussed in Chapter III above. Suffice it, therefore, to set forth once more three of its functions especially influential in promoting or retarding the process.

As lender to the Government the rôle of the Bank has become of such dominant importance that certain interpreters of the French inflation have found in its advances to the State a sufficient explanation of the extraordinary happenings of the period, neglecting altogether the influence of other factors. In the statistical record above (Chapter V) have been set forth the plausible grounds for such a position. For the moment, however, attention will again be called to the fact that advances from the Bank of France to the State were accorded in any amounts [1] required to meet the needs of the Government. Whatever funds the State found itself unable to raise in other ways were borrowed from the Bank of France, which has been throughout the inflation period a ready, if often unwilling, provider of the purchasing power the State has found it necessary there to obtain.

As guardian of the currency supply the Bank of France, as has been seen, likewise plays an all-important rôle. Except for insignificant amounts of small-change currency, its notes, since the disappearance of the gold and silver coins, have made up the entire monetary circulation of the country. It stands ready at all times

[1] There was at all times a legal maximum to such advances but one which was revised frequently as the needs of the State dictated.

to pay out its notes upon the draft of any of its depositors. And, since these depositors, including most of the banks, may increase their accounts by discounting acceptable paper from their portfolios or by otherwise borrowing from the Bank, it must hold itself likewise ready to increase its note circulation to any extent that its depositors provided with eligible paper may demand. The Bank's one available recourse in preventing an undue note expansion is to cut off this demand. This it formerly accomplished by so regulating its discount and loan rates[2] as to discourage excessive borrowing. Recently, however, as explained in Chapter IV, this control has been much weakened by the practice of the banks of keeping large deposits with the Treasury. Reversely, the Bank receives and retires all notes returned by the Treasury, by the banks, by the *Caisse Autonome d'Amortissement*, and by any other of its depositors.

Finally, as banker to the other French banks, the Bank of France once exercised an important influence over their credit policies and consequently over the inflation process itself. The loaning capacity of any bank would once have been very rigidly limited indeed had it not been for the possibility of rediscounting and of otherwise borrowing at all times at the central institution. Moreover, except for the privilege which they hold as depositors of drawing cash at any time from any of the branches of the Bank of France, the other banks would be forced further to restrict their lending capacities by the necessity of holding large cash reserves. It has been seen in Chapter IV above, however, how the recent practice of the banks of keeping large deposits with the Treasury, combined with that of the Bank of France of purchasing large quantities of foreign exchange, has almost completely freed them, at least temporarily, from the necessity of borrowing at the Bank of France. Hence, in this instance, too, the measure of control held by the Bank has been diminished to the extent that its function of banker to other banks has been assumed by the Treasury.

With a view to throwing as much light as possible on the part played by the Bank of France in the inflation and deflation pro-

[2] By charging a premium on the redemption of its notes in gold, wide fluctuations in such rates were at times avoided.

cesses, a statistical analysis of series taken from its monthly statements will be undertaken.

The advances of the Bank of France to the State have been discussed in Chapter V above. It will suffice here to remind the reader of certain conclusions there reached and to add to that discussion several other considerations of importance in understanding the policies followed by the Bank in extending credit to the Government. The size of these advances, as has been seen above, while large, bulk small in comparison with the total of all sorts of government borrowings. In the table below (Table 43), both are given first in paper francs and then in terms of 1913 general

TABLE 43

TOTAL GOVERNMENT BORROWINGS AND ADVANCES FROM THE BANK OF FRANCE *
(In millions of francs)

Date	Total internal borrowings of the Government		Advances of the Bank of France to the State	
	In paper francs	In terms of 1913 purchasing power [a]	In paper francs	In terms of 1913 purchasing power [a]
Dec. 31, 1914	6,834	6,185	3,900	3,529
Dec. 31, 1915	26,317	16,126	5,000	3,064
Dec. 31, 1916	45,803	22,508	7,400	3,636
Dec. 31, 1917	71,302	23,431	12,500	2,432
Dec. 31, 1918	108,200	30,669	17,150	3,543
Dec. 31, 1919	149,278	35,315	25,500	4,057
Dec. 31, 1920	182,598	41,996	26,600	6,118
Dec. 31, 1921	204,690	62,846	24,600	7,553
Dec. 31, 1922	217,490	60,097	23,600	6,521
Dec. 31, 1923	238,114	591,22	23,300	5,081
Dec. 31, 1924	248,043	48,904	22,600	4,456
Dec. 31, 1925	253,786	40,131	35,950	5,685
Dec. 31, 1926	259,646	41,504	36,000	5,755

[a] Nominal francs divided by the index of wholesale prices of the *Statistique Générale de la France* for December of each year.

* Sources: Total internal borrowings of the Government, Robert M. Haig, *The Public Finances of Post-War France* (New York, Columbia University Press, 1929); advances of the Bank of France to the State, 1914–1919, *Journal Officiel*, 1920–1925, *L'Économiste Français*, and 1926, *Bulletin de Statistique et de Législation Comparée*.

purchasing power,[3] the latter figures being established by dividing the amounts in paper francs by the index of wholesale prices (converted to a 1913 base) of the *Statistique Générale de la France* for December of each year.

But, in spite of the relatively small proportion of the State's total borrowings made up of advances from the Bank, they have apparently played a predominant rôle in the process of inflation. Representing, as they do, pure additions to purchasing power without counterpart of saving elsewhere in the system, their expenditure should naturally lead to the purest type of inflation. Moreover, since, until August 1926, changes in their total corresponded almost exactly with increases or decreases in the normal spending of the Government, it is not surprising that an extremely high degree of correlation was found with similar fluctuations of one of the measures of the extent of inflation: currency supplies.[4] Lest the significance of this close correspondence between the movements of advances and of circulation be overestimated, however, let it be borne continually in mind that the long-term movements (secular trends) of the two series were materially different. What is more, the items of the two series are far from alike in amount. Nor does the proportion between corresponding items in any high degree approach constancy. Indeed, as has been observed in Chapter V, the peculiarities of the Paris money market had almost as much to do with the maintenance of the high correlation between the series as did the peculiar character of these extraordinary borrowings themselves. There is ample room, therefore, for other influences in the French inflation.

The deposits of the Bank of France are divided into two distinct parts: those of the Government and those of all other depositors together. The government deposits (*Compte Courant du Trésor*) require but slight consideration. They are characterized by being small and extremely variable (Charts XXVII and XXVIII). With regard to the weekly data, it is seen that peaks occur almost invariably at the month ends. The explanation is an obvious one

[3] Because of the controlled rates prevailing prior to 1919, the data were not reduced to gold francs.

[4] For the full discussion see Chap. V, pp. 60–72.

and lies in the practice of the Government of meeting its salary payments and certain other expenses at the end of each month and also in the custom of many of the depositors of the Treasury of drawing largely on their accounts at the same time. Against these two outgoes the Treasury must provide itself by accumulating ample balances at the Bank of France. The chart of monthly data (Chart XXVIII) shows that throughout the entire period 1914–1927 Treasury deposits averaged very small indeed, being con-

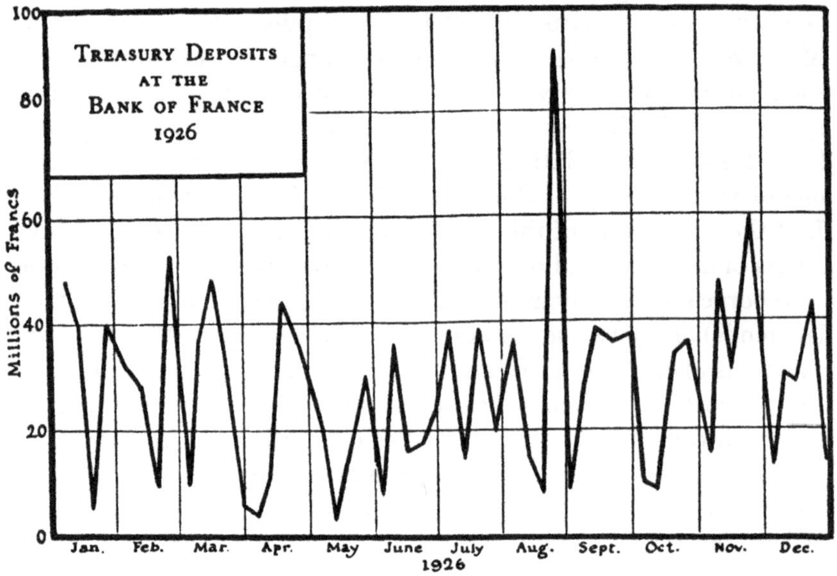

CHART XXVII

sistently less than a hundred millions of francs and often less than twenty millions. It is clear that, especially from 1922 to 1926, the Treasury kept on hand very limited amounts as deposits with the Bank of France. Whatever revenues were received were quickly utilized, if not in meeting current expenses, then in paying off obligations either to the public or to the Bank. The notable exceptions to the small size of the account have simple explanations. In each instance the high points may be related to the large receipts of the Treasury from the flotation of various issues of Government securities. Naturally at these times the account of the Treasury

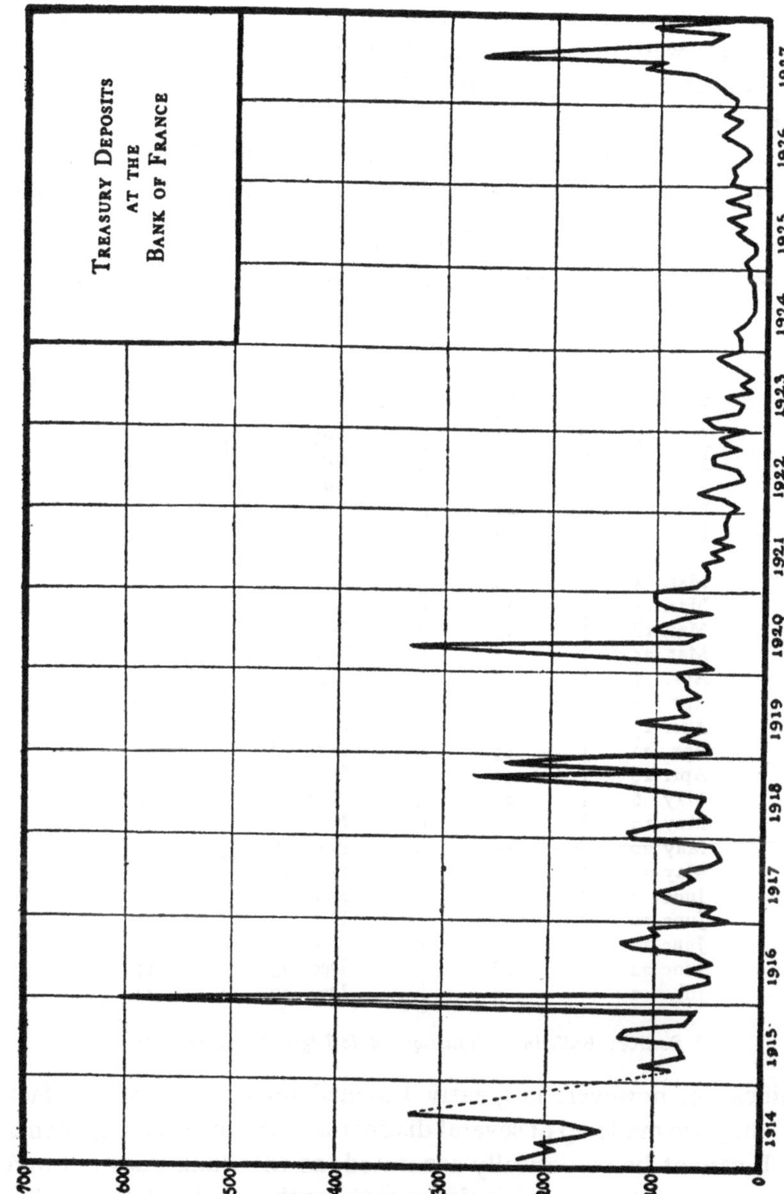

CHART XXVIII

was being swollen daily and consequently appeared large when the reports were made, in spite of the continual pursuance of the policy of using such deposits to reduce advances of the Bank to the State.

The non-governmental deposits of the Bank of France (Chart XXIX) should yield more worth-while information. Their possible

TABLE 44

DEPOSITS OF THE TREASURY AT THE BANK OF FRANCE*

(Weekly data in millions of francs)

1926

Jan. 7	48	July 8	38
Jan. 14	40	July 15	13
Jan. 21	5	July 22	38
Jan. 28	40	July 29	17
Feb. 4	31	Aug. 5	36
Feb. 11	29	Aug. 12	15
Feb. 18	9	Aug. 19	8
Feb. 25	53	Aug. 26	92
Mar. 4	9	Sept. 2	9
Mar. 11	37	Sept. 9	28
Mar. 18	49	Sept. 16	38
Mar. 25	32	Sept. 23	36
Apr. 1	6	Sept. 30	37
Apr. 8	4	Oct. 7	10
Apr. 15	11	Oct. 14	9
Apr. 22	45	Oct. 21	33
Apr. 29	36	Oct. 28	36
May 6	20	Nov. 4	16
May 13	3	Nov. 12	48
May 20	14	Nov. 18	31
May 27	30	Nov. 25	60
June 3	8	Dec. 2	14
June 10	36	Dec. 9	30
June 17	16	Dec. 16	29
June 24	18	Dec. 23	47
July 1	23	Dec. 30	14

* Source: *Bulletin de Statistique et de Législation Comparée.*

significance, however, is greatly lessened on account of the fact that they are made up of several distinct and important components which cannot be statistically separated, as the Bank does not and will not give out the requisite information. After a brief description of the characteristics of the various components, therefore, an examination of the series as a whole must suffice.

In order to be able at all times to make use of the discount and transfer facilities provided by the central institution, most of the banks, as has been pointed out in Chapter III, maintain deposit accounts with the Bank of France. These accounts certainly do not bulk large. No interest is allowed on them, and, since the Bank

TABLE 45

DEPOSITS OF THE TREASURY AT THE BANK OF FRANCE*

(Averages of weekly data for each month in millions of francs)

	1914	1915	1916	1917	1918	1919	1920
Jan.	230	...	78	53	125	45	43
Feb.	190	86	79	41	96	53	53
Mar.	210	112	49	78	43	75	183
Apr.	165	67	51	99	60	52	331
May	156	73	73	76	58	116	74
June	190	76	44	64	53	64	58
July	330	132	61	71	101	75	102
Aug.	...	122	119	43	132	78	80
Sept.	...	69	134	33	274	57	51
Oct.	...	62	97	35	89	67	90
Nov.	...	53	103	38	245	67	102
Dec.	...	606	35	122	160	76	102

	1921	1922	1923	1924	1925	1926	1927
Jan.	62	28	51	23	21	34	26
Feb.	52	40	60	22	12	30	40
Mar.	52	62	26	26	12	32	51
Apr.	56	43	22	20	19	20	67
May	36	22	39	17	28	17	114
June	46	29	19	15	22	19	94
July	25	48	23	15	37	26	267
Aug.	45	47	16	13	19	38	103
Sept.	37	26	25	14	19	30	55
Oct.	38	35	31	15	37	22	36
Nov.	39	44	47	17	25	39	103
Dec.	35	20	22	18	25	27	30

* Sources: 1914–1919, *Journal Officiel;* 1920–1925, 1927, *L'Économiste Français;* 1926, *Bulletin de Statistique et de Législation Comparée.* For Table 44 the data were taken from the weekly reports of the Bank of France, and for Table 45 arithmetic averages were calculated from the weekly reports for each month.

requires only that they be kept large enough to take care of all payments arising from the handling of clearings, collections, and transfers, large balances are not needed. Indeed, there is strong evidence at the present time (December 1927) that all told they amount to little more than half a milliard of francs. Moreover, their proportion to the total deposits of the Bank is probably as high now as has been customary for the past few years.

Likewise, many of the big business establishments — railroads as well as industrials and public utilities — especially those having offices in various parts of the country, keep accounts with the Bank of France. They make continual use of the transfer system, and their distant offices deposit regularly in the local branches of the Bank the funds coming currently into their possession. These accounts form the second component of the non-governmental deposits of the Bank. How much they amount to is impossible to say, though it is certain that their magnitude is far from negligible.

The third component consists largely of the accounts of business firms of various sorts scattered throughout the country. Such firms, some large and others small, but all possessing paper with the requisite three names (or two names supported by acceptable collateral), use the central institution as a bank of loan and deposit. Here also are included the accounts of farmers and of private individuals usually without business connections. They use the Bank of France as most others do the commercial banks. In it they deposit their surplus cash, and from it they borrow to meet their business and personal needs.

With this brief description of the heterogeneous content of the series, the limitations of its analysis are apparent. One is immediately impressed with the fact that unlike most of the other series it has, for the years 1921–1924, a downward trend. Prices, dollar exchange rates, and even the private advances of the Bank itself all showed upward trends during the same period. The most plausible explanation of so strange a movement seems to be that during this period of returning confidence business firms and individuals who during the war period of moratoria and of innumerable uncertainties had for the sake of safety kept considerable balances

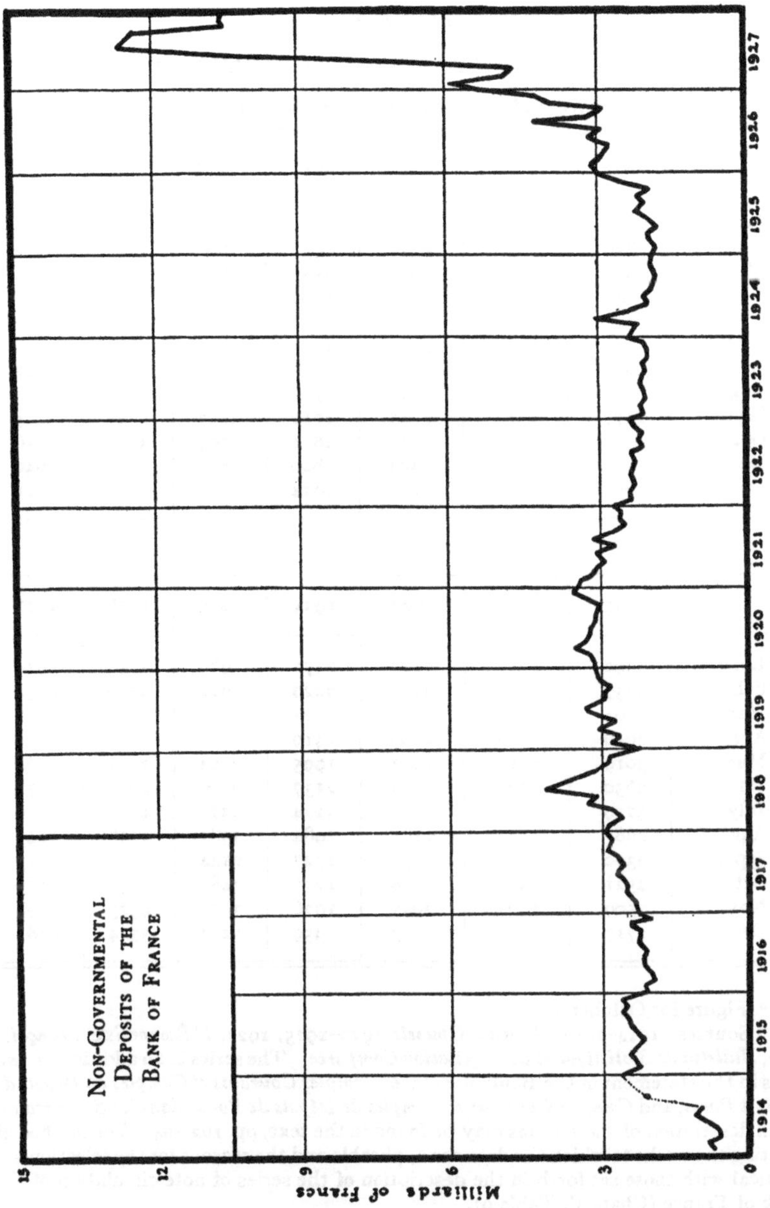
NON-GOVERNMENTAL
DEPOSITS OF THE
BANK OF FRANCE
15
12
9
6
3
0
Milliards of Francs
1914
1915
1916
1917
1918
1919
1920
1921
1922
1923
1924
1925
1926
1927

CHART XXIX

TABLE 46

NON-GOVERNMENTAL DEPOSITS OF THE BANK OF FRANCE *

(Selected end-of-month data in millions of francs)

	1914	1915	1916	1917	1918	1919	1920
Jan.	756	2328	2046	2305	2835	2769	3131
Feb.	830	2356	1942	2452	2608	2648	3232
Mar.	683	2415	2006	2541	2809	3013	3513
Apr.	686	2329	2092	2509	3313	2720	3338
May	846	2201	2109	2629	3162	3200	3639
June	1017	2275	2055	2733	4019	3362	3578
July	943	2380	2273	2588	3845	2952	3307
Aug.	...	2473	2240	2716	3477	2977	3203
Sept.	2177 [a]	2588	2248	2910	3107	2782	3025
Oct.	...	2546	2731	2834	2909	3030	3316
Nov.	...	2671	1852	2800	2816	3089	3640
Dec.	2651	2033	2260	2914	2366	3127	3521

	1921	1922	1923	1924	1925	1926	1927
Jan.	3390	2372	2160	2372	1966	3148	5924
Feb.	3257	2371	2204	2229	2014	2960	4752
Mar.	3104	2311	2041	3223	2039	2802	4457
Apr.	2946	2358	2089	2419	1948	2646	6874
May	3019	2295	2173	1995	2124	3197	10424
June	2630	2276	2142	2137	2409	2909	12677
July	3229	2353	2039	2174	2270	4326	12629
Aug.	2687	2111	2104	1984	2387	3238	12445
Sept.	2390	2179	1974	1727	2144	2958	10575
Oct.	2521	2109	1978	1737	2480	3945	10753
Nov.	2509	2222	2045	1976	3013	4325	10698
Dec.	2717	2289	2363	1959	3244	5324	10481

[a] Figure for October 1.

* Sources: 1914–1919, *Journal Officiel;* 1920–1925, 1927, *L'Économiste Français;* 1926, *Bulletin de Statistique et de Législation Comparée.* The series is an addition of two items in the statement of the Bank of France: *Comptes Courants et Comptes de Dépôts de Fonds à Paris,* and *Comptes Courants et Comptes de Dépôts de Fonds dans les Succursales.* A full description of these items may be found in the text, pp. 162-164. The method of selecting the weeks to which the data are applicable and the reasons for the selection are identical with those set forth in the description of the series of note circulation of the Bank of France (Chap. V, Table 9).

at the Bank of France, were now withdrawing them for deposit in other banks where interest was allowed.

In its minor movements the series shows a noticeable resemblance to circulation and to wholesale prices, and perhaps a slight one to the sight deposits of the "Big Four." Correlation coefficients were not computed, however, as there seemed to be little purpose in so doing.

Beginning in October 1926, the private deposits of the Bank of France became greatly disturbed by the entrance of an entirely new influence. At that time the newly created *Caisse Autonome d'Amortissement* began depositing in the Bank. Its resources are very great, and for some reason the institution has seen fit to maintain literally huge balances with the Bank. By no stretching of terms, however, can these deposits be regarded as anything else than funds of the Treasury, held for the specific purpose of amortizing and retiring the floating debt of the State. Under present laws the *Caisse d'Amortissement* can make use of them for no other purpose. Nevertheless, they cannot but constitute a sort of emergency reserve of the Treasury. A part of the funds were recently transferred to it in connection with the issue of the 6 per cent obligations of July 1927. *Bons de le Défense Nationale* were received by the Treasury in payment for subscriptions to the new issue and at once discounted for the Treasury by the *Caisse d'Amortissement.* Thus the bonds were immediately retired, and the Treasury received funds to a corresponding amount from the deposit resources of the *Caisse* at the Bank.

A rough estimate of the amounts of the deposits of the *Caisse d'Amortissement* at the Bank of France on various dates has been made by subtracting from the non-governmental deposits as reported in the statements of the Bank the sum of 3,500 millions of francs, the approximate level reached at the middle of 1926 a short time before the *Caisse* in its present form came into existence. These estimates are reported in the table on the following page.

Of much greater significance in interpreting the inflation process are the non-governmental advances of the Bank of France. Made up very largely of paper of five days or less to run entrusted

TABLE 47

DEPOSITS OF THE *CAISSE D'AMORTISSEMENT* AT THE BANK OF FRANCE *

(Estimated amounts for selected end-of-month dates in millions of francs)

1926		1927	
October	444	May	6924
November	825	June	9177
December	1824	July	9129
1927		August	8945
January	2424	September	7075
February	1252	October	7253
March	957	November	7198
April	3374	December	6981

* Estimated on the basis of selected end-of-month deposit data.

to the Bank for collection, they include, besides, loans to banks, loans to business firms and loans to private individuals, as well as a considerable volume of rediscounts of the regional offices of the *Crédit Agricole*. Because of the higher rates of interest charged by the Bank of France on commercial paper, big business concerns with unquestioned credit do most of their current borrowing from the commercial banks.

The loans to banks represent, on the whole, a general expansion of bank credit through the economic system. In France, as in other countries where central banking is practiced, houses doing a commercial banking business rely on advances or rediscounts from the central bank to meet the demands of customers for loan accommodations in any considerable excess of normal. Hence, an increase in such lendings by the Bank of France usually indicates an expansion of credit by the commercial banks.

The advances of the Bank to farmers and to small business people, on the other hand, represent simply an unprofitable sort of bank credit, generally quite small in amount, extended to a class of people who would otherwise be practically without banking accommodation. But, so far as inflation is concerned, such loans mean much the same as a like expansion of credit at the commercial banks. So likewise do the borrowings of bigger business firms, which, carrying deposit accounts at the Bank of France, as many

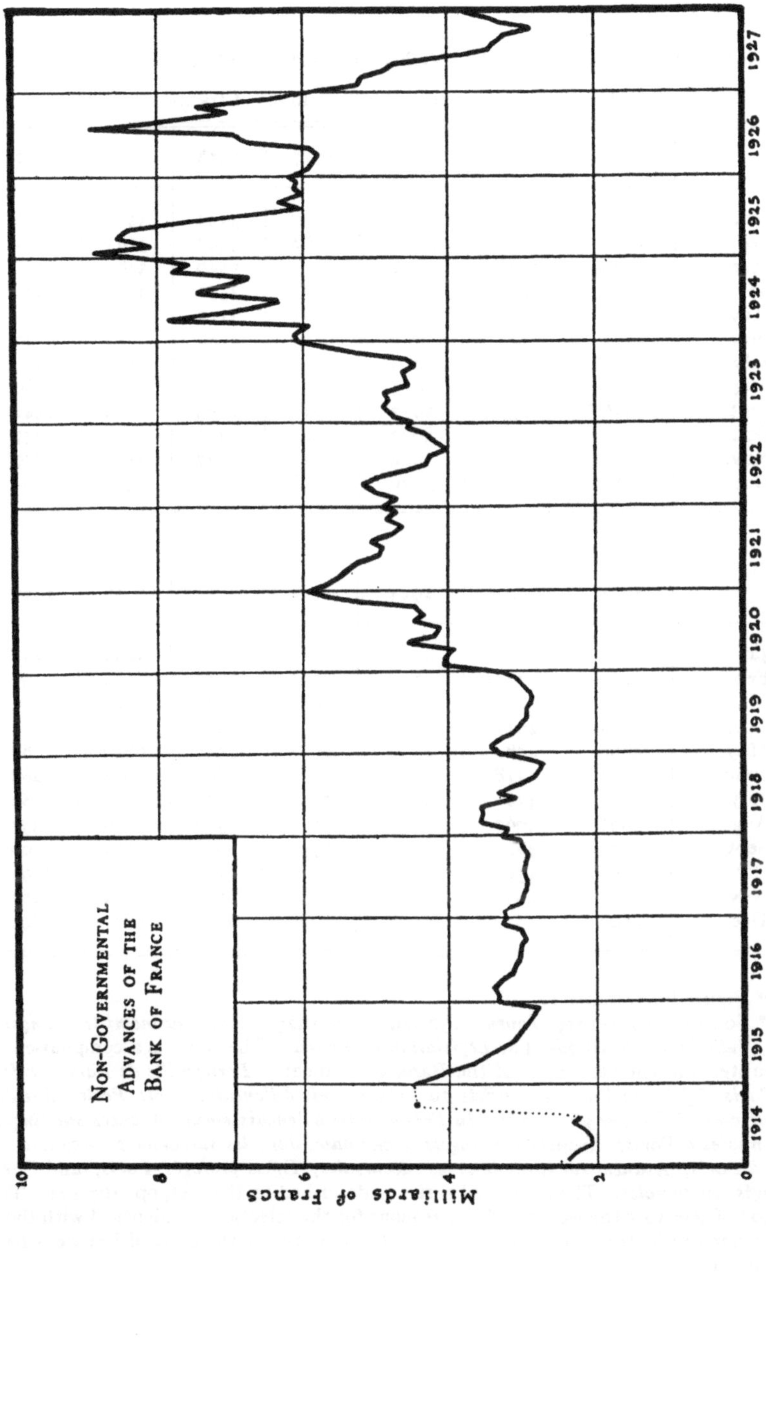
NON-GOVERNMENTAL
ADVANCES OF THE
BANK OF FRANCE
Milliards of Francs
10
8
6
4
2
0
1914
1915
1916
1917
1918
1919
1920
1921
1922
1923
1924
1925
1926
1927

CHART XXX

TABLE 48

NON-GOVERNMENTAL ADVANCES OF THE BANK OF FRANCE *

(Selected end-of-month data in millions of francs)

	1914	1915	1916	1917	1918	1919	1920
Jan.	2403	4155	3392	3297	3244	3474	4022
Feb.	2281	4100	3408	3068	3597	3295	4004
Mar.	2178	3686	3304	3004	3549	3183	3920
Apr.	2177	3472	3204	2923	3551	3025	4526
May	2228	3306	3166	2835	3117	2903	4233
June	2355	3156	3091	2883	3384	2940	4170
July	2280	3018	3073	2876	3065	2884	4474
Aug.	....	2923	3024	2867	2798	2865	4369
Sept.	4476 [a]	2832	2973	2846	2743	2934	4444
Oct.	....	2765	3023	2899	2710	3004	5257
Nov.	....	2736	3324	3011	2947	3127	5739
Dec.	4481	3385	3276	3278	3291	3359	5894

	1921	1922	1923	1924	1925	1926	1927
Jan.	5681	4731	4757	6116	8864	5893	5251
Feb.	5488	5038	4814	5915	8083	5841	5195
Mar.	5346	5210	4782	7853	8579	5762	4793
Apr.	5204	4917	4816	7178	8448	5859	4707
May.	4869	4581	4556	6674	7590	6856	3787
June	4811	4318	4577	6347	6893	7054	3483
July	5024	4306	4605	7404	6037	8998	3382
Aug.	4696	4062	4430	7119	6362	7939	3357
Sept.	4572	4223	4645	6753	6058	7051	2900
Oct.	4769	4307	5304	7735	6189	7495	3296
Nov.	4577	4674	5678	7533	6156	6514	3482
Dec.	4804	4512	6073	8180	6238	5797	3840

[a] Figure for October 1.

* Sources: 1914–1919, *Journal Officiel;* 1920–1925, 1927, *L'Économiste Français;* 1926, *Bulletin de Statistique et de Législation Comparée.* The series is a compilation of eleven items in the statement of the Bank of France: — *Portefeuille de Paris: Effets sur Paris, Effets sur l'étranger, Effets du Trésor remis à l'encaissement; Portefeuille des Succursales: Effets sur place, Effets du Trésor remis à l'encaissement; Avances sur lingots et monnaies à Paris; Avances sur lingots et monnaies dans les succursales; Avances sur titres à Paris; Avances sur titres dans les succursales; Effets prorogés, Paris;* and *Effets prorogés, succursales.* The combined series is described in the text, pp. 167-171. The method of selecting the weeks and the reasons for the selection are identical with those set forth in the descriptions of the series of note circulation of the Bank of France (Chap. V, Table 9).

of them do, use their privilege of borrowing when their holdings of prime paper discountable at the other banks are temporarily insufficient in amount to meet their credit needs.

Unfortunately, these various types of accounts comprising the non-governmental advances of the Bank cannot be separated. Like most other French financial institutions, the Bank of France has not yet learned of the advantages to be gained by taking the public into its confidence. Perhaps because of the impossibility of separating them into their significant components, the non-governmental advances of the Bank of France seem to indicate little during the war period. Reports for two dates during the latter half of 1914 show them high in September and in December of that year. In January 1915 they were also very high. Thereafter they dropped slowly to a level only approximately two-thirds of that prevailing at the end of 1914. This level they maintained with but minor fluctuations until the end of the war. The moratoria[5] of the early days of the war account for the high level then obtaining, the Bank of France naturally having accepted the obligation of taking care of the other banks temporarily burdened with frozen assets. The plentiful supplies of funds put out by the Bank in the form of advances to the State furnish ample explanation for the low level of the war years and for that of 1919. Beginning in early 1920, however, when the advances of the Bank to the State were becoming relatively stable and when business had become very active, the private advances of the Bank rose rapidly, indicating clearly the effect of the business expansion. As was natural for the early stages of business depression, they continued to increase during the latter part of 1920 and to decrease but slowly during 1921. During the following year and three-quarters private advances fluctuated about a nearly horizontal line, while both prices and production recovered slowly.

Beginning in the fall of 1923 and for a year and a half thereafter the private advances of the Bank rose rapidly. Production (Charts XXXI and XXXII), prices, and trade, as indicated by car loadings (Charts XXXIII and XXXIV), continued their upward trends until the fall of 1924. But the precipitate and persistent rise in

[5] See Chap. IX, footnote 6, p. 221.

TABLE 49

THE VOLUME OF PRODUCTION: MONTHLY INDICES OF THE *STATISTIQUE GÉNÉRALE DE LA FRANCE* *

(Base 100 in 1913)

	1919	1920	1921	1922	1923
Jan.	57	65	62	66	88
Feb.	57	64	58	69	83
Mar.	57	64	55	75	83
Apr.	59	63	52	75	82
May	60	60	50	78	82
June	62	63	50	79	87
July	64	62	49	81	88
Aug.	62	64	49	82	91
Sept.	60	65	48	84	92
Oct.	61	68	50	87	95
Nov.	61	68	55	89	97
Dec.	62	67	62	88	98

	1924	1925	1926	1927	
Jan.	102	110	118	117	
Feb.	104	109	122	113	
Mar.	104	108	123	108	
Apr.	102	107	125	106	
May	104	106	126	106	
June	103	105	126	106	
July	107	105	127	106	
Aug.	110	106	128	107	
Sept.	114	107	128	109	
Oct.	117	111	129	110	
Nov.	113	116	129	112	
Dec.	113	118	123	115	

* Source: 1919–1924, *Bulletin de Statistique Générale de la France*, April 1926; 1925–1927, *op. cit.*, July 1927.

This production index prepared by J. Dessirier for the *Statistique Générale de la France* is a weighted arithmetic average of individual production indices for 8 groups of industries. The group indices are computed with the use of various sorts of data, relating, however, always to the physical volume of production. Actual production figures are used only in the construction of the indices for the extractive industries group and for the metallurgical industries group and for the data applying to the cotton and wool industries of the textile group. For the remaining ones other physical criteria are employed. For the indices of the paper and rubber industries and for the production data of particular industries of other groups, monthly import balances of raw materials destined for consumption in the industries in question are utilized after reduction to moving averages. In the construction of the index for the leather in-non-governmental advances, while doubtless partially related to these movements, can hardly be explained entirely by them. As will be pointed out later, part of the rise resulted from certain hidden and indirect advances of the Bank to the State.

Although in pre-war days one of the most sensitive barometers as well as one of the most powerful controls of the credit situation, the discount policy of the Bank of France lost much of its importance as the inflation progressed. The story of its changes during the war period is short and significant. On July 30, 1914 the discount rate was raised from 3½ per cent to 4½ per cent and the rate for advances on collateral from 4½ per cent to 5½ per cent. On the first of August they were again raised to 6 per cent and 7 per cent respectively. Thus, the beginning of the war was marked by a very substantial increase in rates. They were evidently found too

---

dustries group and for the production data applying to the iron and steel industries, composite monthly figures of output plus import balances of raw materials are used, also after reduction to moving averages. The index for the building industry group is based upon the number of building permits issued in certain cities. (It is to be especially noted that building operations in the devastated regions are left out of account.)

Since the production of Alsace-Lorraine is included in the post-war data from which the indices are computed, the production figures for the base year 1913 have been increased for each group of industries to allow for the pre-war production of Alsace-Lorraine. In the absence of reliable production data for all of the industries involved, the weights applied to the group indices going into the construction of the general index are taken, for the pre-war period, as the percentages of active population employed in the respective industrial groups at the time of the 1906 census. These weights, as applied to the indices for the base year and to the indices for the post-war years were modified to take into account the production of Alsace-Lorraine and the relative development or retrogression in each of the respective groups in the course of the years 1906–1913. The corrections were made sometimes on the basis of the actual contribution of Alsace-Lorraine to production, sometimes on the basis of population figures, and sometimes on the basis of the increases in the output of the industries in the respective groups as indicated by the group indices for 1906 and 1913.

A list of the groups of industries considered and of the weights applied to the indices for these groups in the computation of the general index is appended:

Groups of Industries	*Weights*
Extractive	4
Textile	14
Metallurgical	2.5
Mechanical	15
Building	7
Paper	1.6
Leather	5
Rubber	.9

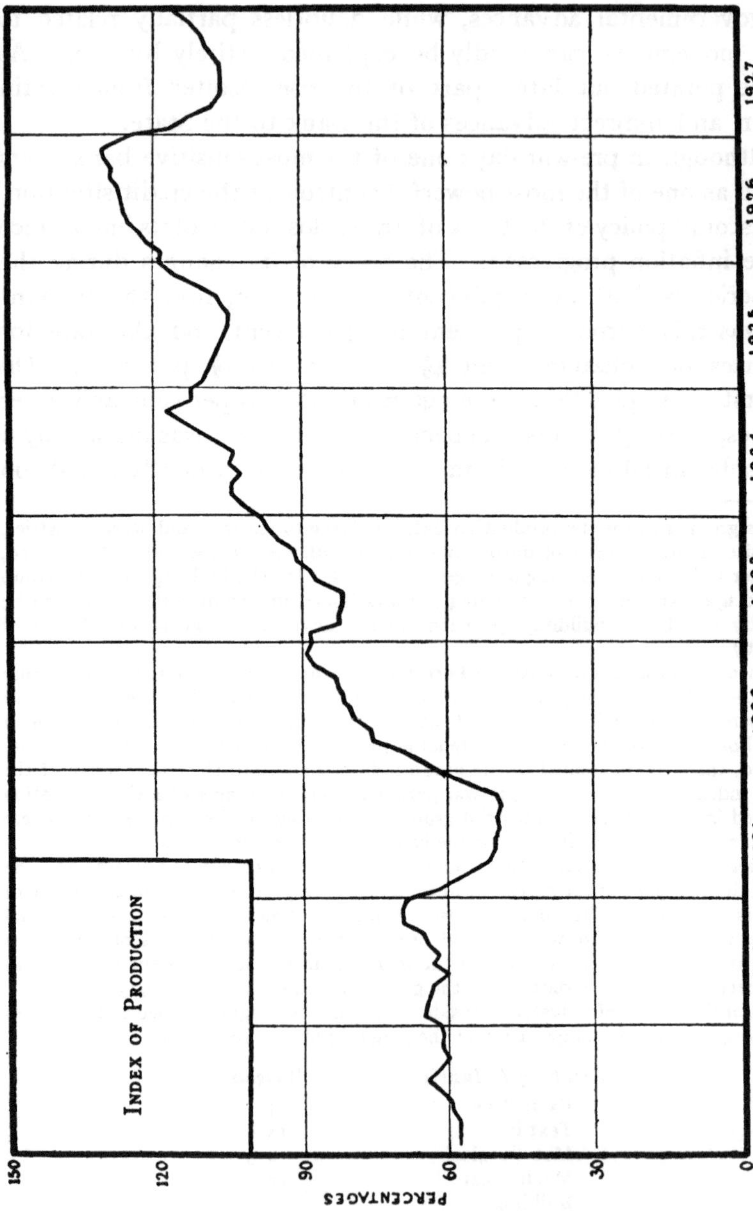
INDEX OF PRODUCTION
PERCENTAGES
150
120
90
60
30
0
1919
1920
1921
1922
1923
1924
1925
1926
1927

CHART XXXI

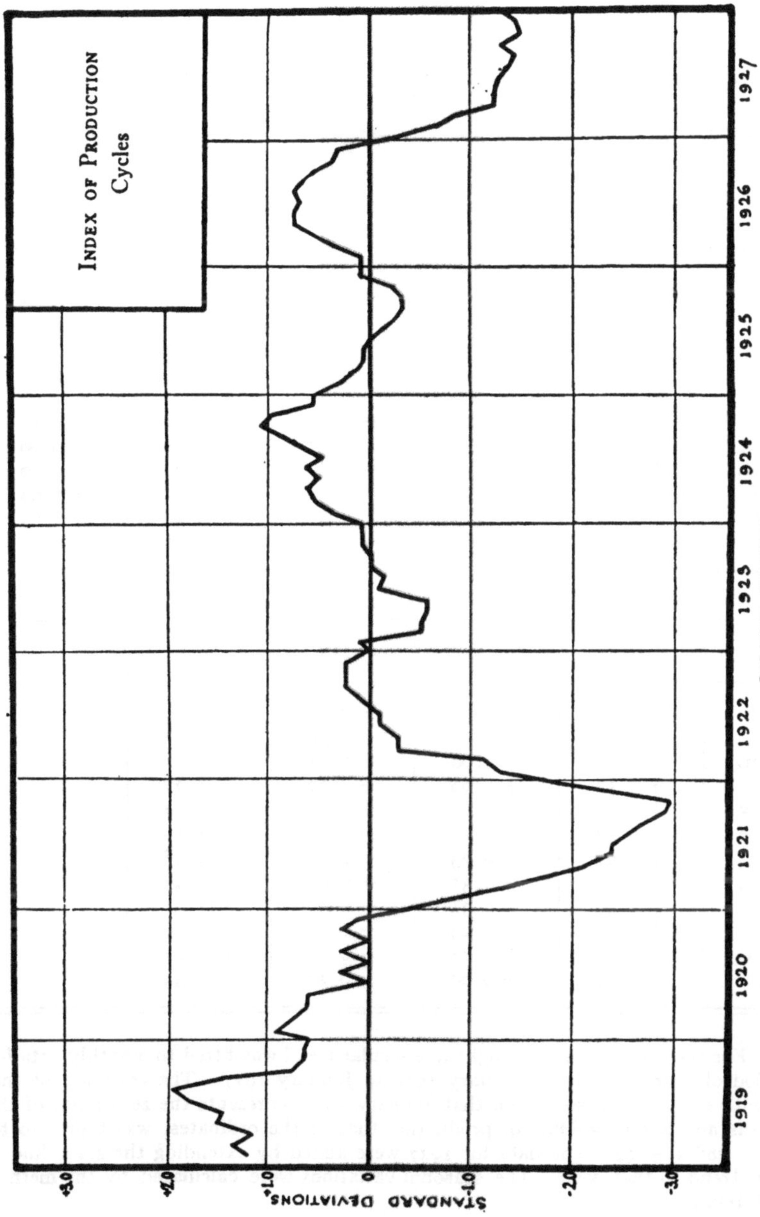
Index of Production
Cycles
1919
1920
1921
1922
1923
1924
1925
1926
1927
+3.0
+2.0
+1.0
0
-1.0
-2.0
-3.0
STANDARD DEVIATIONS

CHART XXXII

TABLE 50

THE VOLUME OF PRODUCTION: MONTHLY INDICES OF THE *STATISTIQUE GÉNÉRALE DE LA FRANCE**

(Percentage deviations from secular trend in terms of standard deviation, allowance made for seasonal variations)

	1919	1920	1921	1922	1923
Jan.	+ 1.21	+ 0.87	− 0.76	− 1.32	+ 0.10
Feb.	+ 1.38	+ 0.72	− 1.25	− 1.09	− 0.48
Mar.	+ 1.19	+ 0.57	− 1.72	− 0.32	− 0.48
Apr.	+ 1.49	+ 0.57	− 2.06	− 0.32	− 0.57
May	+ 1.47	0.00	− 2.39	− 0.11	− 0.57
June	+ 1.80	+ 0.27	− 2.39	− 0.10	− 0.09
July	+ 1.92	0.00	− 2.59	0.00	− 0.19
Aug.	+ 1.42	+ 0.27	− 2.67	+ 0.10	0.00
Sept.	+ 0.77	+ 0.14	− 2.86	+ 0.20	0.00
Oct.	+ 0.60	+ 0.26	− 2.94	+ 0.20	+ 0.09
Nov.	+ 0.60	+ 0.13	− 2.48	+ 0.20	+ 0.09
Dec.	+ 0.59	− 0.25	− 1.79	0.00	+ 0.09

	1924	1925	1926	1927	
Jan.	+ 0.36	+ 0.25	+ 0.08	− 0.62	
Feb.	+ 0.53	+ 0.16	+ 0.36	− 0.88	
Mar.	+ 0.61	+ 0.08	+ 0.51	− 1.21	
Apr.	+ 0.52	+ 0.08	+ 0.72	− 1.27	
May	+ 0.60	0.00	+ 0.72	− 1.14	
June	+ 0.42	− 0.15	+ 0.64	− 1.19	
July	+ 0.67	− 0.23	+ 0.71	− 1.38	
Aug.	+ 0.84	− 0.31	+ 0.64	− 1.43	
Sept.	+ 1.08	− 0.31	+ 0.56	− 1.31	
Oct.	+ 0.99	− 0.23	+ 0.35	− 1.49	
Nov.	+ 0.57	+ 0.08	+ 0.28	− 1.47	
Dec.	+ 0.57	+ 0.08	− 0.20	− 1.34	

* For the calculation, a straight-line secular trend was fitted to monthly data for a period of 97 months from January 1919 to January 1927. The equation of this line, with origin (0, 0) so chosen that January 1919 represents the zero point of the abscissas and a zero volume of production that of the ordinates, was found to be $y = + .788\,x + 49$. The data for 1927 were added by extending the same line of secular trend to that year. The seasonal variations were calculated by the method of link relatives.

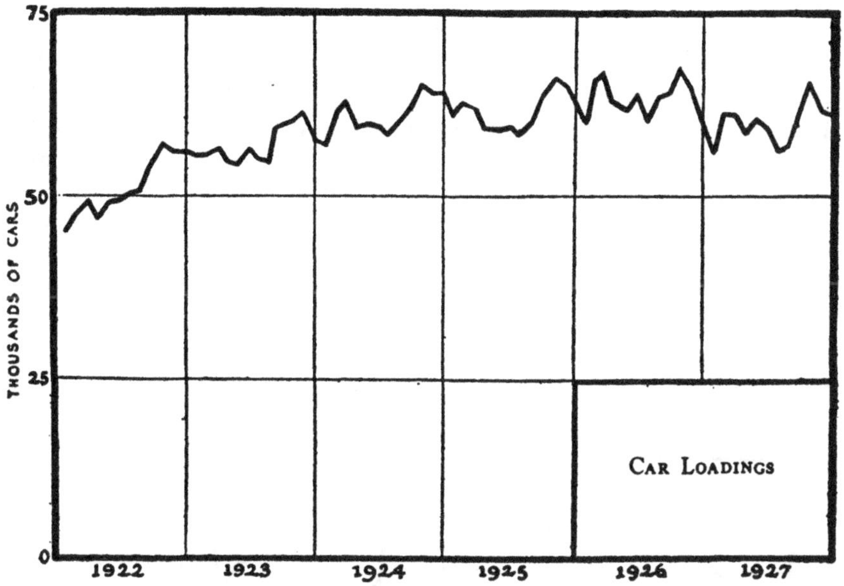

CHART XXXIII

TABLE 51

CAR LOADINGS *

(Averages for each month of daily car loadings)

	1922	1923	1924	1925	1926	1927
Jan.	45584	55052	57362	61361	60808	56663
Feb.	47741	55464	61609	63352	66179	61967
Mar.	49676	56971	63228	62990	67329	61880
Apr.	47225	54930	59126	58944	63193	58817
May	49055	54272	59777	58946	62075	60858
June	49585	56757	59597	59683	64856	59494
July	50031	55073	58708	58037	61478	56549
Aug.	50875	54964	60303	60143	63487	57386
Sept.	54431	59025	62812	64107	64600	61032
Oct.	57185	60517	65471	66542	67923	66507
Nov.	56046	61976	64256	65957	65125	62963
Dec.	55848	57995	64284	63437	60775	61456

* Source: *Bulletin de la Statistique Générale de la France.* The figures represent averages of cars loaded daily on French railroads. The averages are computed by dividing total car loadings for each month (made up of the totals for weeks falling entirely or mostly in each month) by the number of days involved.

high, however, for less than a month later (August 20) they were each reduced by 1 per cent. At these lower levels they were maintained throughout the war period and until April 8, 1920. On that date, in the month of the highest point in prices for the post-war boom, they were again raised to 6 per cent and 6½ per cent respectively. Whether causally connected or not with the adjustment of the rates, there immediately followed the long and precip-

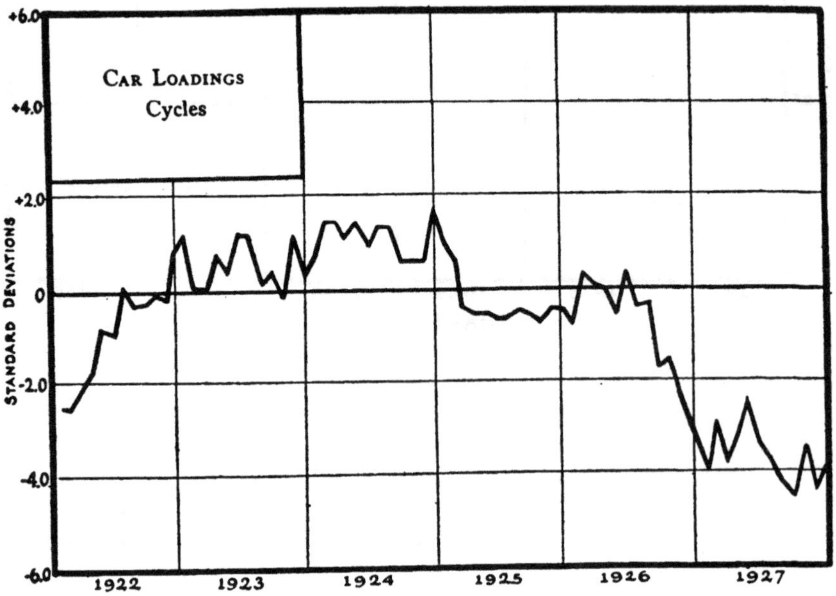

CHART XXXIV

itate decline in prices which continued with but one halt — shortly after the decline began — until the middle of the next year. After November 1920 the volume of production likewise underwent a sharp decline. On July 28, 1921 the discount rate was accordingly again reduced to 5½ per cent. After an insignificant recovery during the following three months, the price decline continued until March of the following year. On the eleventh of that month the discount rate was again reduced to 5 per cent, where it was continued until January 10, 1924. By that time both prices and the volume of business had made substantial recoveries, and — what

TABLE 52

CAR LOADINGS *

(Percentage deviations from secular trend in terms of standard deviation, allowance being made for seasonal variations)

	1922	1923	1924	1925	1926	1927
Jan.	− 2.32	+ 1.21	+ 0.68	+ 1.00	− 0.77	− 3.94
Feb.	− 2.47	+ 0.03	+ 1.44	+ 0.59	+ 0.32	− 2.97
Mar.	− 2.18	+ 0.03	+ 1.44	− 0.38	+ 0.06	− 3.79
Apr.	− 1.79	+ 0.71	+ 1.18	− 0.50	0.00	− 3.26
May	− 0.79	+ 0.32	+ 1.44	− 0.53	− 0.53	− 2.41
June	− 0.91	+ 1.21	+ 0.94	− 0.59	+ 0.32	− 3.35
July	+ 0.09	+ 1.09	+ 1.29	− 0.56	− 0.38	− 3.79
Aug.	− 0.27	+ 0.21	+ 1.27	− 0.38	− 0.29	− 4.21
Sept.	− 0.24	+ 0.41	+ 0.56	− 0.44	− 1.71	− 4.56
Oct.	− 0.06	− 0.15	+ 0.56	− 0.62	− 1.53	− 3.56
Nov.	− 0.09	+ 1.18	+ 0.56	− 0.29	− 2.15	− 4.41
Dec.	+ 0.88	+ 0.24	+ 1.65	− 0.35	− 2.94	− 3.91

* For the calculation, a straight-line secular trend was fitted to monthly data for a period of 59 months from January 1922 to November 1926. The equation of this line, with origin so chosen that January 1922 represents the zero point of the abscissas and a zero volume of car loadings that of the ordinates, was found to be $y = +275.4\ x + 51055$, m being 275.4 and b 51055 cars loaded. The data for 1927 were added by extending the same line of secular trend to that year. The seasonal variations were calculated by the method of link relatives.

was probably of primary importance — note circulation was mounting rapidly and steadily. Under such circumstances the discount rate was once more raised to 5½ per cent only to be pushed up an additional one-half per cent a week later as both circulation and prices continued their upward movements. At the same time the rate for advances on security was raised for the first time since 1920. It was then placed one-half per cent higher and was again increased in September to 8 per cent.

The next change in the Bank rates came on December 11, 1924, when the discount rate was raised from 6 per cent to 7 per cent. This adjustment came at a very critical period indeed. It was later charged (though probably erroneously) that the maximum limit prescribed by law for the advances of the Bank to the State had already been surpassed and that the illegal advances were only

TABLE 53

LOANING RATES OF THE BANK OF FRANCE*

Dates of Change	Discount Rate	Rate for Advances on Security
Jan. 1, 1914	4%	4½%
Jan. 29, 1914	3½%	....
July 30, 1914	4½%	5½%
Aug. 1, 1914	6%	7%
Aug. 20, 1914	5%	6%
Apr. 20, 1920	6%	6½%
July 28, 1921	5½%	....
Mar. 11, 1922	5%	....
Jan. 10, 1924	5½%	....
Jan. 17, 1924	6%	7%
Sept. 11, 1924	....	8%
Dec. 11, 1924	7%	....
July 9, 1925	6%	....
July 31, 1926	7½%	9½%
Dec. 16, 1926	6½%	8½%
Feb. 3, 1927	5½%	8%
Feb. 17, 1927	....	7%
Apr. 14, 1927	5%	6%
Dec. 29, 1927	4%	....

* Source: The data for all years were taken from the records of the Bank of France.

being concealed from the public by misrepresentations in the Bank's statements. In any event, the advances had become dangerously large, and it had begun to appear that with the approach of the new year little less than a miracle could prevent the note circulation from likewise exceeding its legal maximum. The change in the discount rate failed to accomplish the purpose probably intended, but the price level, which had been rising steadily for eight months, became practically stable for the following five, and the volume of production, which had already begun to decrease during the previous month, continued its downward trend for several months thereafter.

The legal limits of both notes and advances were raised by legislative action in April 1925, and on July 9 the discount rate was returned to 6 per cent. This action was taken by the Bank in spite of the fact that prices for two months previous had been rising slowly. The volume of production, on the other hand, had been on a steady decline since October of the preceding year. At these rates — 6 per cent for discounts and 8 per cent for advances on securities — the Bank continued to lend until the desperate crisis of July 1926. On the thirty-first of that memorable month the rates were each raised by 1½ per cent, to 7½ per cent and 9½ per cent respectively. After that time, as the crisis gradually

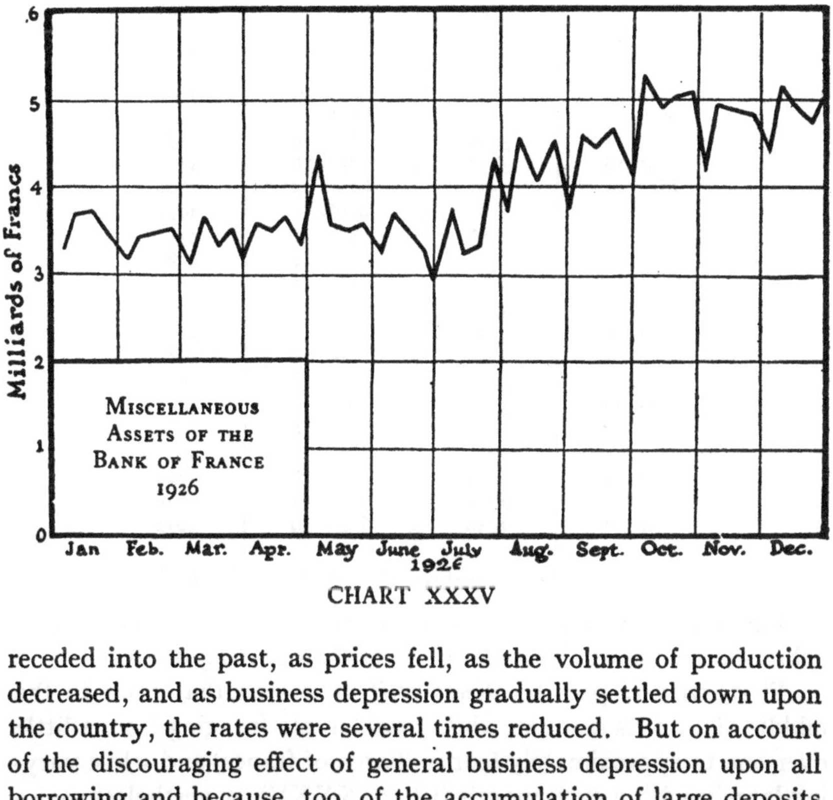

CHART XXXV

receded into the past, as prices fell, as the volume of production decreased, and as business depression gradually settled down upon the country, the rates were several times reduced. But on account of the discouraging effect of general business depression upon all borrowing and because, too, of the accumulation of large deposits of the banks in the Treasury — rendering unnecessary borrowing on their part from the Bank of France — and in view, further, of the continual issue of funds by the Bank for the purchase of foreign exchange, such rates, adjusted partially, no doubt, for moral effects, largely ceased to exert even a sentimental influence over the outside market.

TABLE 54

MISCELLANEOUS ASSETS OF THE BANK OF FRANCE*

(Weekly data in millions of francs)

1926

Jan. 7	3312	July 8	3704
Jan. 14	3677	July 15	3214
Jan. 21	3707	July 22	3376
Jan. 28	3561	July 29	4233
Feb. 4	3183	Aug. 5	3689
Feb. 11	3487	Aug. 12	4555
Feb. 18	3467	Aug. 19	4043
Feb. 25	3529	Aug. 26	4503
Mar. 4	3158	Sept. 2	3787
Mar. 11	3640	Sept. 9	4575
Mar. 18	3367	Sept. 16	4454
Mar. 25	3502	Sept. 23	4602
Apr. 1	3187	Sept. 30	4072
Apr. 8	3586	Oct. 7	5311
Apr. 15	3567	Oct. 14	4984
Apr. 22	3612	Oct. 21	5009
Apr. 29	3353	Oct. 28	5062
May 6	4339	Nov. 4	4189
May 13	3581	Nov. 11	4985
May 20	3543	Nov. 18	4866
May 27	3599	Nov. 25	4832
June 3	3220	Dec. 2	4388
June 10	3655	Dec. 9	5137
June 17	3498	Dec. 16	4892
June 24	3303	Dec. 23	4738
July 1	2948	Dec. 30	5010

* Source: *Bulletin de Statistique et de Législation Comparée.*

Finally, the miscellaneous items of the Bank's statement, both debit and credit, will be found of more than passing interest.

First, with respect to *Divers actif*, it is seen that prior to the middle of 1926 its amount, while considerable (ranging from a little over one to approximately four milliards of francs) and while varying largely within each month (Chart XXXV), nevertheless maintained a remarkable stability from month to month and from year to year (Chart XXXVI). True, there was a noticeable increase from year to year, but one so regular as to be almost calculable. Beginning with January 1927, however, the item began to rise above its former trend so rapidly as to indicate clearly that the content of the item had greatly changed. What had happened

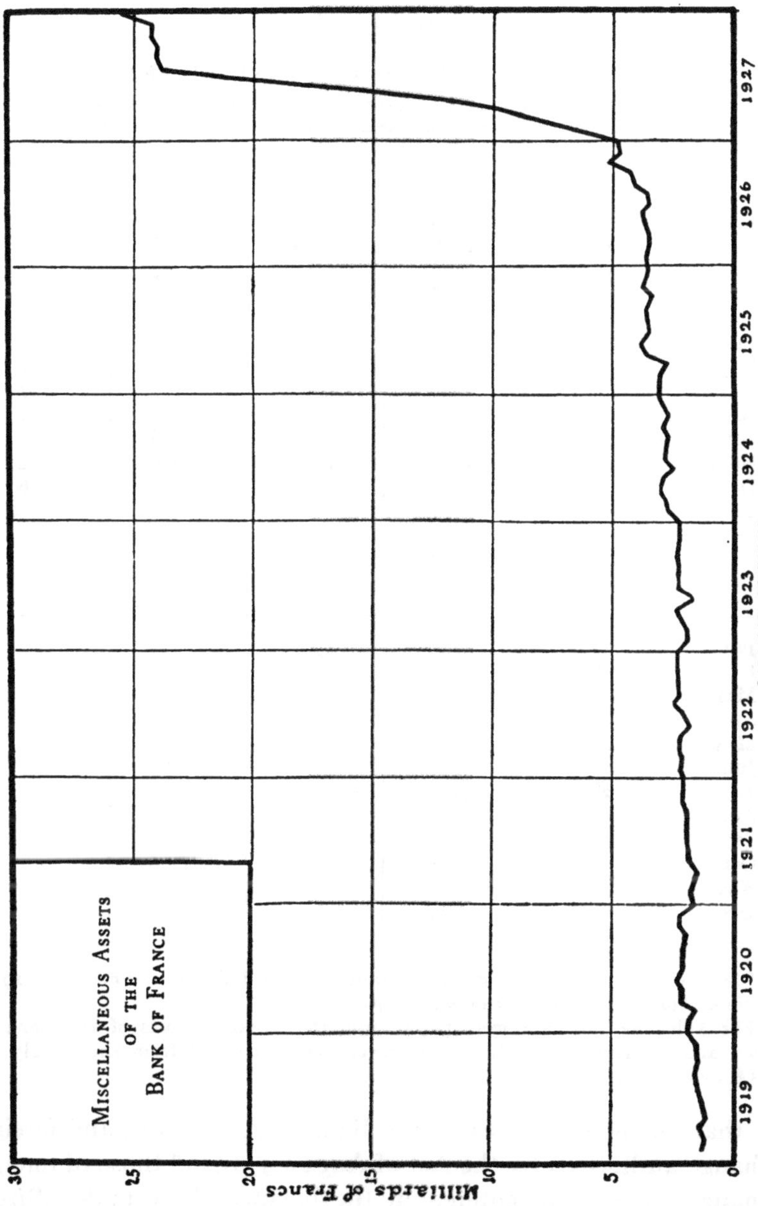

Miscellaneous Assets
of the
Bank of France
1919
1920
1921
1922
1923
1924
1925
1926
1927
30
25
20
15
10
5
0
Milliards of Francs

CHART XXXVI

TABLE 55

MISCELLANEOUS ASSETS OF THE BANK OF FRANCE *

(Averages of weekly data for each month in millions of francs)

	1919	1920	1921	1922	1923
Jan.	1351	1820	1728	2112	1972
Feb.	1336	1778	1640	2008	1926
Mar.	1356	2096	1644	2199	2132
Apr.	1322	2028	1773	2187	2272
May	1467	2276	1901	1913	1677
June	1518	2048	1993	2026	2238
July	1578	2014	1973	2404	2341
Aug.	1661	2018	1929	2126	2237
Sept.	1598	1889	1935	2263	2480
Oct.	1600	2156	2090	2276	2328
Nov.	1731	2062	2059	2252	2224
Dec.	1849	1556	2008	2247	2256

	1924	1925	1926	1927	
Jan.	2741	3029	3564	6451	
Feb.	2829	3039	3417	8459	
Mar.	3146	2801	3417	9963	
Apr.	2964	3839	3461	11830	
May	2681	3926	3765	16893	
June	2962	3670	3419	21165	
July	2853	3640	3495	23727	
Aug.	2807	3725	4192	23864	
Sept.	2952	3499	4298	23867	
Oct.	2818	3751	5091	24396	
Nov.	2959	3527	4718	24372	
Dec.	3066	3504	4833	25547	

* Sources: 1919, *Journal Officiel;* 1920–1925, 1927, *L'Économiste Français;* 1926, *Bulletin de Statistique et de Législation Comparée.*

For Table 54 the data were taken from the weekly reports of the Bank of France, and for Table 55 arithmetic averages were calculated from the weekly reports for each month.

was that, of the purchases by the Bank of gold, silver, and foreign exchange authorized by the Act of August 7, 1926,[6] those of foreign exchange were being entered in the balance sheet under *Divers actif.* The series should, therefore, give us an excellent means of

[6] The date of the enabling *Convention* was September 16, 1926.

estimating the total of such purchases. Accordingly, a linear secular trend for four years beginning with July 1922 was fitted to the series by the method of least squares. The distances above this secular trend line at the times of the last reports of each month were regarded as representing the holdings of foreign exchange purchased under the terms of the above-mentioned law. Adding to these amounts those entered in the statement under the caption "Purchases of gold, silver, and foreign exchange" (*Achats d'or, d'argent et de devises*), estimated totals of the purchases by the Bank of all three items were obtained.

TABLE 56

PURCHASES OF GOLD, SILVER, AND FOREIGN EXCHANGE BY THE BANK OF FRANCE

(Estimated totals in millions of francs)

1926		1927	
September	198	April	10426
October	2207	May	16954
November	2320	June	20258
December	2555	July	22488
		August	21885
1927		September	21649
January	4867	October	22012
February	6819	November	22536
March	8913	December	24437

From the table it is seen that these purchases, beginning a few months[7] after the authorizing act was passed, increased at a rapid rate until the middle of 1927, when they reached the substantial total of approximately twenty milliards of francs. After a slight decrease in August this total continued to increase, though at a much less rapid rate. At the end of December it stood at approximately 24 milliards. This large accumulation of gold and foreign exchange (the amount of silver is very small) of more than 800 million dollars provides a fund of indeed extraordinary dimensions and one which is always available for use in the protection of the franc, should manipulation from abroad again be attempted.

[7] The Bank of France began its purchase of foreign exchange on December 23, 1926.

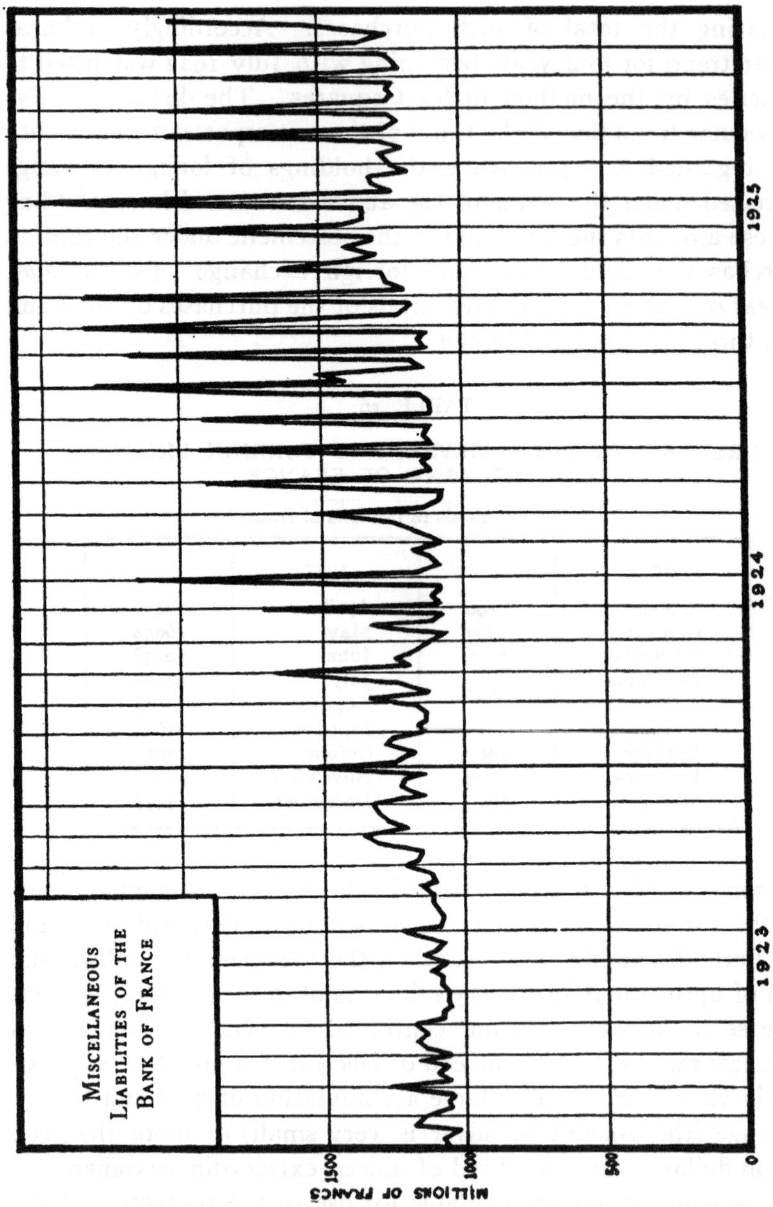

CHART XXXVII

Divers passif, while much more erratic in its movements than *Divers actif*, nevertheless kept a comparatively regular trend from 1919 until the end of 1923. Thereafter it is characterized by a

TABLE 57

MISCELLANEOUS LIABILITIES OF THE BANK OF FRANCE*

(Weekly data in millions of francs)

1923

Jan. 4	1061	May 3	1174	Sept. 6	1117
Jan. 11	1088	May 11	1080	Sept. 13	1133
Jan. 18	1027	May 17	1082	Sept. 20	1115
Jan. 25	1188	May 24	1065	Sept. 27	1120
Feb. 1	1156	May 31	1068	Oct. 4	1205
Feb. 8	1043	June 7	1067	Oct. 11	1167
Feb. 15	1053	June 14	1095	Oct. 18	1152
Feb. 22	1038	June 21	1095	Oct. 25	1306
Mar. 1	1290	June 28	1122	Nov. 2	1366
Mar. 8	1053	July 5	1065	Nov. 8	1204
Mar. 15	1105	July 12	1149	Nov. 15	1277
Mar. 22	1074	July 19	1118	Nov. 22	1310
Mar. 29	1169	July 26	1090	Nov. 29	1326
Apr. 5	1057	Aug. 2	1214	Dec. 6	1161
Apr. 12	1148	Aug. 9	1096	Dec. 13	1211
Apr. 19	1170	Aug. 16	1092	Dec. 20	1202
Apr. 26	1146	Aug. 23	1103	Dec. 27	1156
		Aug. 30	1117		

1924

Jan. 3	1542	May 1	1142	Sept. 4	1526
Jan. 10	1255	May 8	1086	Sept. 11	1129
Jan. 17	1182	May 15	1319	Sept. 18	1097
Jan. 24	1290	May 22	1110	Sept. 25	1095
Jan. 31	1271	May 30	1081	Oct. 2	1894
Feb. 7	1149	June 5	1697	Oct. 9	1223
Feb. 14	1171	June 12	1097	Oct. 16	1113
Feb. 21	1143	June 19	1112	Oct. 23	1135
Feb. 28	1146	June 26	1088	Oct. 30	1109
Mar. 6	1171	July 3	2160	Nov. 6	1921
Mar. 13	1340	July 10	1178	Nov. 13	1114
Mar. 20	1135	July 17	1100	Nov. 20	1149
Mar. 27	1231	July 24	1123	Nov. 27	1137
Apr. 3	1643	July 31	1181	Dec. 4	1914
Apr. 10	1197	Aug. 7	1088	Dec. 11	1121
Apr. 17	1237	Aug. 14	1133	Dec. 18	1127
Apr. 24	1188	Aug. 21	1190	Dec. 26	1162
		Aug. 28	1259		

* Source: *L'Économiste Français.*

TABLE 57

(continued)

1925

Jan. 2	2308	May 7	1399	Sept. 3	2041
Jan. 8	1418	May 14	1301	Sept. 10	1268
Jan. 15	1517	May 22	1407	Sept. 17	1221
Jan. 22	1147	May 28	1316	Sept. 24	1252
Jan. 29	1185	June 4	1995	Oct. 1	2091
Feb. 5	2203	June 11	1406	Oct. 8	1253
Feb. 12	1146	June 18	1352	Oct. 15	1249
Feb. 19	1151	June 25	1351	Oct. 22	1253
Feb. 26	1145	July 2	2514	Oct. 29	1237
Mar. 5	2367	July 9	1259	Nov. 5	1833
Mar. 12	1701	July 16	1325	Nov. 12	1237
Mar. 19	1220	July 23	1332	Nov. 19	1241
Mar. 26	1161	July 30	1198	Nov. 26	1255
Apr. 2	2353	Aug. 6	1240	Dec. 3	2227
Apr. 9	1201	Aug. 13	1289	Dec. 10	1391
Apr. 16	1289	Aug. 20	1205	Dec. 17	1274
Apr. 23	1292	Aug. 27	1283	Dec. 24	1553
Apr. 30	1630			Dec. 31	2032

succession of extremely high peaks appearing approximately monthly and almost invariably in the report for the week including the month end. The explanation of such a change, beginning as it did in the year of increasing financial uneasiness and becoming more pronounced in the critical years of 1925 and 1926, is far from clear. The content of the item is not published, and a direct request for it at the Bank of France failed to yield more than the general explanation that it represented for the most part items in transit between the central office and the various branches. Naturally such items should be larger at month ends. But why they should be so very much larger at month ends (or month beginnings) since 1923 than before, while their general level remained substantially constant, is still unexplained. Since it is generally believed that the note circulation — later admitted by M. Henry Bérenger on the floor of the Senate[8] to have been in excess of the legal maxi-

[8] "A cette date du premier avril 1925, le chiffre effectif des billets en circulation était voisin de 43 milliards, en dépassement d'environ 2 milliards par rapport à la limite légale de 41 milliards autorisée par le décret du 28 septembre 1920, pris par application de la loi du 31 juillet 1920." — *Journal Officiel, Débats Parlementaires, Sénat*, April 16, 1925, p. 865.

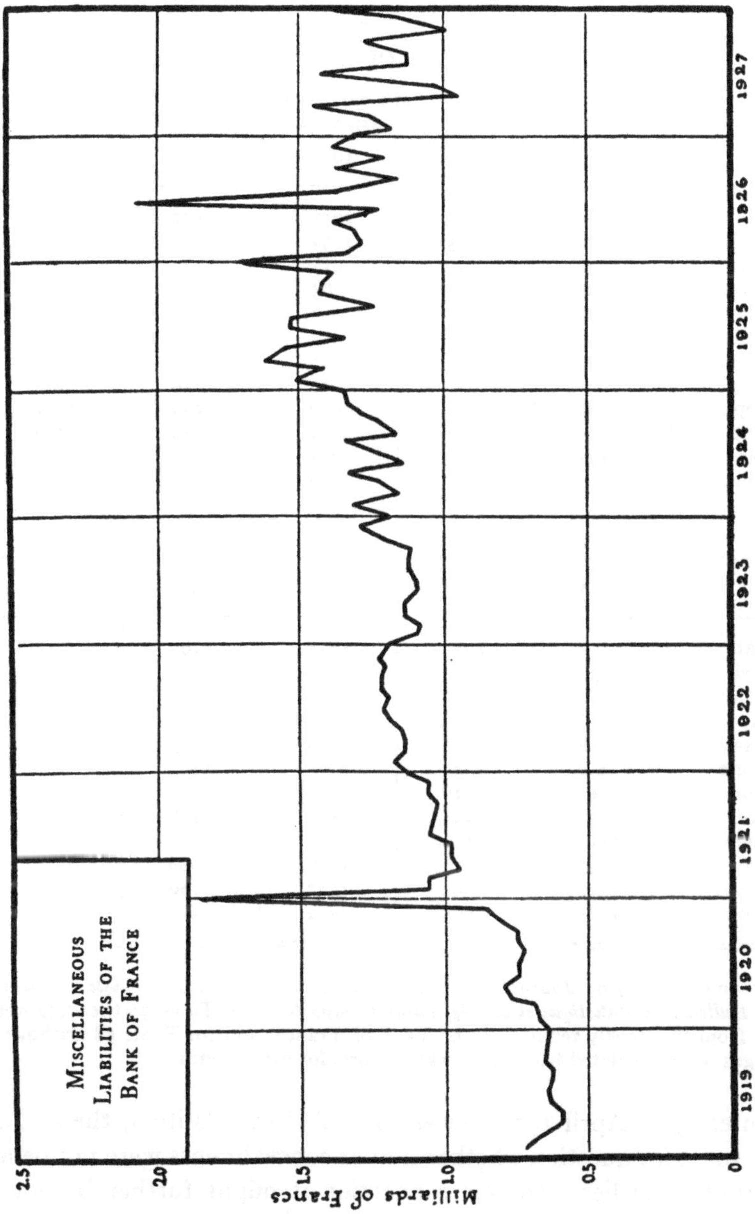

CHART XXXVIII

TABLE 58

MISCELLANEOUS LIABILITIES OF THE BANK OF FRANCE *

(Averages of weekly data for each month in millions of francs)

	1919	1920	1921	1922	1923
Jan.	706	673	1051	1177	1091
Feb.	652	685	1052	1136	1073
Mar.	596	775	953	1133	1138
Apr.	590	800	985	1146	1130
May	628	745	992	1171	1094
June	630	745	1053	1206	1095
July	623	726	1038	1199	1106
Aug.	622	739	1029	1218	1124
Sept.	648	746	1020	1216	1121
Oct.	645	808	1044	1213	1208
Nov.	638	863	1053	1223	1297
Dec.	637	1841	1118	1195	1183

	1924	1925	1926	1927	
Jan.	1308	1515	1334	1196	
Feb.	1152	1411	1294	1269	
Mar.	1219	1612	1321	1439	
Apr.	1316	1553	1373	940	
May	1148	1356	1220	1025	
June	1249	1526	2064	1403	
July	1348	1526	1381	1129	
Aug.	1168	1254	1166	1126	
Sept.	1212	1446	1370	1273	
Oct.	1295	1417	1216	996	
Nov.	1330	1392	1375	1180	
Dec.	1331	1695	1322	1392	

* Sources: 1919, *Journal Officiel;* 1920–1925, 1927, *L'Économiste Français;* 1926, *Bulletin de Statistique et de Législation Comparée.* For Table 57 the data were taken from the weekly reports of the Bank of France, and for Table 58 arithmetic averages were calculated from the weekly reports for each month.

mum early in April 1925 — was concealed in this item, there is at least room for question whether similar concealments were not being resorted to earlier. In this connection it might further be noted that during December 1920, when, there is little reason to doubt, the Bank of France was making indirect advances to the State in excess of the legal maximum for direct advances by discounting for the lending banks paper presented by them for the purpose of making payments to the Treasury, this item increased greatly for several weeks, while the *reported note circulation* — which for the entire period, December 1914 to December 1926, had a correlation with advances of the Bank to the State of +.98(145) — actually declined. For the exact character of these extraordinary movements, the reader is referred to the accompanying graphs (Charts XXXVII and XXXVIII) and tables (Tables 57 and 58).

What then can be said in general with regard to the position of the Bank of France in the various phases of the inflation and deflation processes during the war and post-war years? Certainly its influence has been extremely important. For reasons which have been seen above, however, a quantitative estimate of its importance is very difficult to obtain.

By far the most significant part played by the Bank of France was in its rôle as lender to the Government, to the banks, and to business firms. *And perhaps the most vital question of all is how influential have been the borrowings of the Government from the Bank and the spending resources thus procured, as opposed to the borrowing of private individuals both from the Bank of France and from the commercial banks and their spending of funds thus obtained.*

In a quantitative analysis of the question the close correlation of one of the chief measures of the extent of the inflation, note circulation, with the advances of the Bank to the State becomes again important. It has been observed in Chapter V, however, that, on account of the peculiarities of the Paris money market and the extraordinary borrowing methods of the Treasury, this close correlation does not have the significance which its high coefficient — +.98(145) — would normally indicate. The analysis is directed, therefore, to the loans and advances of the commercial banks, which except in emergencies lend only to non-governmental borrowers.

Here, however, the investigation is largely thwarted by the practice of these banks of reporting in a single item their commercial portfolio and their holdings of short-term Treasury paper. Especially annoying is this policy in view of the further well-established practice of the banks of investing in short-term Treasury paper whatever funds are not demanded by their customers. For, by thus combining in their reports two complementary items, they fall little short of concealing completely their most important loaning operations. Even resort to the *ratio* of "loans plus short-term Treasury paper" and deposits can yield but little. True, in France as elsewhere, loans will expand more rapidly and by greater amounts in periods of business activity than will deposits. And, since the investments in short-term Treasury paper consume funds to exactly the extent of their purchase, the combined item of loans plus holdings of such Treasury obligations should in periods of increasing business activity still be larger than deposits. But, with both sides of the ratio loaded with the extremely heavy[9] dead weight of short-term Treasury paper holdings (or, identically, with the funds consumed in their purchase), its changes cannot but be extremely small. Moreover, deposits of the banks in the Treasury, which are not included with any of the loan items, but with cash holdings, serve as a further distorting element in the ratio; for, while they were doubtless insignificant in magnitude until the middle of 1925, small amounts are able to disturb a ratio based upon such minute differences as is the one under consideration. And in the latter part of the period, when such deposits became very large, the ratio could not but lose all of its normal significance.

[9] The following passages taken from the annual statements of the *Crédit Lyonnais* indicates the large holdings of such obligations in 1920 and again in 1922:

"Le montant des effets de commerce escomptés par votre Siège Central ne s'est pas développé autant qu'il serait désirable, car le vrai et bon papier reste toujours rare. La partie de beaucoup la plus importante de votre portefeuille se compose toujours de Bons du Trésor français et de Bons de la Défense Nationale.

"Nous sommes heureux de constater également l'augmentation du papier bancable escompté par votre Établissement. Cet accroissement déjà notable au cours des précédentes années, n'a pas été inférieur en 1922 à 30% environ du montant enregistré en 1921. Cependant le solde de votre portefeuille commercial, bancable ou non, reste encore très au-dessous du chiffre qu'il devrait atteindre pour permettre de répartir, suivant les proportions d'avant-guerre, entre les divers emplois que peut faire une banque de dépôts, les sommes confiées à votre Société. Les effets émis par le Trésor et n'ayant au maximum que 3 mois à courir forment toujours, de beaucoup, la majeure partie du poste de votre bilan intitulé: Portefeuille et Bons de la Défense Nationale."

By reference to Chart XLI (page 215 below), it is seen that after the middle of 1919 "loans plus holdings of short-term Treasury paper" exceeded deposits of the "Big Four" for almost six years. Presumably during the prosperity period of 1919 and 1920 a considerable portion of the excess of loans resulted from enlarged borrowing on the part of business firms and hence represented increased commercial portfolios. On the other hand, the continued excess during the depression years of 1921 and early 1922 is difficult to explain except on the basis of frozen credits which undoubtedly existed in considerable amounts during that period. The excess of deposits after the middle of 1925 is easily explained by the tendency of the banks to place their funds more and more in investments other than short-term government obligations. In particular, during this period of general "flight from the franc," their accounts with foreign correspondents increased notably, as did likewise those of the investment banks.[10]

The excess of deposits was, without doubt, partly also a result of

[10] The changes in this item, as given by the annual statements of the "Big Four" and of the two largest investment banks are set forth in the table below.

TABLE 59

ACCOUNTS OF FRENCH BANKS WITH FOREIGN CORRESPONDENTS *

(In millions of francs)

	Société Générale	Comptoir d'Escompte	Crédit Industriel	Banque de Paris et des Pays-Bas	Banque de l'Union Parisienne
1922	76	177	16	137	15
1923	92	244	7	207	57
1924	172	292	12	283	99
1925	378	358	34	669	270
1926	638	452	73	463	228

* Source: *Annual Reports of the Councils of Adminstration to the General Assemblies of Stockholders.* All of the banks concerned include their French correspondent balances with their foreign balances, but since the practice of French banks depositing funds with other French banks is neither customary nor wide-spread, the slight proportion of the above amounts which represent balances with French correspondents will not conceal the real increase of foreign credits held. Figures for the *Crédit Lyonnais* are wanting because of the fact that this bank includes its correspondent balances partly in the item *Comptes courants débiteurs* and partly in the item *Espèces en Caisse, chez les Trésoriers et dans les Banques.*

the extensive deposits by the banks in the Treasury. The total of such deposits, including, in addition to those of the banks, those made by private individuals and by business firms, is given in the following table.

TABLE 60

DEPOSITS IN THE TREASURY *

(In millions of francs)

DATE	AT PARIS [a]	TOTAL [b]	DATE	AT PARIS [a]	TOTAL [b]
Jan. 1, 1919	218		Mar. 31		7845
Jan. 1, 1920	646		Apr. 30		7397
Jan. 1, 1921	928		May 1	917	
Jan. 1, 1922	618		May 31		7681
Jan. 1, 1923	676		June 30		8338
Jan. 1, 1924	556		July 31	2167	8378
1925			Aug. 31		7904
Jan. 1	1055		Sept. 30	1717	7833
Jan. 31		7156	Oct. 31	2606	8925
Feb. 28		7430	Nov. 30	2255	8571
Mar. 31		7295	Dec. 31	2629	8975
Apr. 30		7706	1927		
May 31		8240	Jan. 31	2111	8090
June 30		7734	Feb. 28	3330	9630
July 31		7463	Mar. 31	6179	12258
Aug. 31		7385	Apr. 30	6894	13254
Sept. 30		7914	May 31	9214	16010
Oct. 31		7715	June 30	10882	17776
Nov. 30		8756	July 31	9862	16911
Dec. 31		8776	Aug. 31	6349	13457
1926			Sept. 30		13041
Jan. 1	2496		Oct. 31		
Jan. 31		8376	Nov. 30		
Feb. 28		7545	Dec. 31		

[a] "Deposits in the Treasury at Paris" represent deposits at the *Caisse Centrale* and are made up, after 1921, largely of the accounts of the banks. Before 1921 only the accounts of firms and of individuals who furnished supplies to the Government are represented. Many large accounts not those of individuals, of banks, or of business firms, such as the accounts of the City of Paris, of the *Caisse des Dépôts et Consignations*, and of certain other public institutions, are not included.

[b] "Total deposits in the Treasury" include all deposits at the *Caisse Centrale* and, in addition, those at the *Trésoreries Générales* in the provinces.

* Sources: "Deposits in the Treasury at Paris": January 1919–May 1926, *Rapport du Comité des Experts* (Paris, Imprimerie Nationale, 1926); July 1926–September 1927, Chappedelaine, *Rapport du Budget Général de l'Exercise 1928* (Paris, Imprimerie de la Chambre des Députés, 1927). "Total deposits in the Treasury": all data furnished by the Ministry of Finance.

So little progress having thus been made toward answering the important question posed, a reëxamination will be made of the non-governmental advances of the Bank of France, discussed earlier in this chapter (Chart XXX).

This series seems to throw much light on the question. Its rapid rise in August 1914 indicates clearly the immediate relief given by the Bank of France to the other banks, the liquid assets of which had been "frozen" by the government moratoria, while its gradual decline after September of that year bears witness to the slow but steady liquidation of such accounts. The low level maintained from the end of 1915 until late in 1919 indicates further that during that period credit conditions and the inflation were, with little doubt, dominated by the spending of the Government and by the resulting direct borrowings from the Bank by the State and that neither the banks nor business people were borrowing extensively from the Bank of France. The funds liberated by the advances made to the Government naturally flowed soon to the banks and furnished for them the necessary basis for further advances to business. That this was happening during the war period and for at least one year thereafter is brought out by the inverse movements of the governmental and non-governmental advances of the Bank[11] (Chart XXXIX).

It is pretty clear, however, that beginning late in 1919 business spending and borrowing became of influence in continuing the inflation process. It will be remembered that about that time there began a period of rapidly rising prices and of considerable business activity. And what is of interest here is that non-governmental advances increased steadily and rapidly, while those to the State remained nearly constant. It is evident, therefore, (in view of what has been said in Chapter V of the position of the advances of the Bank to the State with regard to government spending) that business purchasing was exerting influence on the credit situation, stimulating prices, expanding deposits, and in general affecting the immediate course of inflation. Somewhat less influential were

[11] It is also significant that the secular trends for the two series move inversely, that for advances to the State being an upward trend and that for non-governmental advances a downward one.

the credit contraction policies of business firms in the depression year of 1921. During that period both governmental and non-governmental advances decreased considerably, the former by somewhat more than the latter, while business activity and prices at the same time declined. That in the activity period extending from late 1922 to the end of 1924 business (as opposed to government) borrowing and spending were usually the major influences

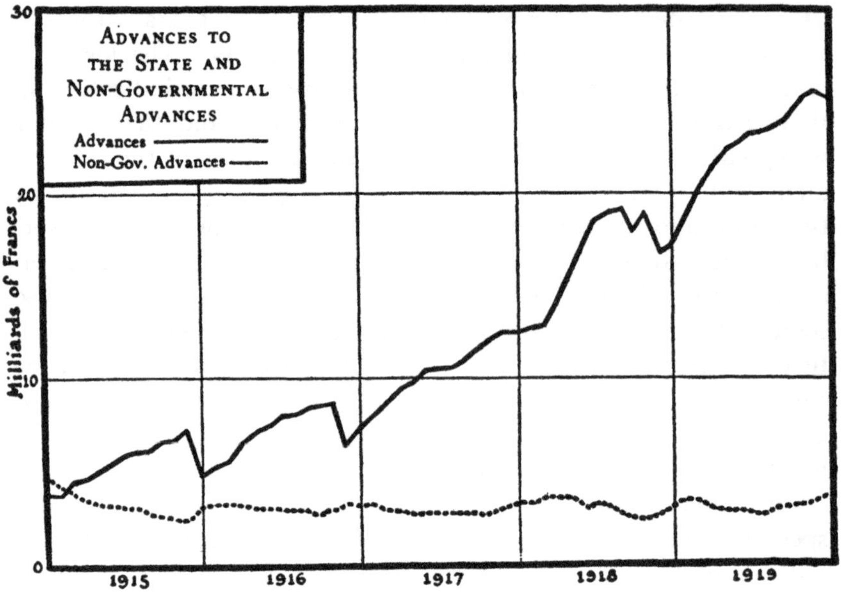

CHART XXXIX

on prices and on circulation there seems little doubt, though at least a portion of the increase in non-governmental advances in 1924 was, as will be explained presently, undoubtedly a result of indirect advances of the Bank to the State. During most of 1925 and until April 1926, it seems even more evident, the large borrowings from the Bank by the State were not only dominating the credit situation but were even so large as to cause the non-governmental advances of the Bank to decrease at a time when prices, circulation, and the pecuniary volume of business were increasing.

Moreover, another important influence made its appearance.

During this last period, as was explained in detail in the preceding chapter, the political uncertainties, bearing as they did directly upon budgets, upon taxes, and, consequently, upon the prospect of future borrowings and even upon the eventual solvency of the State, had stimulated in various foreign exchange centres a large volume of sales of "forward francs" by speculators seeking a profit from the further fall in their value. This speculation necessarily caused the banks handling the forward contracts to protect themselves by making simultaneous sales of like amounts of "spot" francs. Consequently, after the early months of 1925, the franc continued the downward trend which it had abandoned only a year earlier after the debacle of March 1924. This gradual decline of the franc in terms of foreign currency led to increased foreign buying of French goods, to a gradual but lagging rise in prices, and finally, as it became necessary to make the larger payments, to an increase in the currency supply.

To return to the discussion of the relative importance to be attached to government, as opposed to non-government, borrowing and spending in the inflation and deflation processes, it is seen that, in the latter half of 1926 and most of 1927, both types of borrowing decreased rapidly and very greatly, while prices declined until the beginning of 1927 and business activity thereafter. Here again, due credit being given to the salutary effects on the whole population of the country of the new confidence in the Poincaré Government, there seems little doubt that the whole order of events was dominated by the movement in exchange rates, which strengthened gradually at first and then very rapidly until the end of the year. In their train came an inevitable reduction in foreign buying of French goods, a like reduction in prices, and, finally, a diminution of currency and deposits as reduced business activity and lower prices came to prevail. But the extreme decrease in both types of borrowing resulted from still another influence. During this period the Bank of France purchased and still holds large quantities of foreign exchange aggregating approximately 22 milliards of francs (December 1927). The funds put out for these purchases flowed largely to the banks, which in the absence of business demand for credit naturally used of them what was necessary to pay off outstanding indebtedness at the Bank of France and elsewhere and the remainder to deposit in the Treasury. Small amounts were likewise doubtless thus deposited by private individuals and by business firms into whose hands they fell. From whatever source received, they were in turn used by the Treasury to pay off its advances from the Bank of France. The net result was that both government and non-government advances at the Bank were reduced much beyond the point to which the business depression and a lower price level would have brought them.

With this discussion of the relative importance of the chief operations of the Bank of France in the inflation process completed, attention is turned to certain of its extraordinary operations. These consisted (1) of its indirect advances to the State in excess of the legal maximum for direct advances and (2) of its issue of notes in excess of the legal maximum prescribed.

The indirect advances to the State, according to dependable information, have been granted from time to time since 1920. They first received wide publicity and severe public condemnation in April 1925 when they, along with the extra-legal note issues of the Bank of France, came up for discussion in the Senate. The circumstances of the case were that, finding the Treasury in desperate need of funds and at the same time, because of the maximum legal limit to advances from the Bank to the State, unable to secure further direct credit from the Bank of France, the Minister of Finance appealed to other banks to relieve the emergency. A number of them agreed to provide the necessary funds in return for the issue to them of short-term Treasury paper. But this important understanding was included in the agreement: that the Bank of France would at once rediscount for the banks paper in sufficient quantity to pay for the Treasury paper thus purchased — as in the cases made public it actually did on the day following the loan negotiation. Thus the Bank, although in reality lending to the Treasury, was enabled to enter the additional advances under "Portfolio" instead of under "Advances to the State" and, consequently, to fulfill the letter but not the spirit of the law. Just how often such a practice has been followed by the Bank has never been made public.[12] There is statistical evidence, however, of its use on a considerable scale.

During the months October-December 1920 non-governmental advances rose abruptly (Chart XXX), although prices and the volume of production were both declining sharply. During the same period the advances of the Bank to the State remained generally stationary just below the legal maximum prevailing at that time. Again, beginning in the fall of 1923 private advances mounted rapidly while, as reported by the Bank of France, those to the State remained almost constant just below their legal limit. Furthermore, throughout 1924 and the early months of 1925 private advances continued high and generally rising, while during the whole of 1924 advances to the State maintained a dead level and subsequently decreased by a little over a milliard in January 1925.

All of these movements seem very strange indeed and especially so since, during late 1923 and early 1924, circulation (which, as has been seen earlier in this chapter, had for the entire period 1915–1926 a correlation coefficient of + .98(145) with advances to the State), as officially reported, was rising with considerable rapidity. In early 1925 its rise was likewise arrested, however, as it approached the legal maximum prescribed for note circulation. Moreover, prices during this period, while rising, were in general below their normal secular trend, and business, as indicated by the movements of car loadings and the volume of production, while active, averaged not greatly above normal. Also, the peculiar saw-toothed character of the curve of private advances cannot help but be noted, a character which has no counterpart whatever either in prices or in the volume of production and trade. The inference is almost inescapable, therefore, that the much condemned practice of the Government of concealing real advances from the Bank by borrowing directly from the other banks and having the Bank of France actually provide the funds through rediscount was in rather continual use from late 1923 until April 1925, as well as at intervals

[12] A number of instances are cited by Georges Lachapelle in "La Trésorerie et le Budget", *La France économique en 1924* (Paris, Recueil Sirey, 1925) and by Mermeix, *Histoire du Franc* (Paris, Albin Michel, 1926).

earlier.[13] The fact that note issues ceased to increase substantially after approaching very closely their legal maximum in October 1924, while both prices and the volume of business continued their upward trends, would seem to indicate that the misrepresentations in its statements by the Bank of France of the volume of notes might have begun earlier than has been generally believed. According to assurances from the Bank of France, however, they did not occur before January 1925.

The extensive use of such hidden advances, beginning at least as early as May 1924, can be demonstrated by another statistical device. To accomplish this task, the two series, circulation and advances of the Bank to the State, will be reduced to six-month moving averages[14] (Chart XL). Also, attention is once more directed to the long-time relation between advances and circulation discovered in Chapter V above. If the contention there made is correct, it should be expected that, during the long period of gradually more slowly rising advances from 1917 to 1920, the curve of circulation would be continually above that of advances. For, since each ordinate of the circulation series is made up of the sum of two components — one the immediate effect of the new spending by the Government and the other a long-time effect of its spending during several preceding months — when the immediate effect component (which alone operates on advances) has declined with respect to the long-time effect component, the ordinate must be relatively greater for the series having both components than for that having only the immediate. That circulation lies above advances is found to be true for the period mentioned. Moreover, in the period from the early months of 1921 to the middle of 1925, when the decline of both circulation and advances was becoming gradually less rapid all the time, it should be expected that the ordinates of note circulation with one of their components derived from the effects of earlier, more drastic curtailments of expenditures would be continually below those for advances which are affected

[13] See Chap. III, p. 22.

[14] Both series were reduced to percentage deviations from secular trend after seasonal variations had been removed. These percentage deviations were expressed in terms of standard deviations and the results reduced to six-month moving averages.

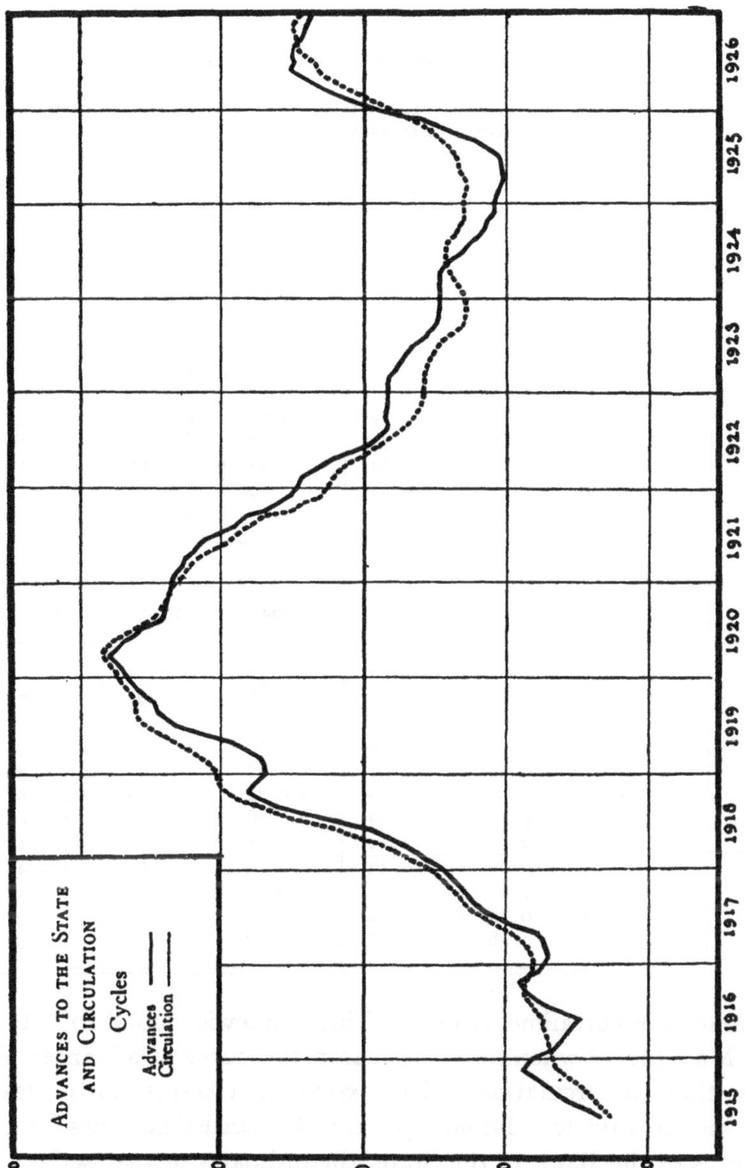
ADVANCES TO THE STATE
AND CIRCULATION
Cycles
Advances
Circulation
1915
1916
1917
1918
1919
1920
1921
1922
1923
1924
1925
1926
+2.0
+1.0
0
-1.0
-2.0
STANDARD DEVIATIONS

CHART XL

TABLE 61

ADVANCES OF THE BANK OF FRANCE TO THE STATE

(Percentage deviations from secular trend in terms of standard deviation, reduced to six-month moving averages)

	1915	1916	1917	1918	1919	1920
Jan.	......	−1.35	−1.30	−0.45	+0.69	+1.68
Feb.	......	−1.42	−1.29	−0.38	+0.72	+1.74
Mar.	......	−1.45	−1.26	−0.29	+0.85	+1.79
Apr.	......	−1.48	−1.22	−0.15	+0.95	+1.74
May	−1.69	−1.54	−1.04	−0.01	+1.14	+1.67
June	−1.58	−1.40	−0.92	+0.22	+1.33	+1.62
July	−1.46	−1.28	−0.85	+0.42	+1.39	+1.54
Aug.	−1.39	−1.18	−0.79	+0.64	+1.44	+1.45
Sept.	−1.31	−1.13	−0.75	+0.75	+1.46	+1.38
Oct.	−1.24	−1.10	−0.69	+0.83	+1.51	+1.37
Nov.	−1.14	−1.20	−0.62	+0.79	+1.58	+1.34
Dec.	−1.25	−1.27	−0.55	+0.69	+1.63	+1.33

	1921	1922	1923	1924	1925	1926
Jan.	+1.32	+0.42	−0.18	−0.56	−0.95	+0.04
Feb.	+1.29	+0.34	−0.19	−0.56	−0.97	+0.21
Mar.	+1.25	+0.22	−0.23	−0.59	−0.99	+0.35
Apr.	+1.19	+0.10	−0.28	−0.62	−0.99	+0.45
May	+1.12	−0.01	−0.31	−0.66	−0.99	+0.50
June	+1.00	−0.10	−0.37	−0.71	−0.95	+0.47
July	+0.91	−0.17	−0.44	−0.76	−0.86	+0.48
Aug.	+0.81	−0.19	−0.49	−0.82	−0.78	+0.47
Sept.	+0.70	−0.17	−0.53	−0.86	−0.66	+0.45
Oct.	+0.62	−0.17	−0.54	−0.89	−0.53	+0.43
Nov.	+0.53	−0.18	−0.56	−0.91	−0.36	+0.41
Dec.	+0.49	−0.18	−0.56	−0.92	−0.12	+0.39

by immediate curtailments only. This is likewise found to obtain until May 1924,[15] when for some reason the curve of advances fell below that of circulation. The explanation seems fairly clear. Since hidden advances did not appear in the statistical series for the advances of the Bank to the State, the ordinates of that series are

[15] In view of the fact that the moving averages are in each case recorded as of the final month, the crossing of the curves appearing in May 1924 is applicable to a date several months earlier.

TABLE 62

NOTE CIRCULATION OF THE BANK OF FRANCE

(Percentage deviations from secular trend in terms of standard deviation, reduced to six-month moving averages)

	1915	1916	1917	1918	1919	1920
Jan.	......	− 1.34	− 1.17	− 0.37	+ 1.08	+ 1.76
Feb.	......	− 1.32	− 1.15	− 0.26	+ 1.15	+ 1.80
Mar.	......	− 1.29	− 1.11	− 0.11	+ 1.25	+ 1.81
Apr.	......	− 1.27	− 1.03	+ 0.06	+ 1.32	+ 1.77
May	− 1.74	− 1.29	− 0.92	+ 0.20	+ 1.45	+ 1.71
June	− 1.68	− 1.22	− 0.84	+ 0.41	+ 1.54	+ 1.63
July	− 1.63	− 1.18	− 0.77	+ 0.59	+ 1.58	+ 1.54
Aug.	− 1.58	− 1.14	− 0.72	+ 0.76	+ 1.59	+ 1.46
Sept.	− 1.53	− 1.13	− 0.68	+ 0.89	+ 1.58	+ 1.41
Oct.	− 1.46	− 1.14	− 0.63	+ 0.99	+ 1.60	+ 1.39
Nov.	− 1.37	− 1.18	− 0.54	+ 1.01	+ 1.66	+ 1.37
Dec.	− 1.36	− 1.18	− 0.47	+ 1.02	+ 1.71	+ 1.31
	1921	**1922**	**1923**	**1924**	**1925**	**1926**
Jan.	+ 1.27	+ 0.21	− 0.43	− 0.71	− 0.72	− 0.09
Feb.	+ 1.21	+ 0.15	− 0.43	− 0.69	− 0.73	+ 0.04
Mar.	+ 1.15	+ 0.07	− 0.44	− 0.65	− 0.73	+ 0.17
Apr.	+ 1.06	− 0.02	− 0.48	− 0.62	− 0.70	+ 0.27
May	+ 0.97	− 0.10	− 0.51	− 0.60	− 0.69	+ 0.33
June	+ 0.89	− 0.18	− 0.56	− 0.61	− 0.68	+ 0.36
July	+ 0.78	− 0.26	− 0.61	− 0.62	− 0.64	+ 0.42
Aug.	+ 0.68	− 0.33	− 0.67	− 0.64	− 0.59	+ 0.47
Sept.	+ 0.56	− 0.35	− 0.71	− 0.68	− 0.53	+ 0.48
Oct.	+ 0.45	− 0.38	− 0.73	− 0.72	− 0.47	+ 0.49
Nov.	+ 0.34	− 0.41	− 0.74	− 0.72	− 0.37	+ 0.48
Dec.	+ 0.27	− 0.43	− 0.74	− 0.72	− 0.22	+ 0.43

evidently too small. And, in all probability, had the total advances of the Bank to the State, including those made indirectly through the other banks, been reported accurately, there would have been no crossing of the curves until late 1925 or early 1926, when the circulation curve should naturally have gone from below, above.

At the same time that the revelations regarding the indirect advances of the Bank to the State came to light, it was also claimed that notes had likewise been issued in excess of the limit set by law. Moreover, it was admitted by M. Henry Bérenger on the floor of the Senate [16] that these violations of the law had been concealed by the manipulation of certain items in the published statements of the Bank of France. This admission made in April 1925 was accompanied by a corrected balance sheet giving, with regard to circulation, the situation at the time. The remaining incorrect balance sheets have never been made public, nor has the exact interval covered been officially stated. From the courses of the series of advances and circulation, however, it would appear (Chart XL) that the understatements began at least as early as January and continued until early in April, when a corrected statement was first issued.

These extra-legal actions of the Bank of France have received such wide condemnation that a few words of explanation should be added with regard to the position of the Bank in the emergency in which they occurred. It must be remembered that gradually during the war the position of the Bank of France as unique source of emergency credit for the Treasury had become firmly established and that in the post-war years this position, far from being relinquished, had come to be generally accepted. In fact, the government borrowing from the Bank during the period since the beginning of the war, as has been observed earlier, had at times so dominated the affairs of the Bank as to give it the appearance more of a department of the Treasury than as a privately owned financial institution. During this period it stood ever ready, though at times perhaps grudgingly so, to lend to the Government whatever proportion of its needs could not be raised in other ways. In 1924 and 1925 the situation affecting this relation between the Govern-

[16] The statement of M. Henry Bérenger, "rapporteur général de la commission des finances," made on the floor of the Senate (April 15, 1925) is referred to: ". . . Quant aux avances directes ou indirectes de la Banque à l'État, elles s'élevaient, le 2 avril, à 25,130 millions, en dépassement de 3,130 millions sur le chiffre de 22 milliards légalement autorisé . . . .

". . . La question qui se pose aujourd'hui est la suivante: le montant des billets émis par la Banque de France est, depuis la publication de sa dernière situation hebdomadaire, en dépassement de plus de 2 milliards sur la limite légale. En ce qui concerne les avances à l'État, le dépassement n'apparaît pas encore dans les comptes, mais il resortira au fur et à mesure de l'arrivée des échéances des valeurs sous la forme desquelles les avances exceptionnelles de la Banque à l'État ont été mobilisées." *Journal Officiel, Débats Parlementaires, Sénat,* April 16, 1925, pp. 865–866.

ment and the Bank was extremely critical. After the severe exchange crisis of March 1924, but a few months passed before both dollar exchange and prices recommenced their upward trends, and there were rumors of ever larger, though illegal, exports of capital. With these developments the position of the Treasury became continually more dangerous. Not only were *Bons de la Défense Nationale* and other short-term Treasury paper increasingly difficult of sale, but the demands for the repayments of those coming to maturity were presented in increasing volume. Furthermore, big issues of 6 per cent *rentes* from three to ten years maturity had been issued in March and April and again in October and November of the preceding year to relieve the floating debt situation. Resort to a 5 per cent ten-year loan in November-December 1924 failed to bring the necessary relief. To attempt still another new issue for the same purpose so soon after the severe crisis of March 1924 would have been, to say the least, a hazardous procedure. In the existing tense political situation, it was almost as hazardous to ask the Chamber of Deputies for increases in the maximum limits prescribed for note circulation and for advances of the Bank to the State. In such an emergency the Bank of France continued to grant the demands of the Treasury for what it was led to believe were very temporary advances. To have refused would have meant at least momentary insolvency for the Government, and to have published its actions would doubtless have precipitated a crisis almost as severe.

Even a very superficial survey of the profits and dividends of the Bank of France will indicate something of the effects of inflation on that important institution itself. In a period of rapid and continued depreciation of the monetary unit all creditors and creditor institutions hold a peculiarly precarious position. In continually lending more valuable to receive at maturity less valuable sums, they almost inevitably lose to the extent of the depreciation of the unit of account. Since the Bank of France was one of the principal creditors of the country throughout most of the inflation period, it is of interest to inquire whether its losses were commensurate with the depreciation of the franc, the unit in which all its lendings and repayments were reckoned. It will also be of interest to see what proportion of the profits came from loans to the Government as opposed to that derived from all other sources.

In the table below (Table 63) are given (1) the total gross profits of the Bank of France, (2) the part of total gross profits received from advances to the State and from the discount of Treasury paper for the Government to provide funds for loans to foreign governments, (3) total expenses, and (4) the deductions made by the State from interest allowed on the advances of the Bank to the State and from the income derived from the discount of Treasury paper for the Government to provide funds for loans to foreign governments.

TABLE 63

PROFITS AND EXPENSES OF THE BANK OF FRANCE *

(In millions of francs)

	Total gross profits	Total expenses	Gross profits from advances to the State, etc.[a]	Deductions made by the State from interest on advances, etc.[b]
1913				
First semester	65.8	31.4		
Second semester	61.5	21.7		
1914				
First semester	58.8	23.6		
Second semester	72.6	34.9	8.6	1.1
1915				
First semester	91.9	41.1	23.6	2.9
Second semester	107.1	58.5	33.2	4.1
1916				
First semester	145.6	66.5	32.2	4.0
Second semester	167.7	95.6	39.2	4.9
1917				
First semester	199.7	63.9	106.6	5.8
Second semester	198.5	59.5	133.0	7.2

[a] For the period 1913–1916 the data represent the interest derived from advances to the State only. For the remaining years the data include also the income of the Bank from the discount of Treasury paper for loans by the State to foreign governments.

[b] Amounts deducted from interest payments by the Government and placed in the Bank's amortization account for the debt of the State.

* Source: *Annual Reports of the General Council of the Bank of France to the General Assembly of Stockholders.*

TABLE 63 (Continued)

	Total gross profits	Total expenses	Gross profits from advances to the State, etc.[a]	Deductions made by the State from interest on advances, etc.[b]
1918				
First semester	257.4	191.7	157.9	127.1
Second semester	240.2	165.0	158.3	110.2
1919				
First semester	311.4	268.8	186.9	125.4
Second semester	334.9	272.6	210.1	140.0
1920				
First semester	390.9	345.2	228.9	157.2
Second semester	459.0	352.9	245.2	170.8
1921				
First semester	742.6	573.9	466.1	391.5
Second semester	676.2	596.9	487.0	414.4
1922				
First semester	648.5	529.5	458.0	386.3
Second semester	644.6	536.7	463.9	391.7
1923				
First semester	637.3	544.6	457.6	385.7
Second semester	660.6	555.6	466.0	393.2
1924				
First semester	748.2	630.3	484.7	408.6
Second semester	803.5	677.5	495.9	418.4
1925				
First semester	862.0	700.3	506.5	426.3
Second semester	834.4	713.7	567.2	487.9
1926				
First semester	950.1	843.1	681.6	594.9
Second semester	1084.9	931.3	757.9	662.5

From the table it is immediately seen that throughout the period a very large portion indeed of the gross profits of the Bank was derived from advances to the State and that only a comparatively very minor part came from all other operations combined. Hence, when the relatively low rates applicable to such advances are taken into account, it is entirely clear how completely the affairs of the Bank throughout most of the period were dominated by the borrowings of the Government. It is to be noted, too, how large a portion of the profits from other operations were consumed by expenses, none of which was charged to the above-mentioned operation for the Government.

A similarly cursory examination of net profits is almost equally illuminating. In the accompanying table (Table 64) are given the total net profits of the Bank and the net profits from operations for the Government (if the latter term may be used for gross profits from operations for the Government minus retractions by the Government from amounts originally allowed the Bank).

It will be seen that in both semesters of 1919 and in the first

TABLE 64

NET PROFITS AND DIVIDENDS OF THE BANK OF FRANCE *

(In millions of francs)

	Total net profits	Net profits from operations other than those for the Government	Net profits from operations for the Government [a]	Dividends
1913				
First semester	34.4	34.4		19.0
Second semester	39.8	39.8		19.0
1914				
First semester	35.2	35.2		19.0
Second semester	37.7	30.2	7.5	17.1
1915				
First semester	50.8	30.1	20.7	17.1
Second semester	48.6	19.5	29.1	20.9
1916				
First semester	79.1	50.9	28.2	22.8
Second semester	72.1	37.8	34.3	22.8
1917				
First semester	135.8	35.0	100.8	23.0
Second semester	139.0	13.2	125.8	23.0
1918				
First semester	65.7	34.9	30.8	23.0
Second semester	75.2	27.1	48.1	23.0
1919				
First semester	42.6	− 18.9	61.5	23.0
Second semester	62.3	− 7.8	70.1	23.0

[a] The data represent the net profits of the Bank of France from operations for the Government. Profits both from advances to the State and from the discount of Treasury paper for the State to provide funds for loans to foreign governments are taken into account, and deduction is made for that part of the profits from these operations going into the Bank's amortization account for the debt of the State. No deduction is made for general operating expenses.

* Source: *Annual Reports of the General Council of the Bank of France to the General Assembly of Stockholders.*

TABLE 64 (Continued)

	Total net profits	Net profits from operations other than those for the Government	Net profits from operations for the Government [a]	Dividends
1920				
First semester	45.7	− 26.0	71.7	24.3
Second semester	106.1	31.7	74.4	27.3
1921				
First semester	168.7	94.1	74.6	27.3
Second semester	79.3	6.7	72.6	27.3
1922				
First semester	119.0	47.3	71.7	27.3
Second semester	107.9	35.7	72.2	29.4
1923				
First semester	92.7	20.8	71.9	29.4
Second semester	105.0	32.2	72.8	29.4
1924				
First semester	117.9	41.8	76.1	30.0
Second semester	126.0	48.5	77.5	30.0
1925				
First semester	161.7	81.5	80.2	30.0
Second semester	120.7	41.4	79.3	34.4
1926				
First semester	107.0	20.7	86.7	32.1
Second semester	153.6	58.2	95.4	34.2

semester of 1920 expenses were actually larger than the return from non-governmental operations. The total net profits, therefore, and part of the expenses of operations were derived from payments by the Government. The large profits from Government operations in 1917 are to be accounted for by the continued enlargement of the borrowings of the State without increase in the percentage deductions made by the Government from interest allowed on such advances. The very great reduction in such income in 1918, on the other hand, is to be explained by new and drastic exactions imposed first in that year. The substantial increase immediately thereafter grew out of the very rapid increases in advances to the State during 1919. The notable increase in profits from non-governmental sources appearing in the second semester of 1923 and continuing through the first semester of 1925 resulted in large part from the great expansion of private advances of the Bank. The increase in the second semester of 1926, on the

TABLE 65

NET PROFITS AND DIVIDENDS OF THE BANK OF FRANCE *

(In millions of gold francs) [a]

	Total net profits	Dividends
1913		
First semester	34.4	19.0
Second semester	39.8	19.0
1914		
First semester	35.4	19.1
Second semester	37.8	17.1
1915		
First semester	48.2	16.2
Second semester	43.0	18.5
1916		
First semester	69.3	20.0
Second semester	64.0	20.2
1917		
First semester	123.5	20.9
Second semester	126.4	20.9
1918		
First semester	59.7	20.9
Second semester	71.5	21.9
1919		
First semester	34.9	18.9
Second semester	30.1	11.1
1920		
First semester	18.9	10.0
Second semester	32.8	8.5
1921		
First semester	71.2	11.5
Second semester	32.4	11.1
1922		
First semester	54.3	12.5
Second semester	40.9	11.1
1923		
First semester	30.5	9.7
Second semester	28.9	8.1
1924		
First semester	32.3	8.2
Second semester	35.6	8.5
1925		
First semester	40.3	7.5
Second semester	23.6	6.7
1926		
First semester	16.3	4.9
Second semester	31.5	7.0

[a] Nominal francs divided by the index of the average of dollar exchange for December of each year. The amounts are not significant for the period of controlled exchange, 1916–1918.

* Source: *Annual Reports of the General Council of the Bank of France to the General Assembly of Stockholders.*

other hand, came largely from the higher discount rates charged and that in the first semester of 1921 from the payment of overdue interest released by the expiration of the moratorium on certain of the Bank's holdings of paper.

By referring next to the figures of net profits reduced to gold values it will be seen that, while they have fluctuated very widely indeed, the general level was not below that in 1913. It seems evident, therefore, that the operating profits of the Bank were not substantially reduced. Also, by reference to the general decline in the gold values of dividends distributed it will be seen that a larger portion of net profits was held to increase the capital fund of the Bank. If any substantial loss was incurred, therefore, it must have come from the shrinkage in some of its assets uncounterbalanced by an appreciation in others. Were there any such shrinkages?

The huge gold reserve of the Bank of France was not only kept intact but was even considerably enlarged. Moreover, its fixed assets were generally kept from depreciation and were gradually increased by new construction. Hence, it would seem not only that there was no reduction in real values in either of these two types of assets but, on the contrary, that there was an actual increase. There is some question, however, whether the profit from the gold reserve will be interpreted as belonging to the Bank.

There remain for consideration the loans and the portfolio of the Bank. Certainly in these items a depreciation would inevitably occur—as, indeed, it did. When it is remembered, however, that the obligations of the Bank in the form of notes and deposits depreciated to the same extent as did its loans and discounts, it is seen that the loss from the shrinkage of assets in gold values must have been largely counterbalanced. It would seem, therefore, that whatever loss may have accrued from this source has been more than offset by the larger proportions of profits held instead of being distributed as dividends.

CHAPTER IX

THE OPERATIONS OF BANKING INSTITUTIONS AND THE MONEY MARKET

In Chapter V the relation of public debts of various sorts to inflation was discussed with the purpose of determining as clearly as possible what types of government borrowing had been most influential in promoting the inflation process. In Chapter VI the magnitudes and orders of movement of the three chief measures of the degree of inflation — prices, circulation, and exchange rates — were examined in detail, in the hope of throwing as much light as possible on the inflation process itself. Finally, in Chapter VIII the operations of the Bank of France, which, as the guardian and bulwark of the financial life of the entire country, naturally played a leading rôle in the inflation process, were studied in some detail. In the present chapter the influences of certain other financial institutions and of the money market and of credit conditions in general will be studied with a view to making as nearly complete as possible the financial story of the inflation period.

As in the earlier parts of this study, the affairs of the four big banks (*grandes sociétés de crédit*) will be taken as representative of those of the commercial banks in general, although, as will be seen in the next chapter, they accomplish only approximately fifty per cent of the commercial banking operations of the country.

By examining the statistics of their capital stock and reserves (Table 66 below) it will be seen that only changes very slight indeed in comparison with those in the value of the franc were made in their stockholder liabilities. While it is true that most of their fixed assets, such as buildings, furnishings, etc., have been marked up little or not at all, there seems little doubt that their total assets measured in gold francs or in purchasing power have actually shrunken during the inflation régime. Moreover, the dividends

TABLE 66

CAPITAL STOCK AND RESERVES OF THE "BIG FOUR" [c]

Date	Millions of francs	Millions of gold francs [a]	In terms of 1913 purchasing power [b]
December 31, 1913	1088	1088	1099
December 31, 1914	1105	1107	1000
December 31, 1915	1122	994	687
December 31, 1916	1049	931	516
December 31, 1917	1054	959	346
December 31, 1918	1059	1007	300
December 31, 1919	1066	515	252
December 31, 1920	1149	356	264
December 31, 1921	1159	473	356
December 31, 1922	1168	443	323
December 31, 1923	1191	328	260
December 31, 1924	1217	344	240
December 31, 1925	1232	241	195
December 31, 1926	1273	261	203

[a] Nominal francs divided by the index of the average of dollar exchange for December of each year. The amounts are not significant for the period of controlled exchange 1916–1918.

[b] Nominal francs divided by the index of wholesale prices of the *Statistique Générale de la France* for December of each year.

[c] Source: *Annual Reports of the Councils of Administration to the General Assemblies of Stockholders.*

paid by these banks to their stockholders have not increased sufficiently to take care of more than a small proportion of the depreciation in the value of the franc.

Hence, in spite of the hesitation which one naturally feels in attempting to draw precise conclusions from statements so general and so evasive as those of most French financial institutions, nevertheless it seems clear that these four commercial banks considered together actually failed to keep up their normal net profit during the inflation period.

Demand deposits and portfolios[1] of the "Big Four" banks have been discussed in some detail in Chapter V above. It will be remembered that in the portfolio item are always included the banks' holdings of *Bons de la Défense Nationale* and other short-term

[1] The descriptions of these series are to be found in Chap. V above, Tables 12 and 14.

TABLE 67

DIVIDENDS PAID TO STOCKHOLDERS BY THE "BIG FOUR"[*]

Date	Millions of francs	Millions of gold francs[a]	In terms of 1913 purchasing power[b]
December 31, 1913	75	75	75
December 31, 1914	34	34	30
December 31, 1915	28	25	17
December 31, 1916	45	40	22
December 31, 1917	48	44	16
December 31, 1918	58	56	17
December 31, 1919	69	33	16
December 31, 1920	90	28	21
December 31, 1921	90	37	28
December 31, 1922	92	35	25
December 31, 1923	100	28	22
December 31, 1924	109	31	21
December 31, 1925	109	21	17
December 31, 1926	129	26	21

[a] Nominal francs divided by the index of the average of dollar exchange for December of each year. The amounts are not significant for the period of controlled exchange, 1916–1918.

[b] Nominal francs divided by the index of wholesale prices of the *Statistique Générale de la France* for December of each year.

[*] Source: *Annual Reports of the Councils of Administration to the General Assemblies of Stockholders.*

Treasury paper which, serving as a sort of secondary reserve, undoubtedly represented during much of the period under discussion the investment of a large portion of the banks' funds which in London or New York would have been placed in highly liquid paper purchased on the money market. The striking similarity of the monthly series of portfolios thus combined with holdings of short-term Treasury paper[2] and that of demand deposits has been commented upon in Chapter V. The items of the two series are almost identical in amounts from December 1914 until May 1925 (Chart XLI). It seems evident, therefore, that during that period these banks were investing their receipts from deposits and nothing more. It can probably be concluded, too, that since the fluctuations of portfolio holdings above those of deposits—even in periods

[2] In the portfolio series are also included advances, Bourse loans, and debit current accounts. It represents, therefore, as completely as possible a total loan series.

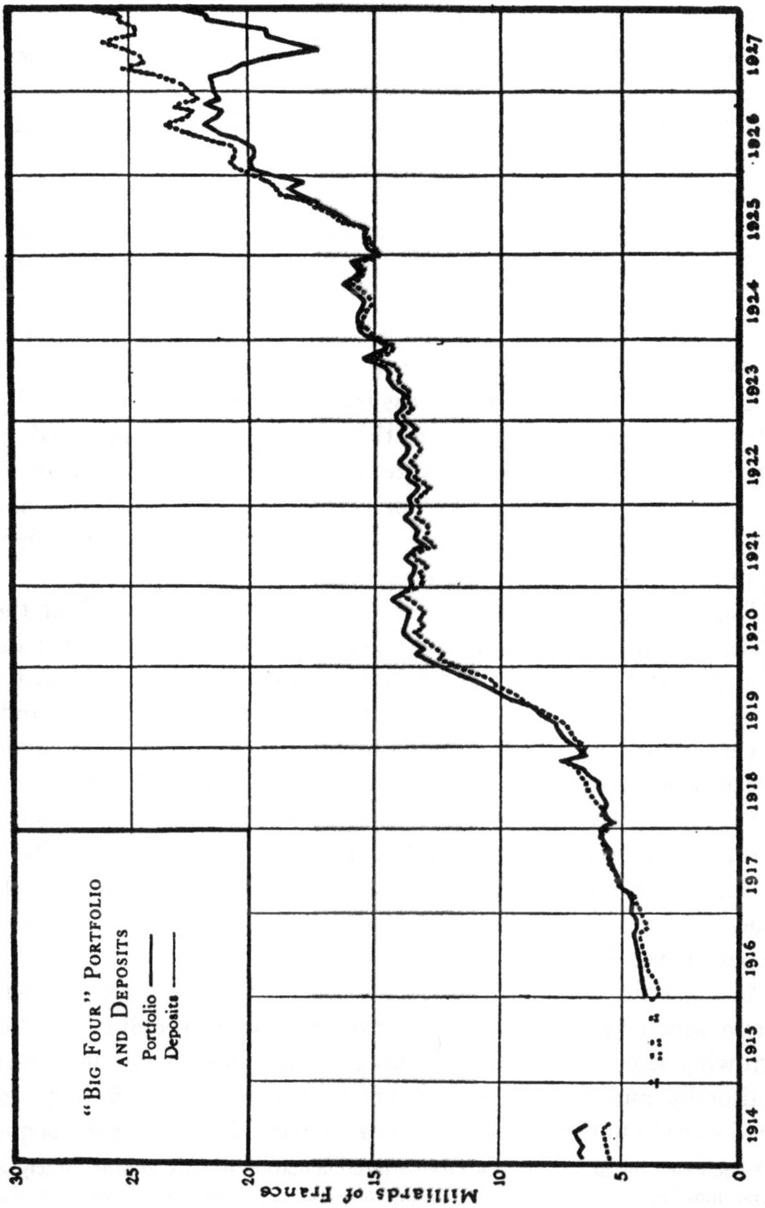
"Big Four" Portfolio
and Deposits
Portfolio
Deposits
Milliards of Francs
30
25
20
15
10
5
0
1914
1915
1916
1917
1918
1919
1920
1921
1922
1923
1924
1925
1926
1927

CHART XLI

of rising prices — were so extremely small the portfolios must have been made up very largely indeed of short-term Treasury paper. Had it been composed mainly of loans, the series would almost certainly have gone considerably above that of deposits at the culmination of the boom period of 1919 and 1920.[3]

After May 1925 the deposits of the banks at the Treasury evidently became of significant magnitudes (Table 60). At that time the curve of "Big Four" deposits, which since the beginning of 1915 had almost coincided with that of "total loans plus holdings of short-term Treasury paper," began to move gradually farther and farther above it. Since cash holdings of the banks — which include deposits at the Treasury — began to increase rapidly at the same time, it is obvious that funds formerly invested in short-term government bonds were being transferred to deposits in the Treasury. Such deposits including those of business firms continued to increase until the middle of 1927, at which time they amounted to 17.8 milliards of francs.

The "Big Four" cash holdings, including cash on hand, at the Bank of France, and in the Treasury, are also of considerable interest (Chart XLII). Beginning low in 1914, they increased greatly during the second half of that year, remained high in 1915, and, after maintaining during 1916 a but slightly lower level, they again increased gradually in 1917 and until August 1918. There was a very sharp decline in the latter half of 1918, then a gradual, though fluctuating, increase until April 1925, after which a precipitous rise set in and continued during the rest of the year. Also, while reduced in rapidity in 1926, this increase proceeded on an even steeper incline during the first half of 1927.

In most respects the movements were expected ones. It will be remembered that very soon after the war began the State started borrowing from the Bank of France. Such borrowings increased continually and rapidly until August 1918, after which they declined sharply until the end of the year (Chart III). With the begin-

[3] Increased quantities of cash flowing into circulation usually appear largely as subtractions from deposits. At the height of a boom period, when loans are very difficult to reduce, lagging prices such as wages and retail prices continue their upward trends, while velocities begin to decline. Hence, more money is drawn into circulation, and deposits are correspondingly reduced with respect to loans.

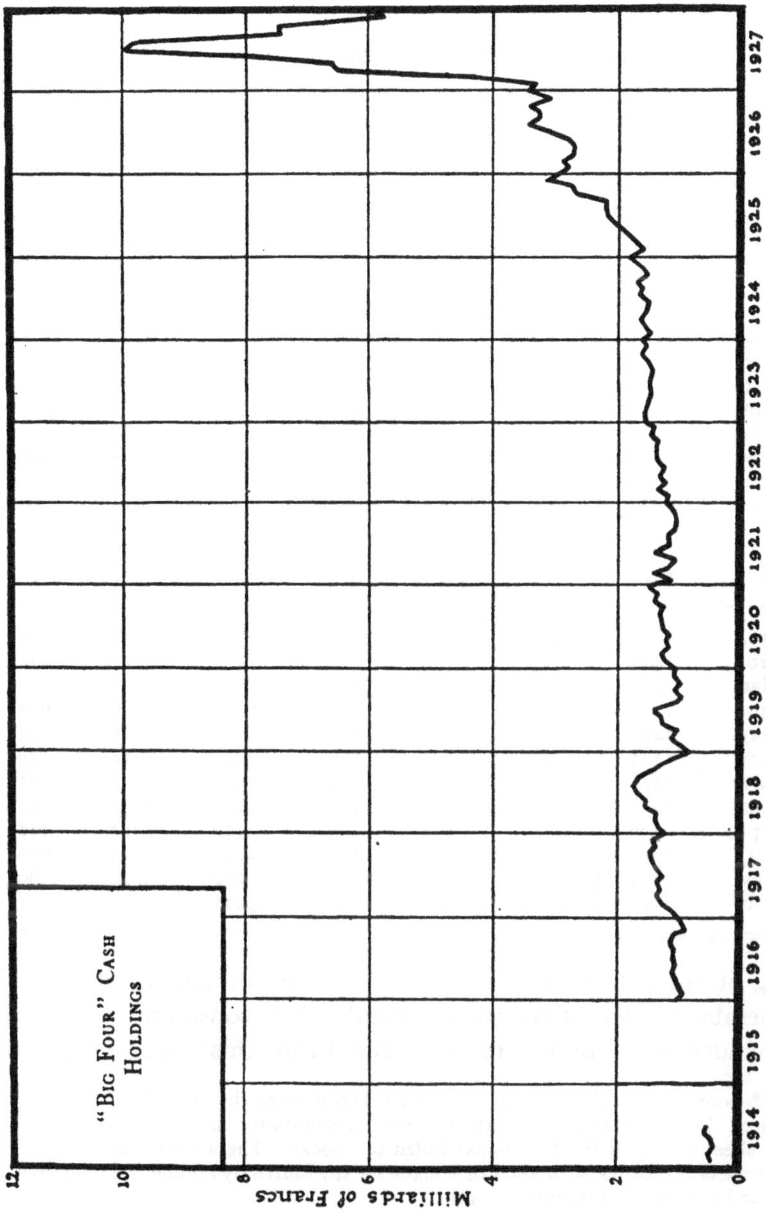
"Big Four" Cash Holdings
Milliards of Francs
12
10
8
6
4
2
0
1914
1915
1916
1917
1918
1919
1920
1921
1922
1923
1924
1925
1926
1927

CHART XLII

TABLE 68

CASH HOLDINGS OF THE "BIG FOUR"*

(Data from end-of-month reports in millions of francs)

	1914	1915	1916	1917	1918	1919	1920
Jan.	502	....	*952*	1243	1369	1024	*1225*
Feb.	541	....	*1024*	1309	1403	1163	1292
Mar.	494	....	1099	1370	1382	1063	1287
Apr.	507	1215	1118	1307	1682	1311	1358
May	654	....	1088	1362	1634	1327	1489
June	617	1315	1115	1278	1736	1458	1246
July	....	....	1100	1349	1804	1044	1403
Aug.	....	....	1191	1457	1750	985	1266
Sept.	....	1323	1184	1467	1449	1087	1252
Oct.	....	....	*915*	*1332*	1309	983	1452
Nov.	....	....	982	1418	*1119*	1096	1791
Dec.	1268	1032	1064	1265	878	1099	1564

	1921	1922	1923	1924	1925	1926	1927
Jan.	1167	1293	1632	1492	1676	2813	3327
Feb.	1408	1338	1630	1576	1770	2946	4318
Mar.	1235	1223	1589	1640	1840	2774	6475
Apr.	1142	1289	1452	1531	1886	2759	6581
May	1449	1243	1472	1468	2114	2875	7736
June	1221	1347	1454	1685	2246	3224	9992
July	1270	1353	1411	1638	2252	3527	9859
Aug.	1220	1356	1484	1701	2252	3307	7420
Sept.	1106	1322	1598	1540	2710	3313	7484
Oct.	1104	1442	1582	1602	2731	3400	6166
Nov.	1113	1409	1523	1778	3280	3214	5803
Dec.	1298	1584	1644	1855	3009	3503	6057

ning of 1919, however, the rapid rise began again. It will be remembered, too, that from several other considerations, it was concluded in Chapter VIII above that during this war period govern-

* Source: The data for all years were taken from the records of the Bank of France. Italicized figures indicate estimated amounts for months in which the balance sheet of one of the four banks failed to appear. The amounts given are those for three of the banks with allowance made for the fourth by adding the cash holdings of that bank for the preceding month.

The item includes cash on hand and funds deposited at the Treasury (beginning with 1921), at the Bank of France, and with correspondent banks in France and abroad.

ment as opposed to business borrowing was dominating the currency and price situation. Under such circumstances the funds put out through the expenditures of the State came continually to the banks, where they furnished a more than abundant resource for advances to business. Moreover, in the second half of 1918, when the advances of the Bank to the State fell off sharply, the cash of the banks did likewise; and again in 1919, when that type of government borrowing increased greatly, so did the cash holdings of the banks. After that time, however, a radical but altogether expected divergence in the movements of the two series began. By the latter half of 1919, while the advances of the Bank to the State continued their upward trend, the cash holdings of the banks dropped sharply. Then in the last month of 1919 and during 1920, with the former series gradually flattening out, the latter increased slowly. What seems to have been happening was that business, which heretofore had been largely nourished from the funds continually accumulating in the banks from government purchases, now became an important influence in the situation. In expanding its purchases, business demanded larger credits at the banks, which, happy to find use for their large reserves, willingly granted the desired advances. As this expansion grew, their increased cash needs led the banks to discount available paper at the Bank of France. Under such circumstances, however, they maintained cash reserves only large enough to meet their gradually expanding deposits and an account at the Bank sufficient to take care of an ever larger volume of clearings. After the culmination of the post-war boom, however, cash again began to accumulate in their vaults and was soon used by them to purchase short-term Treasury obligations and by the Treasury in turn to reduce its borrowings from the Bank of France, which was in its turn enabled to reduce circulation by the amounts of the notes[4] returned.

[4] Not all the funds returned would be in the form of notes. Consequently, the reduction from this source would not be expected to be equivalent to the reduction in advances. Also, the reconstruction activities of the Government in the devastated regions doubtless kept the advances from the Bank from being reduced by an amount equal to the funds returned through the purchase of Treasury paper. For another explanation see Moulton and Lewis, *The French Debt Problem* (New York, The Macmillan Company, 1925), p. 134.

In late 1922, when business began its recovery and prices again turned rapidly upward, cash holdings of the banks likewise increased gradually, largely, it seems, under the influence of business borrowing — the additional funds being derived presumably in large part from the cashing of maturing *Bons de la Défense Nationale.* In the years 1923 and 1924, too, it seems that business rather than government borrowing and spending were dominating the situation, and the cash holdings of the banks increased gradually in response to their need for continually larger balances — the need being partly met by the cashing of *Bons de la Défense Nationale* and by discounting or otherwise borrowing from the Bank of France, though there is reason to believe (Chapter VIII, pp. 198–203) that during most of this period a considerable portion of the increase was coming through indirect advances from the Bank to the State.

There seems little doubt that the significant increases in cash holdings in 1925 came very largely from the further expansions of the borrowings of the Treasury from the Bank. Once spent by the Government, the funds flowed rapidly to the banks, which only gradually invested them in short-term government bonds or deposited them in the Treasury. The notable, but temporary, drop in cash holdings in December 1925 and in the early months of 1926 was probably caused by the rapid rise in both prices and business activity which together caused a drain of cash from the banks to circulation.

Finally, after the crisis of 1926, when the Bank of France began its large purchases of foreign exchange and when deep business depression was settling down upon the country, cash flowed naturally although slowly in large amounts to the banks. The banks, in turn, being unable, on account of the restrictions against the export of capital, to employ the funds in foreign markets and finding short-term Treasury paper becoming ever scarcer — in response to the policy of the Government of reducing its floating debt — invested them very largely as deposits in the Treasury. These deposits were without doubt responsible for much of the enormous volume of cash holdings of the banks in 1927.[5]

[5] In 1927 the cash holdings of the "Big Four" ranged from 3327 millions of francs in January to 9992 millions in June.

In summary, it can be stated that the commercial banks suffered a very serious business setback at the beginning of the war. This slump is accounted for perhaps as much by the fear of new moratoria [6] as by the results of those actually declared. The immediate effects of the declaration were, nevertheless, severe. Not only were many of the most liquid assets temporarily completely frozen, but the jolt to public confidence occasioned by the moratorium on deposits led to a hesitancy on the part of the public to trust to the banks' funds later received. The Bank of France mitigated the situation by discounting, or otherwise lending on the frozen paper of the distressed banks. But it could not remove the shock to public confidence which had resulted from the immoblization of deposits.

Gradually, however, as the distressful recollections of so severe a measure were effaced — as such recollections always are — by the passage of time, and as the Government rapidly increased its war-time spendings, partly through new funds borrowed from the Bank of France, deposits of cash and of cash items increased. The cash holdings of the banks expanded correspondingly and were used, if not to extend loans, then to add to their holdings of government securities. In the latter half of 1919 business became active and prices rose rapidly. With such conditions obtaining, the borrowings of business people from the banks presumably increased greatly. Thus, both loans and deposits of the commercial banks naturally expanded rapidly and greatly, while cash holdings first declined abruptly and then increased gradually as the larger deposits made imperative the holding of larger amounts of till-money and of reserves. To provide such increases in ready cash, the individual banks temporarily had only to make use of

[6] A decree of August 1, 1914 granted a moratorium of 30 days on 95 per cent of all deposits in excess of 250 francs. An exception was granted in the case of funds required for wage payments. On August 29, 1914 the moratorium on deposits was extended 30 days but covered only 80 per cent instead of 95 per cent of accounts. A further exception was then made for funds necessary to continue business and agricultural enterprises. Such funds could be withdrawn up to 60 per cent of their total. Through successive renewals the moratorium on deposits was continued in gradually milder form until March 31, 1919 (Decree of December 29, 1918), but, as a matter of fact, it was practically non-existent after 1915, the four big banks having voluntarily discontinued it by the end of 1914.

the abundant funds which continued to come to them as a result of the extensive borrowings of the State from the Bank of France. By reference to Chart III (Chapter V) it will be seen that such advances continued their steep upward trend.

The Bank of France in according these advances gave the Government a deposit balance which, in being spent, was quickly transferred by the receivers to the banks, which were in turn thus provided with additional funds at the Bank to take care of enlarged clearings as well as to provide a ready source of cash for further till needs. As the volume of business increased, however, and was carried on at ever rising prices, the need for additional funds began to be felt. These funds could be secured by the banks through the liquidation of some of their holdings of government securities or by borrowing directly from the Bank of France. That neither occurred in very fact, however, before the end of the boom, is evidenced by the continued excess of emissions over reimbursements of short-term Treasury paper and by the slightness of the increase in the non-governmental advances of the Bank of France.

After the culmination of the boom was reached a short time before the middle of 1920 and after business depression set in, loans and deposits decreased slightly, and holdings of cash grew appreciably. These movements were not pronounced, however, largely, no doubt, in the case of loans and deposits, because of the considerable volume of frozen credits which existed in France as in the United States at that time and, in the case of cash, because of the alternative use of idle funds for purchasing short-term Treasury obligations. Circulation and advances of the Bank to the State decreased considerably during 1921, showing clearly the effects of the accumulations of funds in the banks and of the resulting purchases of Treasury obligations. 1921 and the first half of 1922 were thus years of extreme ease in the money market. The Bank of France rate was twice reduced, being placed on March 11, 1922 at the war-time rate of 5 per cent, the lowest that had obtained since the close of the war. Later in that same year, however, a business revival, which continued throughout 1923 and 1924, definitely set in, and, with loans and deposits and, consequently, cash requirements of the banks gradually increasing throughout that period, the state of government finances became continually more and more acute. The banks, to meet the needs of their business customers, not only ceased buying short-term Treasury paper, but also, as dates of maturity arrived, cashed, in increasing amounts, those already bought. On February 19, 1923 the rate on three-month ***Bons de la Défense Nationale*** was raised to equivalence with the Bank of France discount rate (5 per cent). This action perhaps led some of the banks to do more discounting at the Bank of France and less cashing of government obligations. Nevertheless, their holdings of short-term Treasury paper, being regarded, as they have always been, as secondary reserves, undoubtedly decreased.[7] Indeed, a radical change in their use was hardly to be expected. Hence, with the growing tenseness of the political situation and with the increasing export of capital during the last two years of this period, there is no doubt that the Treasury felt severely the gradual drain to business use of funds formerly at its disposal.

In view of the lags discovered between the movements of exchange rates and those of prices — lags which showed themselves very clearly for 1923 and 1924 and which perhaps existed in 1922 — it seems fairly certain that at least in the later two years foreign speculation in the franc (to which the precedence in the movements of exchange rates can be attributed) was at the root of many of the economic troubles as well as of some of the advantages to which the French people and their Government were being subjected. The sales of forward francs were depressing first the forward rates of exchange. But, as has been outlined in Chapter VI, a depression of the forward rates inevitably (barring arbitrary restrictions of credit in the country the currency of which is being sold) carries with it an approximately equal depression of "spot" rates. Such reductions in the value of the franc led to increased foreign buying in France of easily exportable goods and started a train of events — among which not the least important

[7] The excess of reimbursements over subscriptions of such bonds was, in 1922, 1291 millions of francs, in 1923, 1350 millions, in 1924, 1312 millions, and in 1925, 8279 millions.

were the eager activities of profiteers of various sorts — which occasioned a rapid and continued rise in prices and which led to a considerable increase in business activity. This notable increase in the pecuniary volume of trade, fortunate as it was for most of those belonging to the business classes in France, drew away to business use the funds formerly at the disposition of the State. It is of course impossible to say how much the speculation of foreigners in French exchange was a result of the tense political situation in France or how much the decline in the franc was itself the cause of the political uneasiness. This much is clear, however: that the declining value of the franc and the emptying coffers of the Treasury were dominant issues in most of the political discussions of the day.

When in April 1925 the sad plight of the Treasury was publicly admitted and at least temporarily relieved by parliamentary action raising the legal limit for the advances of the Bank of France to the State and that for the note circulation of the Bank, the borrowing by the State went on apace. While production and trade in 1925 (Charts XXXI and XXXIII) did not continue to increase as in the two preceding years, they were not greatly reduced. Dollar exchange, prices, and circulation, on the other hand, continued their steep upward trends — with exchange leading prices by at least a month and with circulation by that time moving almost simultaneously with prices. Here again the general movement seemed to come partly from the short sales of francs abroad, though in this case there is good reason to believe that a much more important influence was the purchase of foreign currencies at home. The political uncertainties had by this time caused a large group of French investors themselves to lose faith in their own currency, and an ever increasing number were transferring their investments to foreign securities. In spite of the stringent regulations[8] with regard to the exportation of capital, there is little doubt that the "flight from the franc" during this period assumed very large proportions. Pierre Meynial has estimated the clandestine export of capital at 10 milliards of francs for the years 1924 and 1925 each,[9] and at 17 milliards during the

[8] See Chap. IV, footnote 6, p. 42. [9] P. Meynial, "La Balance des Comptes," *La France économique en 1925* (Paris, Recueil Sirey, 1926), p. 56 *et seq.*

first seven months of 1926.[10] Not only were American and other foreign securities purchased on the Paris Bourse, but the proceeds of exports were frequently left on deposit or otherwise invested in foreign countries. The proceeds of coupons paid in high exchange countries were almost invariably left abroad. Even the smuggling of securities and bank-notes across the Swiss or other borders was rumored to have assumed important proportions, while certain individuals adopted the ruse of entering France with big checks on French banks which they declared on entering in order that they might carry out on their next trip an equivalent sum in some other form.

Under such conditions of rapidly rising exchange rates and prices and of greatly increased borrowings of the State from the Bank, the deposits in the banks increased rapidly, as did likewise the cash reserves. Since business was not expanding in physical volume, however, and since the higher prices at which it was carried on were not sufficiently high to require immediately the *full* utilization by business of the funds thus continually received by the banks through deposits, more and more of these otherwise idle funds began to be transferred to the Treasury, perhaps in small amounts as formerly through the purchase of short-term Treasury paper,[11] but then much more largely as direct interest-bearing deposits.

As might have been forecast, however, production and trade again became active before the end of 1925 and continued so throughout the first half of 1926. But so plentiful had become the funds being put out by the Government, which kept on increasing its borrowings from the Bank of France, that deposits at the Treasury, in spite of the business activity and rising prices, continued generally to grow. Thus is found an extraordinary instance of a period of rapidly rising prices in which money throughout much of the time was becoming continually easier and in which the excess above that required by an increasing volume

[10] P. Meynial, *op. cit.*, p. 91 *et seq.*

[11] The large excess of reimbursements over emissions of such bonds in 1925 coupled with the very large increases in cash holdings of the banks, seems to indicate clearly that funds were being deposited in the Treasury rather than being put to the alternative use.

of business was frequently growing. In the analyses which follow in Chapters XI and XII it will be seen that much the same sort of situation obtained in the boom of 1919–1920.

After the crisis of 1926 and with the beginning of the severe business depression which almost immediately afterward settled down upon the country, the cash deposits in the banks naturally increased, loans diminished, and cash reserves, which, on account of the growing scarcity of short-term Treasury paper,[12] were deposited mainly in the Treasury, became enlarged. The large purchases of foreign exchange by the Bank of France added to the already superabundant funds going continually to the banks. In the absence of business demand for loans and because of the legal restrictions against the investing of any considerable portion of the accumulating funds abroad, the deposits of the banks in the Treasury continued to swell.

In close relation to the operations of the commercial banks were the money market happenings of the period. Accordingly, they will be considered next. In Chapters III and IV above, the peculiar characteristics of the Paris market as contrasted with those of the New York and London markets were discussed in some detail. It was there pointed out that dealings in prime commercial paper, so general in most money centers, are at times in Paris so small in volume as hardly to constitute a market at all. Nevertheless, in order to make this statistical story as complete as possible, the following table of rates furnished by one of the Paris bankers doing an active discount business is here reproduced.[13]

Much more indicative of the rates actually prevailing in the

[12] *Cf.* Chap. V, footnote 12, p. 71.

[13] The table of rates was accompanied by the following observations:

"Paris Discount Market for high-grade trade acceptances: — From August 1914 until some time after the termination of the war, transactions of this kind were indeed quite an exception, and until May 1924 there was no actual market in Paris for discounts.

"Regular transactions between banks through the medium of brokers were resumed in May 1924, but no official rates have ever been quoted, as they vary considerably according to the names on the bills and the endorsing banking institutions or bankers.

"The average rates effective since May 1924 have been as follows:

Paris market are the series of rates for Bourse loans, *reports* (*parquet*), and of those on short-term Treasury obligations. As was seen above in Chapters III and IV, until their gradual suppression beginning late in 1926, Treasury paper of short maturity made up a large portion of the portfolios of the banks. Stock exchange loans were, however, far from negligible. In general, while extremely variable in amount, for the "Big Four" they seem to have ranged roughly between one-fifth and one-tenth of the combined item *avances et reports*,[14] though during the period when Bourse

TABLE 69

COMMERCIAL PAPER RATES IN PARIS

	1924	1925	1926	1927
January	...	$5\frac{3}{4}$	4	$4\frac{1}{2}$
February	...	$5\frac{7}{8}$	4	4
March	...	$5\frac{7}{8}$	4	$3\frac{5}{8}$
April	...	$5\frac{7}{8}$	$4\frac{1}{16}$	3
May	$4\frac{15}{16}$	6	$4\frac{7}{8}$	$2\frac{3}{8}$
June	5	$5\frac{3}{4}$	$5\frac{5}{8}$	$1\frac{7}{8}$
July	5	$4\frac{7}{8}$	$5\frac{5}{8}$	$1\frac{7}{8}$
August	$4\frac{15}{16}$	$4\frac{3}{4}$	$7\frac{1}{8}$	2
September	$5\frac{3}{16}$	$4\frac{5}{8}$	7	2
October	5	$4\frac{1}{2}$	7	...
November	5	$4\frac{1}{2}$	$6\frac{3}{8}$	...
December	6	$4\frac{3}{8}$	$5\frac{1}{2}$	...

[14] The *Crédit Lyonnais* does not separate in its statements the items *reports* and *avances*. For the *Société Générale*, *Comptoir d'Escompte*, and the *Crédit Industriel et Commercial* the combined amounts of *reports* as compared with those of *avances* were as follows:

TABLE 70

(In millions of francs)[a]

	Reports[b]	*Avances*[c]
December 31, 1913	94	588
December 31, 1916	44	399
December 31, 1919	14	558
December 31, 1923	49	486
December 31, 1926	109	462

[a] Source: *Annual Reports of the Councils of Administration to the General Assemblies of Stockholders*.

[b] For the description of this type of loan see page 228.

[c] Loans on the collateral of securities.

operations were largely suspended and when only pre-war contracts were being liquidated, the proportion was at times much smaller. And *avances et reports* for the four big banks have in turn ranged for the period under discussion between 550 and 1400 millions of francs. It is probable, therefore, that for all the banks combined, stock-exchange loans aggregate usually some hundreds of millions of francs. These *reports* are in no sense call loans but are made to brokers usually on the collateral of stock exchange (*parquet*) securities and are settled or renewed every fifteen days. Consequently, while admittedly not sensitive, fluctuations in the rates on this particular type of loan probably represent more accurately than those on any others the varying ease and tightness of the Paris money markets. The rates on short-term Treasury paper, while certainly influenced at times by the needs of the Government and while changed only at long intervals, nevertheless represent, at least roughly, average anticipated rates on highly liquid paper.

The accompanying chart (Chart XLIII) shows the movements of rates on *reports* along with those on prime acceptances and those on *Bons de la Défense Nationale* of three-months maturity.

Relatively little can be told about the rates prior to 1920. According to presumably reliable information obtained from Paris bankers, prime commercial paper, during the war years and before 1924, was sold in such small volume as to preclude the development of anything approaching a current rate in such transactions. *Bons de la Défense Nationale* of short maturity were issued at the same rate throughout the war period and until March 12, 1922. *Reports* fell under the moratorium decree of September 27, 1914 and were fixed at 5 per cent until the end of September 1915, when the *marché à terme* was partially reopened to liquidate the transactions held in an uncompleted state since the beginning of the war. On the day on which settlements were resumed, September 30, 1915, the rate was in the neighborhood of 6 per cent. From that time until the end of 1919, while only previously made contracts were being liquidated, the rates oscillated very closely around 4 per cent.[15] Beginning with January 1920 the

[15] The following information was received directly from the Syndic de la Compagnie des Agents de Change de Paris in a letter addressed to the writer: —

charted rates are actual quotations. Moreover, this much can be said for the earlier period: Certainly money could not have been in any sense tight without affecting the rates on *Bons de la Défense Nationale*, on which the Government was relying for so considerable a subscription of funds.

Although in the latter half of 1918 the rates on *reports* rose from 4 per cent to 5 per cent, it is interesting to note that they slumped to their war-time level with the beginning of 1919 and remained at that point through January 1920. There then ensued a slight rise until the beginning of April — on March 15 the rate going above that of the Bank of France for the first time since September 1915. It is clear, therefore, that the post-war boom was financed with plentiful funds at very easy rates, which did not, in fact, stiffen appreciably until the early months of 1920. On April 20, 1920 the discount rate of the Bank of France was raised from

---

"Paris, le 7 Octobre, 1927

"Monsieur,

Pour répondre à votre lettre du 23 Septembre dernier, j'ai le regret de vous faire connaître qu'il ne m'est pas possible de vous donner les renseignements complémentaires que vous me demandez.

"Le relevé des taux moyens de reports cotés à la Bourse de Paris à chacune des liquidations depuis 1914 ne peut être établi que depuis la réouverture du marché à terme qui a eu lieu le 2 Janvier 1920.

"En ce qui concerne la période antérieure, en effet, je crois devoir vous informer, tout d'abord, que la liquidation du 31 Juillet 1914 ayant été prorogée jusqu'au 30 Septembre 1915, il n'y a pas eu, dans l'intervalle, de reports à pratiquer et par conséquent de taux de reports à déterminer.

"Mais le décret du 27 Septembre 1914, article 1er suspendant toutes demandes en paiement relatives aux ventes et achats à terme antérieurs au 4 Août 1914, de rentes, fonds d'États et autres valeurs mobilières, ainsi qu'aux opérations de reports s'y rattachant, stipulait que les sommes dues à raison de ces ventes, achats et reports seraient augmentées d'un intérêt moratoire de 5% par an.

"À compter du 30 Septembre 1915, en conformité du décret du 14 Septembre 1915, le marché à terme a été rouvert partiellement à seule fin de liquider les opérations demeurées en suspens depuis le début de la guerre.

"Les reports pratiqués se sont, par conséquent, référés à un nombre de transactions de plus en plus restreint et les taux d'intérêts déterminés successivement ne revêtent, dès lors, qu'une signification réduite. Je puis vous signaler que, voisins de 6% à la liquidation initiale du 30 Septembre 1915, ils ont, par la suite, oscillé sans variations appréciables aux environs du taux de 4% l'an.

"Agréez, Monsieur, l'assurance de ma considération très distinguée.

"Le Syndic de la Compagnie des Agents de Change de Paris,

(*Signed*) E. JACOB."

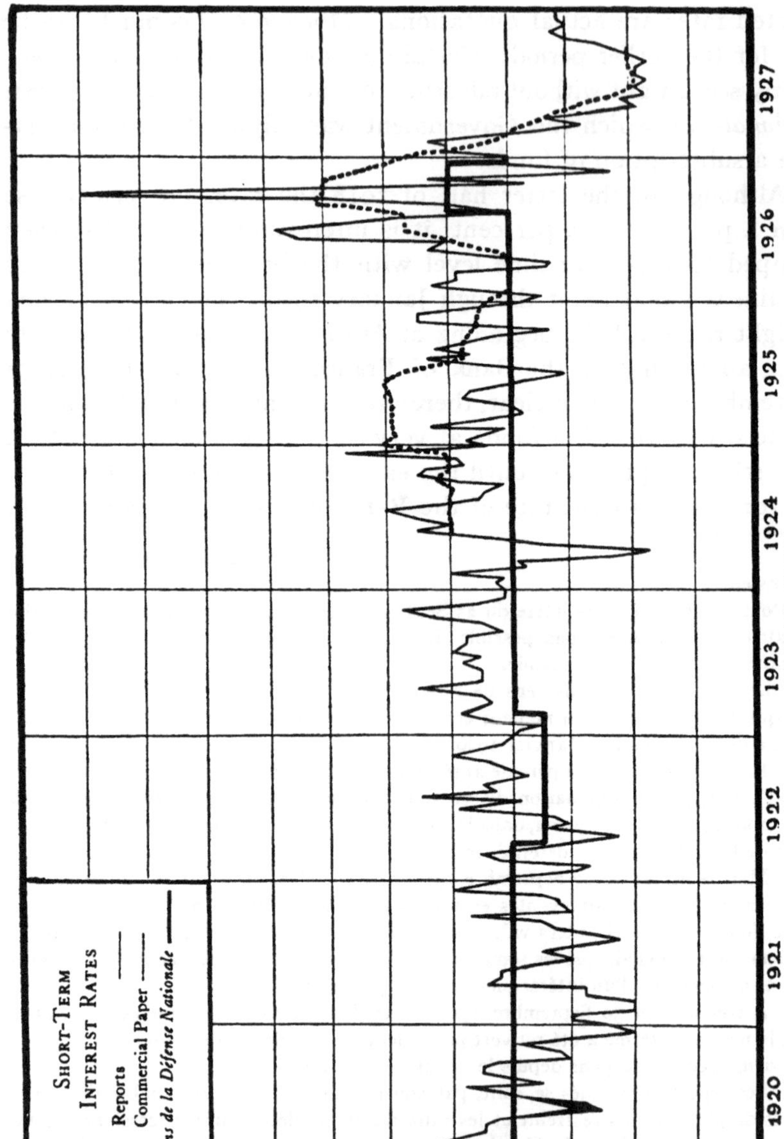
Short-Term
Interest Rates
Reports
Commercial Paper
Bons de la Défense Nationale
Percents
12
11
10
9
8
7
6
5
4
3
2
1
0
1920
1921
1922
1923
1924
1925
1926
1927

CHART XLIII

TABLE 71

RATES ON *REPORTS* *

(Rates on settlement days)

	1918	1919	1920	1921	1922	1923	1924	1925	1926	1927
Jan. 15	4%	4%	4%	3%	4%	3⅞%	4¼%	4¾%	3½%	5%
31	4	4	4	3	3	3½	4⅛	4½	4	5
Feb. 15	4	4	4½ to 4¾	2	2¾	4⅜	5	4⅛	5¼	5¼
28	4	4	4¼ to 4¾	2	4¼	4⅞	3¾	5¼	4⅞	4¼
Mar. 15	4	4	5¼	2¾	4½	4½	3⅞	4¼	4⅞	3⅜
31	4	4	5	2¾	3¾	4⅜	2¼	3¾	3⅜	2¾
Apr. 15	4	4	4½	4½	3⅞	4½	1¾	4	3¼	3⅜
30	4	4	4½	4¼	2¼	5½	3½	4¾	4¼	2¾
May 15	4	4	4¼	4¼	3⅜	4½	4¼	4⅝	5¼	1⅞
31	4	4	2½ to 3	3¾	3	4½	5½	4	5	2⅛
June 15	4&5	4	2¾ to 3¼	3	3¼	4½	5	3¾	7½	1¾
30	5	4	4	3½	4⅞	4¾	5½	3	7⅞	1⅞
July 15	5	4	4¼	2¾	3⅞	4½	6	4	7	1¾
31	5	4	4¾	2¼	5½	5	5⅞	5½	5⅞	1⅞
Aug. 15	5	4	3½	2¾	4¼	4¾	4½	4¾	4	1⅞
31	5	4	4½	3¼	4½	4¾	4⅜	5⅜	5	1¾
Sept. 15	5	4	4½	3½	4⅛	4⅛	4⅛	4¾	7	1⅞
30	5	4	4¼	4¾	3¾	4¼	4⅞	4⅜	11	2⅛
Oct. 15	5	4	3	3	4⅛	4⅜	5½	3⅜	7½	2½
31	5	4	3¼	3¼	4⅜	5¼	5⅜	4¼	3¾	3
Nov. 15	5	4	4	3¼	5	5¾	4¾	5½	5¼	3¼
30	5	4	3	3½	4½	4½	4⅞	5½	2¼	3
Dec. 15	5	4	2	5	4¼	4⅞	6¾	4¾	4	3⅛
31	5	4	2½	4¼	4	4⅞	4⅜	3¾	4	3⅛

* Source: The data for all years were furnished by the Chambre Syndicale des Agents de Change.

The rates are those prevailing on settlement days for loans made on the collateral of Bourse securities for a duration of time between two liquidations on the Bourse. The loans are not callable, but the lender may dispose of the pledged securities. Settlements are made on the 15th and last day of each month. The rates on such loans given in the table are those for advances made upon securities of the official market (*parquet*). The rates for 1918 and 1919 have little significance, for they represent only those applying to loans contracted before August 4, 1914. Consequently, since these loans were gradually being liquidated, the rates applied to a more and more restricted number of transactions. The rates began to take on significance only in 1920 when the *marché à terme* was reopened (January 2).

5 per cent to 6 per cent, but by that time the rates on *reports* had already begun to fall and a month and a half later were down to $2^1/_2$ per cent. Throughout the rest of 1920, all of 1921, and the first half of 1922, money continued easy, as is indicated by the

generally low rates prevailing. With June 1922, however, under the stimulus of business recovery, money tightened considerably, and, when by February 14, 1923 rates still showed no tendency to decrease, those paid on *Bons de la Défense Nationale* were raised by one-half of one per cent.[16] Throughout 1923 and 1924 (with the exception of March and April 1924) rates continued high. With the waning of business activity and with the growing tenseness of the political situation in the early months of 1925, however, rates on *reports* showed a tendency to weaken, while those on commercial paper continued at the high level reached at the end of 1924. As the heavy advances of the Bank of France to the Government began again in April 1925, rates on commercial paper eased considerably, and those on *reports*, though showing much irregularity, averaged somewhat lower than in the latter half of 1924. The year 1926 thus began with both rates low, but they rose rapidly and greatly as the 1926 crisis approached — probably on account of the great uncertainty as to the exchange value of the franc at the maturity of loans then negotiated. Nevertheless, the high point was not reached until the end of September 1926, more than two months after the Poincaré Cabinet assumed power. After that time both rates declined rapidly, at first, no doubt, because of the returning confidence in the franc, but later more largely because of the growing business depression and because of the issue of funds by the Bank of France in its purchase of foreign exchange, all coupled with the stringent restrictions on the export of capital.

Another excellent indicator of the relative ease and tightness of the money market is to be found in the data of the excesses of issues over reimbursements of short-term Treasury paper. It will be remembered that until late in 1926 *Bons de la Défense Nationale* were issued in any desired amounts whenever applied for. Their use by the banks as a form of investment for otherwise idle funds has been commented upon frequently and at length in the pages which have gone before. The relative ease or tightness of the money market, as well as the waning confidence in the Government, should be indicated, therefore, by the excess of issues over

[16] Exception was made for bonds of one month maturity, which continued to be issued at 3 per cent.

TABLE 72

EXCESS OF EMISSIONS OVER REIMBURSEMENTS OF BONS DE LA DÉFENSE NATIONALE AND SHORT-TERM TREASURY PAPER *

(In millions of francs)

	1915	1916	1917	1918	1919	1920
Jan.	859	844	833	735	2501	1668
Feb.	540	764	932	975	1924	1460
Mar.	952	725	1000	779	1910	− 11
Apr.	368	721	1035	601	1569	110
May	776	1231	1115	1545	2073	1316
June	479	838	1012	547	2602	1760
July	825	1074	1104	881	2619	2220
Aug.	559	1016	1142	1511	2588	− 6225
Sept.	717	899	870	1620	2606	1245
Oct.	839	− 3484	907	2678	2308	858
Nov.	284	591	1136	2266	1993	2624
Dec.	− 1854 [b]	393	− 4153	− 10820	491	− 764
Yearly [a]	5387	5612	6933	3318	25183	6261

	1921	1922	1923	1924	1925	1926
Jan.	531	1393	↑	704	753	132
Feb.	1277	201	− 4546 [c]	136	− 345	529
Mar.	2282	393		− 255	58	− 251
Apr.	2506	485	↓	1191	− 1961	339
May	1803	1751	1706	393	− 929	83
June	614	1130	2677	329	− 204	− 161
July	− 230	− 1163	658	1282	1035	− 2110
Aug.	1223	412	421	221	2	1340
Sept.	1377	1011	447	− 372	733	134
Oct.	873	− 2919	− 1627	− 2999	− 5304	− 1558
Nov.	692	− 3209	− 1441	1552	− 1864	2315
Dec.	1163 [d]	− 775	355	− 3494	− 253	404
Yearly	13049	− 1291	− 1350	− 1312	− 8279	1196

[a] The yearly figure for 1914 is 1619 millions.

[b] Minus signs indicate excesses of reimbursements.

[c] Total for the first quarter of the year.

[d] Deduction was not made for an error of 7 milliards found by the Ministry of Finance and deducted as of this date.

* Source: Georges Lachapelle, "*L'Évolution de la Circulation*," etc. (Paris, Société d'Études et d'Informations Économiques, 1926 and 1927).

reimbursements during the various phases of the period under discussion. By reference to the table on page 233 it will be seen that until 1922 there was always an annual excess of issues over reimbursements. The excess in 1919 — the largest for any year of the period — is especially interesting in view of the fact that during that year the post-war boom got under way. Under the influence of the rapidly increasing advances of the Bank to the State, funds during that year were evidently extremely plentiful, at least until December, when the excess of subscriptions reached its lowest point of 491 millions. In 1920, likewise, money rates evidently continued generally easy, for, while the excess of subscriptions over reimbursements was reduced from 25 milliards to 6 milliards, it was still of significant magnitude. Certainly it can be said, therefore, that the entire post-war boom was financed under conditions of extremely easy money, with rates tightening only slightly just before the culmination of activity in 1920.

In 1921, as might have been anticipated, the excess of subscriptions was again very large. The development of industrial depression released funds formerly utilized by business, and, on accumulating in the banks, these funds were naturally used either by their owners or else by the banks to purchase the short-term obligations of the Government.

Beginning with 1922, there was each year until 1926 an excess of reimbursements over subscriptions. In 1922 and 1923, it is pretty evident that reviving business activity and rising prices, in the absence of further increases in the advances from the Bank to the State, were tightening money conditions and causing the banks to cash their short-term Treasury obligations as they came due. In 1924, however, when it is fairly certain that the Bank of France had begun making indirect advances to the Treasury and when the political situation was already becoming tense, it is not clear whether the continued excess of reimbursements was resulting principally from the loss of confidence in the Government by private investors or whether the continued rapid expansion of business under an ever rising price level was bringing about a further liquidation of the holdings of Treasury obligations by the banks. Both influences were probably at work. The indirect advances of the Bank of France to the State, it is true, passed through the hands of the other banks. But, remaining there only momentarily, as they did, not only did they not reduce the banks' further lending power but, on the contrary, as the proceeds were rapidly spent by the Government, led to an inflow of cash deposits. It is also true that 1924 was the most active business year in France since 1920. It seems probable, therefore, that the expanding business needs were at least partially causing the banks to continue their liquidation of government bond holdings and that their actions in turn were forcing the Government, in the absence of an authorization to increase its advances from the central bank, to resort to the subterfuge of borrowing directly from the other banks while arranging with the Bank of France to discount sufficient paper from their portfolios to provide the funds required for the advances.

The big excess of reimbursements in 1925, on the contrary, seems to have resulted very largely from the growing distrust of the Government and of the franc, a feeling which undoubtedly became aggravated by the disclosures on the floor of the Senate early in April with regard to the indirect advances of the Bank of France to the State and to the issue of notes in excess of their legal maximum.[17] By reference to the table of monthly data it will be seen that in the month of April alone the excess of reimbursements over issues was 1961 millions and in May 929 millions. Funds were evidently being withdrawn for investment in other forms of values or even for hoarding. The rapid decline of the franc, beginning early in the year and becoming more marked in the later months, seems to point definitely to the form many of these new investments were taking. In spite of the restrictions on the export of capital, the balances of French banks with foreign correspondents increased greatly — and in the case of some of the big banks they much more than doubled.[18] Moreover, it is an open secret [19] that during this period many private individuals followed the same policy as their bankers and con-

[17] See Chap. VIII, pp. 203–204. [18] See Chap. VIII, Table 59, p. 193.

[19] P. Meynial estimates that during the year 1925 alone such exportation of capital amounted to more than 10 milliards of francs. — P. Meynial, *op. cit.* p. 56 *et seq.*

verted their government bonds into foreign securities as rapidly as they dared. The Government, being forced to turn elsewhere for funds with which to meet its maturing obligations, increased its advances from the Bank of France. Notes were evidently withdrawn to a somewhat smaller amount to make the purchases of foreign securities, of domestic stocks, and of whatever other objects of value the frightened investors decided to acquire, for the circulation of the Bank of France increased similarly, though not so greatly, as the advances to the State.[20]

The general feeling of uncertainty seemed likewise to affect the business situation. In spite of the continued rise in prices, the volume of production, car loadings, and bank clearings all slumped below their normal secular trends, thus providing another reason why the increase in currency supplies should not be so great as that of advances of the Bank of France to the State.

Late in 1925 both dollar exchange rates and prices mounted rapidly, and the excesses of reimbursements over issues of short-term government obligations became very large, especially in October when the fall of the franc was most rapid. In early January 1926, on the other hand, dollar exchange declined slightly and in February moved upward by only a similarly small amount. Quick in their response, issues of short-term Treasury paper in both of these months exceeded reimbursements. For the three following months of rapidly rising dollar and sterling exchange rates, reimbursements exceeded in the first, and issues in the other two. Then, in June and July, as the crisis approached, the excess of

[20] During this period the indirect advances of the Bank of France to the State were being converted into direct ones and the formerly concealed issues of the Bank of France were brought to light, so that quantitative comparisons of the increases in note circulation and in advances of the Bank to the State are somewhat unsatisfactory. Nevertheless, it seems clear that the increase in advances was actually considerably greater than that in notes, as indeed, one would expect when it is recalled that the funds being withdrawn were largely for investment. Probably some of the government *mandats* (as well as *virements*) would not be cashed but be deposited with the Bank of France and checked against in paying for the new investments. Even if all were cashed, however, the note circulation would be expected to decrease again almost as soon as the new expenditures for securities had been made, since such expenditures do not, as do most others, stimulate a long train of further purchases and thus keep money in circulation.

reimbursements mounted rapidly. After the establishment of the Poincaré Government, with the single exception of October, when exchange rates again rose rapidly, there was during 1926 a continued excess of issues.

After 1926 the gradual suppression[21] of *Bons de la Défense Nationale* of short maturity caused all such obligations, at least temporarily, to lose significance on the money market. In the future they will probably not be sought by the banks until within three months of maturity,[22] when they become rediscountable at the Bank of France.

Before closing this discussion of the Paris money market something should be said of the severe exchange crisis of 1924. Apparently growing out of the large short sales of francs in various foreign exchange centers of the world, it seemed to come most largely from Central European centers. It was rumored that the same group of speculators which had profited so greatly from the Austrian and Germany currency debacles had centered their attention on Paris. Certainly many of the Viennese banks were themselves involved.

As has been pointed out in Chapter VI, the short-sales of future francs involved an almost equivalent sale of "spot" francs by the speculators' banks. This necessary cover was secured by the banks in various ways. Some ordered their Paris correspondents to buy the desired foreign exchange on the Paris market. The regulations against the export of capital, however, interfered seriously with such transactions on a large scale. Other banks operated through correspondents in remote money centers. Especially important was Amsterdam, for example, in negotiating the sales of francs, though there is little doubt that most of the

[21] In October 1926 there were in circulation and being issued from day to day bonds with maturities of one, three, six, and twelve months. Those with two-year maturities began to be issued in January 1927. The *arrêté* of December 16, 1926 suppressed the issue of bonds of one month; that of December 22, 1926, bonds of three months; that of January 29, 1927, bonds of six months; and that of June 2, 1927, bonds of one year. The two-year bonds continue to be issued, but their maturities at times of issue are too long for general use by the banks as liquid assets.

[22] Since the last of the one-year bonds matures on June 2, 1928 and the first of the two-year bonds on January 1, 1929, there will be an interval of a little more than six months during which no maturities will occur.

transactions had their origin somewhat farther east on the Continent. Still other banks simply sold directly "spot" francs in the centers in which they were located.

But, however the operations were arranged in detail, they required franc balances against which franc drafts could be sold or with which foreign drafts could be bought. Some such balances were actually secured from persons and institutions speculating for a rise in francs. Such persons or institutions were glad to exchange their francs for some of the foreign currencies offered. In a period such as that of early 1924, however, comparatively small quantities could be expected from these sources. To the extent that the required balances could not be thus obtained, they had to be borrowed, and naturally most of such borrowing took place in Paris. Banks desiring to sell French exchange in their home markets or elsewhere simply arranged to draw upon their Paris correspondents. At first no difficulty was encountered, as such arrangements were frequently made in the normal order of business.

When the extent of the exchange manipulation coming from abroad began to be realized in Paris, however, various steps were taken to meet the crisis. Not only was the rapid and drastic decline of the franc causing prices to rise rapidly and the general economic situation to be disturbed, but the little understood movements were directing public attention to the fundamental weakness of the position of the franc and to the reckless financial and foreign policies of the Government itself. Nevertheless, any effective means of arresting the movements without disturbing the delicate mechanism of the modern financial organization of economic activities was difficult to find. So various were the forms of the loans utilized in securing the desired franc credits that a prohibition against all the usable types would have brought the credit machinery practically to a halt. Moreover, so informal are often the extensions of credit between correspondents that no mere regulations with regard to forms of loans could possibly prove effective. Accordingly, the one available method was used. In a letter of January 21, 1924, addressed by the Minister of Finance to the president of the *Union Syndicale des Banquiers de Paris et de la Province*, all the bankers of the country were requested to coöperate in bringing the movement to an end. In particular they were asked not to allow overdrafts to their clients or to foreign correspondents against any foreign currencies, but above all their coöperation was solicited in the endeavor to make unavailable in any form the credit requisite to a further damaging sale of francs.

That this appeal bore fruit is indicated by the wide separation in the rates on "spot" and forward exchange in the various foreign exchange centers. In New York, for example, on at least two days in March 1924 the spread on 90-day contracts was more than half a cent (10 per cent of the franc's value). Such a separation could not possibly have occurred had credit in the Paris market been easily available on the terms there quoted at the time.

The reason for the separation is not difficult to discern. It will be remembered from the discussion of exchange rates above (Chapter VI) that the differentials between forward and "spot" rates are almost completely determined by the differences in the money rates prevailing in the two centers concerned. Should the discount on forward francs in New York, for example, become greater than that corresponding to the difference in interest rates between New York and Paris, immediately it would become profitable to arbitragers to buy forward francs at the big discount prevailing and to cover by selling "spot" francs at the correspondingly higher rate. To be in a position to sell "spot" francs, however, a balance must be borrowed or otherwise secured in Paris. Since, however, the deal gives the operator the dollar proceeds of the draft in New York, its chief cost consists of the difference in having the funds in New York rather in Paris. And, since by hypothesis the difference in money rates in the two centers is less than that corresponding to the discount on forward francs in New York, a profit is realized from the transaction. Arbitragers seeking to avail themselves of such profits would increase the demand for forward francs while enlarging the supply of "spot" francs. Since, too, these operations would continue so long as there was a profit to be made, the discount on francs in New York would be forced to substantial adjustment with the difference in money rates between Paris and New York.

It is evident, therefore, either that lending rates in the Paris market were extremely high on funds required for the sales of francs or else that sufficient funds were at times actually unavailable and that the banks handling the speculative sales were making a heavy charge to cover their risk while searching for the necessary balances in Paris. According to French bankers, rates as high as 30 per cent were charged on advances for the tabooed purpose and even up to 60 per cent on back payment adjustments. But, besides being discouraged by the high rates, many speculators without doubt were forced to restrict operations because of the unavailability of franc credits in sufficient volume to provide the balances against which the necessary "spot" sales could be made. Furthermore, since money rates for ordinary purposes in Paris at the same time were not substantially higher than usual, it is clear that the spread between "spot" and forward rates was being produced by the actions of Paris bankers in their attempts to render much needed assistance to the Government.

On March 10, 1924 there were rumors of a hundred million dollar loan made by J. P. Morgan and Company of New York to the French Government. The proceeds of the loan, formally announced after the close of business on March 12, were to be used to prevent a further fall of the franc. The recovery was immediate. Many of those who a few days before were feverishly placing orders for the sale of forward francs began in their desperate run for cover just as eagerly to purchase the same currency. Within ten days the rates on dollar exchange were below those prevailing at the beginning of the year, and the decline continued until the end of April.

The effects of the crisis on the economic and credit situations are of interest. Wholesale prices rose almost as quickly and almost as rapidly as did dollar exchange rates. Non-governmental advances of the Bank of France showed a sharp rise and even the note circulation a slight one. Clearings, too, increased rapidly, and security prices rose abruptly. It is certain therefore that the disturbance was considerable and widespread. Strange as it may seem, however, money rates were little affected. Rates on *reports* (Bourse loans) reached a slight peak on February 15, but at the end of the month they were below their normal, as they were also on the next settlement day (March 15). Rates on paper discounted at the banks seem to have changed little. On the other hand, long-term interest rates moved up rapidly and, unlike the other phenomena discussed, remained high after the crisis had passed.

From these movements several things are evident. Not only is it clear that by this time prices were already being moved up with any drastic decline of the franc but also that they were being marked down as soon as the franc recovered. The big increase in clearings probably represents little more than the effects of the operations connected with the selling of francs in foreign countries and with the purchase of foreign securities and foreign currencies in France. The notable rise in long-term interest rates, on the other hand, is probably in part attributable to the increased uneasiness with regard to the future of the franc — a feeling which from that time until the middle of 1926 had much to do with the large export of capital as well as with many of the financial difficulties of the Treasury and with other political troubles of the Government. The continual threat of a capital levy increased in turn the incentive to transfer investments from French to foreign securities.

Nevertheless, by far the most interesting deduction that can be drawn from the March 1924 crisis concerns the extent of the manipulation produced by foreign speculators in the franc. If the operations of foreign speculators were sufficient to cause the franc to lose one-fourth of its value, to what extent is the currency of a country subject to foreign manipulation? Certainly the question is a vital one. Not only are the resulting movements of exchange rates extremely harmful to the country the currency of which is attacked, but the probability of the appearance of the danger is much increased by the fact that a fabulous profit[23] awaits the successful attacker and his accomplices. Moreover, if the type of offensive is dependable, wars might be fought with its extensive use and enemies dependent on outside sources for any large proportion of their supplies might be reduced to practical

[23] In order for the profit to be realized some means would have to be found for borrowing extensively in the country the currency of which was being attacked.

impotence by the loss in outside purchasing power of their monetary units. The answer will throw new light, too, on the potential power of the very wealthy — the real kings of this financial age — in determining the affairs of whole nations.

How great was the volume of the speculative sales of francs it is impossible to state. Coming as it did mostly from such poverty-stricken centers as Berlin and Vienna, it was probably not large — at least not in the Anglo-Saxon sense of the term. How much the movement was aggravated by the activities of capital exporters in France itself must also remain unanswered, though it is certain that it bulked small in dollars or in pounds. On the other hand, the franc at that time had none of the normal protection usually surrounding the currency of a big and important country. Furthermore, for political as well as for financial reasons its position was extremely weak. Many were already anticipating a further fall in its international value without outside impetus. So perhaps what manipulators could do with the franc in March 1924 gives but slight indication of what might have been done at other times or with other currencies. The consternation that was thrown into the camp of the manipulators by the announcement of the Morgan loan of $100,000,000 is nevertheless indicative of the estimated potency of relatively so small a sum — at any rate when provided by so powerful a banking firm.

The normal protection against such manipulation is of course to be found in the metallic reserves behind the currency of a country and in the accumulation of actual or potential balances in foreign centers. In order to be effective in time of danger, however, the protective resources must be used. Unusable gold reserves held only for sentimental purposes can accomplish nothing. Furthermore, even under the gold standard where the redeemability of all moneys is maintained, the protection furnished by the reserve is to the extent of its magnitude only. Hence, in the absence of foreign balances and of the possibility of borrowing them, the outside purchasing power of practically any small country — even though it were on the gold standard — could be wrecked[24] by any

[24] Even the securing of credits within the country attacked would not be necessary if the cost of the operations was not of prime importance.

one of a number of big banking interests. Foreign credits, though in many ways more convenient and more readily available in time of danger, can likewise prove effective only to the extent of their magnitudes. Certainly, however, had it been politically, sentimentally, and otherwise possible in March 1924 for the French Government to use the accumulated reserves of the Bank of France, the depreciation of the franc could have been quickly arrested. The present (December 1927) large holdings of foreign exchange furnish ample protection for at least an $800,000,000 drive against the value of the franc.

CHAPTER X

INVESTMENT BANKING, SAVINGS, AND INVESTMENTS

As was pointed out in an earlier part of this study, the *Banque de Paris et des Pays-Bas* and the *Banque de l'Union Parisienne* together do a very large portion indeed of the primary investment banking business in France. The affairs of these two banks will, therefore, be taken as representative of those of the *banques d'affaires* in general. The scanty and diverse reports of the private investment banks (*la haute banque*) are of such a nature as to make an analysis of their operations of doubtful validity.

By reference to the statements of these two largest of the investment banks proper it will be found that, as in the case of the commercial banks, when the depreciation in the purchasing power or in the gold value of the franc is taken into account, neither earnings nor capital items were maintained at their pre-war levels. The table below gives in terms of paper francs, of gold francs, and of 1913 purchasing power both capital liabilities and dividends for the years covered in this report. In spite of the fact that fixed assets such as buildings and furnishings were not marked up to correspond with the depreciation of the franc, and in spite, too, of the indefinite character of the statements of all French banks, a reference to the table seems to show not only that profits paid out as dividends were reduced, but that capital liabilities actually shrank in gold or purchasing power values. However, it is also evident that the shrinkage in each case was less than in like items of the commercial banks.[1]

A very important change in the affairs of these banks occurred during the inflation régime. Both have increased very greatly their commercial banking operations. The demand deposits of the *Banque de Paris et des Pays-Bas*, for example, which before the

[1] See Chap. IX, Tables 66 and 67, pp. 213–214.

TABLE 73

CAPITAL STOCK, RESERVES, AND DIVIDENDS OF THE *BANQUES D'AFFAIRES* [*]

Date	Millions of francs	Millions of gold francs [a]	In terms of 1913 purchasing power [b]
	Capital and Reserves		
December 31, 1913	384	384	388
December 31, 1914	331	332	300
December 31, 1915	328	291	201
December 31, 1916	338	300	166
December 31, 1917	343	312	113
December 31, 1918	345	328	98
December 31, 1919	·449	217	106
December 31, 1920	531	164	122
December 31, 1921	616	252	189
December 31, 1922	608	230	168
December 31, 1923	612	169	133
December 31, 1924	615	174	121
December 31, 1925	620	121	98
December 31, 1926	625	128	100
	Dividends		
December 31, 1913	23	23	23
December 31, 1914	4	4	4
December 31, 1915	9	8	6
December 31, 1916	11	10	5
December 31, 1917	13	12	4
December 31, 1918	15	14	4
December 31, 1919	20	10	5
December 31, 1920	33	10	8
December 31, 1921	30	12	9
December 31, 1922	38	15	11
December 31, 1923	43	12	9
December 31, 1924	47	13	9
December 31, 1925	49	10	8
December 31, 1926	55	11	9

[a] Nominal francs divided by the index of the average of dollar exchange for December of each year. The amounts are not significant for the period of controlled exchange, 1916–1918.

[b] Nominal francs divided by the index of wholesale prices of the *Statistique Générale de la France* for December of each year.

[*] Source: *Annual Reports of the Councils of Administration to the General Assemblies of Stockholders*. The *Banque de Paris et des Pays-Bas* and the *Banque de l'Union Parisienne* only are considered.

war were carried almost exclusively for investment-banking customers, have in the past seven years been invited from everyone. On December 31, 1926 the item for this bank was several times as large as the corresponding one for the *Crédit Industriel et Commercial*, the smallest of the "Big Four," and almost half as large as that of the *Comptoir d'Escompte*. Its commercial loan and discount business has expanded correspondingly, as has also that of the *Banque de l'Union Parisienne*.

TABLE 74

PORTFOLIO, DEPOSITS, AND ACCOUNTS WITH CORRESPONDENT BANKS OF THE *BANQUES D'AFFAIRES* *

(In millions of francs)

Date	Portfolio [a]	Deposits [b]	Correspondent Accounts
December 31, 1913	946	485	...
December 31, 1914	720	360	...
December 31, 1915	558	233	...
December 31, 1916	644	324	...
December 31, 1917	797	511	...
December 31, 1918	883	569	...
December 31, 1919	1230	885	...
December 31, 1920	1752	1395	...
December 31, 1921	1922	1508	...
December 31, 1922	2125	1672	152
December 31, 1923	2454	2129	264
December 31, 1924	2606	2437	382
December 31, 1925	3161	3654	939
December 31, 1926	3055	3281	691

[a] The item includes holdings of *Bons de la Défense Nationale* and short-term Treasury paper, of other longer-term securities, and of commercial paper, *reports*, loans on the collateral of securities, participation in syndicates, and debitor current accounts.

[b] The item represents both sight and time deposits.

* Source: *Annual Reports of the Councils of Administration to the Assemblies of Stockholders*. The *Banque de Paris et des Pays-Bas* and the *Banque de l'Union Parisienne* only are considered.

One other change in the business of these banks is worthy of note, as it seems to have come about largely as a result of the depreciation of the franc. The story is told by the very great increases, shown in the statements of these two banks, as in those of the "Big Four," of accounts with correspondent banks. In the case of the investment banks much of the increase undoubtedly came as a result of their extension of commercial banking operations, but a very large part, too, is admittedly a result of the enlargement of balances with *foreign* correspondents. The *Banque de Paris et des Pays-Bas* in particular has greatly increased the

TABLE 75

BOND EMISSIONS [e]

GOVERNMENTAL [a]

YEAR	MILLIONS OF FRANCS	MILLIONS OF GOLD FRANCS [b]	IN TERMS OF 1913 PURCHASING POWER [c]
1914	804	806	791
1915	15033	13315	9753
1916	11184	9924	5939
1917	12237	11125	4678
1918	27359	26007	8066
1919	4857	3509	1363
1920	30963	11194	6078
1921	15102	5853	4377
1922	12176	5172	3727
1923	22873	7215	5459
1924	9397	2543	1924
1925	− 454 [d]	− 112	− 83
1926	2960	607	472

[a] The data represent the nominal value of the excesses of issues over reimbursements of government bond emissions and include all securities of this category except *Bons de la Défense Nationale*, other short-term Treasury paper, and government obligations given in settlement of war indemnity claims. The obligations of the *Crédit National* are included.

[b] Nominal francs divided by the index of the average of dollar exchange for December of each year. The amounts are not significant for the period of controlled exchange, 1916–1918.

[c] Nominal francs divided by the index of wholesale prices of the *Statistique Générale de la France* for December of each year.

[d] Minus signs indicate excesses of reimbursements over emissions.

[e] Sources: Governmental emissions, R. M. Haig, *The Public Finances of Post-War France* (New York, Columbia University Press, 1929). Non-governmental emissions: issues of railroad companies, *Annuaire Statistique de la Statistique Générale de la France*, 1926, p. 334; issues of other non-governmental organizations: 1914–1919, *Annuaire de l'Association Nationale des Porteurs Français de Valeurs Mobilières* for 1915–1920; data for 1920–1924 furnished by the same organization; 1925–1926, *Bulletin de la Statistique Générale de la France.*

TABLE 75 (Continued)

NON-GOVERNMENTAL [a]

YEAR	MILLIONS OF FRANCS	MILLIONS OF GOLD FRANCS [b]	IN TERMS OF 1913 PURCHASING POWER [c]
1914	2816 [d]	2822	2769
1915	328	291	234
1916	470	417	250
1917	2102	1911	803
1918	1129	879	332
1919	9242	6677	2594
1920	9130	3301	1792
1921	9039	3504	2620
1922	5139	2183	1573
1923	6055	1910	1445
1924	4311	1167	882
1925	2550	628	463
1926	4206	696	598

TOTAL

YEAR	MILLIONS OF FRANCS	MILLIONS OF GOLD FRANCS [b]	IN TERMS OF 1913 PURCHASING POWER [c]
1914	3620	3628	3560
1915	15361	13606	9987
1916	11654	10341	6189
1917	14339	13036	5481
1918	28488	26886	8398
1919	14099	10186	3957
1920	40093	14495	7870
1921	24141	9357	6997
1922	17315	7355	5300
1923	28928	9125	6904
1924	13708	3710	2806
1925	2096	516	380
1926	7166	1468	1144

[a] The data represent the nominal value of all *other than government* bond emissions and include those of French corporations operating at home and abroad, those of municipalities, those of foreign corporations and governments floated in France, those of the *Crédit Foncier*, and those for colonies and protectorates. Issues of foreign bonds are excluded in 1925 and 1926. Issues of private and state railway companies are included.

[b] Nominal francs divided by the index of the average of dollar exchange for December of each year. The amounts are not significant foı the period of controlled exchange, 1916–1918.

[c] Nominal francs divided by the index of wholesale prices of the *Statistique Générale de la France* for December of each year.

[d] No emissions were made during the last five months of 1914.

number of its foreign correspondents as well as the total held on deposit with them. By reference to the table below it will be seen that the large increases in this item came during the crucial years 1923, 1924, and 1925. The inference cannot but be drawn, therefore, that these increases were probably not unconnected with the "flight from the franc." It is not certain, however, just how much of the increased foreign balances was carried for the accounts of customers and how much for those of the banks themselves.

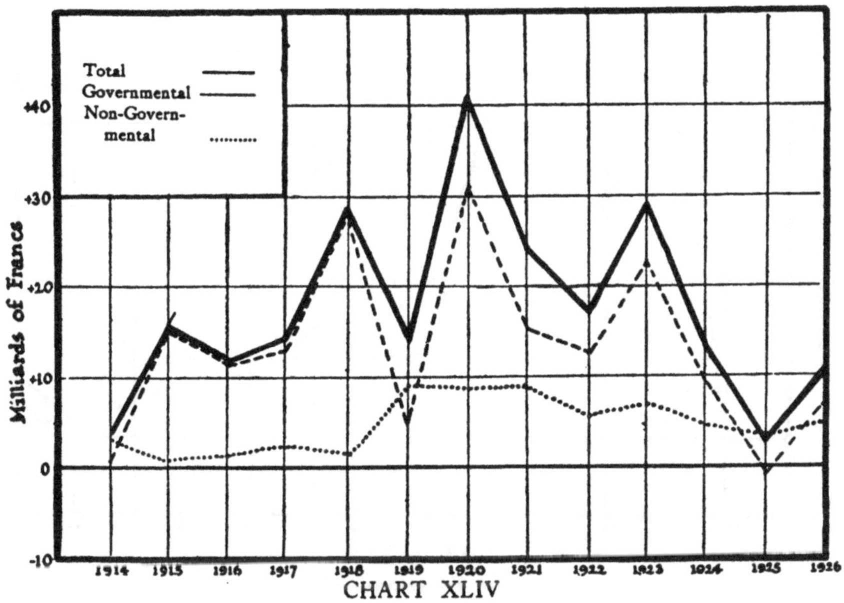

CHART XLIV

BOND EMISSIONS — I

With this brief discussion of the changes in the affairs of the investment banking institutions themselves in mind, attention will be directed to the volume of security emissions and to the rates of yield to their purchasers. In Table 75 will be found, classified into governmental and non-governmental emissions, the total issues of bonds each year since 1914. In order to enable the reader to take account of the variations in the value of the franc, the data are given in terms of 1913 purchasing power and in gold francs as well as in paper francs.

By reference to the accompanying chart (Chart XLIV) it will

at once be observed how overwhelmingly large the issues of the Government — even exclusive of its short-term obligations — were in comparison with those for all other organizations. The Government was evidently claiming a very large portion indeed of the total investment credit available, and during the entire period it is clear that business borrowers were continually in competition with the Government for the existing supply. And, on account

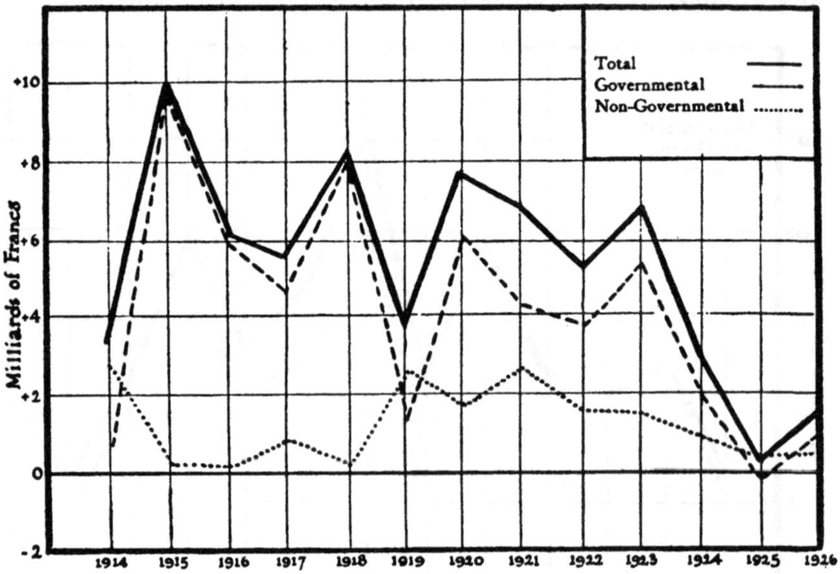

CHART XLV

BOND EMISSIONS — II
1913 Purchasing Power

of the high taxes applicable to the interest on corporation bonds and from which government issues were exempt, business borrowers were placed at a great disadvantage.

It will be further noted that in terms of paper francs the government as well as the total bond emissions during the middle years of the period were considerably higher than in either the earlier or the later years. With the same series reduced to purchasing power units[2] (Chart XLV), however, it is apparent that

[2] The gold values are unusable for this comparison because of the fact that prior to March 1919 the exchange value of the franc was artificially controlled.

the government issues as well as the total, which they almost completely dominated, after 1915 showed downward secular trends throughout the rest of the period. In 1924 and in 1925 there ensued abrupt falls followed by only a comparatively slight rise again in 1926.

For the non-governmental issues the movement was entirely different. At the beginning of the war they dropped off immedi-

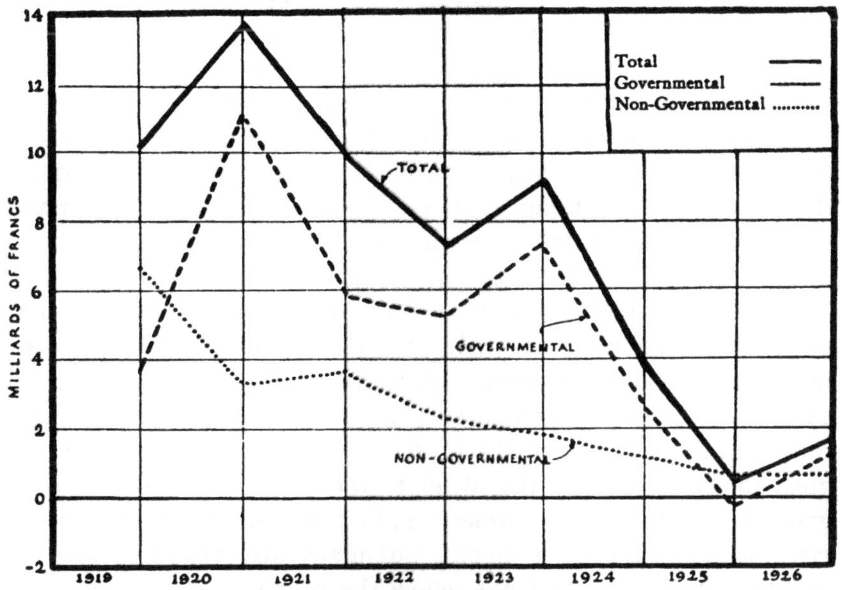

CHART XLVI
Bond Emissions — III
Gold Francs

ately and very greatly, and continued low in terms of purchasing power units as well as in nominal francs until the close of hostilities. In 1919, however, they increased greatly, continued high in 1920 and in 1921, and then decreased gradually to a low point, both in nominal francs and in purchasing power units, in 1925. A slight rise followed in 1926.

What is the explanation of these diverse movements? Evidently 1925 was an extremely bad year for bond flotations of all sorts in France. And 1924 was one only slightly better. The explanation seems clear. Undoubtedly French investors had by 1924 lost much of their natural patriotic confidence in their monetary unit. From the beginning of the war until early in 1920 they had seen the value of their fixed-return investments continually dwindle away. Nevertheless, during that period the ever rising prices, which were the chief cause of their loss, were gradually accepted as one of the inevitable consequences of the war. After the financial crisis of 1920, however, relief seemed finally to have arrived. Prices declined rapidly for more than a year; for another year they continued almost stable — as did likewise the exchange value of the franc. The ultimate return to the gold standard was not only confidently expected by the great masses of the people, but all voters were also continually confirmed in this belief by the utterances of politicians high and low of most parties. Consequently there was no hesitation on the part of investors in placing their savings in government or other bonds.

Shortly before the middle of 1922, however, both prices and dollar exchange resumed their gradual but continued and disquieting upward movements. Then early in 1924 came the severe exchange crisis, which demonstrated clearly to thinking people the fundamental weakness of the position of the franc. Not only did great uncertainty as to the ultimate return to the gold standard gradually displace the former implicit confidence in the financial policies of the Government, but many also began to wonder whether the franc might not follow the courses of the crown and of the mark, so recently and so disastrously plunged to their ruin.

Under such circumstances, especially when they were combined, as they were, with an ever growing tenseness in the political situation, is there any wonder that purchases of the bonds of the Government, as of all other organizations issuing them in terms of francs, should have been made with greatest hesitation? The big slump in bond emissions in 1925, as to a less extent, perhaps, the smaller one in 1924, seems to be completely explained by the disappearing confidence in the value of the franc, by the fear of the imposition of the capital levy continually advocated by the parties of the Left, and by the resulting large exportation of capital. The slight rise in such emissions in 1926, almost all of which appeared in the latter half of the year, is equally explicable on the basis of the great increase in confidence which came with the almost uninterrupted succession of beneficial measures which followed the crisis of July 1926 and of the disappearance once for all of the threat of a capital levy.

The notable rise in non-governmental emissions just after the close of the war is probably attributable to the great demand for funds by private companies. So small had been the flotations during the war period that the capital needs of many business concerns were undoubtedly large, and some of them naturally attempted to supply such needs as soon as the return of peace enabled them to do so. It should be remembered, too, that business was very active during 1919 and early 1920, while money continued extremely easy. The enlarged business activity was of course increasing the need for capital equipment, and the easy money conditions — in 1919 combined with a scarcity of government flotations — invited immediate issues. It seemed, in fact, to be the deliberate policy of the Government in 1919 to finance itself with *Bons de la Défense Nationale* and with borrowings from the Bank of France rather than with long-term issues.

With the development of business depression in the latter half of 1920 and with its continuance in 1921, the ease in the money market persisted in intensified form. Under such favorable conditions of issue the emissions continued large in spite of the discouragement to further credit expansion occasioned by the declining business activity.

Again in 1923, under the stimulus of a new and continued advance in prices accompanied by an increase in production and trade, non-governmental emissions rose slightly, though the great increase in total emissions during that year was almost completely accounted for by the much enlarged issues of the Government. By that time, however, the waning confidence in the future of the franc had apparently already begun to be felt. Under this new and important influence, in the year of prosperity of 1924 as in that of depression of 1925, issues of both private and government borrowers declined rapidly.

A consideration of the data of stock emissions (Chart XLVII) will throw additional light on the trend of investments. As in the case of bond emissions, the data are given in terms of 1913 purchasing power units and in gold as well as in paper francs.

TABLE 76

STOCK EMISSIONS [*]

YEAR	MILLIONS OF FRANCS	MILLIONS OF GOLD FRANCS [a]	IN TERMS OF 1913 PURCHASING POWER [b]
1914	419 [c]	412	420
1915	18	13	16
1916	160	85	142
1917	598	229	544
1918	618	182	587
1919	1514	425	1094
1920	4104	806	1484
1921	2380	690	922
1922	1378	422	585
1923	2277	543	718
1924	3694	756	1000
1925	2705	492	667
1926	3020	430	499

[a] Nominal francs divided by the index of the average of dollar exchange for December of each year. The amounts are not significant in the period of controlled exchange, 1916–1918.

[b] Nominal francs divided by the index of wholesale prices of the *Statistique Générale de la France* for December of each year.

[c] There were no issues during the last five months of 1914.

[*] Sources: 1914–1919, *Annuaire de l'Association Nationale des Porteurs Français de Valeurs Mobilières* for 1915–1920; 1920–1924, data furnished by the same organization; 1925 and 1926, *Bulletin de la Statistique Générale de la France.* The data include the issues of French corporations operating at home and abroad and those of foreign corporations floated in France, the latter being omitted, however, in 1925 and 1926. For the years 1914–1924 the data supposedly represent *émissions réalisées,* and for the years 1925 and 1926 *émissions annoncées.* All the figures represent nominal values.

It will be noticed that after the initial drop in emissions at the beginning of the war the general movement of the volume of stock issues (in terms of paper francs) was usually upward. It will be further observed, however, that when the depreciation of the franc is taken into account the upward movement was for the

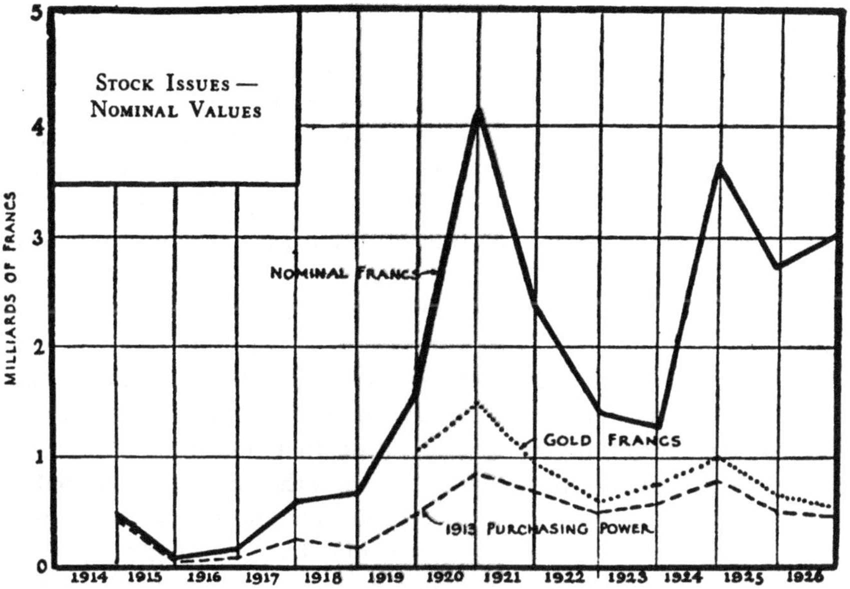

CHART XLVII

years 1915 to 1920 only and that after that time the general trend was nearly horizontal. Important peaks occur in 1920 and in 1924. Moreover, both the peaks and the troughs appeared likewise when the data were reduced to 1913 purchasing power and to gold francs. Also, both peaks and troughs correspond with those in bond emissions, except that the second peak occurred for stocks in 1924 and for bonds in 1923.

It seems that the continued and generally accelerated increase in stock flotations appearing during the war years and lasting until the end of 1920 (whether measured in gold francs, in 1913 purchasing power units, or in paper francs) and accompanied by a general tendency of bond emissions to decline in real value indicates very clearly a turning away of the investing public from bonds to stocks. The change was certainly a natural one. Under conditions of continually and rapidly rising prices, such as those which characterized most of the period under discussion, along with the inevitable and growing loss to all bond holders, there was, in the absence of extraordinary adverse counteracting circumstances, an almost equally inevitable gain accruing to stockholders.[3] Hence even so conservative an investing public as that of France is reputed to be gradually came to realize that conservatism in investments was no longer to be found in the purchase of bonds, but rather in that of well chosen stocks. The especially rapid increase in such emissions in 1919 and 1920 evidences likewise the expanding needs of business in a period of high and profitable activity.

The decline of stock emissions in 1921 and 1922 was likewise one which might have been anticipated in view of the prolonged business depression which settled down upon the country at that time. Also, the rise in such emissions in the years of increasing prosperity, 1923 and 1924, was altogether natural. The comparatively slight decline in 1925, on the other hand, can probably be attributed to two very important influences. Not only was it a year of relative business depression, but the "flight from the franc" had by that time undoubtedly reached important proportions. Indeed it is the slightness rather than the fact of the decline which causes surprise. In 1926 the slight increase in stock emissions can probably be related to the enlarged business activity of the first half of the year, while the increase in bond issues would seem traceable to the return of confidence in the last six months of the year and to the resulting repatriation of capital.

The appearance of the peak for bond issues in 1923, while that for stocks came a year later, is perhaps an indication that in France, as in the United States, bonds are more easy of sale in the early months of prosperity and stocks in the later.

So much for the emissions of securities during the period under consideration. What can be said of the long-term interest rates at which the bonds were issued and the prices at which the stocks were sold?

Unfortunately, dependable information on the first of these subjects is extremely scanty. For the years 1922–1924 the *Association Nationale des Porteurs Français de Valeurs Mobilières* computed a mean monthly rate on emissions. This rate was obtained,

[3] For the extent of the gain see below, Table 79 and Chart LIII.

however, by dividing, for each emission, the nominal rate by the emission price regardless of the maturity date of the bond. Hence, in addition to lacking comparability with the latter part of the series, these rates are capable of considerable misrepresentation. It is true, however, that most of the issues taken into account were of sufficiently long maturities to reduce such errors to small proportions. The movements of these rates monthly[4] since the

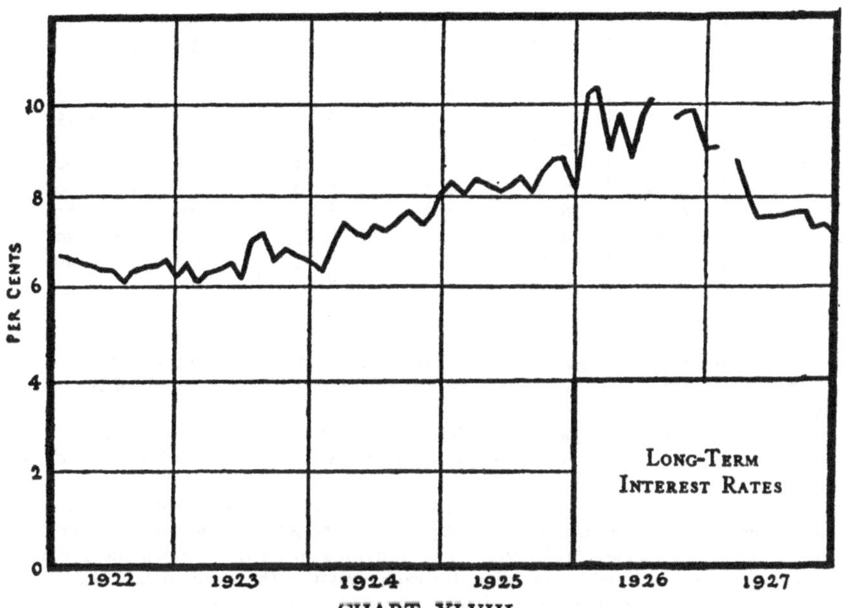

CHART XLVIII

beginning of 1922 are shown in the accompanying table (Table 77) and graph (Chart XLVIII).

The general movements of the curve are very significant. It will be noted that from the low level of the depression year 1922 the rates increased gradually and progressively until the middle of 1926 and then dropped off sharply and continued to decline throughout most of 1927. It will be remembered that the period July 1923 to July 1926 was one of rapidly rising prices, of continued decline of the franc, of frequent threats of a capital levy, and of

[4] For August 1926 there was not a sufficient number of emissions to permit of the computation of a significant rate. The same was true for February 1927.

TABLE 77

LONG-TERM INTEREST RATES [*]

VARIATIONS MENSUELLES DU TAUX MOYEN DES ÉMISSIONS D'OBLIGATIONS ET DES BONS

(Average monthly rates on bonds)

	1922	1923	1924	1925	1926	1927
Jan.	6.66	6.57	6.35	8.30	10.20	9.20
Feb.	6.61	6.11	7.02	8.05	10.30	.... [b]
Mar.	6.57	6.26	7.49	8.45	9.05	8.75
Apr.	6.45	6.32	7.29	8.35	9.80	8.05
May	6.37	6.40	7.23	8.10	8.85 [a]	7.55 [a]
June	6.30	6.15	7.42	8.20	9.80	7.60
July	6.02	7.03	7.38	8.45	10.10	7.60
Aug.	6.32	7.20	7.51	8.10	.... [b]	7.70
Sept.	6.36	6.71	7.77	8.60	9.75	7.75
Oct.	6.41	6.83	7.46	8.85	9.80	7.30 [c]
Nov.	6.59	6.70	7.70	8.85	9.85	7.40
Dec.	6.22	6.61	8.12	8.25	9.15	7.15

[a] The interest on obligations of the *Crédit Foncier* is not taken into account.

[b] The issues during these months were of too small volume to admit of the calculation of an average rate.

[c] The interest on obligations of *Denain-Anzin* is not taken into account.

[*] Source: *Bulletin de la Statistique Générale de la France,* April 1926, and the following issues.

For the period January 1922 to December 1924 the data represent for each month the average rate on bonds as computed by the *Association Nationale des Porteurs Français de Valeurs Mobilières.* The individual rates from which the averages were made were obtained by dividing, for each emission, the nominal rate of interest by the issue price, neither dates of maturity nor conditions of amortization being taken into account.

The rates for the period after December 1924 are those prepared by the *Statistique Générale de la France* and represent likewise average rates for each month. In these computations, unlike in the earlier ones, account was taken of maturity dates, and actual *yields* were computed on the basis of the issue price and the nominal rates of interest. Allowance was also made for all taxes except that of transmission. For a detailed description of the series the reader is referred to the *Bulletin de la Statistique Générale de la France* (April 1926).

gradually waning confidence in the Government and in its financial policies. Impelled by all these adverse influences, the rates rose perhaps less than might have been expected. The second half of 1926, on the other hand, was a period of rapid recovery of the franc, of abrupt decline in prices, and of growing confidence

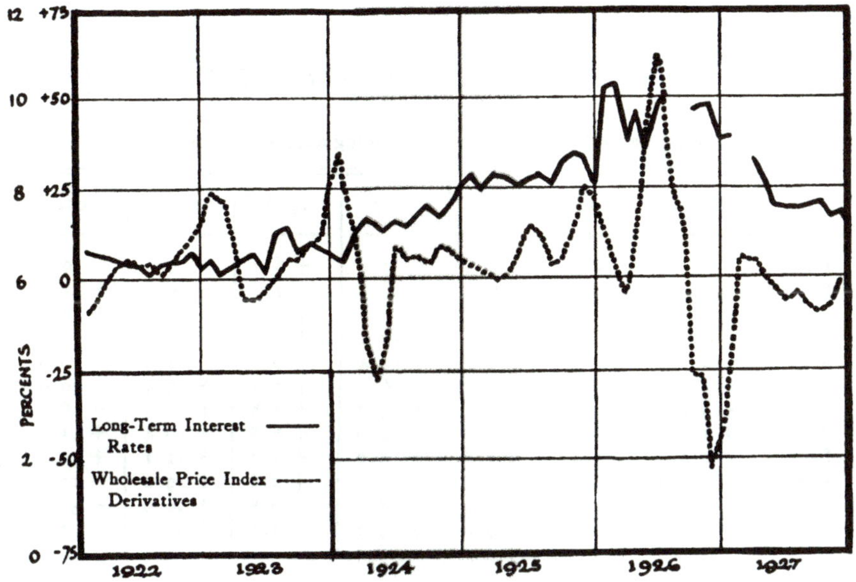

CHART XLIX

LONG-TERM INTEREST RATES AND DERIVATIVES OF WHOLESALE PRICE INDEX

in the Government and in its actions. The sharp fall in the rates during this period has been noted.

To obtain an estimate of how much the *rapidity* in the rise of prices was influencing long-term interest rates, a comparison was next made of the above series with that of the first derivative of prices[5] (Chart XLIX). By reference to the chart a very striking likeness will be observed not only in the minor fluctuations of the series but, what is more significant, also in the directions of the long-time movements themselves. It is evident that during this period at any rate there was a very close connection indeed between the two phenomena. Moreover, on careful examination it will be found that there was a distinct lag of the movements of interest rates behind those of the derivative of prices, indicating probable causal relationships. It is further evident that this lag diminished as the price rise became more rapid. In the drastic

[5] First derivatives of a three-months moving average of the index numbers of wholesale prices of the *Statistique Générale de la France* were used in the comparison.

TABLE 78

WHOLESALE PRICE INDEX OF THE *STATISTIQUE GÉNÉRALE DE LA FRANCE*

(First derivatives, three-month moving average centered)

	1914	1915	1916	1917	1918	1919	1920
Jan.	.....	+ 5.9	+ 6.3	+ 9.4	+ 8.7	− 5.8	+ 39.0
Feb.	.....	+ 6.3	+ 7.6	+ 8.5	+ 7.6	− 5.7	+ 43.9
Mar.	− 0.1	+ 4.5	+ 6.1	+ 10.8	+ 6.9	− 5.1	+ 33.6
Apr.	− 0.1	+ 3.6	+ 4.2	+ 10.1	+ 5.4	− 5.1	+ 9.4
May	− 0.1	+ 2.6	+ 0.8	+ 12.4	+ 0.5	− 2.3	− 20.6
June	− 0.3	+ 2.3	− 2.1	+ 6.7	+ 1.3	+ 5.5	− 30.6
July	+ 0.9	+ 1.8	− 1.5	+ 4.7	+ 4.8	+ 7.5	− 16.3
Aug.	+ 1.2	+ 2.4	+ 0.1	+ 4.6	+ 8.8	+ 10.4	+ 11.0
Sept.	+ 2.0	+ 3.8	+ 2.8	+ 5.2	+ 7.5	+ 11.1	+ 2.0
Oct.	+ 1.5	+ 6.1	+ 3.8	+ 7.7	+ 2.6	+ 19.2	− 13.5
Nov.	+ 2.5	+ 6.2	+ 4.9	+ 8.1	− 0.8	+ 20.9	− 30.3
Dec.	+ 5.2	+ 7.1	+ 7.6	+ 9.7	− 4.1	+ 35.0	− 31.7

	1921	1922	1923	1924	1925	1926	1927
Jan.	− 27.8	− 8.5	+ 23.2	+ 33.6	+ 3.8	+ 10.0	− 17.4
Feb.	− 25.0	− 6.1	+ 20.7	+ 13.6	+ 2.1	− 0.2	+ 5.0
Mar.	− 19.8	0.0	+ 9.3	− 14.7	− 0.5	− 5.5	+ 4.8
Apr.	− 16.0	+ 3.5	− 5.1	− 28.4	+ 1.6	+ 17.4	− 1.1
May	− 11.6	+ 5.9	− 5.1	− 11.3	+ 9.7	+ 35.5	− 6.3
June	− 5.7	+ 3.8	− 2.7	+ 10.3	+ 14.7	+ 62.0	− 5.5
July	+ 0.6	+ 4.8	+ 2.2	+ 6.0	+ 12.5	+ 27.2	− 3.5
Aug.	+ 6.3	+ 1.4	+ 5.0	+ 6.8	+ 4.4	+ 16.2	− 7.4
Sept.	+ 0.4	+ 4.1	+ 4.6	+ 5.4	+ 5.2	− 28.2	− 10.8
Oct.	+ 0.2	+ 7.0	+ 9.9	+ 9.0	+ 16.1	− 28.6	− 7.8
Nov.	− 6.1	+ 10.9	+ 11.7	+ 7.2	+ 25.6	− 53.5	+ 1.3
Dec.	− 5.8	+ 16.5	+ 24.5	+ 5.8	+ 20.4	− 43.2	......

decline in the rates which began immediately after the middle of 1926 and which continued throughout most of 1927, however, the lag apparently lengthened materially.

Some similarity is likewise discovered between the movements of long-term interest rates and those of the first derivatives of dollar exchange rates[6] (Chart L), though it is much less marked

[6] First derivatives of a six-month moving average of end-of-month averages of dollar exchange rates (Table 8) were used in the comparison.

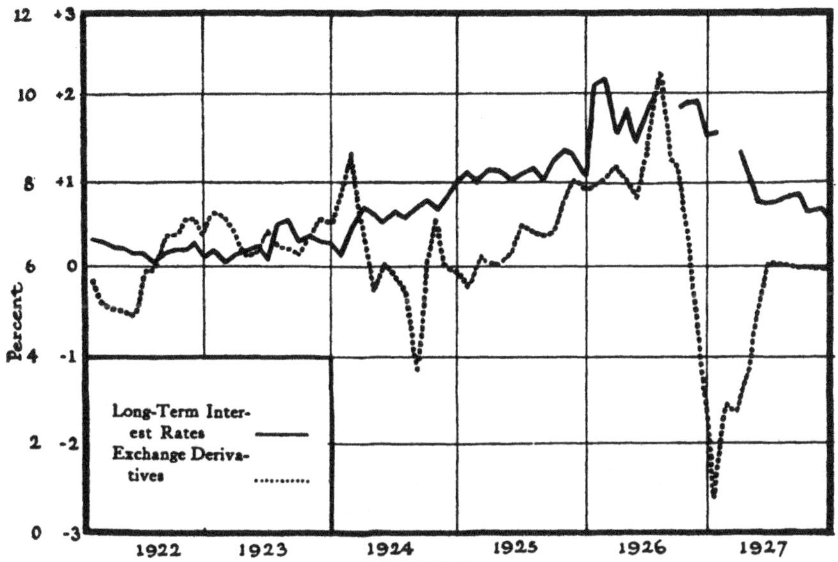

CHART L

LONG-TERM INTEREST RATES AND DERIVATIVES OF EXCHANGE RATES

than that between the same rates and the first derivatives of wholesale prices. The directions of the long-term movements, which are the really significant ones, were nevertheless very similar.

It can be concluded, therefore, that the changes in interest rates during the period under consideration are probably largely to be attributed to the rapid rises in prices and in exchange rates. Such rapid rises, continued over a considerable period, gradually stimulated a general anticipation of a further rise in prices and of a further fall in the exchange value of the franc — two phenomena which by that time naturally and rightly were closely associated in the minds of most investors. And, with such anticipations on the part of investors, bonds inevitably lost their popularity and interest rates moved upward accordingly. With the rapid and continued falls in prices and in dollar exchange rates which followed the crisis of July 1926, reverse expectations led equally naturally to increased popularity of bonds and to correspondingly falling yields.

That the rapid and long-continued rise in interest rates from 1922 until the middle of 1926 reflects the changed attitude of the French investing public toward bonds and other fixed interest-bearing investments can hardly be questioned. It would seem likewise true, however, that the rising interest rates in turn probably caused many of the more conservative firms to resort in their financing to stock rather than to bond issues. Hence the general shift from bonds to stocks during the period was probably accounted for by both influences. With the return of lower rates in the latter half of 1926 and in 1927 the return to popularity of bonds was, for reverse reasons, naturally to be expected.

The general tendency, too, of total emissions — stocks and bonds — to decline sharply but irregularly after 1920 and until the middle of 1926 indicates clearly the inclination during that period for industries as well as for the Government to finance with short-term rather than with long-term credit. This inclination probably accounts for much of the shift from investment to commercial banking on the part of the large *banques d'affaires*.

It remains to discuss the movements of the prices of stocks. Fortunately a very carefully constructed index of such prices has been compiled by the *Statistique Générale de la France*.[7] Representing now 288 different stocks separated into twenty distinct groups, it is probably as comprehensive an index of security prices as is at present published. While constructed on a 1913 base, a special device was used in making the computations to eliminate inevitable distortions which would otherwise (because of the remoteness of the base year) appear in some of the *group indices*. To accomplish this the indices of separate stocks for January 1926, for example, were first compiled on a 1925 base. The index of each *group* was then made on the 1925 base by taking a simple arithmetic average of the indices of the component individual stock prices. The *group* index was then transferred to the 1913 base, and for the index as a whole the result was the same as though the separate indices had been computed on that base at the outset.

The movements of the general index for the period 1919 to 1927 are pictured in Chart LI. For the years prior to 1919 no seriously compiled index seems to be available.

A study of the long-term movements of the series indicates clearly the pronounced upward trend of stock prices during the en-

[7] For the full description of the index see Table 79.

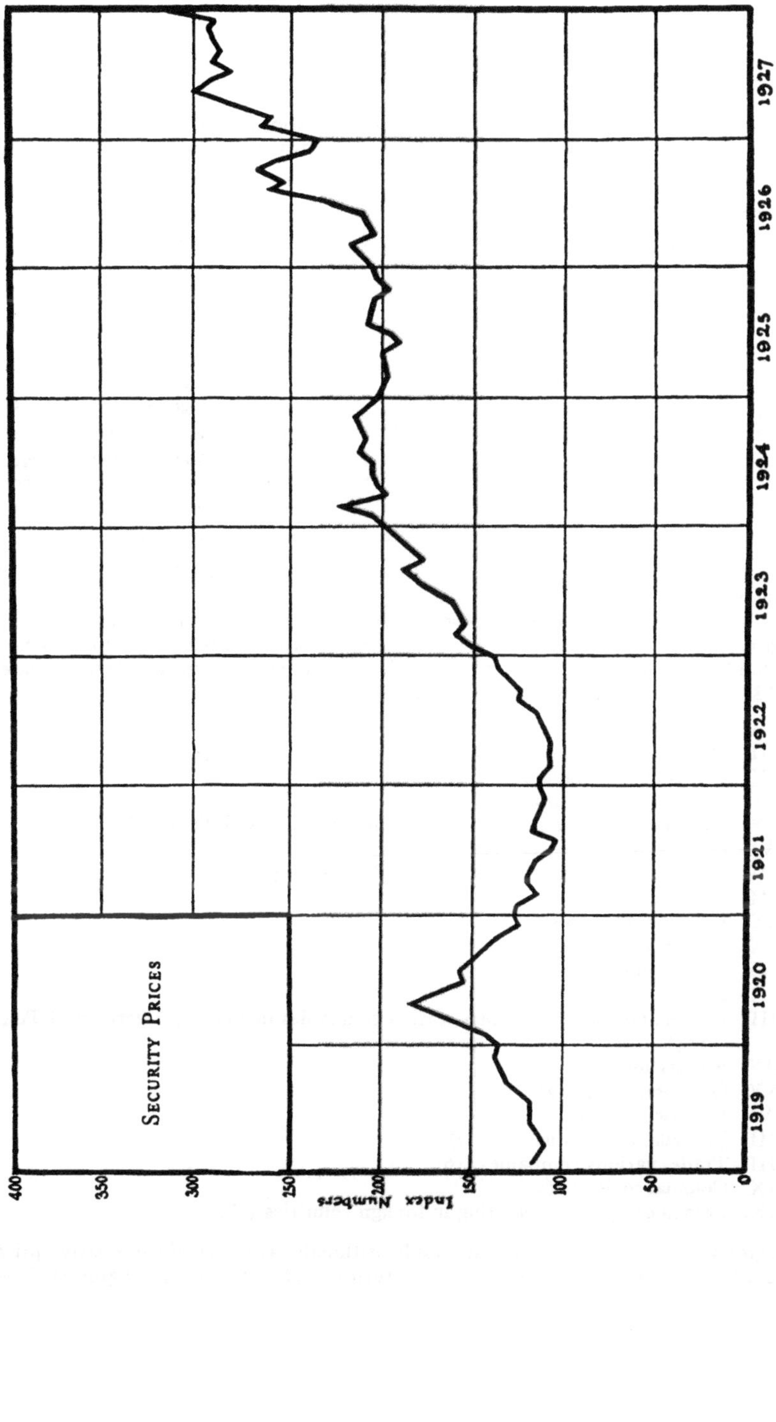
Security Prices
Index Numbers
400
350
300
250
200
150
100
50
0
1919
1920
1921
1922
1923
1924
1925
1926
1927

CHART LI

TABLE 79

SECURITY PRICE INDEX OF THE *STATISTIQUE GÉNÉRALE DE LA FRANCE—COURS DES VALEURS FRANÇAISES À REVENU VARIABLE* *

(Index numbers based on end-of-month quotations. Base 100 in 1913)

	1919	1920	1921	1922	1923	1924	1925	1926	1927
Jan.	117	141	124	112	152	208	200	211	265
Feb.	114	153	114	108	158	222	197	216	262
Mar.	111	170	119	108	154	199	199	205	280
Apr.	114	181	119	106	158	202	200	207	301
May	119	170	113	110	160	204	190	211	293
June	119	154	107	111	170	204	194	229	281
July	119	156	104	115	180	212	208	260	291
Aug.	123	152	114	125	186	210	208	254	288
Sept.	131	145	114	124	177	211	204	269	292
Oct.	136	136	111	131	182	216	198	259	294
Nov.	138	123	110	137	192	208	202	239	290
Dec.	137	126	112	139	198	202	206	232	315

* Source: *Bulletin de la Statistique Générale de la France*, July 1927 and the following issues.

Until 1927 the index was composed of 194 prices of different stocks divided into 25 groups. Since the beginning of 1927, however, the number of groups has been reduced to 20, while the total number of prices taken into account has been increased to 288. The present 20 groups are the following:

I. Banks (13 securities).
II. Insurance companies (15).
III. Central coal companies (7).
IV. Northern coal companies (11).
V. Various extractive industries in France, Algeria, and Tunis (9).
VI. Forge and steel works (13).
VII. Metal, mechanical, and electrical industries (24).
VIII. Shipbuilding (7).
IX. Building materials (11).
X. Chemical products (16).
XI. Textile industries (13).
XII. Railways (6).
XIII. Various railway and transportation companies in France, Algeria, and Tunis (14).
XIV. Navigation (9).
XV. Gas companies (12).
XVI. Electricity (23).
XVII. Miscellaneous industries (22).
XVIII. Trade, various companies (16).
XIX. Colonial societies (25).
XX. French companies operating in foreign countries (18).

The group indices are in every case simple arithmetic averages of the relative prices included in each, and the general index is in turn a similar average of the group indices.

tire period and especially after early 1922. It is interesting to note, too, that the same upward trend persisted throughout the depression period of late 1926 and 1927. The minor movements of the series show a highly cyclical character. In the prosperity period of late 1919 and early 1920 stock prices rose rapidly. Then as depression developed they fell almost equally rapidly until the middle of 1921, remained for a year substantially at the low level reached, and then rose rapidly again a little in advance of the returning prosperity of 1922–1924. They turned distinctly downward again in late 1924 with the development of depression, continued low in 1925 while business activity was also reduced, but failed to recover with the nervous activity and rapidly rising prices which characterized the early months of 1926. They increased very rapidly, however, as the crisis approached, remained high until October, and then broke sharply at the end of the year, only to rise even more sharply and more considerably during the first four months of 1927. A slight drop ensued, but the high level was substantially maintained throughout the rest of the year. In general it can be said, therefore, that until 1926 the movements of security prices, at least in direction, corresponded with the varying business conditions of the period.

On comparing the movements of stock prices with those of wholesale prices in general (Chart LII) it will be seen that the two series show an astonishing likeness. With close examination it will be observed, too, that the similarity does not hold solely for the minor movements, but that the long-time trends are also much alike. In order to obtain a clear idea of the relative movements of the two series, therefore, stock prices were reduced to wholesale prices as a base. Since the indices of both series are already relatives on

---

Formerly on a 1901–1910 base, the present index has been transferred to a 1913 base. In order, however, to make the group indices as significant as possible, an ingenious device has been used to eliminate the distortions arising from the remoteness of the base year. The indices of the separate stocks for January 1926, for example, were first compiled on a 1925 base. The index of each group was then made on a 1925 base by taking the simple arithmetic averages of the component indices. The group index was then transferred as a whole to a 1913 base. For the general index the result is the same as though all of its component prices had been computed on a 1913 base at the outset. For a complete description of the index the reader is referred to the *Bulletin de la Statistique Générale de la France* (July-September 1927).

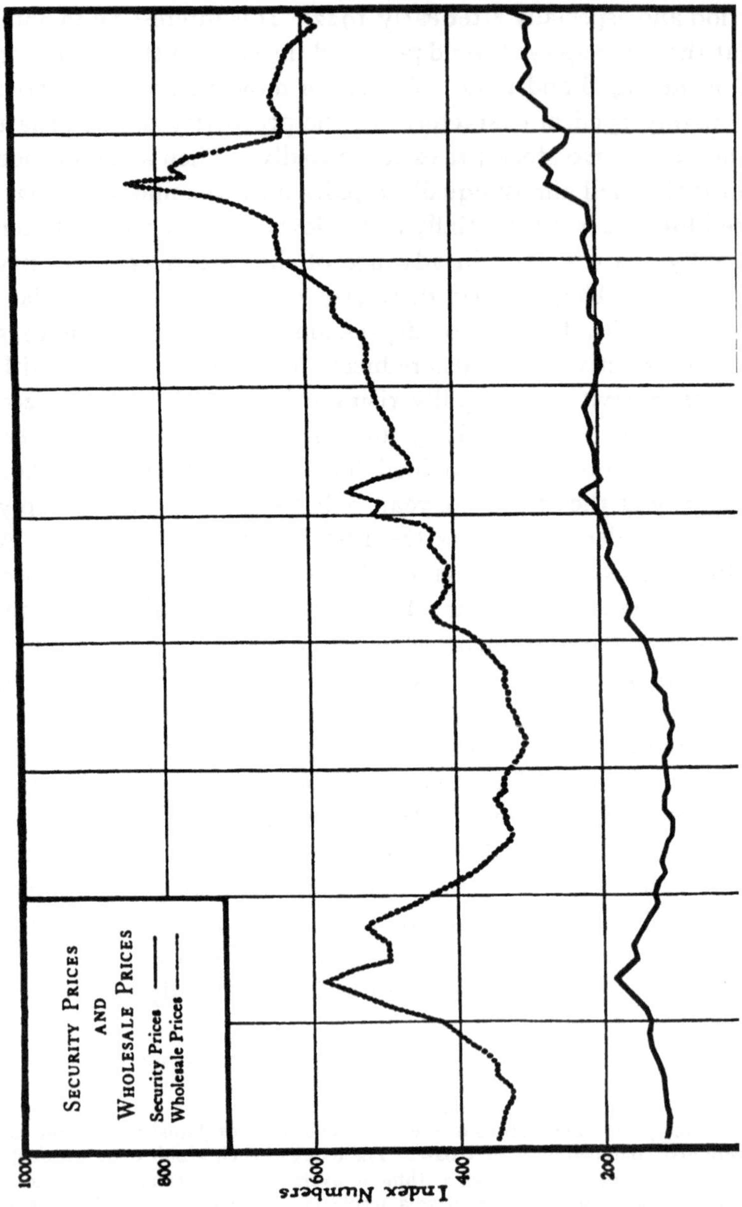
Security Prices
and
Wholesale Prices
Security Prices
Wholesale Prices
1000
800
600
400
200
Index Numbers

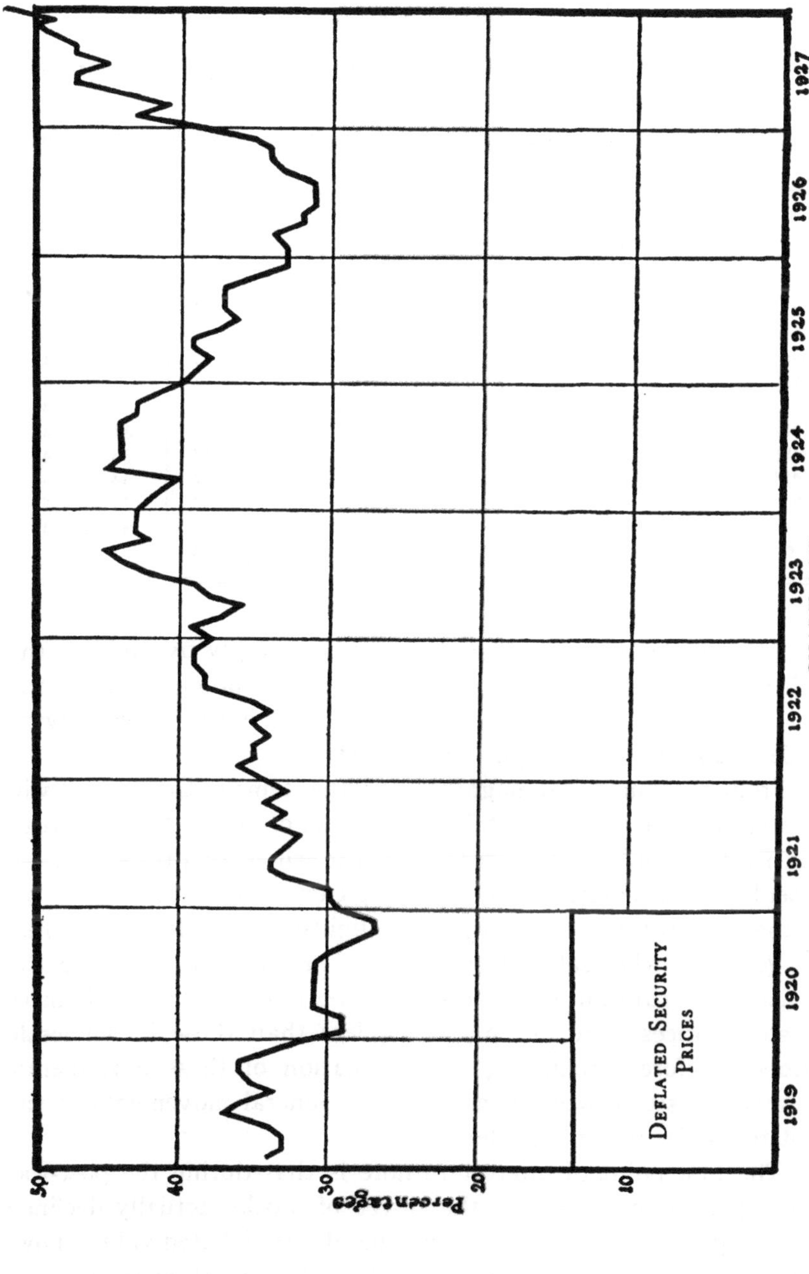
Deflated Security Prices
Percentages
50
40
30
20
10
1919
1920
1921
1922
1923
1924
1925
1926
1927

CHART LIII

TABLE 80

DEFLATED SECURITY PRICE INDEX OF THE *STATISTIQUE GÉNÉRALE DE LA FRANCE*

(Index numbers of security prices divided by the indices of wholesale prices for corresponding months)

	1919	1920	1921	1922	1923	1924	1925	1926	1927
Jan.	.34	.29	.30	.36	.39	.42	.39	.33	.43
Feb.	.33	.29	.30	.35	.37	.41	.38	.34	.41
Mar.	.33	.31	.33	.35	.36	.40	.39	.32	.44
Apr.	.34	.31	.34	.34	.38	.45	.39	.32	.47
May	.37	.31	.34	.35	.39	.44	.37	.31	.47
June	.36	.31	.33	.34	.42	.44	.36	.31	.45
July	.34	.31	.32	.35	.44	.44	.37	.31	.47
Aug.	.35	.30	.34	.38	.45	.44	.37	.33	.47
Sept.	.36	.28	.33	.38	.42	.43	.37	.34	.49
Oct.	.36	.27	.34	.39	.43	.43	.35	.34	.50
Nov.	.34	.27	.33	.39	.43	.41	.33	.35	.49
Dec.	.32	.29	.34	.38	.43	.40	.33	.37	.52

1913 bases, the desired result was attained simply by dividing the indices of the stock prices' series by corresponding items of the other series. The resulting quotients are given in the accompanying table (Table 80) and graph (Chart LIII).

From the numerical magnitudes of the items of the series it will be seen at once that the total rise in prices of stocks between 1913 and 1927 was only half as great as that in wholesale prices. On the other hand, as is indicated by the rising trend of the series from 1919 to 1927, the price rise after 1918 was slightly greater for stocks than for goods at wholesale. It is evident, therefore, that during the period 1913–1918 for which no stock index is available the advances in stock prices were in total much less than those in wholesale prices. Before attempting an explanation of these movements, however, a study will be made of the general movements of the deflated series under consideration.

The first point of interest to note is that during the post-war boom period of 1919–1920 the prices of stocks actually declined with respect to those of goods in general. In deflated values, however, they began increasing again before the end of 1920 and continued to rise throughout the depression years of 1921 and 1922 and until the fall of 1923, a year after the new period of general business activity had begun. Then, beginning in April 1924, they declined steadily with respect to prices in general until the crisis month of July 1926. From that time until the end of 1927 they rose first rapidly and then more slowly relatively to prices although not always absolutely.

What can be divined from all of these extremely various movements? The failure of stock prices to rise as much as others in late 1919 and early 1920 is difficult to explain. Perhaps the fact of their failure to do so during the war years was a deterring factor. That they should fall farther and more rapidly as soon as depression set in would tend to confirm such a guess, though, in the United States at least, stock prices show a tendency to move more rapidly and more drastically than almost any other kinds of prices. Consequently, perhaps little confidence is to be placed in the opinion hazarded. Their early and persistent rise with respect to other prices after late 1920, however, would certainly seem to indicate the growing popularity with the French investing and speculating public of stocks as opposed to bonds — a popularity which was clearly evident from the statistics of security emissions and interest rates discussed earlier in this chapter. It is evident that they were in great demand until the fall of 1923 and that this demand, while not increasing thereafter, was not materially diminished until the middle of 1924. For the latter portion of that year, as for all of 1925 and the first half of 1926, it is clear that, in spite of the continued preference for stocks over bonds, the general fear of all French investments was exerting an important influence on the further course of their prices.

With the return of confidence after July 1926 came not only the rapid repatriation of French capital, but likewise a considerable inflow of foreign funds destined for investment in French securities. Hence the pronounced rise of stock prices with respect to prices in general after that time was only to be expected.

A clear estimate of the movements of savings in France during the period under consideration is extremely difficult to obtain.

While French savings banks publish monthly data of deposits and withdrawals and while annual statistics of insurance premiums are available within two years after they are paid, there are reasons for discrediting both of these series as accurate indicators of the accumulation and the dissipation of savings. The savings banks of both categories (*la Caisse Nationale* and *les caisses d'épargne ordinaires*) have a set maximum of 12,000 francs for the account of any one individual and hence can give indication of the saving dispositions of small savers only. Moreover, since deposits can be withdrawn from these banks on any day without previous notice, they have come to be used extensively for the deposit of business funds by small tradespeople, who — especially in the periods of low interest rates recently prevailing — have sought to profit by the relatively high return there received. Insurance premiums, on the other hand, were subjected to a moratorium from August 1, 1914 to August 1, 1919 and move otherwise too regularly to give much indication of the changing effects of various economic situations on the savings habits of the people.

So diverse and so reputedly undependable are the reports of business firms that the laborious task of attempting to draw from their statements of surplus and reserves any well-defined idea of the movements of their savings — important as are those from a like source in the United States — was abandoned as impracticable.

Finally, it should be pointed out that under progressively increasing inflation the mere reduction of data to purchasing power units (especially when an index of *wholesale* prices has to be used for the conversion), or to gold francs, distorts almost as frequently as it corrects the indicated changes in savings habits. Nevertheless, the savings series will be studied in an attempt to discover any general tendencies which may thereby be revealed.

In the accompanying chart (Chart LIV) are represented the monthly excesses of deposits or of withdrawals in terms of paper francs for each group of savings institutions[8] separately.

In spite of the highly seasonal character of both the series, their general movements are easily discernible. In the first three years,

[8] For descriptions of the two types of savings institutions, the reader is referred to Chap. III, pp. 29–31.

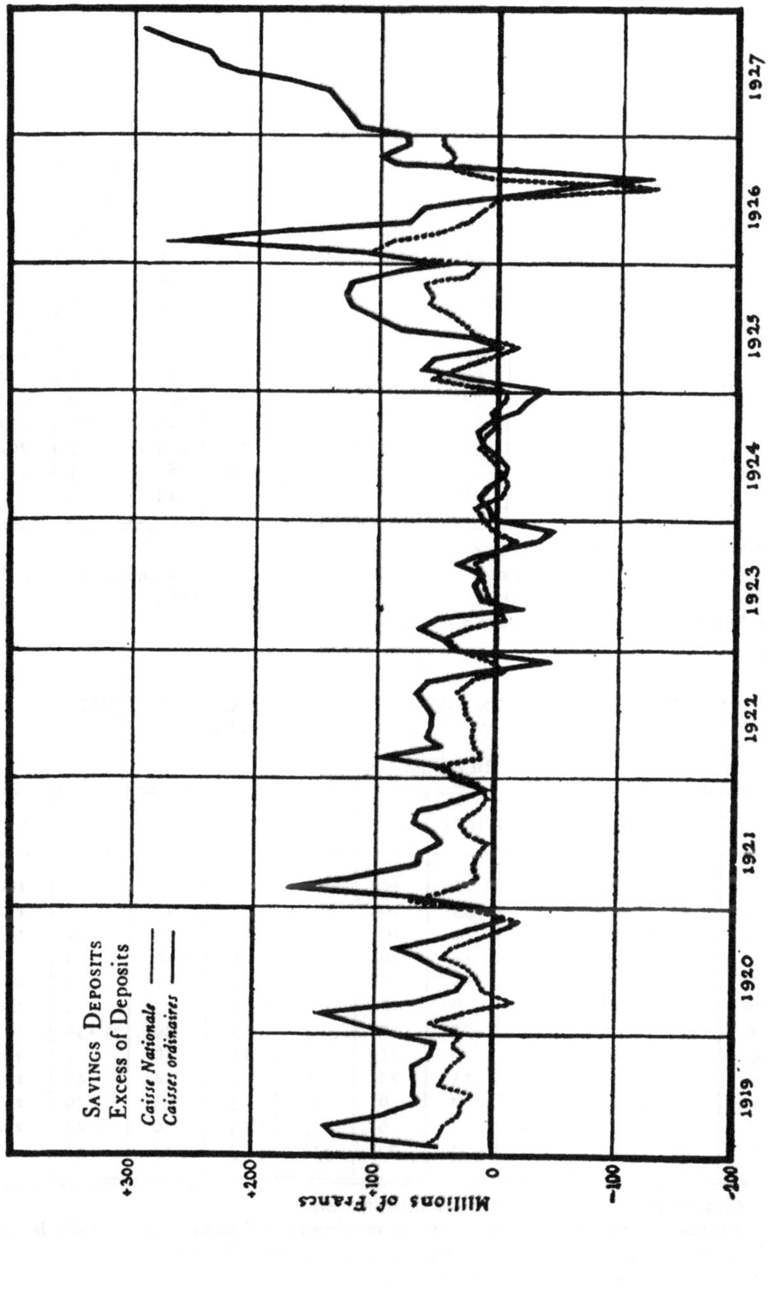
Savings Deposits
Excess of Deposits
Caisse Nationale
Caisses ordinaires
1919
1920
1921
1922
1923
1924
1925
1926
1927
+300
+200
+100
0
-100
-200
Millions of Francs

CHART LIV

TABLE 81

EXCESS OF DEPOSITS OVER WITHDRAWALS* AT THE *CAISSES D'ÉPARGNE ORDINAIRES*†

(In millions of francs)

	1918	1919	1920	1921	1922	1923	1924	1925	1926	1927
Jan.	..	43	44	70	40	44	4	21	114	119
Feb.	..	134	150	170	100	64	16	68	279	358
Mar.	..	142	65	111	48	44	8	55	170	197
Apr.	..	96	29	66	58	− 23	− 6	− 2	73	137
May	..	62	26	63	55	14	− 7	25	61	166
June	..	68	45	45	53	22	0	81	55	214
July	..	67	68	52	62	12	15	104	− 54	232
Aug.	..	67	86	72	66	35	20	125	− 129	235
Sept.	..	68	46	68	58	19	3	128	84	273
Oct.	..	52	17	33	17	− 33	− 16	125	99	292
Nov.	..	47	− 7[a]	1	− 43	− 49	− 24	82	74	...
Dec.	27	80	12	38	33	3	− 39	45	75	...

[a] Minus signs indicate excesses of withdrawals.

* Funds accumulated in excess of the maximum and used automatically for the purchase of government obligations are considered as withdrawals.

† Source: *Journal des Caisses d'Épargne.*

TABLE 82

EXCESS OF DEPOSITS OVER WITHDRAWALS* AT THE *CAISSE NATIONALE D'ÉPARGNE*†

(In millions of francs)

	1918	1919	1920	1921	1922	1923	1924	1925	1926	1927
Jan.	..	59	53	71	49	42	19	53	110	160
Feb.	..	45	22	33	10	23	− 1	33	89	124
Mar.	..	40	−19[a]	14	16	− 8	− 8	16	50	107
Apr.	..	29	10	15	20	− 1	− 5	− 18	23	81
May	..	26	14	14	19	8	0	17	11	121
June	..	18	21	6	28	9	7	25	3	149
July	..	45	44	24	27	13	15	39	− 134	157
Aug.	..	40	33	29	31	19	11	56	7	200
Sept.	..	31	15	15	22	6	2	54	46	197
Oct.	..	23	− 3	6	− 6	− 18	3	63	36	237
Nov.	..	33	− 22	8	9	5	− 5	30	43	268
Dec.	29	26	29	23	32	15	− 5	17	45	...

[a] Minus signs indicate excesses of withdrawals.

* Funds accumulated in excess of the maximum and used automatically for the purchase of government obligations are considered as withdrawals.

† Source: *Journal des Caisses d'Épargne.*

1919, 1920, and 1921, the excesses of deposits were high and of similar proportions, though in 1920 a slight sag is to be noted. After 1921 came a steady decline in such excesses until the end of 1924, in which year reimbursements exceeded deposits. Then, in the depression year of 1925 and at the beginning of the activity period of the first half of 1926, the excesses of deposits increased rapidly. In July 1926 for the national savings institutions and in August for the private ones there was a great excess of withdrawals following a progressive decline in excesses of deposits during the five preceding months. Thereafter an excess of deposits reappeared and continued on a rapidly increasing scale.

These movements are, to say the least, interesting. On the assumption that they indicate roughly the movements of savings of the poorer classes, it would seem that during the period of prosperity and of rapidly rising prices in 1920 these people actually saved less than in the marked depression periods of early 1919 and of 1921. Again, with the return of business prosperity and of rising prices in 1922, their monthly savings were reduced; and the more pronounced the business activity and the price rise became, the greater was the reduction. At the height of business activity in 1924 withdrawals considerably exceeded deposits. In 1925, however, as business activity waned, while prices continued to move even more rapidly upward and while, besides, there is reason to believe that the export of capital was taking place at an increasing rate, monthly deposits of cash in the savings banks increased notably. Deposits continued much in excess of withdrawals throughout most of 1926 and all of 1927. Only in the crisis months of July and August 1926 were withdrawals greater than deposits.

One conclusion seems entirely clear: Certainly the depositors in the savings banks were not appreciably affected by the general loss of confidence in the policies of the Government, or, at least, not to the extent of joining the "flight from the franc" until the very crisis months themselves. It would also seem that the savings of small gentry, even in terms of paper francs, were much more affected by changes in business activity than by those even in the level of prices itself. And strange as it may seem to those unfamiliar with the thrifty habits of the French people, the more active business became, the less was the inclination to save, and the deeper the business depression, the larger were the amounts laid aside for a rainier day.

The extremely large excesses of deposits in 1927 doubtless represent, for the early months, the redeposit of funds withdrawn a few months previously. For the later months, however, another explanation appears. Interest rates on deposits at most of the banks during that period, as has been mentioned frequently in the pages which have gone before, were extremely low. At the same time the rates on deposits at the savings banks continued relatively much higher. Moreover, for small tradespeople making and receiving all payments in cash, the disadvantages of carrying accounts with the savings institutions rather than with the commercial banks were very slight indeed. No notice is required for withdrawals and, while perhaps a slightly greater amount of time is spent in waiting in line before windows while the industrious clerks register a sufficient number of times the details of the withdrawals, the slight inconvenience thus occasioned is much more than counterbalanced by the attractiveness[9] of the return. Hence, there is little doubt that in 1927 a considerable item of business deposits was included in the total.

In the accompanying graph (Chart LV) the total monthly excesses of deposits or of withdrawals for the two groups of savings institutions are represented in terms of paper and of gold francs. These new series reveal little that has not already been drawn from the earlier ones. A notable reduction in the magnitudes of deposits as well as of withdrawals becomes evident, however. While part of this reduction can doubtless be traced to the failure to increase the maximum limits[10] set for the individual accounts sufficiently to counterbalance the depreciation of the franc, it is clear that much of it must be attributed to other influences.

[9] During 1927 the rate was 3.75 per cent at the national institutions and 4–4.25 per cent at the private ones, while those at the commercial banks were rarely above $1^1/_2$ per cent.

[10] The maximum limits for the account of any one individual were as follows:

Prior to October 18, 1919	3000 francs
October 18, 1919 to April 25, 1925	5000 francs
April 25, 1925 to August 20, 1926	7500 francs
After August 20, 1926	12000 francs

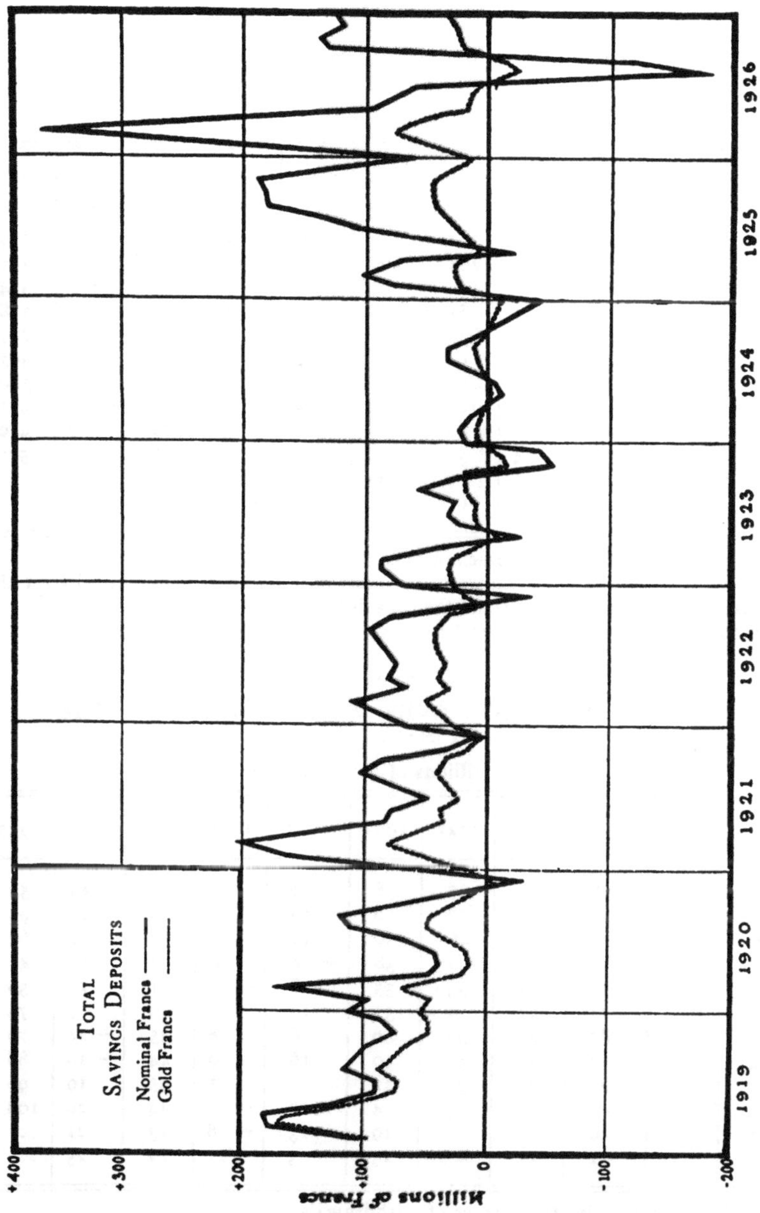
Total
Savings Deposits
Nominal Francs
Gold Francs
1919
1920
1921
1922
1923
1924
1925
1926
+400
+300
+200
+100
0
-100
-200
Millions of Francs

CHART LV

TABLE 83

EXCESS OF DEPOSITS OVER WITHDRAWALS* AT THE FRENCH SAVINGS BANKS†

(In millions of francs)

	1918	1919	1920	1921	1922	1923	1924	1925	1926	1927
Jan.	..	102	97	141	89	86	23	75	224	279
Feb.	..	179	171	204	109	86	15	101	368	482
Mar.	..	182	46	125	64	36	0	71	220	304
Apr.	..	126	39	81	78	− 24	− 11	− 21	96	218
May	..	88	40	78	74	23	− 7	41	71	287
June	..	86	65	50	81	31	7	105	59	363
July	..	112	112	76	88	25	30	144	− 187	389
Aug.	..	107	119	101	97	54	30	181	− 121	435
Sept.	..	99	61	82	80	24	5	182	130	470
Oct.	..	75	14	39	10	− 51	− 13	188	135	529
Nov.	..	81	− 30[a]	7	− 34	− 44	− 29	113	117	...
Dec.	56	106	41	61	65	19	− 45	62	120	...

[a] Minus signs indicate excesses of withdrawals.

* Funds accumulated in excess of the maximum and used automatically for the purchase of government obligations are considered as withdrawals.

† Source: *Journal des Caisses d'Épargne.*

TABLE 84

EXCESS OF DEPOSITS OVER WITHDRAWALS* AT THE FRENCH SAVINGS BANKS

(In millions of gold francs) †

	1918	1919	1920	1921	1922	1923	1924	1925	1926	1927
Jan.	..	98	43	47	38	30	6	21	44	57
Feb.	..	173	63	77	50	28	4	28	71	98
Mar.	..	165	17	46	30	12	0	19	41	62
Apr.	..	110	13	31	38	− 8	− 4	4	17	44
May	..	73	14	34	35	8	− 2	11	12	58
June	..	71	27	21	37	10	2	26	9	74
July	..	85	47	31	40	8	8	35	− 24	79
Aug.	..	72	45	41	40	16	9	44	− 18	88
Sept.	..	62	22	31	32	7	1	45	19	96
Oct.	..	46	5	15	4	− 16	− 4	44	20	108
Nov.	..	46	−9[a]	3	19	− 13	− 8	23	21	...
Dec.	53	51	13	25	25	5	− 13	12	25	...

[a] Minus signs indicate excesses of withdrawals.

* Funds accumulated in excess of the maximum and used automatically for the purchase of government obligations are considered as withdrawals.

† Nominal francs divided by the index of dollar exchange for each month.

A superficial study of the amounts of premium payments on old-age and life insurance policies seemed to indicate so little with regard to the accumulation and dissipation of savings that the investigation was not pursued. A similar cursory examination of the time deposits of the four big commercial banks led likewise to the abandonment of a further study.

CHAPTER XI

THEORETICAL ANALYSIS

FISHER EQUATION OF EXCHANGE

WITH the use of the *equation of exchange* as developed by Irving Fisher the analysis of the data can be carried somewhat further. For its accomplishment, however, a brief description of this useful piece of machinery and its reduction to forms suitable for attacking the problems at hand are essential.

This equation, which is usually written in the form:

$$MV + M'V' = PT,$$

is made up of a very great number of little equations of values, each arising from the fact that in every purchase and sale transaction the money, or money substitute, used in making payment is equal in value[1] to the price of the goods multiplied by the quantity sold. Thus, if one buys two pounds of sugar at 6 cents a pound, paying for it in cash, there obviously arises the little equation of values:

$$12 \text{ cents} = 6 \text{ cents} \times 2 \text{ pounds of sugar}.$$

Likewise for every other purchase and sale transaction there arises a similar little equation of values. Payment, however, is not always made in cash but very frequently by check or draft — or, in France, by *virements*[2] — on an account in a bank or other financial institution. In our present-day economic society, payments made in any other way than by cash or by check or draft may be disregarded as being usually negligible in amount.

[1] By definition, the value of anything is its price per unit multiplied by the number of units which it contains.

[2] *Virements* is the technical term used for transfers made by means of the *giro* system in general use in France. See the description of the system (Chap. III, p. 21).

For the derivation of the equation of exchange the data must necessarily be limited to a given period, say the year 1927, and to a given locality, as, for example, to the United States of America. To accomplish this task there must be taken into account, at least mentally, every purchase and sale transaction that took place in the locality and during the period considered. Each, as has been seen above, will give rise to a little equation of values, which will be written in one of two ways according as payment is made (1) *in cash*, or (2) by check or draft upon a bank deposit.

With the use of the example given above, in which was assumed the purchase of two pounds of sugar at 6 cents a pound, *payment being made in cash*, the equation of values:

$$12 \text{ cents} = 6 \text{ cents} \times 2 \text{ pounds of sugar}$$

will be written in the general form:

$$m = pq,$$

in which m is the 12 cents *paid in cash*, p the price per pound of the sugar sold, and q the number of pounds sold. Suppose, on the other hand, that an exporter of grain buys 1000 bushels of wheat at $1.50 a bushel, *paying for them with a check on his bank account* for $1500. In this case the little equation of values:

$$\$1500 = \$1.50 \times 1000 \text{ bushels of wheat}$$

should be written in the general form:

$$m' = pq,$$

in which m' is employed instead of m to indicate that payment was made by check or draft upon a bank account instead of by cash.

With the use of the notation just described, the little equations of values may be written for every purchase and sale transaction that took place in the United States in 1927. Suppose that there were n transactions effected with cash and k with check or draft upon some bank account. Then the equation may be indicated as follows:

$$
\begin{array}{lcl}
m_1 & = & p_1q_1 \\
m_2 & = & p_2q_2 \\
\vdots & & \vdots \\
m_n & = & p_nq_n \\
\quad m_1' & = & p_{n+1}q_{n+1} \\
\quad m_2' & = & p_{n+2}q_{n+2} \\
\quad \vdots & & \vdots \\
\quad m_k' & = & p_{n+k}q_{n+k} \\
\hline
E + E' & = & \sum_{x=1}^{x=n+k} p_xq_x
\end{array}
$$

Although the little equations thus indicated, equaling in number the purchase and sale transactions which took place in the United States in the year 1927, probably number many milliards or even trillions, yet their total is finite. Hence, when added, their sums are likewise equal.

If the sum of the m's be written as E and the sum of the m''s as E', it is seen immediately that E represents the sum total of the *expenditures in cash* for all goods and services sold in the United States in the year 1927, while E' is the sum total of *expenditures in bank deposits*. And it is further seen (it is, in fact, self-evident) that these two quantities together aggregate the sum total of the $n + k$

products of the form pq. In this elemental form, however, the equation of exchange is of little use. It can be put into more serviceable shape by factoring each of the above quantities into two other more usable and more significant magnitudes.

For one of the factors of E, which, as has been seen, represents the total expenditures in cash for the period and locality designated, the average quantity of money in circulation in this locality for the given period may be chosen.

This quantity will be indicated by M. Then the other factor of E must of necessity be $\frac{E}{M}$. It is observed that on account of its constitution this magnitude necessarily represents the average number of times that the money in circulation (M) was turned over against goods and services during the course of the year 1927. In order to indicate its general character, therefore, it will be called the velocity of circulation of money in the United States in 1927 and will be designated by V.

E' likewise breaks easily and naturally into two very useful factors, one the average deposits subject to check in the banks of the country during the period considered (M') and the other the number of times that these average deposits were turned over against goods and services during the year. This magnitude will in turn be designated by V'.

It remains to factor the right-hand side of the equation, which is made up of the sum of the very great number of little products of the form pq. With the left-hand member of the equation written in the form to which it has just been reduced and with the right-hand side indicated in more detail, the equation becomes:

$$MV + M'V' = p_1q_1 + p_2q_2 + \ldots\ldots + p_{n+k}q_{n+k}.$$

The task now becomes that of splitting into two factors the sum of the products:

$$p_1q_1 + p_2q_2 + \ldots\ldots\ldots + p_{n+k}q_{n+k}.$$

For one factor it would be desirable to have a quantity representing, in some usable unit, the total of the q's or the total *quantity* of goods and services transferred by sale during the period. It is at once evident, however, that there must be devised a common unit of measure for goods as diverse as bales of cotton and horses on the one hand and the services of cooks and dentists on the other. Thus is taken as the unit of measure for each quantity the quantity of that particular type and grade of commodity which, at the average price prevailing during some recent year chosen as a base year, a dollar would purchase. With the use of the two examples of sales transactions given above:

12 cents = 6 cents × 2 pounds of sugar

and

$1500 = $1.50 × 1000 bushels of wheat

and with the average price in 1913 of sugar of the grade involved in the transaction being assumed to be 4 cents and that of the wheat $.50, the above equations can be written in the new forms with quantities measured in units of a dollar's worth in 1913 and with prices changed to correspond:

12 cents = $1.50 × .08 (dollars' worth of sugar in 1913)

and

$1500 = $3.00 × 500 (dollars' worth of wheat in 1913).

By changing the quantities involved in all the purchase and sale transactions to similar units, by changing likewise their prices to correspond to the changed sizes of the units of quantity, and by indicating such changes by placing ‾'s over the p's and the q's, the equation of exchange may be written thus:

$$MV + M'V' = \bar{p}_1\bar{q}_1 + \bar{p}_2\bar{q}_2 + \ldots\ldots + \bar{p}_{n+k}\bar{q}_{n+k}.$$

In this form its members have identically the same magnitude as formerly; the only difference is that the units of quantities have been changed and those of prices likewise changed to correspond.

Now, however, the $\bar{q}$'s, being in uniform units of quantity (dollars' worth in the base year), may be added. Hence, the operation of factoring may now be accomplished and the equation accordingly written in the form:

$$MV + M'V' = \frac{\bar{p}_1\bar{q}_1 + \bar{p}_2\bar{q}_2 + \ldots + \bar{p}_{n+k}\bar{q}_{n+k}}{\bar{q}_1 + \bar{q}_2 + \ldots\ldots + \bar{q}_{n+k}}(\bar{q}_1 + \bar{q}_2 + \ldots + \bar{q}_{n+k}).$$

The first factor will be called P and the second T. More exactly, by the selection of one factor, T, the other, P, is determined automatically. It should be remarked that T, being the sum of the $\bar{q}$'s, represents the total physical volume of trade for the United States in 1927. Also, it should be further noted that the units of quantity for T are dollars' worth[3] in the base year, so that its magnitude depends on the base year chosen. Furthermore, it is evident that the various quantities are counted each time they are sold. Consequently, the methods of distribution, determining, as they do, the number of times that commodities of various sorts are sold, may be even more influential than the total production itself in fixing the magnitude of T.

The other factor, P, as mentioned above, is established by the fact that, when it is multiplied by T, the product must be equal to the sum of the products making up the right-hand side of the equation. Upon observation of its algebraic expression:

$$\frac{\bar{p}_1\bar{q}_1 + \bar{p}_2\bar{q}_2 + \dots\dots\dots\dots + \bar{p}_{n+k}q_{n+k}}{\bar{q}_1 + \bar{q}_2 + \dots\dots\dots\dots + \bar{q}_{n+k}},$$

it is noted that it is a weighted arithmetic average of the p's, the weights in every case being the corresponding q's. Or, more explicitly, P is the weighted arithmetic average of all the prices at which goods and services were sold in the United States in 1927, each price being weighted by the quantity of goods sold at that price. Let it be borne in mind, however, that the prices in every case are the prices of quantities of various articles which could be bought for one dollar at the average price which prevailed for each in the base year. Hence, the individual prices represent multiples of the corresponding base year prices, and P, the price level, in turn represents the average multiple which the 1927 prices were of those of the base year.

[3] Should anyone question the physical quality of these units, let him consider for a moment the following case: A man returns to his native town after a long sojourn in another country. It will be assumed that in 1913, during his original stay in the given town, he had developed the habit of buying each month a dollar's worth of sugar. On returning, he goes to the same grocer and asks for the amount of sugar which he once received in 1913 for one dollar. Can the physical quality of such a unit be contested?

Had the statistical material in France made such a procedure possible, it would have been of interest to follow for the period since the beginning of the war the actual magnitudes of all the quantities entering into the equation of exchange. In the present state of the available data, however, such an undertaking would prove entirely fruitless. With respect to M and M', fairly good estimates are available. Accordingly, actual values will be used for these two magnitudes. For V', however, no trustworthy numerical estimates seem possible, and for V there are no dependable directly derived indices of even the movements themselves. The absolute magnitudes of T, as might be expected, are completely beyond the reach of approximation. It will be necessary, therefore, to use indices only for four of the six magnitudes. Accordingly, the equation will be written in the form:

$$M\bar{V} + M'\bar{V}' = C\bar{P}\,\bar{T}$$

in which the ¯'s indicate that indices instead of actual magnitudes are used, and in which C is an obviously necessary factor introduced on account of the employment of indices to make the balance appear.

In making the monthly[4] series for M it was decided to use the note circulation of the Bank of France without correction for the metallic *jetons*,[5] for the Chamber of Commerce notes and the local coins which accompanied them, or for the silver coins which only gradually disappeared after the war began. Allowance was made, however, for cash actually held in the vaults of the banks. To accomplish this a deduction of 3 per cent[6] of estimated demand deposits for each month was made from each of the monthly items of

[4] For the inaccuracies involved in monthly series of the various quantities entering into the equation of exchange, see footnote 25, p. 304.

[5] The proportions of *jetons* to the note circulation were computed for several years. In 1925 and again in 1926 they amounted to but 1.8 per cent of the total note circulation. In the other years the proportion was similarly insignificant — as was presumably that of the displaced types of emergency currency to note circulation. On the other hand, it is clear that the silver circulation made up during the first years of the war probably a much larger percentage of the total.

[6] A number of bankers were consulted as to the approximate percentage. All agreed that it was probably very small. Three per cent was named by several, and none of the estimates varied widely from that one.

the series of outstanding Bank of France notes. This estimate is doubtless too low for the early years of the period covered, in view of the fact that for a considerable time after the outbreak of the war and after the moratorium on deposits, all of the banks were forced to keep on hand much larger quantities of cash than usual. But, since no allowance has been made for the metallic money which continued in circulation during the early years of the war, it is difficult to say whether M in 1914 and 1915 was actually larger or smaller than the amounts reported. The series should perhaps also be corrected to take care of the misrepresentations of the statements of the Bank of France in the early months of 1925. As a matter of fact, however, the corrected figures have never been published and, consequently, cannot be given. It is certain that the corrections, if inserted, would make little difference in the general appearance of the series.

For M' an estimate based on the sight deposits of the "Big Four" commercial banks was made. The method first tried was a refinement of that employed by Jacques Rueff in his recent study of the equation of exchange with the use of French data.[7] To perform the computations it was necessary first to find as nearly accurately as possible the proportions the sight deposits of the four big banks were of the total volume of deposits for the country. Accordingly, through the helpful coöperation of the Paris Clearing House (*Chambre de Compensation des Banquiers de Paris*) the total monthly clearings of the four big banks since 1917 were secured. A direct comparison of these totals with the total clearings[8] for all the banks participating in the clearing operations of the Paris Clearing House would mean little because of the changing number of member banks — especially since many of the recent entrants are very large. Consequently, clearings for each of the banks entering since December 1917 were secured for the months of August and

[7] Jacques Rueff, *Théorie des Phénomènes monétaires* (Paris, Payot et Cie., 1927).

[8] The clearings of the Paris Clearing House alone were taken into account. The branches of the four big banks use the provincial clearing houses for local clearings. Consequently, in order to render the provincial clearings usable in the estimates being made, it would have been necessary to separate them into the two categories made for the Paris clearings. In view of the reticence of French officials in giving out the necessary information, such an undertaking was considered an infeasible one.

September 1927, and the proportions which the clearings of each bore to the total during those two months were used for scaling up the total clearings for each year. Thus was obtained a series of monthly total clearings corrected so as to represent what clearings would have been if all the present members of the Clearing House had belonged to it during the entire period under discussion. Finally, the proportions which the clearings of the "Big Four" bore to these corrected totals were computed.

These percentages naturally varied somewhat from month to month and from year to year. In particular, it was observed that in periods of business depression the proportions of total clearings attributable to the "Big Four" were considerably above those during periods of prosperity. It was further noted that the percentages had a distinctly downward secular trend. In other words, the proportion of the clearings done by the four big banks declined gradually throughout the period 1918–1926, for which the trend was fitted. The equation of the linear trend for monthly data, in terms of percentages, with origin at June 1918 was found to be:

$$y = -0.0561\,x + .241.$$

It was hoped that the monthly ordinates of this trend could be used as the estimated percentages for each month of the "Big Four" demand deposits to total deposits subject to check. By comparison of the estimates of deposits thus obtained with the actual deposits on December 31, 1926 of the 21 largest banks of France, however, it was found that the method had yielded figures large beyond all possibility of reason. Evidently the very large clearings of the big foreign banks, which have, without any doubt, been playing a larger and larger rôle in Paris banking and which have a clientele accustomed to the use of checks, had distorted greatly and in a downward direction the estimated percentages of the deposit banking done by the "Big Four." The failure of the method to take account likewise of clearings as between head offices and branches (important with three of the "Big Four" banks) had led to a further distortion in the same direction.[9]

[9] A similar method of estimating total deposits in France, it has been learned, was also tried by the Bank of France with equally unsatisfactory results and was by it also discarded.

Accordingly, on the basis of information from various banking officials, and from the Bank of France with regard to its collections and to other of its operations with the "Big Four" as compared with those with all the other banks, it was determined that a fairly accurate estimate of total deposits subject to check for the entire period under consideration could be obtained by simply doubling the deposits of the "Big Four." The estimates were accordingly made in this simple way; but, in order to avoid the appearance of greater accuracy than could possibly be expected from the method, only milliards were taken into account. The estimates thus arrived at are given in the accompanying table (Table 85).

For *P* the index of wholesale prices compiled by the *Statistique Générale de la France*[10] was used. This index is made up of the prices of 45 commodities at wholesale, of which 16 are of imported and 29 of domestic goods. The question whether any index of wholesale prices is sufficiently representative of the general average of all prices naturally arises, with the evident answer that there is no reason to believe that it is. Nevertheless, in most cases, it probably gives a fairly accurate indication of all important general movements with which this study is chiefly concerned. Moreover, since the index chosen is, without any serious doubt, the best constructed of the indices available for the entire period, there could be little hesitation in adopting it.

For *T* there was the choice of two possible series, that for the volume of production and that for car loadings.[11] The production index of the *Statistique Générale de la France* excludes entirely the building operations in the devastated regions and, consequently, cannot but give a wrong impression of production activity during parts of the period covered. The car loadings series, on the other hand, contains many inaccuracies and possible distortions. In capacity the cars vary from 6 to 40 metric tons and, as in most other countries, are loaded to any fraction of their capacity, often at the whim of the loader. Nevertheless, there seems to be enough uniformity even in these whims to give certain meaning to the series. After all, a Frenchman, because he is loading cars, is not likely to

[10] For a full description of this index, see Chap. V, Table 7.

[11] For the complete descriptions of these series, see Chap. VIII, Tables 49 and 51.

lose his ingrained parsimony and pay for a sixth car when five will accommodate his shipment. And, as for small parcels, human inertia would probably in general cause them to be carried in a smaller rather than a larger number of cars.

By comparing the two series (Chart LVI) it will be seen that, while their broad movements are roughly similar, those of production are much smoother than those of car loadings. On the other

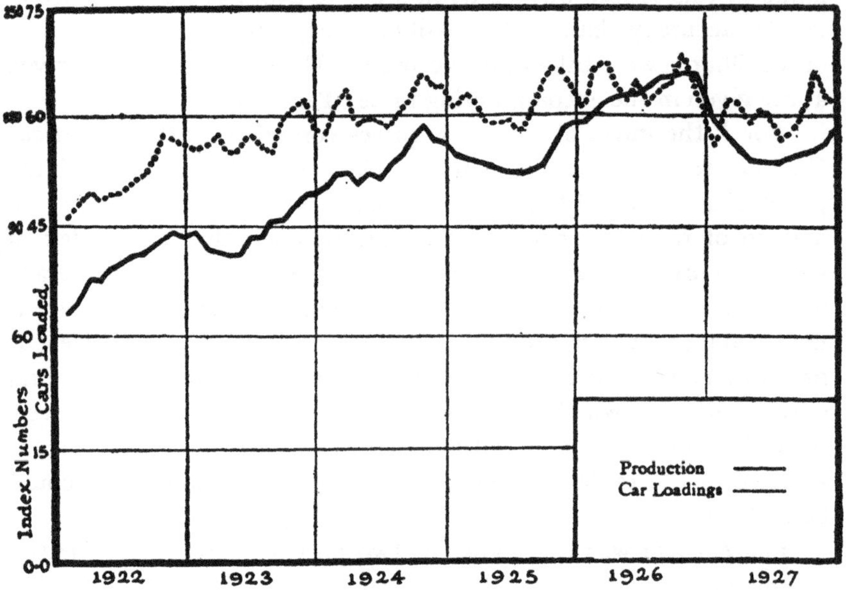

CHART LVI

INDEX OF PRODUCTION AND CAR LOADINGS

hand, car loadings prove to be highly seasonal and seem to bear in their minor fluctuations at least a remote resemblance to velocities of circulation of deposits. The car loadings series also takes into account automatically the building operations in the devastated regions. On the whole, it constitutes a much better measure of the volume of trade than does the index of production. Unfortunately, however, it has not been compiled for data prior to January 1922. Both series will be used in the analysis to follow.

For France V' cannot be estimated in actual values. Nevertheless, a fairly satisfactory index seems to be calculable. For each month beginning with August 1917, an index was computed by dividing each item of the series of Paris bank clearings (corrected[12] to take account of the varying number of member banks in the Clearing House during the period under discussion) by the corresponding items of the series of total bank deposits subject to check.[13] Inasmuch as the numerators in these divisions are evidently only a small portion of the total expenditures by check, while the denominators are presumably nearly accurate in magnitude, the resulting quotients are necessarily far smaller than the actual values of the velocities sought. Nevertheless, the movements of the resulting series should correspond very closely indeed with those of the actual velocities of circulation of deposits. They will be used, therefore, as indices only.

Finally, for V, there seems to be no way of securing directly even an index, though it can probably be safely assumed that its movements are at least remotely similar to those of V'. How remote the similarity turns out to be will be estimated as the discussion proceeds.

The movements of the series representative of the quantities entering into the equation of exchange are pictured in the accompanying graph (Chart LVII).

A comparison will first be made of prices (P) and circulation (M). As in the comparison of total circulation with prices, it will be noted that the long-term movements of the two series are strikingly similar.[14] The short-term movements, on the other hand, are very different, those of prices being more frequent and much more pronounced than those of money circulation. Striking differences in the general movements of the two series are found for the period extending from May 1919 to May 1921 and again for that from November 1922 to April 1924. During the former of these periods prices first rose rapidly and greatly and then declined almost as rapidly to their earlier level, while, during much of the period, the amount of money in circulation remained nearly constant.

[12] For the details of the method of making this correction, see above, pp. 285–286.

[13] For the construction of this series, see above, pp. 285–287.

[14] The similarity of the long-term movements of the two series is even more apparent in the logarithmic curves (Chart LVIII).

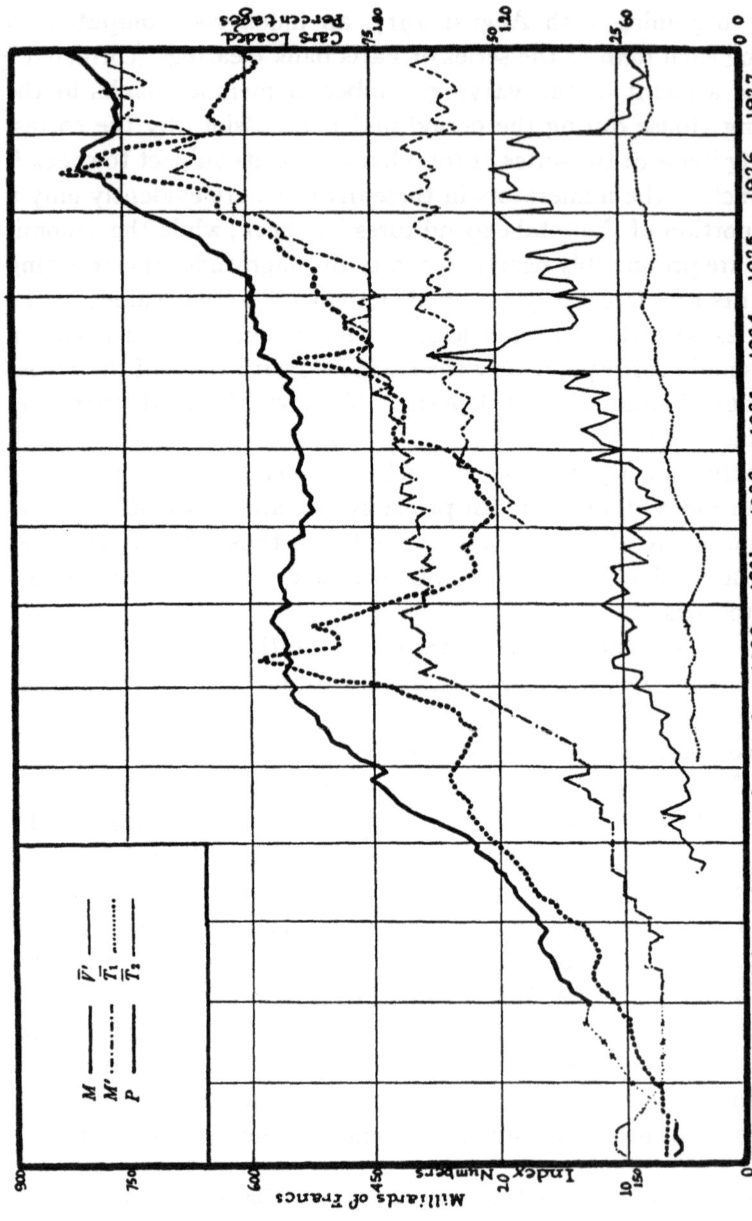

CHART LVII

Fisher Equation of Exchange

TABLE 85

M

(End-of-month * estimates in millions of francs)

	1914	1915	1916	1917	1918	1919	1920
Jan.	5594	.....	13648	17088	22833	31374	36863
Feb.	5433	.....	14085	17619	23656	32072	37109
Mar.	5413	.....	14637	18190	24849	33352	36819
Apr.	5475	11330	15068	18710	26035	33528	36547
May	5482	.....	15225	19095	26713	33654	37105
June	5552	11895	15495	19523	28190	33932	36764
July	....	.....	15851	19902	28758	34392	36916
Aug.	....	.....	16136	20139	29044	34520	37125
Sept.	....	13100	16474	20665	29502	35187	37880
Oct.	....	.....	16379	21375	30271	36139	38274
Nov.	....	.....	15712	22084	28682	36764	37967
Dec.	9833	12991	16439	22007	29860	36585	36664

	1921	1922	1923	1924	1925	1926	1927
Jan.	37133	35653	35940	37429	39616	49388	50822
Feb.	37028	35371	36245	37965	39892	49761	50287
Mar.	37383	34532	36378	39020	39992	50292	50412
Apr.	37431	34977	35738	38924	41762	50784	50740
May	37423	34894	35546	38503	41743	51445	50330
June	36744	35042	35849	38765	42010	51753	50607
July	36161	35240	36089	39152	43171	54642	51196
Aug.	36033	35271	36271	39074	43652	53797	51232
Sept.	36171	35793	36726	39439	44447	53187	52303
Oct.	36344	35884	36830	39560	45569	53198	53710
Nov.	35556	35009	36319	39517	46945	51943	53432
Dec.	35707	35549	37035	39734	48823	50914	54991

* Calculated from *selected* end-of-month circulation data. See footnote to Table 9.

In the later period there again appeared a marked divergence in the movements of the two series, but one which became much reduced after the spring of 1924.

What is the explanation of these important divergences in the movements of the two series? To discover it, other of the series must be taken into account and that of *M′* in particular. It will be noticed that after January 1916 — the earliest date following the

TABLE 86

M'

(End-of-month estimates in milliards of francs) *

	1914	1915	1916	1917	1918	1919	1920	1921	1922	1923	1924	1925	1926	1927
Jan.	10	..	7	8	11	14	24	26	26	28	30	30	41	45
Feb.	11	..	7	9	11	14	26	26	26	27	31	30	41	47
Mar.	11	..	7	9	11	14	25	25	25	27	31	30	40	50
Apr.	11	7	7	10	12	15	26	26	27	27	30	30	41	49
May	11	..	7	10	12	16	27	27	26	28	30	32	43	49
June	10	7	8	10	12	17	26	25	27	28	30	33	44	50
July	..	..	8	10	13	18	26	26	27	28	31	35	46	52
Aug.	..	..	8	11	13	19	26	25	26	28	32	35	45	48
Sept.	..	7	8	11	14	20	27	25	27	30	30	37	44	49
Oct.	..	..	7	11	15	21	27	27	27	28	30	37	46	51
Nov.	..	..	8	11	13	22	28	26	26	28	31	38	44	51
Dec.	7	7	8	11	13	23	26	26	27	29	29	39	44	52

* See text, pp. 285–287.

TABLE 87

V'

(Estimated monthly indices) *

	1917	1918	1919	1920	1921	1922	1923	1924	1925	1926	1927
Jan.	...	.30	.31	.50	.66	.48	.69	1.24	.80	.91	.67
Feb.	...	.31	.29	.50	.57	.46	.72	1.21	.83	.92	.61
Mar.	...	.36	.34	.63	.61	.51	.78	1.52	.98	1.19	.53
Apr.	...	.28	.36	.63	.63	.38	.69	1.17	.94	1.09	.54
May	...	.41	.38	.58	.62	.47	.62	1.13	.80	1.13	.54
June	...	.30	.37	.59	.64	.45	.70	1.04	1.04	1.13	.48
July	...	.25	.37	.59	.44	.51	.70	.82	.85	1.22	.46
Aug.	.20	.26	.34	.59	.51	.51	.73	.79	.70	1.03	.50
Sept.	.19	.27	.43	.55	.60	.48	.65	.81	.67	.96	.42
Oct.	.25	.25	.43	.58	.45	.55	.87	.83	1.09	.98	.48
Nov.	.23	.27	.43	.64	.51	.74	.84	.72	1.12	1.13	.52
Dec.	.24	.28	.52	.69	.55	.60	.76	.94	1.20	.99	.51

* See text, pp. 288–289.

outbreak of the war at which the various series began to approach normality — deposits moved in general similarly to prices and to money in circulation. With early 1919, however, deposits began to rise rapidly, preceding by almost six months the corresponding rise in prices. On the other hand, the amount of money in circulation, as we have seen before, continued its less abrupt upward trend with no apparent relation whatever to the movements of prices and comparatively little to those of deposits. Then, beginning in May 1920, when prices started their rapid decline, M' first rose slightly and thereafter moved almost horizontally for two years, while M continued its earlier level for another year.

Such a combination of movements is certainly most extraordinary and seems to fit almost equally badly all the existing theories of money. A study of the movements of the velocity of circulation of deposits (V') seems to bring the explanation no nearer. As might have been anticipated, that series rose considerably during the boom period of late 1919 and early 1920, but, strange to note, it only began to decline materially after June 1921. V, on the other hand, most certainly decreased much earlier. In the analysis of the same data with the use of the Keynes equation (Chapter XII), the movements of k indicate clearly a decrease in the magnitudes of V during the period April 1920 to May 1921. The solution of the riddle, however, must be sought elsewhere. As for so many other problems of this study, it is to be found in government finance and in the extraordinary relations between the Treasury, the banks, and the Bank of France.

By reference to the series of advances of the Bank of France to the State it will be seen that during 1919 such advances rose very rapidly, their total increases aggregating for that year the significant sum of 8.4 milliards of francs. Moreover, from the table below it will be seen that the net additions to the outstanding short-term Treasury paper were greater during that year than in any other during the entire period. This form of government indebtedness was actually increased during the year by a total of 25.2 milliards. It will be remembered, too, that during the same period (late 1919 and early 1920) not only were prices rising rapidly, but business activity was high and increasing. Thus there arises what appears at first sight another contradiction, but one which disappears with analysis. How was it possible for a business boom, accompanied, as this one was, by rapidly rising prices, to be financed while at the same time funds[15] were being taken in by the Treasury in considerably greater amounts than they were being put out by the Bank?

TABLE 88

ANNUAL EXCESS OF EMISSIONS OVER REIMBURSEMENTS OF *BONS DE LA DÉFENSE NATIONALE* AND OTHER SHORT-TERM TREASURY PAPER *

(In millions of francs)

1914	1619	1921	13049
1915	5387	1922	— 1291 [a]
1916	5612	1923	— 1350
1917	6933	1924	— 1312
1918	3318	1925	— 8279
1919	25183	1926	1196
1920	6261	....	......

[a] Minus signs indicate excesses of reimbursements.

* Source: G. Lachapelle, *L'Évolution de la Circulation*, etc., (Société d'Études et d'Informations Économiques, 1926 and 1927).

What seems to have been happening was this. Through its advances to the State, the Bank of France was putting out continually and in large amounts funds which were quickly spent[16] by the Government. These funds, as soon as they were spent, drifted naturally in large part to the banks. Especially was this true during the first half of 1919 before the price rise had begun and while business was temporarily depressed. Funds thus deposited — as well as certain other resources in the hands of the public — were quickly used to purchase short-term Treasury obligations, the issue

[15] It should be borne in mind that a very large proportion indeed of these funds were Bank of France notes.

[16] Since both the floating and the permanent debt of the State were increasing during this period, the advances from the Bank would not have been requested had not the funds received been needed for cash expenditures. For the complete discussion of this subject the reader is referred to Chap. V.

of which — as had previously been the case with the deposits of the banks — began to increase greatly. But how reconcile the amounts? The funds put out by the Bank of France in the form of advances to the State were only 8.4 milliards, and those deposited in the banks were approximately 10 milliards, while the increase in short-term Treasury paper was 25.2 milliards. The answer is clear if the above analysis is carried one step further. The funds received by the Treasury as subscriptions to government obligations were again spent in large part, again drifted at least in part to the banks, and were again, to the extent that they were not claimed by business borrowers, used to buy Treasury obligations and thus to start the cycle anew. Thus is explained not only the excess of deposits over advances of the Bank to the State and that of the increase in short-term Treasury obligations over deposits, but also the source of the funds used in financing the enlarged volume of business at ever rising prices. Moreover, it is also seen why deposits did not decrease after the fall in prices commenced and after business activity became reduced. For the funds released by business likewise flowed to the banks, as they always do, and, unclaimed by further business borrowings, continued to swell the purchases of short-term Treasury paper. Thus in 1921, the year of deepest business depression, the increase in that form of government obligation outstanding amounted to 13.0 milliards, as opposed to an increase of 6.3 milliards in 1920 and a decrease of 1.3 milliards in 1922.

It remains to explain the divergences in the movements of prices and of money in circulation appearing in late 1922. For this purpose, as well as to bring out certain other relations between the movements of the two series, the logarithms of the items of each were plotted and compared (Chart LVIII).

It will at once be noticed that during most of the long period of rapidly rising prices beginning in late 1915 and continuing with but slight interruptions until November 1918, there was a persistent tendency for prices to increase faster than the quantities of money in circulation. The same tendency may likewise be observed in the other long period of rapidly rising prices from late 1922 until the middle of 1926, as well as for the period from the middle of 1919 until April 1920 already discussed. In the periods of falling prices, on

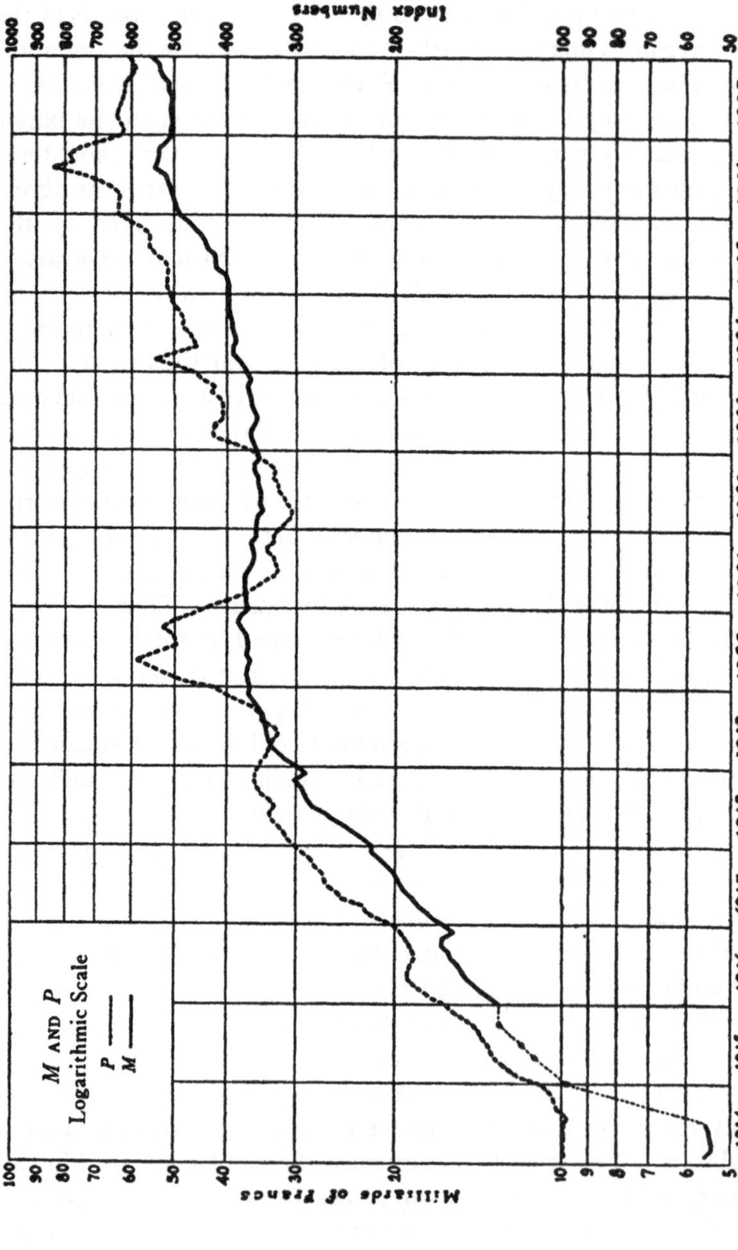
Index Numbers
1000
900
800
700
600
500
400
300
200
100
90
80
70
60
50
M AND P
Logarithmic Scale
P
M
1914
1915
1916
1917
1918
1919
1920
1921
1922
1923
1924
1925
1926
1927
Milliards of Francs
100
90
80
70
60
50
40
30
20
10
9
8
7
6
5

CHART LVIII

the other hand, prices seem in general to fall faster than the quantities of money in circulation.

In order to interpret these relative movements the equation of exchange will be reduced to a more convenient form.

Let $\frac{M'}{M} = K$ [K is not constant. Its magnitudes are given below (Table 89).]

Then the equation of exchange may be written:

$$MV + KMV' = PT$$

or

$$M(V + KV') = PT$$

or

$$M = \left(\frac{T}{V + KV'}\right) P.$$

With the equation in this form it will be seen that if the quantity in parentheses, $\frac{T}{V + KV'}$, is constant, then there is a direct proportionality between M and P. In other words, P moves proportionally to M, or M moves proportionally to P — the quantity theory hypothesis without causal relationships. It is, therefore, of interest to investigate the conditions under which this significant quantity approaches constancy and — what is even more important for interpreting the movements of prices and of money circulation under consideration — the conditions under which it decreases and those under which it increases.

That the quantity is always positive and always greater than one is immediately obvious. Hence, if it increases above its usual amount, prices will no longer keep their former proportionality to money in circulation but will move less rapidly upward or more rapidly downward; while, if, on the other hand, it decreases, P will move correspondingly more rapidly upward and less rapidly downward than M. This statement can probably be more readily understood if both sides of the equation are reduced to logarithms:

$$\log M = \log P + \log \frac{T}{V + KV'}.$$

If $\frac{T}{V + KV'}$ is constant, the equation may be written in the form:

$$\log M = \log P + \log c; \quad c > 1$$

which signifies that the log M series is always a constant distance above[17] the log P series, the movements of the two series being otherwise exactly similar. If, however, $\frac{T}{V + KV'}$ is not constant but increasing, the log M series will continually separate from[18] the log P series by a greater and greater amount. In other words, M will increase continually faster than P or decrease continually more slowly. If, on the other hand, $\frac{T}{V + KV'}$ is decreasing, the log P series will move continually closer to the log M series above. Otherwise expressed, P will increase continually faster than M or decrease continually more slowly.

It is, therefore, important to make an analytical study of the quantity $\frac{T}{V + KV'}$.

Unfortunately, the absolute magnitudes of all the quantities involved, except K, are completely unknown. This much is known, however: that T was very large, amounting doubtless to hundreds of milliards of francs' worth of goods at their 1913 prices; that V and V', on the contrary, were probably not less than 15 nor greater than 30;[19] and that K, as computed by dividing each item of the

[17] It should be remembered that in absolute magnitudes the items of the M series are always much larger than those of the P series.

[18] See footnote 17.

[19] V has been frequently estimated for the United States by Irving Fisher (see his annual articles in the June numbers of the *American Economic Review* for 1911 to 1913). These estimates were usually between 20 and 25. V' for the United States has been more recently computed by Randolph Burgess of the Federal Reserve Bank of New York. (Randolph Burgess, "Velocity of Bank Deposits," *Journal of the American Statistical Association*, June 1925.) His estimate of V' over a number of years was approximately 30. Still more recently an apparently even more dependable computation of the velocity of bank deposits in the United States has been made by Professor Wesley C. Mitchell in his *Business Cycles, the Problem and Its Setting* (New York, National Bureau of Economic Research, 1927). According to his estimates this velocity varies from about 25 to approximately 29 per annum.

On account of the far-famed hoarding habits of the French people, both V and V' probably average lower in France than in the United States.

series of M' by corresponding items of the series for M, was, at least after the beginning of 1915 and until the end of 1926, always less than 1 (Table 89).[20]

What then can be said with regard to the constancy or to the variability of the magnitude of $\frac{T}{V + KV'}$ in France during the period under consideration? Certainly, by no stretch of the imagination could V — the one unindexed factor — be conceived of as moving in ways to keep the factors constant. In fact, there is almost completely conclusive evidence from the analysis of the data with the use of the Keynes monetary equation (Chapter XII) that the movements of V, usually similar to those of V', were sometimes greater in magnitude. (This evidence will be discussed in Chapter XII below.) The problem will be attacked, therefore, by attempting to discover the magnitudes and directions of movement of the fraction away from constancy. The above estimates of the orders of magnitude of the various quantities involved, combined with the indices of each (except of V), should certainly throw some light on the movements of the fraction as a whole. The task is lightened by the almost exact similarity which appears between the secular trends of V' and T.

Assuredly, in the period of rapidly rising prices from late 1915 until early 1918, during which analysis as well as statistical evidence[21] indicates gradually increasing V's and V''s, while T presumably did not increase radically and while K continued almost constant, the fraction $\frac{T}{V + KV'}$ would be expected to decrease. Thus, the faster rise of the log P series during this period could have been

[20] The estimates are not dependable prior to 1916. Because of the impossibility of determining accurately the quantities of silver and other coins in circulation, no allowance whatever for them has been made in computing M. In the latter part of the period, a very extraordinary combination of circumstances has given rise to extremely large deposits, so that care must be taken in interpreting the resulting high ratios.

[21] The statistical evidence, other than that given by the computed values of V', is found in the movements of k and k' in the Keynes monetary equation treated in the following chapter. Falls in k and k' — as will there be explained — almost invariably mean corresponding rises in V and V'.

expected. Moreover, as soon as the price rise became less rapid after May 1918 and as the velocities of money and of deposits turned downward, $\frac{T}{V + KV'}$ (in the absence of an unusual reduction in the volume of business[22]) would necessarily increase. The tendency of the two curves to come together at that time would indicate that such an increase actually occurred. Finally, the explanation of the continual convergence of the two logarithmic curves appearing after the middle of 1922 and continuing until July 1926, as that of their tendency to separate thereafter, becomes immediately apparent. The period prior to July 1926 was likewise one of rapidly rising prices, of clearly increasing V's,[23] and of mildly increasing V''s, while T moved upward and at about the same rate as V'. It seems evident, therefore, that during this period $\frac{T}{V + KV'}$ decreased somewhat — a fact that might have been anticipated from analysis. As a consequence, prices rose more rapidly than the quantity of money in circulation.

In the absence of the data necessary for constructing a time series of the magnitudes of $\frac{T}{V + KV'}$, the use of the fraction for a detailed analysis of the movements of P and M would probably be unwarranted. It may be pointed out, however, that the separation of the two logarithmic curves in the rising price period of 1919–1920 was of a sort which corresponds completely with the undoubted considerable decrease which might have been anticipated in $\frac{T}{V + KV'}$. Likewise the more rapid decline in prices than in monetary circulation in the interval April 1920 to February 1922, as well as its more rapid rise thereafter, tallies exactly with the easily predictable movements of the fraction in such highly disturbed periods.

Much is being brought out in detail, however, which might more

[22] It is not at all certain that the reduction at that time was not extremely great. It will be remembered that the period coincided with the most critical stage of the war.

[23] See graph of k, Chart LXII.

profitably be discussed in general. Let us look, therefore, at the equation of exchange in the form:

$$M = \left(\frac{T}{V + KV'}\right) P.$$

As mentioned in another connection above, it is immediately apparent that the necessary and sufficient conditions for the holding of the quantity theory, *without causal relationships*, is that $\frac{T}{V + KV'}$ be constant. In undisturbed periods of but mildly and slowly changing prices it might — in the absence of an increase in trade resulting, as is likely, from the very stability itself — approach constancy. That in periods of rapidly or even moderately rising prices it is sure to diminish and in periods of falling prices equally sure to increase is clearly indicated for the post-war years in France by the foregoing comparisons. *In fact, it may be said in general — at least for the recent years in France and probably for all modern countries — that, when prices rise substantially and continue rising over a considerable period, their rise will be proportionately greater than the increase in monetary circulation and that, when prices fall materially and keep falling over any considerable period, their fall will be proportionately greater than the reduction in the quantity of money in circulation.*

Should a finance minister set out, therefore, to finance a war, or any other venture, by currency inflation, he may be very sure that the resulting rise in prices, with all the important consequences of such a rise, will be more than in proportion to the accompanying increase in monetary circulation. In general, too, in view of the smallness of the change which might be anticipated in the ratio $\frac{M'}{M}$, it may be added with assurance that the rise in prices would be more than in proportion to the increase in the total funds in use.

A few words of discussion should be added with regard to the series of deposits and of the velocities of their circulation. Deposits in French banks should not be regarded as are demand deposits in the United States. While they are subject to check, a very large

TABLE 89

$$\frac{M'}{M}$$

(Estimated ratios of end-of-month data) *

	1914	1915	1916	1917	1918	1919	1920
Jan.	1.79	....	0.51	0.47	0.48	0.45	0.65
Feb.	2.02	....	0.50	0.51	0.46	0.44	0.70
Mar.	2.03	....	0.48	0.49	0.44	0.42	0.68
Apr.	2.01	0.62	0.46	0.53	0.46	0.45	0.71
May	2.01	....	0.46	0.52	0.45	0.48	0.73
June	1.80	0.59	0.52	0.51	0.43	0.50	0.71
July	....	....	0.50	0.50	0.45	0.52	0.70
Aug.	....	....	0.50	0.55	0.45	0.55	0.70
Sept.	....	0.53	0.49	0.53	0.47	0.57	0.71
Oct.	....	....	0.43	0.51	0.50	0.58	0.71
Nov.	....	....	0.51	0.50	0.45	0.60	0.74
Dec.	0.71	0.54	0.49	0.50	0.44	0.63	0.71

	1921	1922	1923	1924	1923	1926	1927
Jan.	0.70	0.73	0.78	0.80	0.76	0.83	0.89
Feb.	0.70	0.74	0.74	0.82	0.75	0.82	0.93
Mar.	0.67	0.72	0.74	0.79	0.75	0.80	0.99
Apr.	0.69	0.77	0.76	0.77	0.72	0.81	0.97
May	0.72	0.75	0.79	0.78	0.77	0.84	0.97
June	0.68	0.77	0.78	0.77	0.79	0.85	0.99
July	0.72	0.77	0.78	0.79	0.81	0.84	1.02
Aug.	0.69	0.74	0.77	0.82	0.80	0.84	0.94
Sept.	0.69	0.75	0.82	0.76	0.83	0.83	0.94
Oct.	0.74	0.75	0.76	0.76	0.81	0.86	....
Nov.	0.73	0.74	0.77	0.78	0.81	0.85	....
Dec.	0.73	0.76	0.78	0.73	0.80	0.86	....

* See text pp. 298–299.

portion of them are never drawn upon except by depositors cashing checks. Moreover, they do not represent to nearly the same extent as in America the counterparts of advances made to customers. Many of the banks' business clients borrow regularly through the use of overdrafts on a prearranged line of credit, so that deposits appear in their accounts only to the extent that cash and cash items are brought to the banks in excess of drawings. Furthermore, as has been pointed out many times in the pages which have preceded, a very large proportion of the funds on deposit are often invested in government bonds and securities other than those representing loans to business. In fact, *in some respects* they are more like savings than commercial deposits. Very frequently, recently, they have risen during periods of business depression, as idle funds drifted into the banks; and it is at least conceivable that they might decline in a period of increasing business activity and of rising prices.

V' is naturally affected by the peculiar character of French demand deposits. The fluctuations in its magnitude during the period under consideration were probably, therefore, far from normal. The extremely high peak of March 1924 was undoubtedly a result of the large operations and settlements incident to the exchange speculation of that month and of those preceding. Such peaks, as also those appearing in similar data for the United States during periods of heavy stock speculation, are misleading unless account is taken of the high velocities of deposits used in accomplishing the originating transactions.[24]

In the above analyses the indices of V' were continually used with some suspicion. Not only were many of their movements the reverse of what might have been expected of them from analysis (the movements in the last two-thirds of 1920 and in the first half of 1921, for example), but they also often appeared different from those indicated by the movements of k and k' to be discussed in the next chapter. And for March 1924 it would be preposterous to regard the magnitude of V' as that indicated by the estimated index for that month — unless speculative deals in foreign exchange and all French operations connected with handling them were also included in T. Moreover, since no direct estimates of V appeared possible, the indices of V' were used to represent those of V also. Hence, whatever error was involved in V' would naturally be magnified. Before using the indices of V' in any essential part of the analysis, therefore, it was thought desirable to estimate the error involved.

[24] For a computation of the velocity of circulation of funds used in stock speculation in New York, see James Harvey Rogers, *Stock Speculation and the Money Market* (Columbia, Missouri, Lucas Brothers, 1927).

Accordingly, in the equation of exchange, which, it will be recalled, was finally written in the form:

$$M\bar{V} + M'\bar{V}' = C\bar{P}\,\bar{T}.$$

$\bar{V}'$ was substituted for $\bar{V}$, and the equation became:

$$M\bar{V}' + M'\bar{V}' = \bar{C}\,\bar{P}\,\bar{T}.$$ [The changed balancing factor is designated by $\bar{C}$.]

Computations were then made of the values of $\bar{C}$ from the expression:

$$\bar{C} = \frac{\bar{V}'\,(M + M')}{\bar{P}\,\bar{T}}.$$

If all the estimated indices were true indicators of the magnitudes of their respective quantities and if in addition there were no lags in any of the series with respect to any of the others,[25] $\bar{C}$ would be a constant. How far from constancy it actually is can be seen from the accompanying table (Table 90). The errors involved in the use of at least one of the series are, therefore, obviously considerable.

TABLE 90

$\bar{C}$

	1919	1920	1921	1922	1923	1924	1925	1926	1927
Jan.	.71	.96	1.65	1.43	1.30	1.66	.98	1.10	.88
Feb.	.69	.94	1.64	1.34	1.30	1.48	1.03	1.08	.83
Mar.	.84	1.10	1.92	1.32	1.40	2.05	1.24	1.38	.77
Apr.	.89	1.06	2.21	1.00	1.27	1.76	1.23	1.23	.80
May	.97	1.13	2.43	1.16	1.18	1.62	1.07	1.23	.81
June	.92	1.19	2.43	1.09	1.26	1.49	1.37	1.16	.73
July	.87	1.21	1.69	1.21	1.25	1.12	1.14	1.16	.72
Aug.	.86	1.16	1.92	1.15	1.25	1.07	.93	1.03	.75
Sept.	1.10	1.04	2.22	1.09	1.11	1.02	.92	.93	.65
Oct.	1.05	1.11	1.72	1.18	1.41	.99	1.42	1.00	.77
Nov.	1.02	1.35	1.72	1.44	1.26	.89	1.35	1.23	.82
Dec.	1.18	1.48	1.68	1.18	1.12	1.13	1.41	1.22	.79

[25] Here also are included inaccuracies in the equation arising from the failure of payments to be made at the time of purchase. (After this manuscript was written it was discovered that many of the observations here made had been stated admirably by Professor Wesley C. Mitchell in his *Business Cycles, the Problem and Its Setting*, pp. 130–133.) While it is only *differences* in the amounts of the carry-over of unpaid purchases from month to month which are of importance, nevertheless in certain types of periods such differences may be sufficiently large to throw the equation completely out of balance.

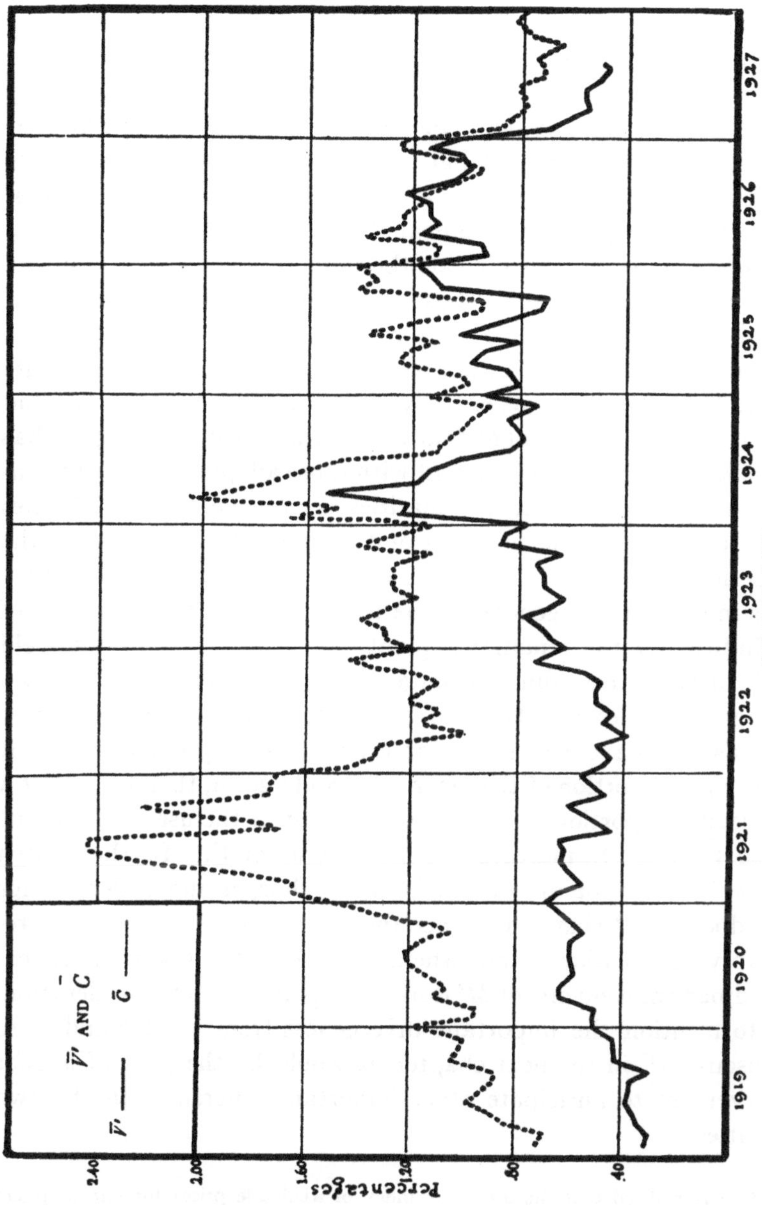

$\bar{V}'$ AND $\bar{C}$
$\bar{V}'$ ——
$\bar{C}$ ——
2.40
2.00
1.60
1.20
.80
.40
Percentages
1919
1920
1921
1922
1923
1924
1925
1926
1927

CHART LIX

On plotting the values of $\bar{C}$, it becomes at once apparent that the movements of the new series correspond extraordinarily closely with those of $\bar{V}'$ (Chart LIX, $\bar{V}'$ and $\bar{C}$). It will be noted, too, that in 1921, when the indices of V' moved in a particularly unexpected way, the values of $\bar{C}$ increased greatly above their normal level, thus giving evidence of a very large error in at least one of the indices. Another very large error is indicated in March 1924 and evidently one in $\bar{V}'$. It seems fairly clear, therefore, that however excellent the other indices, certainly those of V' cannot be depended upon for the double use to which they have been put. Either there has been a gross error in the estimates made of V' or else the use of its indices for those of V was entirely unwarranted. In February and March of 1924 it is evident that the method of computing $\bar{V}'$ has led to values entirely inconsistent with those adopted for T. In general, however, most of the peculiarities of movement of the $\bar{V}'$ series seem to be explicable in terms of the unusual movements of the M' series, and the method of its computation inspires confidence in its movements in general. The inaccuracies in the estimates of the indices for the remaining quantities could certainly not yield much of the extraordinarily large error discovered.[26] Nor could the lags in the movements of the series with respect to one another — great as they have been shown at times to be — probably account for any great portion of the error. It would seem, therefore, that a very large proportion of the error arises out of the use of the items of the $\bar{V}'$ series to indicate the movements of V. In the United States V' undoubtedly moves in much sharper and wider swings than does V. Perhaps in France they are likewise sharper but presumably not so wide. And, when, too, account is taken of the extraordinary movements of M' during the period under consideration, not to mention the important divergences from V' of k and k' to be discussed[27] in the next chapter, it would be the part of a poor observer not to anticipate other important differences in the two velocities.

[26] It is realized that the use of an index of wholesale prices for one of prices in general may introduce during certain periods an error of considerable magnitude.

[27] k and k' refer to magnitudes used in the Keynes monetary equation to be discussed in full in the next chapter.

For the moment, therefore, it will be assumed that the entire error responsible for the extraordinary movements of $\bar{C}$ is attributable to the estimates made of the indices of V' and to their use as indicators of the movements of V. If this assumption approaches accuracy, a very large portion of the error can be elimiated.

The equation from which the values of $\bar{C}$ were computed took the following form:

$$M\bar{V}' + M'\bar{V}' = \bar{C}\,\bar{P}\,\bar{T}$$

from which is derived the equation:

$$\bar{C} = \frac{\bar{V}'\,(M + M')}{\bar{P}\,\bar{T}}.$$

If both sides of this equation are divided by $\bar{C}$, the result is:

$$1 = \frac{\frac{\bar{V}'}{\bar{C}}\,(M + M')}{\bar{P}\,\bar{T}}$$

or

$$\frac{\bar{V}'}{\bar{C}}(M + M') = \bar{P}\,\bar{T}.$$

Hence, if $\frac{\bar{V}'}{\bar{C}}$ is used instead of $\bar{V}'$ as an index of both V and V', the equation *in terms of indices for four of the magnitudes* will balance *without the insertion* of a variable factor. Accordingly, $\frac{\bar{V}'}{\bar{C}}$ will be used instead of $\bar{V}'$ as an index of both V and V'.

But before proceeding with the analysis it will be necessary to discover the characteristics of $\bar{V}'$,[28] the quantity for which the new index just obtained is to be used. To accomplish this, it will be necessary to revert to the original equation:

$$MV + M'V' = P\,T$$

[28] It will be remembered that $\bar{V}'$ has been used as an index for both V and V'.

and to the equation in which indices were substituted for real magnitudes for four of the quantities:

$$M'\bar{V} + M'\bar{V}' = \bar{C}\,\bar{P}\,\bar{T}.$$

By equating the left-hand side of the second equation with the same side of the first one *multiplied* by a constant K to take care of the differences involved in using indices in one member and actual numbers in the other, it is found that the equality holds if, and only if,

$$\bar{V}' = K\,\frac{MV + M'V'}{M + M'}.$$

In other words, $\bar{V}'$, as it is being employed in the double use of indicator of movements both of $\bar{V}$ and of V', is an *index* of the weighted arithmetic average of V and V' wherein V is weighted by M and V' by M'.

Accordingly, a monthly series was computed for $\frac{\bar{V}'}{\bar{\bar{C}}}$ and its movements carefully noted.

With all of its virtues — and they are many — this series possesses one outstanding fault. It accomplishes too much. It absorbs not only all the errors involved in the computation of the indices of V' but all those likewise in the computation of all the other series. Moreover, its movements are further distorted by the absorption of all the inaccuracies resulting from the varying lags of the series one with another, and from the lack of coincidence in times of purchases and payments. Its movements should therefore prove of much interest. If, in spite of so manifold an opportunity for distortion, its movements still bear any resemblance to what those of a velocity of circulation could reasonably be expected to be, confidence in the validity of the other indices should be much enhanced.

By comparing the curves pictured in Chart LX, it will be seen that the new corrected index of average velocities of circulation moves, with very few exceptions, as would be expected of a curve of velocities. The movements are perhaps too even and its fluctuations not wide or frequent enough for an index of velocities of de-

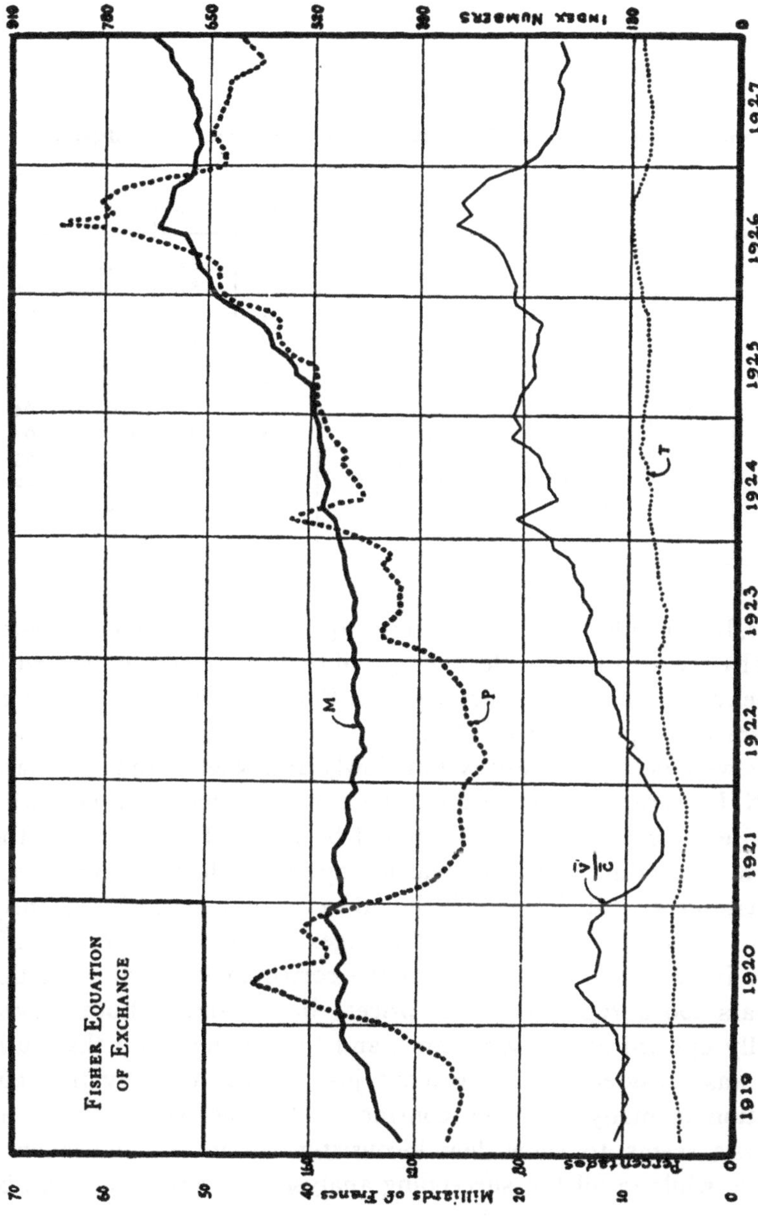
Fisher Equation
of Exchange
Index Numbers
Milliards of Francs
Percentages
M
P
T
1919
1920
1921
1922
1923
1924
1925
1926
1927

CHART LX

TABLE 91

$$\frac{\bar{V}'}{C}$$

(Corrected monthly indices of combined velocities of money and of deposits)

	1919	1920	1921	1922	1923	1924	1925	1926	1927
Jan.	.44	.52	.40	.34	.53	.75	.82	.83	.76
Feb.	.42	.53	.35	.34	.55	.82	.81	.85	.73
Mar.	.40	.57	.32	.39	.56	.74	.79	.86	.69
Apr.	.40	.59	.29	.38	.54	.66	.76	.89	.68
May	.39	.51	.26	.41	.53	.70	.75	.92	.67
June	.40	.50	.26	.41	.56	.70	.76	.97	.66
July	.43	.49	.26	.42	.56	.73	.75	1.05	.64
Aug.	.40	.51	.27	.44	.58	.74	.75	1.00	.67
Sept.	.39	.53	.27	.44	.59	.79	.73	1.03	.65
Oct.	.41	.52	.26	.47	.62	.84	.77	.98	.62
Nov.	.42	.47	.30	.51	.67	.81	.83	.92	.63
Dec.	.44	.47	.33	.51	.68	.83	.85	.81	.65

posits, but such fluctuations could be expected to be smoothed somewhat by the inclusion, in the average, of the velocities of money with the heavy weights which they carry in France. One or two strange movements appear. From December 1921 to February 1922, when prices were declining steadily but slowly and when k and k' (Chapter XII) were both increasing, the corrected index of velocities likewise increased slowly. It should be noted, however, that the volume of production was increasing rapidly at the same time, and, at least in the United States, it should be remembered, V' frequently follows in its minor movements changes in the volume of trade.[29] Early in 1919 also the decline in the corrected index of velocities appears too abrupt for that in prices; but k and k' both moved rapidly upward at the same time, and there is no doubt that business was considerably disorganized just at that time by the cancellation of many war-time contracts. On the whole, therefore, analysis seems to show few inconsistencies in its movements. Hence, while in all the succeeding analyses its movements will be

[29] *Cf.* unpublished records of the Department of Research and Statistics of the Federal Reserve Bank of New York.

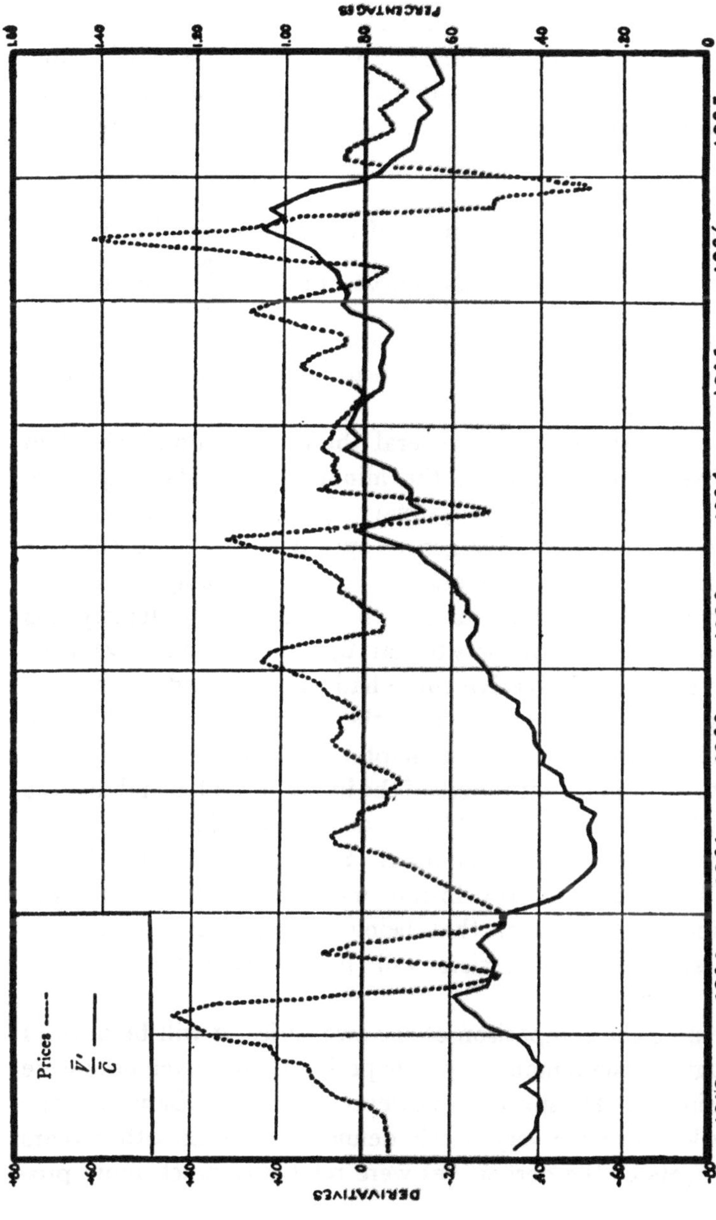

CHART LXI

Fisher Derivative of Prices and $\frac{\bar{V}'}{C}$

carefully checked against those of k and k', the new series will be used as an indicator of the combined movements of V and V'. But, most important of all, the analysis may be continued with greatly enhanced confidence in the accuracy of the indices of the remaining series.

A comparison will next be made of the new index of combined velocities with the first derivative curve of prices $\frac{dp}{dt}$. In order to facilitate the undertaking, three-month moving averages of the latter curve have been plotted instead of the month-to-month derivatives (Chart LXI).

It will be noticed that in general the movements of the two series are very similar. Even the minor movements frequently appear in both series. From January 1921 until January 1922, however, very important divergences appear. Beginning early in 1921 the derivative of prices started climbing rapidly, while the new index of velocities for four months declined but slightly less rapidly and then leveled out only to start upward again in November, one month after the derivative curve had again started downward. By turning, as a matter of check, to the curves of k and k' (to be defined and discussed in the next chapter), it will be seen that their movements correspond with those of the index of the V's and diverge completely from those indicated by the derivatives of prices. Hence, some special explanation is required. Since, however, the movements of k and k' naturally inspire more confidence than those of so artificial an index as that being used for the movements of the V's, further discussion will be deferred to the next chapter.

In pursuing the comparison of the two series, it will be noticed that throughout the remainder of the period their movements were generally similar. During 1922, however, the minor changes of the index of velocities were very poorly defined, and in the other years the movements of the derivatives were relatively much more pronounced.

One further observation which will be found usable in arriving at the explanation given in the next chapter can be made. In late 1919, when the derivatives of prices were moving rapidly upward, the index of velocities increased comparatively slowly. This latter movement of the average of the velocities, however, will be found to correspond exactly with the diverse movements of k and k' calculated for the same period and used in the comparisons described in the following chapter. Weight is thereby added to the indicated necessity of the special explanation there set forth.

CHAPTER XII

THEORETICAL ANALYSIS (*continued*)

KEYNES MONETARY EQUATION

IN the last chapter certain of the important series connected with the inflation process in France were analyzed from the standpoint of the Fisher equation of exchange. In the present chapter the same data will be attacked with the use of the Keynes monetary equation. This equation, unlike that of Irving Fisher, which deals with periods of time, rates of turnover, total flows and average magnitudes, represents instantaneous cross-sections of the monetary situation. It is hoped, therefore, that an analysis made with its aid will throw new light on the important happenings of the period under consideration.

The equation is written in the form:

$$N = p(k + rk')$$

and represents little more than the instantaneous divisions of the monetary supplies of the country. It is an identity, and consequently all discussion relative to its truth or falsity is simply beside the point. The question of importance is: Is it of any use? As to its value for the purpose of analyzing the data under consideration, the reader will be better able to judge as the discussion proceeds.

The terms of the equation may be defined[1] as follows:

N = the total money in the country outside the vaults of the Bank of France.[2]

p = the index of prices used as an indicator by inversion of the purchasing power of money to a group as varied as the

[1] A very slight change in Keynes's definitions has been made in order better to adapt the equation to French institutions and to French data.

[2] Hoarded gold and silver have for all practical purposes ceased to be money and are accordingly excluded.

population itself. In the present investigation the general index of wholesale prices is used for the simple reason that there is no other available measure.[3]

k = the number of purchasing-power units[4] carried by the entire population and its organizations (other than the banks) in the form of cash. (The small Treasury holdings are included.) Numerically, it will be taken as the total amount of money in circulation divided by the general index of wholesale prices of the *Statistique Générale de la France* reduced to a 1913 base.[5]

k' = the number of similar purchasing-power units carried by the population and its organizations as deposit accounts subject to check in the banks and banking institutions.

r = the ratio of reserves of actual cash kept by the banks to their outstanding demand deposits subject to check.[6]

With these definitions before him, it will be entirely obvious to the reader that the algebraic equation above written is a mathematical identity.

Statistical series of the various quantities — N, k, k', and p — have been computed monthly[7] for France during the entire period

[3] Any index of prices suitable for any one individual or for any group of persons is preposterous for all taken together. Each of us is personally interested in the purchasing power of our money over the goods for which we spend it. To an ordinary investigator of economic subjects living modestly on his charity-endowed earnings, the purchasing power of the dollar, meaning, as it does, the capacity for securing food, clothing, books, shelter, and a few other worth-while things of life is certainly an entirely different sort of concept from that to the financial managers of the Steel Corporation buying alike unskilled labor, crude mineral products, and the scientific intelligence of the world.

[4] On account of fluctuating price levels, the dollar in 1927 represents an entirely different amount of purchasing power from a dollar in 1913 or from that in almost any other year chosen at random. In order, therefore, to establish a standard unit of measure for so important a magnitude, the device of purchasing power units has been resorted to. Such units represent in terms of commodities in general the purchasing power of the monetary unit over commodities, not at prevailing prices, but at those which held during some earlier year chosen as a base.

[5] For the detailed description of this index and the method of its conversion, see Chap. V, Table 7.

[6] It is assumed that no actual cash reserves are held against deposits not subject to check. The error in such an assumption is probably negligible.

[7] The data for each are for approximately the ends of months.

1914–1927, and in their compilation the data used and the methods of computation employed were selected to accord as nearly as possible with the above definitions.

For N the total volume of Bank of France notes outstanding on selected end-of-month dates was used.[8]

For p the monthly wholesale indices of the *Statistique Générale de la France* were used without modification.[9]

For k it was necessary first to estimate the total money in the hands of the public at the end of each month. These estimates were made by subtracting from the totals of the Bank of France notes outstanding at the end of each month[10] the estimated amounts of cash actually held by the banks as reserves and till-money against their demand deposits.[11] The remainders were divided by the indices, for corresponding dates, of the wholesale price index of the *Statistique Générale de la France.*

For k' the estimated[12] total deposits subject to check in French banks at the end of each month were divided by the wholesale price indices for the ends of corresponding months.

For r the ratio 3 per cent[13] was taken.

The movements of the monthly series thus obtained are represented in the accompanying graph (Chart LXII).

In spite of the relative undependability of the data of money in circulation during 1914 and 1915 and in spite of the infrequency of the reports of deposits during those years, reference to the movements of k and k' shows very clearly the great change which came about in the monetary habits of the French public at the outbreak of the war. There is no doubt whatever that after the declaration of the moratorium on deposits,[14] not only did hoarding

[8] The reason for the selection of dates is set forth in Chap. V, Table 9. The infeasibility of correcting the series to allow for the metallic money in circulation is discussed in Chap. XI, pp. 284–285 and accompanying note.

[9] The data actually employed are the index numbers of the *Statistique Générale de la France* on the base 100 in 1913 as published in the *League of Nations Bulletin of Statistics.*

[10] Selected end-of-month data were used for reasons given in Chap. V, Table 9.

[11] See Chap. XI, pp. 284–285 and accompanying note.

[12] The method of arriving at these estimates is described in Chap. XI, pp. 285–287.

[13] See Chap. XI, pp. 284–285 and the accompanying footnote.

[14] See Chap. IX, p. 221, footnote 6.

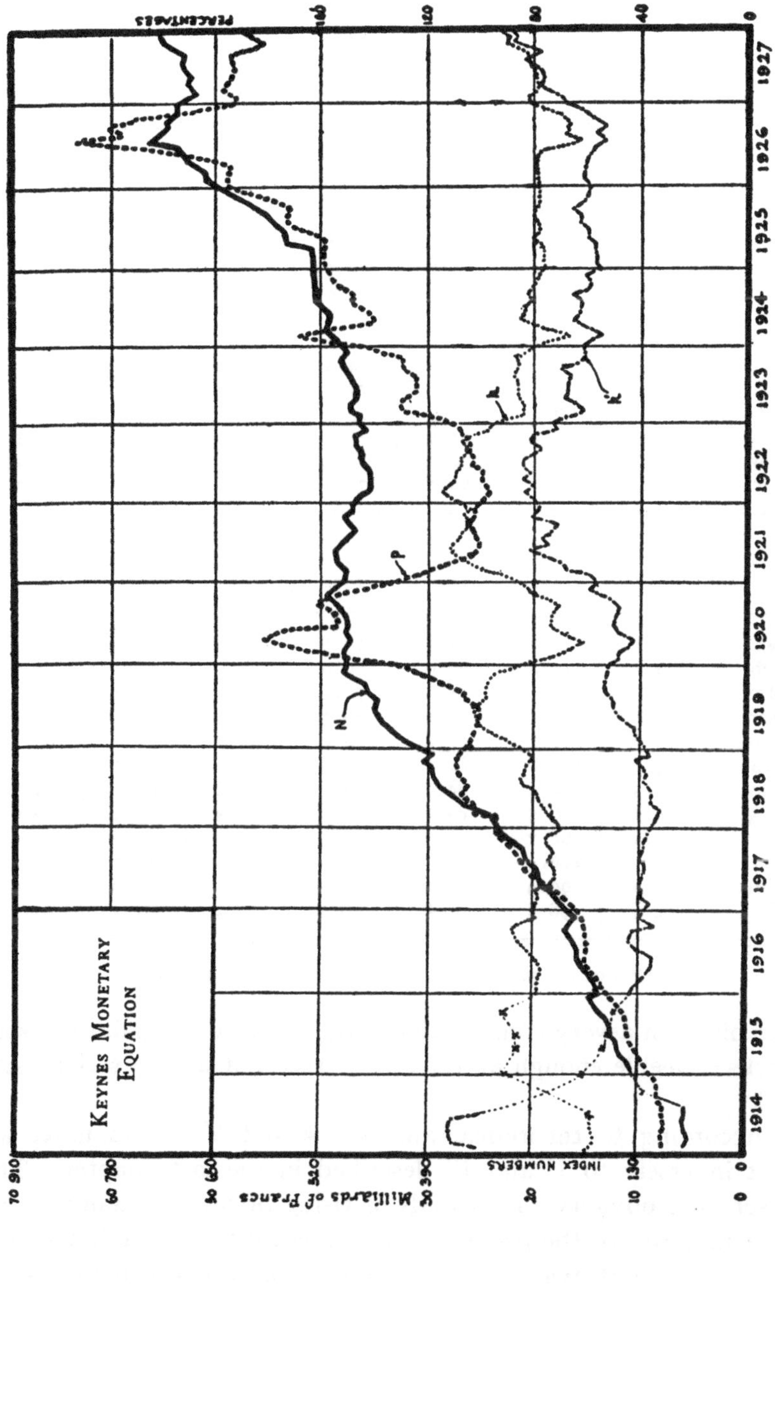
Keynes Monetary
Equation
PERCENTAGES
INDEX NUMBERS
Milliards of Francs
1914
1915
1916
1917
1918
1919
1920
1921
1922
1923
1924
1925
1926
1927
N
P
k
k'

CHART LXII

TABLE 92

k

(Estimated values for end-of-month dates; hundreds of millions of 1913 francs) *

	1914	1915	1916	1917	1918	1919	1920
Jan.	56.5	....	79.0	79.3	73.0	90.3	75.7
Feb.	54.4	....	79.2	78.1	74.1	94.2	71.1
Mar.	54.4	....	78.7	79.5	76.0	99.4	66.4
Apr.	55.5	85.2	78.9	75.4	78.1	100.9	62.2
May	55.0	....	80.0	74.6	79.6	103.5	67.5
June	55.9	86.6	82.2	73.3	85.8	103.2	74.6
July	....	....	85.9	74.3	85.3	98.7	74.5
Aug.	....	....	86.8	74.6	83.0	99.3	74.1
Sept.	....	90.7	87.3	73.8	83.1	97.7	72.1
Oct.	....	....	84.9	75.4	84.1	94.7	76.3
Nov.	....	....	79.6	75.3	80.1	90.8	82.4
Dec.	89.0	79.6	80.8	72.3	84.6	86.6	84.3

	1921	1922	1923	1924	1925	1926	1927
Jan.	91.3	113.6	92.9	75.8	77.0	78.0	81.7
Feb.	98.1	115.4	85.9	69.8	77.5	78.3	79.6
Mar.	103.9	112.3	85.8	78.1	77.9	79.6	78.6
Apr.	107.8	111.5	86.2	86.5	81.4	78.1	79.7
May	113.6	110.1	87.4	84.0	80.3	74.8	80.1
June	113.1	107.8	87.7	83.3	77.4	70.1	81.3
July	109.5	108.4	88.7	81.4	77.5	65.3	82.6
Aug.	108.8	106.5	87.8	82.0	78.3	69.9	82.9
Sept.	105.1	108.7	86.7	81.2	80.0	67.6	87.1
Oct.	109.7	106.4	87.6	79.6	79.6	70.8	90.5
Nov.	107.2	99.4	82.0	78.5	77.5	76.0	89.9
Dec.	109.6	98.2	80.8	78.3	77.2	81.4	91.0

* For the method of computation see text, p. 315.

take place on a very considerable scale, but also the habit of using checks — feeble enough at its best — received a very serious setback.

According to theoretical analyses k and k' should move almost inversely to V and V' described in the last chapter. The reasons are obvious. In periods of rising prices, for example, the great majority of the people can be expected to change but slowly their habits with regard to the amounts of cash which they keep

TABLE 93

k'

(Estimated values for end-of-month dates; hundreds of millions of 1913 francs) *

	1914	1915	1916	1917	1918	1919	1920
Jan.	101.0	....	40.5	37.1	35.2	40.3	49.3
Feb.	110.1	....	39.3	39.9	34.4	41.1	49.8
Mar.	110.6	....	37.7	39.3	33.6	41.7	45.1
Apr.	111.4	52.6	36.7	40.3	36.0	45.2	44.3
May	110.4	....	36.8	39.1	35.8	49.2	49.1
June	100.7	50.9	42.5	37.6	36.5	51.7	52.8
July	....	....	43.4	37.3	38.5	51.6	52.5
Aug.	....	....	43.0	40.7	37.1	54.7	51.9
Sept.	....	48.4	42.4	39.3	39.4	55.6	51.4
Oct.	....	....	36.3	38.8	41.7	55.0	53.8
Nov.	....	....	40.5	37.5	36.3	54.3	60.8
Dec.	63.3	42.9	39.3	36.1	36.8	54.4	59.8

	1921	1922	1923	1924	1925	1926	1927
Jan.	63.9	82.9	72.4	60.7	58.3	64.7	72.4
Feb.	68.9	84.9	64.0	57.0	58.3	64.5	74.4
Mar.	69.5	81.3	63.7	62.1	58.4	63.3	78.0
Apr.	74.9	86.1	65.1	66.7	58.5	63.1	77.0
May	82.0	82.1	68.9	65.4	61.6	62.5	78.0
June	76.9	83.1	68.5	64.5	60.8	59.6	80.3
July	78.8	83.1	68.8	64.4	62.9	55.0	83.9
Aug.	75.5	78.5	67.8	67.1	62.8	58.5	77.7
Sept.	72.7	82.0	70.8	61.8	66.6	55.9	81.6
Oct.	81.5	80.0	66.6	60.4	64.7	61.2	86.8
Nov.	78.4	73.8	63.2	61.6	62.8	64.3	85.8
Dec.	79.8	74.6	63.2	57.2	61.7	70.3	86.1

* For the method of computation, see text, p. 315.

on hand. Prices that are usually paid in cash, as we have seen before, are among those which lag most in both the rise and the fall. Hence there is no need for enlarged cash holdings until some time after the rise in wholesale prices has begun. Perhaps, too, most people have to get "caught" a time or two without enough pocket change before they are jarred free from so firmly fixed a notion as that twenty dollars is enough for a man to carry around in his pocket. Under falling prices a similar inertia in adjusting cash holding habits to the changes in the price level brings about opposite movements in k. One only gradually becomes aware of the fact that he is carrying more cash than is necessary. Consequently k rises. For reasons less potent and less certain, k' can be expected to move similarly to k.

For readers more familiar with the equation of exchange analyses it should perhaps be remarked that the explanations given above of the movements of k and k' inverse to those of changes in prices are almost identical with ones which might have been given for the movements of V and V' similar to those of changes in prices. When expenditures increase or decrease while cash and deposits on hand temporarily fail to change in like proportions, V and V' necessarily move in the same direction as prices.

A study of the movements of the two series in France during the period 1914–1927 reveals that in general, when prices moved upward, k and k' moved downward and vice versa. There were, however, certain exceptions, and, since it is the exception rather than the rule which often yields the more interesting story, they will be investigated with care.

First, it will be noticed that the k' series, which at the end of June 1914 was very much above that of k, dropped rapidly to a level much below it as soon as the war broke out. In fact, by the beginning of 1916 the items of the deposits series had become reduced to but little more than half those of the cash series. Thereafter the curves kept approximately a constant distance apart and moved almost exactly similarly until May 1919, when they began again to converge rapidly. By the spring of 1920 the two curves were again fairly close together. The separation increased, however, in 1921 and in 1922 and then lessened gradually in the succeeding four years and very rapidly in 1927. Throughout the entire period after the end of 1915 their minor movements were, nevertheless, strikingly similar.

What explanation can be given for this unexpected variety of movements? The great change in the relative magnitudes of k and k' at the beginning of the war seems, as was mentioned above, to indicate clearly not only the changed attitude of the public toward the bank check but also its readiness to hoard cash coming into its possession. The continued high level of k and the low level of k' attest to the disinclination of many to give up either position.

But why should the two series begin to converge so rapidly after April 1919? By referring to the unaltered data of money in circulation and of deposits subject to check discussed in the last chapter (Chart LVII, page 290), it will be seen that the separation was a result almost exclusively of a rise in deposits rather than of a fall in circulation. With this in view it will be seen clearly that until October 1919 deposits were actually increasing faster than by enough to counterbalance the rise in prices and that only after the beginning of 1920 did their further rise conform with price movements. If the comparatively slight increase in the volume of business (Charts XXXI, XXXII, XXXIII, and XXXIV, pages 174, 175, 177 and 178) during this period may be neglected, it may be said with substantial accuracy that only after September 1919 did business spending play even a perceptible rôle in causing the price rise and that only after the end of the year did it begin to play one on an equality with that of the Government in the further progress of the inflation. The extraordinary character of the above deductions demands perhaps a fuller explanation.

This much seems obvious. The rapid rise in deposits which began early in 1919 (while perhaps very slightly connected with the moderate increase in production at that time) seems to be almost exclusively a result of the large advances of the Bank of France to the State. As was observed earlier in this study (Chart III, page 53) and commented upon at length in Chapter IX, such advances increased greatly in 1919, especially during the first part of the year. Representing, as they did, expenditures by the Government of new and entirely inflationary funds, in flowing to the banks they inevitably caused deposits to swell greatly. The resulting accumulation of funds, being temporarily unclaimed by business borrowers, was turned to the alternative use of purchasing short-term Treasury obligations. Once more in the possession of the Government, that they were almost immediately re-spent is indicated by the fact that the Treasury continued to increase rapidly its borrowings from the Bank of France. Coming again, in turn, to the banks, they again swelled deposits, and the swelling process continued until the funds were absorbed by business and other demands. There seems little doubt, therefore, that the continued rise in k' after April 1919, while k was decreasing, was a result of this kind of an accumulation of deposits. By the end of August 1919, however, the rise in prices had become extremely rapid, and after September k' began falling slightly, but not nearly so fast as k. Only after the beginning of 1920 did the movements of k' again come into their normal correspondence with those of k. Only then, therefore, can it be said that k' was no longer being dominated by the extraordinary cash deposits growing out of the peculiar methods of finance employed by the Government combined with the peculiar character of the Paris money market. And only then, therefore, did deposits begin to play their normal rôle in the continued business and price expansion.

The increase in the private advances of the Bank of France beginning gradually in September 1919 and becoming very rapid after November of that year,[15] as well as the somewhat delayed rise in the rates on *reports*,[16] lend support to the above contentions. With the drop in prices that came after April 1920 both k and k' increased rapidly.

In the succeeding prosperity period from late 1922 until the end of 1924, during which time the direct advances of the Bank to the State were actually reduced (though indirect ones were several times resorted to), k and k' moved similarly and in almost exactly parallel directions, though the gradual reduction toward pre-war levels in the public's holdings of cash purchasing power diminished slightly their separation.

The very great increase in the advances of the Bank to the State, beginning early in 1925, by again increasing rapidly deposits at the banks, caused the k' series again to move toward that of k. Furthermore, the gradual rise of k' during the middle months of that year in a period of generally rising prices, while k was practically constant, shows very clearly indeed that at that time

[15] See Chap. VIII, Chart XXX, p. 169 and the accompanying discussion.
[16] See Chap. IX, Chart XLIII, p. 230 and the accompanying discussion.

the impetus toward inflation was coming from government financial methods[17] rather than from business buying. The more normal decline of k' thereafter until the middle of 1926 indicates equally clearly that private spending and borrowing were again playing more important rôles.

After July 1926 the fast developing business depression, with the resulting accumulation of idle funds in the banks, would alone have been sufficient to cause a considerable further convergence of the two series under discussion, but, when there were added the funds arising from the heavy purchases of foreign exchange by the Bank of France,[18] the very close convergence in 1927 causes no surprise.

In the study of k and k' thus far made it was intimated on several occasions that their movements were very closely connected with the rapidity of the changes, either up or down, of prices. A comparison will next be made, therefore, of each of these series with the first derivative[19] of the index of prices (Chart LXIII).

By comparing the movements of k and k' with those of the first derivative of prices it will be seen that the inverse correlation between the k curves on the one hand and the derivative curve on the other is very clearly defined. Even the minor movements of the k curves almost invariably carry counter movements in the other. There is a tendency, however, for the movements of k and k' to lag slightly behind those of $\frac{dp}{dt}$. A striking divergence from the inverse movements appears in 1921 during a period of gradually more slowly falling prices. Under such circumstances the first derivative of prices was naturally rising. But at the same time k and k' also rose. The explanation is that, although prices had been falling for a considerable period, money

[17] This statement is not inconsistent with the small lags discovered for this period between the movements of prices behind exchange rates or with the explanations given in Chapter VI. Naturally, in the tense political situations of 1925 and 1926, much of the speculation in exchange preceded the easily foreseen increases in the borrowings of the State from the Bank of France.

[18] See Chap. VIII, pp. 182–185.

[19] A three-month moving average (centered) of the derivatives was used.

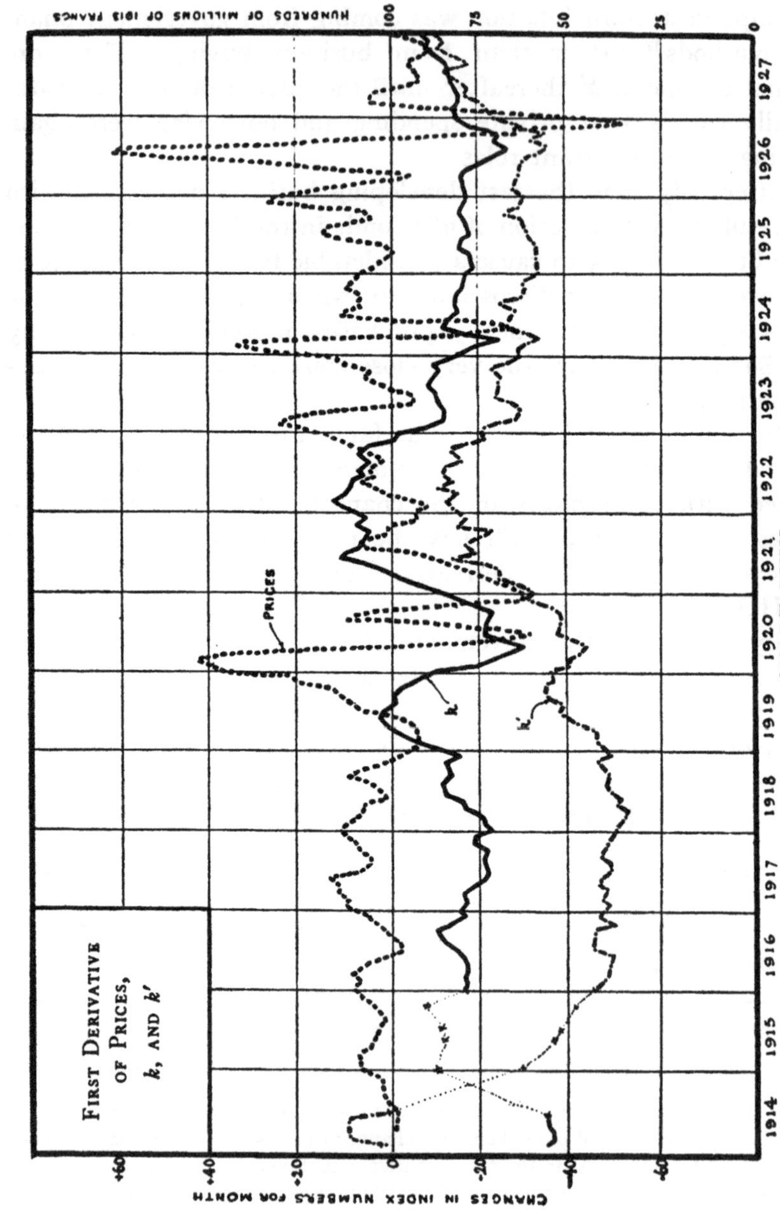
FIRST DERIVATIVE OF PRICES, k, AND k′
PRICES
k
k′
HUNDREDS OF MILLIONS OF 1913 FRANCS
100
75
50
25
0
1914
1915
1916
1917
1918
1919
1920
1921
1922
1923
1924
1925
1926
1927
+60
+40
+20
0
-20
-40
-60
CHANGES IN INDEX NUMBERS FOR MONTH

CHART LXIII

in circulation was very slow in being reduced and deposits showed no tendency toward reduction at all. Hence the divergences can be explained by the hoarding habits of the French public and by the peculiar character of deposits — already described at length in Chapter XI — which kept them from decreasing. That this explanation is the proper one is further indicated by the fact that, while the magnitudes of the falls of k and k' were generally about equal to the corresponding rises of $\frac{dp}{dt}$, those of the rises in response to falls in $\frac{dp}{dt}$ were usually much slighter.

One additional significant result may be derived from the analysis with the use of the derivative curve. In the latter half of 1919, as has already been pointed out, k' continued to move upward while k turned downward. By examining the inverse movement of the derivative of prices it can be concluded at once that the movements of k were the normal ones. An investigation of k' yields the interesting story outlined above (pp. 321–322) that the whole movement was being financed by the large borrowings of the State from the Bank of France.

CHAPTER XIII

THE PRESENT FINANCIAL SITUATION IN FRANCE JANUARY 1928

BEFORE closing this report of the Process of Inflation in France, something should be said with regard to the applicability of the findings to the present financial situation. For this purpose first a very brief review of some of the financial events leading up to the crisis of July 1926 will be attempted. Then will be described equally briefly certain of the outstanding changes in the financial situation which followed the advent to power of the famous Poincaré Ministry. Finally will be added a few words with regard to certain elements of strength and of weakness in the existing (January 1928) situation.

Early in 1925, it will be remembered, the value of the franc in the foreign exchange centres of the world began its steepest and most long-continued decline. Not only had the chaotic political conditions rendered extremely uncertain the financial status of the Treasury itself, but at this juncture also appeared the disturbing revelations on the floor of the Senate of misrepresentations in its published statements of certain extra-legal operations by the Bank of France. In the face of the dire government necessity this highly respected institution had been led, by the use of a subterfuge, again to extend indirect advances to the State in excess of the maximum allowed by law and, in so doing, was forced a little later to increase its note circulation likewise beyond its legal maximum. Moreover, a capital levy seemed continually more imminent.

Under such circumstances it is not surprising that foreign selling of francs should again start, or, what is more important, that the "flight from the franc" on the part of frightened French investors should take on disturbing proportions. Hence the depreciation of French exchange continued to move at a generally accelerated rate.

Following the upward movements of dollar and other stable money exchange rates, usually at an interval of somewhat less than a month, prices likewise rose rapidly, carrying with them the almost inevitable stimulus to business as well as the altogether certain distress to those living on small and fixed incomes. But more important still were the effects on government finances and, consequently, on the continuation of the whole movement itself. Much of the capital being exported was that hitherto invested in government securities. Thus arose the increasing demands for repayment of government obligations as the movement grew in volume and in intensity. The data of the excess of reimbursements over emissions of short-term Treasury paper (Table 72, Chapter IX, page 233) indicate the effect of this influence.

But even this is not all. The condition of the Treasury was further aggravated by the growing business prosperity itself. It will be remembered that until the reorganization of the *Caisse Autonome d'Amortissement* into its present form (October 1, 1926) the Treasury was accustomed to receive a considerable portion of its working funds from subscriptions to short-term government paper, as more recently from the direct deposit of funds in the Treasury itself. It will be remembered, too, that the banks were not only large subscribers to such obligations, which were issued daily in any amounts desired, but were also the most important of the depositors in the Treasury. In fact, they were at times responsible for most of the funds thus received by the Government. With the development of business activity, the banks, to take care of the demands of their customers, were obliged to withdraw most of their funds loaned in either way to the Treasury. As a consequence the Treasury was in turn forced to increase its borrowings from the Bank of France, and such advances accordingly increased rapidly. With the increase in advances of the Bank to the State, partly as cause and partly as effect, went a corresponding increase in note circulation: as cause in so far as the withdrawals from the Treasury were increasing the advances of the Bank to the State and as effect in so far as the new advances were in turn causing new notes to be drawn into circulation.

With the precarious position of the Treasury thus being continually aggravated, the political situation grew more and more strained. And the increasing uncertainty furnished to the disillusioned French investors a more and more powerful incentive to escape — illegally though it were — from the impending ruin, while to the Central European speculator it presented another golden opportunity to profit at the expense of his country's most hated enemy. Thus each fall in the franc set in motion forces destined almost inevitably to bring about another fall. The process, once set going, not only found no resistance to its movement, but itself exerted influences causing it to gather momentum as it went.

During all this period of rapid exchange-rate and price movements and of dramatic political happenings, short-term interest rates continued low and generally declining until May 1926. With new funds being continually put out in large quantities by the Bank of France, it was hardly possible for them to rise materially. Long-term interest rates, on the other hand, moved rapidly and continually upward, showing clearly the increasing borrowing difficulties of business as well as of the Government in a period of fast waning confidence in the position of the franc.

Under these disquieting circumstances Poincaré assumed control at the head of his renowned National Union Cabinet. While he apparently had to "encourage" his measures through Parliament by a general increase in salaries, no such primitive form of inducement was required to win the support of the people. His reputation for irreproachable honesty and his scrupulous regard of the Constitution and of the law seemed to stimulate sufficiently wide-spread confidence to afford the much needed period of respite during which constructive legislation could be passed and be put into operation.

Old taxes were raised, new ones imposed, and all taxpayers were asked to pay in advance their direct assessments, while the venerable *Caisse d'Amortissement*, with much pomp and ceremony, was reorganized into its present form and charged with the duty of applying certain specialized revenues to the amortization and retirement of the floating debt of the State. The increase in revenue from the new taxes, as well as the reduction in the floating debt by the *Caisse d'Amortissement*, were, however, in the future. What was of immediate importance in addition to the passage of legislation promising future benefits, provided the franc could be kept from further depreciation long enough for the benefits to accrue, was to prevent the further depreciation. This the initial confidence in the Poincaré Government, coupled with that added by its success in getting the beneficial measures passed, seemed to accomplish.

Almost immediately the franc ceased its decline and began to rise, at first rapidly, then more gradually, and finally more rapidly again as the movement gained momentum. As soon as it began to appear that the movement was not merely a temporary one, two important influences tending to make the recovery more rapid came into play. Foreign speculators who had sold francs for future delivery began to cover their sales by buying "spot" francs, and frightened French investors, who a few months previously were hurriedly converting their funds from francs into dollars or pounds, just as hurriedly and with equal fright began to reconvert them into francs. So this movement also gained momentum as it progressed.

Accompanying the improvement in French exchange came a number of other movements, some the direct results of the exchange movements themselves, others growing out of the return of confidence — itself in no small part a result of the continued rise in the value of the franc and of the partially resultant movements of other important economic factors.

In August 1926 alone the excess of emissions over reimbursements of Treasury paper reached the substantial total of 1340 millions of francs, as opposed to an excess of reimbursements of 2110 millions in July. Moreover, with one exception, there was a continued excess of emissions during each of the remaining months of the year. That one exception proves as interesting as the general movement itself. Occurring, as it did, in the one period during which the franc had again shown weakness, it indicates clearly how significant had become the movements of exchange in their effects on government finances and how important it was, therefore, that further depreciation should be avoided.

Along with the increase in subscriptions to short-term Treasury obligations came a corresponding decrease in the advances of the Bank of France to the State. And, with the reduced spending accompanying the enlarged investing in government obligations, prices (perhaps even more largely influenced, too, by the movements of exchange themselves) began likewise to fall. Moreover, with the fall in prices came a reduced volume of business. And, with a reduced volume of business being transacted at continually lower prices, a somewhat correspondingly reduced quantity of circulating media was required for its handling. The surplus funds were either invested directly by their holders in government obligations or were deposited by them in the Treasury, or else they flowed naturally to the banks, which used them for the same purposes. In any event the return flow to the Treasury continued as long as these potent forces continued their significant actions. With the new cash thus received, a new reduction in the advances of the Bank to the State was accomplished, the reduction, in turn, giving new cause for increasing confidence in the Government and in its policies. And this ever growing confidence brought to the already sleepless speculator in francs increasing alarm and to the faithless French capital exporter and to his abetting institutions an ever more haunting shame. Thus this movement, too, once set in motion, continued to cumulate and to gain impetus as it progressed.

By October 1926 the situation had sufficiently improved to permit of the flotation of a seven per cent forty-year loan to retire a little over three milliards of *Bons de la Défense Nationale* and in December an additional ten-year loan was floated to take care of 1293 millions of bonds of the *Crédit National* which had been deposited for payment in February. This loan was likewise placed, however, at the high rate of seven per cent.

So marked and so rapid had become the recovery of French exchange by December 1926 that some action seemed necessary to prevent a further damaging rise. Not only had the drastic increase in the value of the franc in foreign markets had a very serious effect on certain export industries in France, but a further rise threatened to bring the already growing business depression to disastrous proportions. Accordingly, on December 23, 1926, the Bank of France under the authorization provided in the Act of August 7 made its entrance into the foreign exchange market as a purchaser of foreign currencies. The desired effect of arresting the upward movement of the franc was immediately attained, and since that time dollar exchange has fluctuated within very narrow limits around the value of 25.50 francs to the dollar.

The policy adopted for the purpose of avoiding a disastrous rise in the franc, however, has had other important effects on the financial conditions not only of the Government and of the Bank of France, but also of the banks and to a certain extent of business firms and of the public. In making the purchases the Bank of France inevitably put into the market entirely new funds just as does the Bank of England or any one of the Federal Reserve Banks in its purchases of commercial paper or of government securities on the open market. These funds issued in payment for foreign exchange fell into the hands sometimes of exporters and of others receiving due payments from abroad, but under the existing circumstances much more largely into those of persons bringing back their previously exported holdings for reinvestment in France or, on an increasingly large scale during the late winter and spring of 1927, into the hands of agents of foreign purchasers of the fast appreciating securities on the Paris Bourse.

Under such circumstances, since funds expended for existing securities do not in general stimulate a long train of further purchases — as is usually the case when goods or services are bought — most of the funds became idle again as soon as they had been exchanged once against the securities transferred. As always they inevitably drifted in large part to the banks. Hence, both deposits and cash holdings of the receiving banks were correspondingly swelled.

In the face of the stringent restrictions against the export of capital, which since the advent to power of the Poincaré Government had been much more scrupulously observed, and in the continued absence of an enlarged business demand for funds, the banks had little choice but to trust their funds to the Government either through the purchase of its obligations or by direct deposit in the Treasury, or else themselves to join the group speculating in the purchase of the apparently attractive Bourse securities. That they did both is evidenced by the continued rise, throughout most of the spring, of security prices as well as of deposits in the banks and in the Treasury. Because of the fact that beginning in December 1926, the issue of *Bons de la Défense Nationale* was being gradually discontinued[1] and because to the extent that funds were spent for outstanding securities they returned quickly to the banks, such deposits in the Treasury continued to assume larger and larger proportions.

All of these happenings just described had wrought marvelous changes in the apparent condition of the Treasury. The large subscriptions to government obligations as well as the growing volume of deposits in the Treasury provided the means for a very significant reduction in the advances of the Bank of France to the State. After February 1927 two other long-term (fifty-year) refunding loans aggregating almost 3 milliards of francs were placed by the Government at net rates of 6.98 per cent and 6.67 per cent respectively, as opposed to 8.67 per cent and 8.51 per cent respectively for the ones preceding. Moreover, the gradual suppression of the shorter-term *Bons de la Défense Nationale* had by July 29, 1927 left in circulation only one- and two-year paper, and by June 2, 1928 there will continue in circulation only those originally issued with two-year maturities. Between June 1928 and January 1929 there will be no maturities of these now historic trouble-makers.

By May 1927 it was a matter of general observation that life in Paris had taken on a more nearly normal aspect than had been known since the outbreak of hostilities in 1914.

Meanwhile, however, short-term interest rates had become extremely low, and the banks began justly to complain bitterly of the narrow limits of the money market in which, because of the stringent restrictions against the export of capital, they were forced to operate. In view of the fact, therefore, that by midsummer 1927 the holdings of foreign exchange by the Bank of France had reached the substantial total of some 20 milliards

[1] See Chap. V, p. 71, footnote 12.

of francs, an important revision of the capital export restrictions was granted. While the laws have been in no way amended, by special permission of the Government a sort of temporary export of capital has been arranged between the banks on one hand and the Bank of France on the other. Under this special arrangement, which is revokable at any time at the pleasure of the Government, a bank desiring to invest funds *temporarily* in London or New York, for example, may do so by approaching the Bank of France and buying the necessary exchange. When the demand exchange is sold to the requesting banker, however, the Bank of France will require him at the same time to sell to it for *forward* delivery (of not more than ninety days) an equivalent sum of dollars or pounds. In this way the banker is forced to bring back to Paris within ninety days and to reconvert into francs funds thus invested. And, since the forward dollars (or pounds) are not paid for until delivered, the Bank of France meanwhile suffers no further extension of its credit. In the practical operation of the arrangement forward contracts can naturally be renewed from time to time, and hence the funds may be kept in the foreign centre as long as there is no reason why they should be brought back to Paris. Thus, while the present superabundance of funds continues to exist in the Paris market, the banks are allowed to profit by the higher rates in other centres, and the Government is at the same time completely protected against a damaging outflow of capital. By these measures, too, the burden of preventing a further rise in the franc has been largely transferred from the Bank of France to the other banking institutions.

Such are some of the outstanding features of the existing (January 1928) financial and monetary situation in France. What are its elements of strength, and what are the dangers — if any — which threaten its continuance? Certainly, in spite of the continued business depression, the betterment in the economic life of the entire French people since July 1926 has been nothing short of remarkable. Moreover, very substantial progress indeed has been made toward safeguarding the situation against a relapse into that existing prior to the coming to power of the present Government. As a guarantee against a further fall in French exchange the Bank of France has in addition to its large holdings of gold (somewhat increased over their high pre-war level) approximately 22 milliards of foreign exchange. Certainly any temporary tendency toward depreciation could be arrested with the aid of a fund of such magnitude. Also, as is explained in detail later in this chapter, the floating debt has been brought — in the absence of extraordinary happenings — to manageable proportions. Moreover, the price level has adjusted itself downward to substantial equilibrium with the international value of the franc without occasioning too severe business depression. Nevertheless, these changes have come about through such an extraordinary combination of circumstances that it cannot but prove fruitful to inquire into the effects of possible changes in some of the fundamental conditions which have contributed to its creation.

To begin with the most obviously likely happening, suppose, for example, that, under the extraordinarily easy money conditions which have now existed for more than a year and which have been intensified recently by the disinclination of the Treasury to encourage further deposits, a considerable increase in business activity should appear. As has been observed earlier in this investigation, such an increase in activity, causing serious embarassment to the Treasury, grew out of strikingly similar economic conditions in 1922. What changes might be anticipated if a similar revival of business came at this time? Certainly, with the necessarily accompanying expansion of credit, the banks, as soon as their idle cash and the funds temporarily invested abroad were exhausted, would draw upon their deposits at the Treasury, and the Treasury, in order to meet their demands, would in turn increase its borrowings from the Bank of France. Thus again the dreaded advances of the Bank to the State could be expected to increase. Claims for payment of maturing *Bons de la Défense Nationale* and other short-term Treasury paper, still carried in considerable amounts as secondary reserves by the banks, would no longer have the same effect. The funds held in foreign markets, however, combined with those kept actually idle in the vaults of the banks, undoubtedly amount to a sufficient sum to provide for a considerable expansion before such advances to the State would need to be greatly increased — unless, let it be clearly understood, the greater activity in business carries with it a considerable rise in prices.

With the expansion of the volume of business, especially if accompanied by rising prices, as, indeed, it is most likely that it would be, the note circulation of the Bank of France might be expected to increase somewhat more slowly but with equal certitude and ultimately by amounts roughly proportional to the increases in the *pecuniary* volume of trade. Under such circumstances there would be a tendency, therefore, for the note circulation to approach its legal maximum. Since, however, it has been especially provided by law[2] that the additions to note issues occasioned by the purchase of foreign exchange by the Bank of France may be deducted from the total outstanding circulation in determining the application of this maximum, and since this deduction might with almost general support[3] be interpreted as being equivalent to the amounts of the purchases themselves, no embarrassment to the Government is apt to come from this source.

On the assumption that the franc is to be maintained in the foreign exchange markets of the world at approximately its present value, it should be added with all the emphasis at our command that an increase in note circulation, unless accompanied by a substantial price rise, should cause no concern whatever. It is to be hoped and expected that the volume of business will continue to expand in the future as in the past, and the attendant increased needs for funds must naturally be taken care of with increased amounts of money and of bank credit.

Moreover, an increase in the advances of the Bank of France to the State, even though it necessitated, as it might likely do, a raising of the legal limit of such advances,[4] must not be re-

[2] By terms of the Act of August 7, 1926.

[3] As a matter of fact, on account of the economic situation existing throughout the period of heavy purchases of foreign exchange by the Bank of France, it can be said with assurance that such purchases have had an almost negligible effect upon the present (January 1928) quantity of outstanding notes.

[4] To escape the necessity of resorting to this highly undesirable measure it is possible that a means would be found of transferring to the Treasury the large resources (approximately 7 milliards) of the *Caisse d'Amortissement* at the Bank of France.

garded with too much concern if it represents simply the necessary action of the Treasury in response to withdrawals of funds by the banks or others in their efforts to meet the enlarged credit demands of business. Practically no interest is paid upon such advances by the State, and, provided their increase for the above-described reason is unaccompanied by a sufficient rise in prices to threaten again a necessary increase in expenditures or a reduction in revenues of the Government, it should prove of little economic importance. Just as the reduction in advances of the Bank to the State through a corresponding increase in deposit liabilities — important as it was in the circumstances under which it took place — was nothing more than a sentimental advantage, so likewise any increase in such advances accompanied by a corresponding reduction in Treasury deposit liabilities is nothing more than a change from a more to a less pressing and from a costlier to a less expensive obligation.

What is of fundamental importance is that the total debt of the country be continually reduced. It should be always borne in mind that an almost entirely negligible reduction in the total debt has been so far accomplished.[5] Mostly what has happened is that the extremely large and ever threatening current debt burden has been partially transferred to the future. Barring extraordinary happenings, however, such as the possible outbreak of war or other events causing a large increase in government expenditures, a considerable reduction in revenues, or a return of the old fright as to the future of the franc, the Government is not likely to be faced with impossible demands upon its resources. Nevertheless, as long as its total debt is as large as it is, the great proportion of the yield from its already extremely onerous tax exactions must continue to be used in meeting the attendant interest charges. Hence, any unexpected considerable increase in expenditures or any even temporary reduction in revenues may make necessary a resort to former inflation policies so recently but so intelligently escaped.

[5] The most recent computation available is that of August 31, 1927. Hence the statement applies to that date.

CHAPTER XIV

SUMMARY

With the outbreak of war in 1914 began the most severe test to which our institutions of credit and finance have ever been subjected. Instead, however, of the war failing — as many prophets forecast — because of the lack of funds with which to prosecute it, finances were forced to adjust themselves to the demands of war. The far-reaching and long-continued inflation of prices, of currency, and of foreign exchange rates growing out of this extraordinary and forced adjustment in France furnishes the subject of this investigation.

Inflation is not a word which has been explicitly defined, but has reference almost equally generally to expansions in prices, in circulation, and in rates of foreign exchange. For the purposes of this study it is defined as *an increase in the general level of prices growing out of an increase in expenditures while goods available for purchase are not correspondingly increased in amount.* By the terms of this definition a rise in prices, however great, unaccompanied by an increase in expenditures — as in the case of famine conditions, for example — would not constitute inflation. Nor would a great increase in expenditures, even though accompanied by considerable additions to the monetary circulation, be called inflation if also accompanied by a corresponding increase in the amounts of goods available for purchase, so that there was no resultant general rise in prices. On the other hand, larger expenditures by the Government, by business firms, or by private individuals or by any of their organizations, so long as the enlargement leads to a general increase in prices, will be regarded as inflation.

The part played by the banks in such an enlargement of expenditures is an important and, under our present financial organization, an inevitable one. When a government needs to increase its expenditures beyond the limits of its immediate revenues, it must borrow. And, while such borrowing is usually done in large part from the public through the intermediacy only of some of its financial institutions, almost invariably recourse is also had to direct borrowing from one or more of the banks themselves. Business firms and credit-worthy individuals, too, once additional expenditures become expedient or necessary, borrow sometimes *through*, but equally often *directly from*, the banking institutions with which they deal.

The importance of such borrowing in a study of inflation is that it provides prospective spenders with the wherewithal to make their purchases. For, as anticipated above, it is the increase in expenditures which provides the motive force not only for getting the inflation process started, but also for maintaining it once it is under way. But, even though the proceeds of any loan, no matter what its form, provide the prospective spender with immediately available purchasing power, it has been seen throughout the study that the form the borrowing takes is of utmost importance in determining its inflationary influence. Some loans are made in such a way as to take from one spender as much as is given to the other. Thus, in the case of a loan from one boy to another, the first cuts his expenditures by the same amount that the second increases his. Identical is the situation when a government or business firm floats a loan which is subscribed to by persons from funds which otherwise would have been soon spent. Very different is the case, however, of subscriptions in no way related to savings. Of this sort are the purchases of government bonds by the hounded spendthrift, who immediately re-borrows the amount of his "patriotic" purchase and carelessly continues his unrestrained consumption.

But far more important from the standpoint of inflation is the fact that bank loans *in general* partake of much of the same character. To meet the credit needs of their clients, banks, within comparatively wide limits, expand readily their loans and deposit currency. And the limit of this expansion is very greatly raised when — as was true throughout much of the inflation period in France — new funds were being continually provided by the central bank or other outside agency. Unless they lead to a speedy and sufficient increase in the production of goods, such loans, providing, as they do, an almost equivalent increase in purchasing power[1] in the hands of ready spenders without any counterbalancing reduction in purchasing power elsewhere, represent a direct and inevitable inflation.

Besides providing a large portion of the credit required by business and private individuals as well as a portion of that demanded by governments, the banks have a further function of supplying most of the requirements for circulating media. In many countries the deposits issued directly by almost all of the banking institutions themselves make up a large portion indeed of the total currency supply. But even when this is not true, one or more of the so-called issuing banks provide in their circulating notes a large portion of the monetary supplies. In France, at the present time, while circulating deposits are actually smaller in amount than total monetary circulation, the notes of the Bank of France make up more than 98 per cent[2] of the stocks of money outside the vaults of the Bank itself.

To understand the process of inflation in France a general acquaintance with the peculiar characteristics of the French banking system is of prime importance. Accordingly, a very brief summary of the outstanding features of the Bank of France, of the commercial banks, and of the Paris money market was attempted.

The position of the Bank of France is unique. Probably no banking institution in the world, with the possible exception of the Bank of England, has ever commanded more general respect and esteem. A Frenchman may lose faith in his Government — as he often does — but never in his Bank. Founded under Napoleon, it has ever since remained a private institution. Nevertheless, its chief control is in the hands of a governor and two deputy-governors, all appointed by the *Chef de l'État.*

The functions of the Bank of France are varied and important.

[1] To the extent that prices rise before the expenditures are accomplished, the purchasing power is reduced. On account of the inertia of prices, however, the quick spenders usually get the advantage of existing prices.

[2] For the years 1925 and 1926 the metallic *jetons* amounted to approximately 900 and 951 millions of francs respectively, and constituted in each case somewhat less that 2 per cent of the total circulation.

As sole holder of the privilege of note issue it has come to be the guardian of the monetary supplies of the country. Its issues of notes and grants of loans put funds into circulation or into the possession of the banks, and payments to it lead to corresponding reductions in funds at the disposition of the banks or of the public. As banker to other French banks it not only takes care for them of clearings and collections in distant parts of the country but also, in coöperation with the Post Office, operates for them as for all its other depositors a money transfer system which reaches to almost every village in the country. Besides, it stands in a position at all times to rediscount for the banks any acceptable paper which they may have in their portfolios. As banker for the public it functions much as do the commercial banks, except that it pays no interest on deposits and that it requires three signatures on all paper which it discounts. In this capacity it does an extensive business not only with railroad companies and other large business concerns having numerous offices in various parts of the country, but also with smaller firms engaged in all sorts of operations, and, through the branches of the Bank, even with farmers in the remote country districts. Finally, as banker for the Government, besides managing for it all fiscal operations unassigned to any of the various bureaus of the Ministry of Finance, it holds itself in readiness at all times to advance to the State whatever needed funds it has been otherwise unable to raise. So large were such advances during most of the period studied that they almost completely dominated the affairs of the Bank itself, and consequently very largely determined the credit conditions prevailing throughout the country. More recently the very large purchases of foreign exchange by the Bank have exerted a powerful influence toward loosening further the already extremely easy money rates prevailing since the fall of 1926.

About half of the commercial banking business in France is transacted by four big banks, three of which have numerous branches scattered over the country. Besides loaning to clients by discount, by acceptance, and by various kinds of secured advances, they also allow to many of their business customers extensive overdraft facilities. Each of these banks makes a monthly report of its operations, and from these reports were compiled much of the statistical data used in interpreting the course of their affairs. Unfortunately, however, there is so little uniformity even in the content of the items used that important quantitative conclusions were found difficult to draw.

Of much more interest is the Paris money market. Not only are its operations very different from those of the New York and London markets, but its peculiarities have proved of unforeseen importance in interpreting the course of inflation in France. Unlike those in London and in New York, the banks in Paris do not carry in their portfolios any large quantity of paper purchased on the open market. Instead, throughout the period under discussion until the end of 1926, they relied almost exclusively on the purchase of short-term Treasury paper, which, until the recent change beginning in December 1926, was issued in any desired amounts and with maturities from one to twelve months. All idle funds were quickly utilized in its purchase, and most additional cash needs were met by cashing the paper at maturity or sometimes by discounting[3] it at the Bank of France. Since the gradual suppression of the issue of *Bons de la Défense Nationale* of short maturity, the banks, in order to place otherwise idle funds, have relied more and more largely on their privilege of depositing in the Treasury. Thus is explained the great increase in the amounts of such deposits and in the importance which they have assumed in the credit situation of the country.

So generally has the recent inflation process in France been related to the great volume of public debts accumulated during the war and post-war years that the statistical study of the period was begun with the comparison of the amounts of the total debt and of each of its subdivisions with the various measures of the degree of the inflation — exchange rates, prices, and monetary circulation. In this way it was discovered that while the movements of all the series were at least remotely similar, those of advances of the Bank of France to the State and of its note circulation bore an extraordinary likeness. In fact, not only were their long-term movements generally similar, but the coefficient of correlation between the

[3] When within three months of maturity they are acceptable for discount by the Bank of France.

fluctuations of the two series about their respective secular trends was found to be +.98(145) for the entire period December 1914 to December 1926. The similarity was likewise close between the Bank's advances to the State and the other two measures of inflation — prices and foreign exchange rates — but by no means so strikingly close. The movements of other forms of public indebtedness, on the other hand, showed only remote and often unrecognizable kinship with all three of the measures alike.

A careful investigation was accordingly made of the two series of "advances" and of circulation. This study revealed, with regard to advances, that they differed in many respects from other sorts of government borrowing. In their use the purchasing power turned over to the Government was balanced by no reduction in purchasing power elsewhere in the economic system, while in most other types of government borrowing the purchasing power placed at the disposition of the Government represented a substantially equal amount of savings on the part of subscribers to loans. An important difference was found in subscriptions by the banks of otherwise idle funds to *Bons de la Défense Nationale* and other short-term Treasury paper. Through these subscriptions, funds being freed from business or personal use were passed on to the Treasury. In the absence of a direct use for them in making further payments, the Treasury in turn passed on the funds to the Bank of France in liquidation of its indebtedness to that institution. Hence, to the extent that subscriptions to such issues did not represent savings, they did represent idle funds of the banks, and, to the extent that the proceeds were not used for further government purchasing, they were used to reduce the advances of the Bank to the State.

With these observations in mind, the close correlation between the movements of advances and of circulation becomes at once explicable. Although the proceeds of all other types of government borrowings increased in the same way as did advances from the Bank, the spending resources of the Treasury, all except subscriptions by banks to short-term government obligations, carried with them a corresponding decrease in spending elsewhere in the system. But, in the instance of the excepted subscriptions by banks, the funds turned over to the Government represented those just released from business and private uses, and, to the extent that such funds were not immediately put out again by further purchasing on the part of the Government, they were used to reduce advances. Hence, to the extent that note circulation varied with increased or reduced spending, it necessarily varied likewise with such advances. And, on account of the large use in France of notes rather than of deposits for almost all sorts of payments, increases and decreases in spending naturally produced similar changes in the quantity of the medium with which most payments were made.

The long-term movements of the series of advances and of circulation, while similar, did not correspond nearly so closely as did their minor fluctuations. The reasons are just as clear, but since their further use for the purposes of this summary are not so important, the reader is referred to Chapter V for their exposition.

But what of the effect of business spending on the French inflation? If the movements of note circulation corresponded so closely with changes in the amounts of the advances of the Bank to the State, how was it possible for them likewise to adjust themselves to changes in the volume of business spending? The explanation takes us once more into the interconnections between the states of business, the purchases by the banks of short-term Treasury paper, and changes in the amounts of advances from the Bank of France to the State. When the volume of business increased or was done at higher prices, the demands upon the banks for supplying the needs of business customers were naturally correspondingly enlarged. The banks, with large holdings of Treasury paper usually maturing daily, met these additional demands by cashing, instead of renewing, a sufficient quantity of the maturing paper. Should maturities not occur properly for such a procedure, paper with but a short time to run was discounted at the Bank of France and, in turn, cashed by that institution at dates of maturity. In any event, the Treasury found itself with resources reduced by the amounts of the drafts upon it of the banks, and, in order to provide itself with the funds requisite for meeting the enlarged demands for payment, increased its borrowings from the Bank of France.

Furthermore, unlike the situation in a check-using country like the United States,[4] the amounts demanded by the banks of the Treasury would be nearly equivalent to the amounts demanded by business customers of the banks. Hence the increase in advances of the Bank to the State would in turn correspond in amount to the new purchasing power placed in the hands of the business buyers.

Reversely, a reduction in the pecuniary volume of business, leading to a paying of loans at the banks, resulted in the purchase by the banks or by others of short-term Treasury obligations and, consequently, in a reduction of advances of the Bank to the State. Hence, in this case, too, the changes in business spending were automatically accompanied by corresponding changes in advances of the Bank to the State.

Thus, for the entire war and post-war periods until October 1, 1926, when the *Caisse Autonome d'Amortissement* began its important operations, expansions and contractions in business spending, through the mechanism of subscriptions and repayments of short-term Treasury paper, had effects on advances almost identical with those of similar changes in uncounterbalanced government spending. After October 1, 1926 receipts from such subscriptions accrued not to the Treasury but to the *Caisse d'Amortissement*, and repayments were effected likewise by the same institution. Nevertheless, on account of the gradual disappearance of all *Bons de la Défense Nationale* of short maturity after December 1926, a similar but less close relationship has been built up by the deposit in the Treasury by banks and others of funds for which they have no immediate use and by their withdrawal when again needed.[5]

During the period under discussion, therefore, the movements of the series of advances of the Bank of France to the State reflected almost as faithfully the changes in the volume of expenditures of business firms and of private individuals as they did similar changes in the purchasing of the Government. Accordingly, indications of the relative importance of the various types of bor-

[4] For a full explanation the reader is referred to a forthcoming publication entitled "A Third Approximation in Monetary Theory."

[5] This mechanism, it is true, operated during the entire period after the Treasury began to receive deposits in 1921. It became important, however, only after the suppression of short-term *Bons de la Défense Nationale*.

rowing in advancing or retarding the inflation process must be sought elsewhere.

A study was next made of the movements of prices, circulation, and exchange rates. Under the metallic standards existing prior to the war there were close and easily but variously explained relationships among the movements of the three phenomena. So close were the connections, in fact, that no considerable change could occur in one without creating some sort of a disturbance in the others. Being, as it were, joined together by the measures maintaining the metallic standards, their relative movements were extremely small indeed. With the partial break-down of the metallic standards, however, and with their replacement in certain countries by inconvertible paper standards, a much greater freedom of movement has resulted. The movements of each of these important quantities may be regarded, in fact, as separate measures of the degree of inflation, and hence their relative movements take on an added interest.

In the movements of dollar exchange rates and of wholesale prices, a very close similarity was found to persist throughout the entire post-war period. Moreover, their fluctuations seemed in general to be synchronous. But, with a careful study of the movements of *domestic* goods' prices and dollar exchange rates, there appeared, for the years 1919–1922, a slight tendency for the prices to precede exchange rates by approximately one month. The result, however, was not a clearcut one. A comparison of simultaneous items indicated almost as high a similarity as that found when prices of one month and exchange rates of the following were compared. For the period 1923–1926, on the other hand, a more definite result was obtained. The correlation process showed a clear lag averaging approximately one month of domestic goods' prices behind dollar exchange rates. A point-to-point comparison revealed, however, that the lag was sometimes one month, sometimes two months, and sometimes zero or less than one month. With respect to the relative movements of exchange rates and imported goods' prices and wholesale prices in general, while no lag of prices behind exchange or of exchange behind prices could be discovered by the use of the correlation process, point-to-point comparisons seemed to indicate a general tendency for the movements of both price series to lag slightly behind those of exchange rates.

As for the movements of wholesale prices as compared with those of circulation, the results obtained were much more definite and seem to be established beyond question. For the entire period December 1914 to December 1926 there was apparent a distinct though varying lag of circulation behind prices. For the final period of rapid inflation, December 1924 to December 1926, however, the lag seemed almost completely to disappear. On the other hand, during the war period, December 1914 to December 1918, the lag, while variable, clearly averaged approximately five months; and in the period of rapidly falling prices during 1920 and 1921 the average lag even lengthened to six or seven months. In the following period of rising prices of 1922–1924, however, the lag was reduced to one or two months and in the final period of rapid inflation, as mentioned above, either disappeared or else became too short to be discoverable by the correlation process.

The explanation of these discovered lags in the movements of one of the series behind those of another are not only of importance in themselves and from the standpoint of monetary theory, but they likewise seem to indicate much with regard to the influences behind the inflation process itself.

The general tendency of prices to lag slightly behind exchange rates would seem to signify that during much of the period under discussion the exchange value of the franc was moving under influences unconnected directly with internal price movements in France and that the changing rates of exchange, on the contrary, were causing prices to adjust themselves to new international values of the franc. This view is further substantiated by the fact that the lag was evident only in domestic goods' prices and failed to appear clearly in the prices either of imported goods or of commodities in general. What seems to have been happening, at least after the middle of 1923 and until the middle of 1926, was that the selling of "forward" francs in foreign countries[6] and, in the latter

[6] For the explanation of the immediate effect on "spot" rates, see Chap. VI, p. 126.

part of the period, the buying of foreign currencies in France, were causing the exchange value of the franc gradually to depreciate. To the extent of its depreciation came an added advantage to foreign purchasers for buying in France, as well as an added incentive to French sellers to put up their prices. Evidently the first influence should operate almost immediately on imported goods' prices, and both should act with almost equal celerity on the prices of exported goods, though with somewhat less promptness on those of domestic goods.

For the period from 1919 to 1922, when, on the other hand, prices seemed in general to be preceding exchange rates, it is fairly clear that no such unusual influences were causing exchange values of the franc to depreciate. During those three years exchange rates appeared to be adjusting[7] themselves normally and quickly to the existing level of prices after the artificial exchange control had been raised in early 1919.

The long lags of circulation behind prices suggest a much more fundamental explanation — one, in fact, which goes to the very basis of the causal relations between money and prices themselves. So important, indeed, were these lags considered that, at the expenditure of a great deal of time and labor, statistics from the German inflation régime were gathered and analyzed. The results with respect to the lags both between exchange rates and prices and between prices and circulation were qualitatively so entirely similar (though the lengths of the lags varied considerably) that of the basic facts there seemed to be no longer any reasonable doubt. The explanation of the usually slight lag of prices behind exchange rates was apparently identical with that given for the same tendency in France. But, most important of all, the long and varying lags of circulation behind prices — as in the French data — made their appearance in all stages of the inflation process examined, except — also as for the French data — in the final stages of most rapid inflation. In the last few months in Germany, when the daily increases in both prices and circulation reached almost stellar magnitudes, there was some indication of a possible

[7] For a general discussion of the mutual adjustments between exchange rates and prices, the reader is referred to Chap. VI, pp. 89–91.

precedence of circulation over prices. The following explanation of the lags of circulation behind prices would, in the absence of a detailed study of the accompanying economic conditions, seem to be applicable to the German inflation also. In fact, when the explanations are written, their general applicability to all modern industrial countries operating under existing credit and currency systems appears almost certain.

Most goods are purchased in advance of payment. With government purchases this is almost invariably true. Many, during the period under consideration, were purchased in France as in the United States long before they were produced and, in cases, even before the tools or the raw materials to be used in their manufacture were in existence. Payment was generally required only after the delivery of the purchased goods. It is evident, therefore, that there was no need for the means of payment until the times of payment had arrived. And in the cases of government purchasing as of that of business firms and individuals, the means were not sought until the times of their use approached. On the other hand, the effects on prices were in general coincident with the buying of the goods to which they applied. It was at that time that the demand became effective, and it is the demand in connection with existing supplies which determines the prices at which all goods are sold. Hence, that the changes in the amounts of circulation should follow those in the prices of the goods in payment for which they were used seems not only altogether natural but almost inevitable as long as our credit machinery functions as it does.

The investigations above described, however, have given but a partial explanation of the process of inflation itself. Of extreme importance is the question of the relative influence of government as opposed to business buying in stimulating or retarding the process in the various phases through which it passed during the period studied. Numerous statistical series were examined and various methods of analysis used in the attempt to find a satisfactory answer to this question.[8] In this way certain important conclusions were reached.

If the war and post-war years are considered together, it may

[8] The reader is referred especially to Chapters VIII, IX, XI, and XII.

be said that they covered two distinct periods of inflation and two equally distinct ones of deflation. Those of inflation extended from the beginning of the war until early 1920 and from late 1922 until July 1926, and those of deflation from early 1920 to early 1922 and from August 1926 until early 1927.

In the war period and until the beginning of 1920, there is ample evidence that the continued purchases of the Government were made with funds secured in the form of advances from the Bank of France to an extent sufficient for keeping money conditions at all times exceedingly easy. Even during late 1919, when prices were rising extremely rapidly and when business activity was high, so great were the continued increases in the advances of the Bank to the State that money rates became even easier and credit evidently more plentiful. Only after the beginning of 1920 did short-term interest rates show any tendency to rise. Furthermore, that it was the borrowing of the Government from the Bank which was furnishing funds for business rather than the borrowings of business forcing an enlargement of the advances of the Bank to the State was made evident by the accompanying large excess of subscriptions over reimbursements of short-term Treasury paper. Had business required more funds than were currently flowing to the banks, there would have been a heavy demand for reimbursements of the securities making up so large a part of the secondary reserves of most of the banks.

In the second inflation period beginning in late 1922 and continuing until the severe crisis of July 1926, the relative importance of the two factors seems to have varied greatly. There is little doubt that in its early stages at any rate the expansion was dominated by business rather than by government spending and that the business expansion in turn, because of the demand on the part of the banks that more and more of their holdings of short-term Treasury paper be paid at maturity, was continually increasing the financial difficulties of the Government. These difficulties were much magnified by the narrow margins between the existing volume of outstanding advances of the Bank to the State and the legal maximum set to their amount. Indeed, so acute did they become that by the end of 1923, it is fairly certain, the Government had already been forced to resort to the later much condemned policy of borrowing directly from the commercial and other banks while arranging with the Bank of France to rediscount an equivalent amount of paper for the lending banks. After April 1925, however, the rapid expansion of the advances of the Bank of France to the State for government use increased so greatly the inflow of new funds to the banks that rates soon began to decline greatly, and it was only at the approach of the crisis of July 1926 that the great plethora of funds put out the previous year in the form of advances of the Bank to the State seemed to be fully utilized.

In the depression period of late 1920, 1921, and the first three-quarters of 1922, as in that following the crisis of July 1926, the release of funds by business necessarily had much to do with the easy money conditions which prevailed. The forces which set in motion and maintained the process of deflation are, however, not so easily determined. About the same time in 1920 came similar crises and similar beginnings of deflation in both England and the United States as well as in certain other countries. Even in the Anglo-Saxon countries there is far from general agreement on the causes which turned rapidly rising prices to equally rapidly falling prices and business prosperity into business depression within the course of a very few months. Under such circumstances it would be rash indeed to attempt with the use of the meagre French statistical data to explain causally similar happenings in France. With regard to the dominating influences starting the 1926 deflation, the determination seems somewhat clearer. With the outstanding large holdings by French investors of foreign investments of various sorts and with the existing large volume of uncovered short sales of francs in the various foreign exchange centres of the world, all that was needed to start a rapid recovery in French exchange was something to frighten the capital exporters and the speculators. This the unanticipated confidence in the new Poincaré Government seemed to provide. The resulting rapid recovery of the franc immediately set in motion numerous influences tending to maintain and intensify the process. The higher value of the franc in other countries tended to discourage foreign buying in France, while the lower values of foreign currencies in France tended to stimulate French purchasing abroad. But immediate and doubtless much more important in its effects was the hesitation which came to French importers, exporters, and other business operators alike. Business began to stagnate; with the stagnation came cuts in prices; and with the cuts in prices, combined with the reduced volume of business, came a gradual shrinkage in bank credit, a gradual accumulation of idle funds in the banks and a corresponding increase in subscriptions to short-term Treasury obligations, a gradual enlargement of deposits at the Treasury, and a steady reduction of the advances of the Bank to the State and of the note circulation of the Bank of France. All these happenings in turn stimulated a further rise in the franc. The movement once set in motion began to cumulate and to gain momentum as it went.

So marked and so rapid had become the recovery of French exchange by December 1926 that some action was deemed necessary to prevent a further damaging rise. Accordingly, acting under an earlier authorization, the Bank of France made its entrance into the foreign exchange market as a purchaser of foreign currencies. Not only was the desired effect immediately attained and the value of the franc thereafter held at approximately 124 to the pound sterling, but the Bank of France also accumulated a volume of foreign balances sufficient to guarantee it against any temporary tendency, however pronounced, toward renewed depreciation.

Certain worthwhile theoretical conclusions make their appearance. Besides the almost invariable lag of changes in the volume of circulation behind those in the level of prices and the usual lag of the movements of domestic goods' prices behind those of dollar exchange rates, the varying rapidity of adjustment among the different factors was observed. In particular, it was found that in the one doubtful case where circulation seemed to precede prices, as in the several fairly certain cases in which prices preceded exchange rates, the adjustment in every case was extremely rapid. In the more usual precedences above noted the adjustments were in general much slower — especially as between circulation and prices — but tended to become more rapid as the inflation process itself gained in momentum.

With regard to the equation of exchange, one incidental but

important result made its appearance. In spite of the ample opportunity for the equation to be thrown continually out of balance by the long and varying lags between purchases and payments and by the resulting largely varying amounts of unsettled contracts carried over from one period to another, there was little evidence of important distortions from such failures to balance. The well established custom of cash payments in France probably accounts for the smallness of the disturbances. It could certainly be anticipated that under similarly disturbed conditions in any of the Anglo-Saxon countries the distortions would prove much greater.

Finally, it was established very clearly indeed that under rising as under falling prices the changes in the volume of money in circulation were much less than in proportion to the changes in prices and that the more rapid the movements in prices the greater was the distortion of their normal ratio to money circulation.

The great improvements in the financial situation in France since July 1926 are real, and there is no apparent reason why they should not be lasting. In fact, as soon as it is clear that the budget can be kept in equilibrium and that foreign payments large enough to upset the international balance of payments are not going to be required, there is no reason why the gold standard should not be reëstablished at approximately the present value of the franc. While from a financial standpoint the task would have been much easier with a three-cent rather than with a four-cent franc, the great accumulation of foreign exchange and of gold holdings at the Bank of France furnish an ample protection against any temporary and not too persistent tendency of the franc to depreciate. Should, however, exceedingly large payments be demanded and received by foreign creditors, or should the French Government again resort to the slovenly financial policies so characteristic of most of the post-war years prior to July 1926, the gold standard would prove but a feeble and fruitless check against the powerful forces of inflation so recently brought under control.

It should not be forgotten that it was in connection with the accumulation of the huge public debt that the original forces behind the inflation process came into action. Moreover, while the ever threatening current debt burden has been in large part transferred to the future, in the total of the national debt there has been only an entirely negligible reduction. And, while the total is as great as it is, so large a proportion of the income of the Government is required for meeting the attendant interest charges that any unexpected increase in expenditures or any substantial reduction in revenues might so disturb the balance of the budget as to make necessary another resort to inflationary financial measures.

Let it be remembered, too, that there is always in the background another inflationary force which so far the French have not been required to face. In spite of the utterances of French politicians to the contrary — especially when addressing American audiences — the extremely difficult transfer problem, which was one of the major influences in the German inflation, has not yet really presented itself in France. For estimates of the margin of safety against the appearance of this problem, the reader is referred to the able but somewhat differing computations made by Pierre Meynial in his *Créances et Dettes internationales* (*Balance des Comptes*) and by Harold G. Moulton and Cleona Lewis in *The French Debt Problem*.[9] Of its overwhelming importance, should external payments in considerable excess of current incoming payments be required and actually attempted by the French Government, there is no possible question. Nor would the proposed return to the gold standard in itself offer any more than a sentimental resistance to its effects. True, the existing large gold and foreign exchange holdings of the Bank of France are sufficient to check any temporary tendency toward further depreciation of the franc whether arising from unfavorable balances of payments or from budgetary deficits. In fact, so large are these holdings that, provided they could be used for the purpose, combined they are sufficient to discharge immediately substantially half of the total debt to both the English and American Governments. Gold reserves have to be kept for sentimental but none the less important reasons, however, and, to the extent that the foreign exchange fund is used to ward off the effects of one influence, it ceases to serve as safeguard against

[9] Pierre Meynial, *Créances et Dettes internationales* (*Balance des Comptes*) (Paris, Librairie Dalloz, 1926); Harold G. Moulton and Cleona Lewis, *The French Debt Problem* (New York, The Macmillan Company, 1925).

another. With the budget kept in balance, however, it would seem an entirely ample protection against the disturbing influence of probable unfavorable international balances of payments.

Against certain false alarm-signals a further note of warning may be sounded. The French public should be prepared to see certain things happen which under most circumstances would presage danger but which under the present (January 1928) extraordinary conditions would prove almost inevitable concomitants of a return of business prosperity.

With an increase in business activity, especially if accompanied by rising prices, a considerable expansion of bank credit might be anticipated. The banks, as soon as their idle cash and funds invested abroad were exhausted, would be obliged to draw upon their deposits at the Treasury, and the Treasury, in order to meet their demands, would in turn be forced to increase its borrowings from the Bank of France. Thus again the dreaded advances of the Bank to the State, which have caused so much trouble in the recent past, could be expected to increase. Also, along with such an increase in advances to the State would almost inevitably go a somewhat corresponding increase in note circulation, likewise a time-honored danger signal. Should business activity become very great and the price rise considerable, it is not unlikely that the legal limit to advances might have to be raised — though this might be avoided if the large balance of the *Caisse d'Amortissement* at the Bank of France could be temporarily deposited in the Treasury.

Nevertheless, if merely results of business expansion, all of these apparently hazardous happenings might occur not only without presaging trouble, but even as indicating a general betterment in the economic life of the whole country. There is, however, one important danger signal which should be watched with the greatest care. Should, during such a business revival, the price level rise continually for any considerable period of time, disaster might quickly return. While increased purchasing abroad, combined with reduced foreign purchasing in France, would be gradually reducing the foreign exchange reserve, such a rise would likewise almost inevitably increase government expenditures without correspondingly raising revenues, and the really dangerous Treasury deficits would again appear.

BIBLIOGRAPHY

BIBLIOGRAPHY

In the making of the above study of the process of inflation in France, the works of a number of authors, both French and foreign, were consulted.

I

The following books were of especially valuable assistance:

Albert Aftalion, *Monnaie, Prix et Change* (Paris, Recueil Sirey, 1927).

In this work the author has made a searching statistical analysis of the relations between exchange rates and prices and of those between prices and monetary circulation. He concludes that prices in France have in general followed the movements of the external purchasing power of the franc and that circulation has lagged on the average approximately five months behind prices. He attacks the quantity theory and emphasizes the importance of the psychological factors in the movements of exchange rates.

Maurice Bloch, *Dictionnaire de l'Administration française* (Paris, Berger-Levrault, 1905).

This work has provided a good and much needed historical study of French governmental financial institutions.

J. R. Cahill, *Report on the Economic and Industrial Conditions in France, revised to June 1924* (London, His Majesty's Stationery Office).

——, *Report on the Economic and Industrial Conditions in France, revised to July 1925* (London, His Majesty's Stationery Office).

——, *Report on the Economic and Industrial Conditions in France, 1925–1926* (London, His Majesty's Stationery Office).

In his several reports, the author, who is an attaché of the British Embassy in Paris, has given a very enlightening and comprehensive story of the industrial conditions existing in France. His comments on financial happenings take on added importance because his treatment of them is always in connection with the many other economic and political happenings. He emphasizes the importance of the movement for the capital levy in aggravating the "flight from the franc." He also shows how the disastrous effects of inflation were being escaped by many through the purchase of land and of various other sorts of material goods.

Marcel Chaminade, *L'Expérience financière de Monsieur Poincaré* (Paris, Emile-Paul Frères, 1927).

The writer is a serious critic of the Poincaré régime in general. His analysis of certain phases of the financial situation shows a clear insight into many of the recent events.

Jacques Duboin, *La Stabilisation du Franc* (Paris, Librairie des Sciences Politiques et Sociales, 1927).

Apparently written primarily as propaganda for the stabilization of the franc, this book nevertheless presents a thoughtful analysis of the situation existing in 1926. Special emphasis is laid on the evils of instability and on the importance of a return to the gold standard.

Gaston Giustiniani, *Le Commerce et l'Industrie devant la Dépréciation et la Stabilisation monétaire. L'Expérience allemande* (Paris, Félix Alcan, 1927).

The author makes a good historical study of certain phases of the German inflation. His statistical study of the banks and of several of the industries is of special interest.

Georges Lacout, *Le Retour à l'Étalon-or* (Paris, Payot, 1926).

This book is a serious and well considered plea for the return to the gold standard. After discussing the disadvantages experienced by the British in their return to the old gold parity of the pound, he advocates the return to the gold standard but at a greatly reduced value of the monetary unit.

Richard Lewinsohn, *Histoire de l'Inflation, Le Déplacement de la Richesse en Europe* (Paris, Payot, 1926).

The writer makes a historical study of certain phases of the German inflation, followed by an abridged discussion of the French situation. He especially emphasizes the destructive effects of inflation on many types of wealth.

Germain Martin, *Les Finances publiques de la France et la Fortune privée* (Paris, Payot, 1925).

——, *La Situation financière de la France, 1914–1924* (Paris, Le Cours de Droit, 1925).

Of the two important works of this eminent French writer, the one entitled *La Situation financière de la France* has the more direct bearing on this study. His discussion of the relative movements of exchange, prices, and circulation takes on added importance because of its early appearance. Qualitatively his results anticipate some of those of Aftalion and of the present study. His work *Les Finances publiques de la France* is concerned primarily with the discussion of fiscal problems and with the change of France from the position of a creditor to that of a debtor nation.

Pierre Meynial, *Créances et Dettes internationales* (*Balance des Comptes*) (Paris, Librairie Dalloz, 1926).

This book constitutes probably the most searching study that has yet been made of the international balance of payments. Careful estimates of such balances have been made, not only for France, but also for England, Germany, Austria, and the United States. Except for the investigation of the problem by H. G. Moulton and Cleona Lewis, included in their study entitled *The French Debt Problem*, Meynial's book seems to be unique in its field. His methods of arriving at the estimates are of especial interest.

Harold G. Moulton and Cleona Lewis, *The French Debt Problem* (New York, The Macmillan Company, 1925).

This book, well known in America as well as in France, is a careful and comprehensive study of the French financial situation as it existed in 1924.

Bertrand Nogaro, *La Monnaie et les Phénomènes monétaires contemporains* (Paris, Marcel Giard, 1924).

——, *Finances et Politique* (Paris, Marcel Giard, 1927).

In his two important works, the author has analyzed many of the financial aspects of the inflation process in a number of countries. Of especial interest are his conclusions with regard to the sequences of movement of prices, circulation, and exchange rates. His works, while largely descriptive, carry much importance because of the number of countries included in his investigation.

George Peel, *The Financial Crisis of France* (London, Macmillan and Company, Ltd., 1926).

The writer presents a popular but extremely interesting story of the financial happenings in France prior to 1926. Of especial interest is his description of the critical conditions existing in 1925.

Louis Pommery, *Changes et Monnaies* (Paris, Marcel Giard, 1926).

Written by a person engaged in the practical interpretation of events for one of the French banks specializing in foreign commercial transactions, this work gives a banker's plea for a return to the gold standard. He gives a detailed description and history of the monetary systems of all the important countries of the world. The book is evidently written for the business man, and primarily for importers and exporters.

Jacques Rueff, *Sur une Théorie de l'Inflation* (Paris, Berger-Levrault, 1925).

——, *Théorie des Phénomènes monétaires* (Paris, Payot, 1927).

In his two works above-cited, the author has turned his mathematical abilities to the analysis of certain aspects of inflation. The extraordinary relationships which, in his earlier work, he discovers between the advances of the central banks to the State and the note circulation are of much interest. In his later work, his theoretical analysis of the French inflation with the aid of Fisher's equation of exchange is also of much interest, though he makes little use of the analysis to interpret the situations to which it refers.

Robert Wolff, *Note sur le Système monétaire français* (Paris, Gauthier-Villars, 1927).

In this work, the author has made a careful and detailed study of the important interrelations of the operations of the Bank of France and of the Treasury. In particular, he follows with great care the changed relationships which have come with the extensive use of the Treasury as a sort of bank of deposit. This book is one of the most significant studies of financial interrelationships which has yet appeared.

Anonymous, *L'Inflation allemande* (Strasbourg, Istra, 1926).

Although the author has not seen fit to sign his name to the work, its importance is not to be neglected. Rather popular in style, it gives an interesting study of certain of the outstanding effects of the German inflation.

II

In addition to the above-mentioned works, the following books, many of them of interest and of importance, have been consulted:

L'Allemagne depuis la Guerre: Sketch by Alfred Beucourt on "Salaires et Stabilisation monétaire en Allemagne"; sketch by M. C. Brouilhet on "La Situation économique et financière de l'Allemagne à la fin du second trimestre de 1925" (Paris, Librairie Générale de Droit et de Jurisprudence, 1925).

Pierre Bayart, *Les Effets de l'Inflation sur le Bilan au Point de Vue fiscal* (Lille, H. Morel, 1924).

Victor Cat, *L'Inflation — Ses Profiteurs — Ses Victimes* (Paris, Bureau d'Éditions, de Diffusion et de Publicité, 1926).

Albert Despaux, *L'Inflation dans l'Histoire* (Paris, Imprimerie Spéciale de l'Information, 1922).

Charles Dupuis, *Comment sauvegarder l'Avenir du Franc* (Paris, Plon, 1924).

Harvey E. Fisk, *French Public Finance in the Great War and Today* (New York, Bankers Trust Company, 1922).

Octave Homberg, *Le Financier dans la Cité* (Paris, Grasset, 1926).

Georges Lachapelle, *La Vérité sur notre Situation financière* (Paris, Georges Roustan, 1921).

Jean Lorin, *La Politique des Banques françaises de Dépôts et ses Rapports avec la Situation du Marché monétaire* (Paris, Presses Universitaires de France, 1923).

Léonce Magnien, *Les Caisses d'Épargne ordinaires en France (1914–1924)* (Paris, Éditions du Bureau Central des Caisses d'Épargne, 1926).

Mermeix, *Histoire du Franc depuis le Commencement de ses Malheurs* (Paris, Albin Michel, 1926).

Achille Mestre et Emile James, *La Clause-Or en Droit français — Étude juridique* (Paris, Nouvelle Librairie Nationale, 1926).

H. Montarnal, *Manuel des Opérations commerciales et financières de Banque et de Bourse* (Paris, Librairie des Sciences Politiques et Sociales, 1924).

——, *Les Salaires, l'Inflation et les Changes* (Paris, Librairie des Sciences Politiques et Sociales, 1925).

Gilles Normand, *Les Sociétés de Crédit et Banques à Succursales en France* (Paris, Perrin et Cie., 1924).

P. C. Raffegeau et A. Lacout, *Établissement des Bilans-Or* (Paris, Payot, 1926).

J. Ruotte, *Opérations et Travaux de Banque* (Paris, Marcel Rivière, 1920).

Société des Nations, *Mémorandum sur les Monnaies et les Banques centrales*, 2 vols., 1913–1924 (Geneva, Albert Kundig, 1925).

Henry Terrel et Henri Lejeune, *Traité des Opérations commerciales de Banque* (Paris, Masson et Cie., 1921).

Henri Truchy, *Les Finances de Guerre de la France* (Paris, Presses Universitaires de France, 1926).

Georges Valois, *L'État, les Finances et la Monnaie* (Paris, Nouvelle Librairie Nationale, 1925).

J. S. de Villefaigne, *Manuel pratique du Change des Monnaies étrangères* (Paris, chez l'Auteur, 1926).

Yves-Guyot et Arthur Raffalovich, *Inflation et Déflation* (Paris, Félix Alcan, 1921).

Nicolas Zvorikine, *Étude sur le Papier-Monnaie* (Paris, Rapid-Imprimerie, 1927).

III

The following booklets, each dealing with one or more of the phases of the French inflation, are also of interest:

Maurice Bokanowski, *La Crise financière: Conséquences d'Erreurs monétaires* (Paris, Imprimerie des Journaux Officiels, 1925).

Albert Buisson, *De la Validité des Clauses tendant à parer, dans les Contrats, aux Inconvénients de l'Instabilité monétaire* (Paris, Librairie Générale de Droit et de Jurisprudence, 1926).

L. Charles-Bellet, *Vers la Stabilisation du Franc* (Toulouse, Imprimerie Coöperative du Sud-Ouest, 1926).

F. François-Marsal, *Comment sauver la Fortune française* (Paris, La Revue Hebdomadaire, 1926).

Octave Homberg, *Politique et Finance, Conférence faite le 2 février 1926 à l'École des Hautes Études Sociales* (Paris, E. Desfossés, 1926).

Georges Lachapelle, *L'Évolution de la Circulation, des Changes, des Prix et de l'Émission des Valeurs à court terme du Trésor, de 1914 à 1926* (Paris, Société d'Études et d'Informations Économiques, 1926).

——, *L'Évolution de la Circulation, des Changes, des Prix et de l'Émission des Valeurs à court terme du Trésor, en 1926* (Paris, Société d'Études et d'Informations Economiques, 1927).

Paul Marion, *La Crise financière, la Faillite du Cartel, le Programme communiste* (Paris, Bureau d'Éditions, de Diffusion et de Publicité, 1926).

Anonymous, *L'Inflation et ses Conséquences* (Paris, Société d'Études et d'Informations Économiques, 1926).

Annuals and Reports

I

Association Nationale des Porteurs Français de Valeurs Mobilières, *Annuaire, 1915-1920* (Paris).

Caisse Nationale d'Épargne, *Rapport à Monsieur le Président de la République sur les Opérations. Années 1918 à 1924* (Paris, Imprimerie Nationale).

——, *Rapport à Monsieur le Président de la République sur les Opérations. Année 1925* (Paris, Imprimerie Nationale).

Caisse d'Amortissement et la Caisse des Dépôts et Consignations, *Rapport fait au Sénat et à la Chambre des Députés par la Commission de*

Surveillance sur les Opérations de l'Année 1925 (Paris, Imprimerie de la Chambre des Députés, 1926).

Caisses d'Épargne Ordinaires, *Rapport à Monsieur le Président de la République sur les Opérations. Année 1921* (Paris, Imprimerie Nationale, 1927).

Comité des Experts, *Rapport* (Paris, Imprimerie Nationale, 1926).

Councils of Administration of: Le Crédit Lyonnais, La Société Générale, Le Comptoir National d'Escompte, La Société Générale de Crédit Industriel et Commercial, La Banque de Paris et des Pays-Bas, and L'Union Parisienne; *Annual Reports to the General Assemblies of Stockholders, 1913 to 1926.*

Crédit Foncier de France, *Compte-rendu présenté au Nom du Conseil d'Administration, exercise 1926* (Paris, Imprimerie et Librairie Paul Dupont, 1927).

Crédit National pour Faciliter la Réparation des Dommages causés par la Guerre, Assemblée Générale ordinaire des Actionnaires, *Compte-rendu des Opérations sociales, Rapports pour 1920-1924* (Paris, Imprimerie et Librairie Centrales des Chemins de Fer, Imprimerie Chaix, 1921–1925).

La France économique en 1922, 1923, 1924, 1925, 1926. Annuaire de la Vie économique française (Paris, Recueil Sirey, 1923–1927).

Statistique Générale de la France, *Annuaire Statistique, 1926* (Paris, Imprimerie Nationale, 1927).

II

The following articles, taken from the above publications, have in many cases proved of aid in compiling this study:

Marcel Bourbeau, "La Bourse des Valeurs," *La France économique en 1924, 1925, 1926.*

L. Duge de Bernonville, "Le Mouvement des Prix et des Salaires," *La France économique en 1926.*

Georges Lachapelle, "La Trésorerie et le Budget," *La France économique en 1924, 1925, 1926.*

Marcel Lenoir, "Le Mouvement des Prix et des Salaires," *La France économique en 1924, 1925.*

Jean Loriot, "Les Banques," *La France économique en 1924, 1925, 1926.*

Pierre Meynial, "La Balance des Comptes," *La France économique en 1925, 1926.*

Charles Rist, "La Trésorerie et le Budget, Partie II, Aperçu statistique," *La France économique en 1925.*

Henri Ulmer, "Les Échanges intérieurs," *La France économique en 1925, 1926.*

Jean Vergeot, "Les Caisses d'Épargne," *La France économique en 1924, 1925, 1926.*

——, "Les Émissions," *La France économique en 1924, 1925, 1926.*

Robert Wolff, "Le Marché monétaire et les Changes," *La France économique en 1925.*

Anonymous, "Le Marché monétaire et les Changes," *La France économique en 1924, 1926.*

PERIODICALS

I

Bulletin de la Statistique Générale de la France (Paris, Félix Alcan, 1924–1927). April, 1924–1927, "Les Émissions de Valeurs mobilières en France en 1923, 1924, 1925, 1926."

——, April, 1924, "Cours, Taux de Capitalisation et Revenu net des Valeurs mobilières en France de 1919 à 1924."

——, July, 1925, "Cours, Taux de Capitalisation et Revenu net des Valeurs mobilières en France de 1919 à 1925."

——, April, 1926, "Cours, Taux de Capitalisation et Revenu net des Valeurs mobilières en France de 1919 à 1926."

——, July 1927, "Cours et Revenu des Valeurs mobilières en France de 1919 à 1927."

——, Oct., 1927, "La Comparaison des Indices des Prix de Gros et de Détail."

Bulletin de Statistique et de Législation Comparée (Paris, Imprimerie Nationale).

L'Économiste Français (Paris).

L'Europe Nouvelle (Paris).

Journal des Caisses d'Épargne (Paris).

Journal des Économistes (Paris, Félix Alcan, 1926). July 15, 1926, "Rapport du Comité des Experts — Résumé officiel."

Journal Officiel de la République Française, Lois et Décrets (Paris, 31 Quai Voltaire).

Revue d'Économie Politique (Paris, Recueil Sirey).

II

The following articles, taken from the above periodicals, have in many cases proved of aid in compiling this study:

Albert Aftalion, "Les Expériences monétaires récentes et la Théorie quantitative," *ibid.*, March–April 1925.

——, "Les Expériences monétaires récentes et la Théorie du Revenu," *ibid.*, May–June 1925.

——, "Les Expériences monétaires récentes et la Théorie psychologique de la Monaie," *ibid.*, Sept.–Oct. 1925.

——, "Prix, Circulation et Change en France de 1916 à 1924," *ibid.*, Nov.–Dec. 1925.

——, "Les Théories dominantes du Change," *ibid.*, March–April 1926.

——, "Théorie psychologique du Change," *Revue d'Économie Politique*, May–June 1926.

Benjamin M. Anderson, "La France et l'Étalon-Or," *L'Europe Nouvelle*, Oct. 24, 1925.

Roger Auboin, "Le Redressement financier est-il à la merci d'une Surprise politique?" *ibid.*, Nov. 5, 1927.

——, Editorials, *ibid.*, 1925–1927.

Henry Bérenger, "La Capacité de Paiement de la France. Mémoire presenté aux membres de la War Debt Funding Commission," *ibid.*, May 8, 1926.

Maurice Bokanowski, "Le Problème financier et la Technique de la Confiance," *ibid.*, May 29, 1926.

M. J. Bonn, "Les Leçons de l'Inflation allemande," *ibid.*, Jan. 2, 1926.

George Bonnet, Editorials, *ibid.*, 1925–1927.

S. H. Bousquet, "Observations sur l'Intérêt du Capital," *Revue d'Économie Politique*, July–Aug. 1927.

Pierre Cauboue, "L'Évolution des Sources de Bénéfice des Banques," *ibid.*, Nov. 15, 1925.

——, "Du Caractère des Opérations de Banque dans les principaux Pays européens," *ibid.*, March 15, 1926.

——, "Les Banques et l'Inflation," *ibid.*, July 15, 1926.

——, "La Technique bancaire," *Journal des Économistes*, Dec. 15, 1926.

Marcel Cavelier, "Les Achats d'Or et de Devises par la Banque de France," *ibid.*, Oct. 15, 1926.

B. L. Chlepner, "La Dépréciation et la Stabilisation du Franc belge," *Revue d'Économie Politique*, Jan.–Feb. 1927.

Jean Dessirier, "Indices mensuels de la Production industrielle en France," *ibid.*, April 1926.

——, "Les Finances publiques et l'Activité économique en divers Pays de 1919 à 1926," *Bulletin de la Statistique Générale de la France*, April 1927.

François Divisia, "L'Indice monétaire et la Théorie de la Monnaie,"

Revue d'Économie Politique, July–Aug. 1925, Sept.–Oct. 1925, Nov.–Dec. 1925 and Jan.–Feb. 1926.

B. Eliacheff, "Stabilisation et Crédit extérieur," *ibid.*, Nov.–Dec. 1926.

M. Lamoureux, "Un Exposé des Créances de la France sur l'Étranger," *L'Europe Nouvelle*, March 20, 1926.

Jean-Pierre Lazard, "Les récentes Théories monétaires anglaises," *Revue d'Économie Politique*, March–April and July–Aug. 1926.

N. Mondet, "Le Ministère Poincaré," *Journal des Économistes*, Oct. 15, 1926.

M. Piétri, "Une Évaluation des Dettes françaises à l'Étranger," *L'Europe Nouvelle*, March 20, 1926.

Alfred Posé, "La Théorie de la Parité des Pouvoirs d'Achat et les Faits," *ibid.*, May–June 1926.

——, "Billets de Banque et Crédits de Banque," *Revue d'Économie Politique*, Sept.–Oct. 1927.

Charles Rist, "La Stabilisation en Allemagne et en Tchécoslovaquie," *L'Europe Nouvelle*, May 29, 1926.

René Roy, "Les Index économiques," *Revue d'Économie Politique*, Sept.–Oct. 1927.

F. Sauvaire-Jourdan, "Le Rapport du Comité des Experts et la Revalorisation du Franc," *ibid.*, Nov.–Dec. 1926.

Yves-Guyot, "L'Inventaire de la Situation financière de la France," *ibid.*, Jan. 15, 1925.

——, "Aperçus historiques sur les Rapports de la Banque de France et de l'État," *ibid.*, Nov. 15, 1925.

——, "À propos du Rapport de la Banque de France," *ibid.*, Feb. 15, 1926.

——, "Projet du Comité des Experts et de M. Caillaux," *Journal des Économistes*, July 15, 1926.

Anonymous, "L'Œuvre de la Caisse Autonome d'Amortissement," *L'Europe Nouvelle*, May 28, 1927.

——, "Le Budget de 1927 et la Stabilisation," *Journal des Économistes*, Nov. 15, 1926.

——, "Le Budget de 1928 et la Dette," *ibid.*, Nov. 15, 1927.

INDEX

SOCIAL AND ECONOMIC STUDIES OF POST-WAR FRANCE

EDITED BY

CARLTON J. H. HAYES

VOL. I. **The Public Finances of Post-War France.** By ROBERT M. HAIG, Professor, School of Business, Columbia University. 8vo, cloth. *In press.*

VOL. II. **The Process of Inflation in France, 1914–1927.** By JAMES HARVEY ROGERS, Professor of Economics in the University of Missouri. 8vo, cloth, pp. 378. $5.00 net.

VOL. III. **The Development of French Industry and Agriculture, 1918–1927.** By WILLIAM F. OGBURN, Professor of Sociology in the University of Chicago, and WILLIAM JAFFÉ, Assistant Professor of Economics in Northwestern University. 8vo, cloth. *In press.*

VOL. IV. **The French Labor Movement since the War.** By DAVID J. SAPOSS, Professor of Trade Unionism in the Brookwood Labor College, and A. D. MEURIG EVANS, Fellow of the Social Science Research Council. 8vo, cloth. *In press.*

VOL. V. **National Psychology in Contemporary France.** By CARLTON J. H. HAYES, Professor of History in Columbia University. 8vo, cloth. *In press.*

VOL. VI. **The French Parliamentary System, 1918-1928.** By LINDSAY ROGERS, Professor of Public Law in Columbia University. 8vo, cloth. *In press.*

VOL. VII. **The Foreign Policies of France, 1918-1928.** By PARKER THOMAS MOON, Professor of International Relations in Columbia University. 8vo, cloth. *In press.*

VOL. VIII. **Social and Economic Effects of Inflation in Contemporary France.** A volume of studies by various members of the staff. 8vo, cloth. *In press.*

COLUMBIA UNIVERSITY PRESS
COLUMBIA UNIVERSITY
NEW YORK

FOREIGN AGENT
OXFORD UNIVERSITY PRESS
HUMPHREY MILFORD
AMEN HOUSE, LONDON, E.C.

Bei Fragen zur Produktsicherheit wenden Sie sich bitte an:
If you have any questions regarding product safety,
please contact:

Walter de Gruyter GmbH
Genthiner Straße 13
10785 Berlin
productsafety@degruyterbrill.com